AWS Certified Cloud Practitioner

Technology Workbook

www.ipspecialist.net

Document Control

Proposal Name	:	AWS Certified Cloud Practitioner Workbook
Document Version	:	1.0
Document Release Date	:	15 Nov 2018
Reference	:	CLF-C01

Copyright © 2018 IPSpecialist LTD.

Registered in England and Wales

Company Registration No: 10883539

Registration Office at: Office 32, 19-21 Crawford Street, London W1H 1PJ, United Kingdom

www.ipspecialist.net

All rights reserved. No part of this book may be reproduced or transmitted in any form or by any means, electronic or mechanical, including photocopying, recording, or by any information storage and retrieval system, without written permission from IPSpecialist LTD, except for the inclusion of brief quotations in a review.

Feedback:

If you have any comments regarding the quality of this book, or otherwise alter it to better suit your needs, you can contact us through email at info@ipspecialist.net.

Please make sure to include the book title and ISBN in your message.

About IPSpecialist

IPSPECIALIST LTD. IS COMMITTED TO EXCELLENCE AND DEDICATED TO YOUR SUCCESS.

Our philosophy is to treat our customers like family. We want you to succeed, and we are willing to do anything possible to help you make it happen. We have the proof to back up our claims. We strive to accelerate billions of careers with great courses, accessibility, and affordability. We believe that continuous learning and knowledge evolution are most the important things to keep re-skilling and up-skilling the world.

Planning and creating a specific goal is where IPSpecialist helps. We can create a career track that suits your visions as well as develop the competencies you need to become a professional Network Engineer. We can also assist you with the execution and evaluation of proficiency level based on the career track you choose, as they are customized to fit your specific goals.

We help you STAND OUT from the crowd through our detailed IP training content packages.

Course Features:

- *Self-Paced learning*
    - Learn at your own pace and in your own time
- *Covers Complete Exam Blueprint*
    - Prep-up for the exam with confidence
- *Case Study Based Learning*
    - Relate the content to real-life scenarios
- *Subscriptions that suit you*
    - Get more while paying less with IPS subscriptions
- *Career Advisory Services*
    - Let the industry experts plan your career journey
- *Virtual Labs to test your skills*
    - With IPS vRacks, you can testify your exam preparations
- *Practice Questions*
    - Practice questions to measure your preparation standards
- *On Request Digital Certification*
    - On request, digital certification from IPSpecialist LTD.

About the Authors:

This book has been compiled with the help of multiple professional engineers. These engineers specialize in different fields, e.g., Networking, Security, Cloud, Big Data, IoT, etc. Each engineer develops content in his/her specialized field that is compiled to form a comprehensive certification guide.

About the Technical Reviewers:

Nouman Ahmed Khan

AWS-Architect, CCDE, CCIEX5 (R&S, SP, Security, DC, Wireless), CISSP, CISA, CISM, Nouman Ahmed Khan is a Solution Architect working with a major telecommunication provider in Qatar. He works with enterprises, mega-projects, and service providers to help them select the best-fit technology solutions. He also works closely with consultants to understand customer business processes and helps select an appropriate technology strategy to support business goals. He has more than 14 years of experience working in Pakistan/Middle-East & UK. He holds a Bachelor of Engineering Degree from NED University, Pakistan and M.Sc. in Computer Networks from the UK.

Abubakar Saeed

Abubakar Saeed has more than twenty-five years of experience, managing, consulting, designing, and implementing large-scale technology projects, extensive experience heading ISP operations, solutions integration, heading Product Development, Presales, and Solution Design. Emphasizing on adhering to project timelines and delivering as per customer expectations, he always leads the project in the right direction with his innovative ideas and excellent management.

Muhammad Yousuf

Muhammad Yousuf is a professional technical content writer. He is a Cisco Certified Network Associate in Routing and Switching, holding a Bachelor's Degree in Telecommunication Engineering from Sir Syed University of Engineering and Technology. He has both technical knowledge and industry sounding information, which he uses perfectly in his career.

Saima Talat

Saima Talat is a postgraduate Computer Engineer working professionally as a Technical Content Developer. She is a part of the team of professionals operating in the E-learning and digital education sector. She holds a Bachelor's Degree in Computer Engineering accompanied by Masters of Engineering in Computer Networks and Performance Evaluation from NED University, Pakistan. With strong educational background, she possesses exceptional researching and writing skills that has led her to impart knowledge through her professional career.

Free Resources:

With each workbook you buy from Amazon, IPSpecialist offers free resources to our valuable customers.

Once you buy this book, you will have to contact us at info@ipspecialist.net to get this limited time offer without any extra charge.

Free Resources Include:

Exam Practice Questions in Quiz Simulation: IP Specialists' Practice Questions have been developed keeping in mind the certification exam perspective. The collection of these questions from our technology workbooks is prepared to keep the exam blueprint in mind, covering not only important but necessary topics as well. It is an ideal document to practice and revise your certification.

Career Report: This report is a step by step guide for a novice who wants to develop his/her career in the field of computer networks. It answers the following queries:

- Current scenarios and future prospects.
- Is this industry moving towards saturation or are new opportunities knocking at the door?
- What will the monetary benefits be?
- Why get certified?
- How to plan and when will I complete the certifications if I start today?
- Is there any career track that I can follow to accomplish specialization level?

Furthermore, this guide provides a comprehensive career path towards being a specialist in the field of networking and also highlights the tracks needed to obtain certification.

IPS Personalized Technical Support for Customers: Good customer service means helping customers efficiently, in a friendly manner. It is essential to be able to handle issues for customers and do your best to ensure they are satisfied. Providing good service is one of the most important things that can set our business apart from the others of its kind.

Great customer service will result in attracting more customers and attain maximum customer retention.

IPS is offering personalized TECH support to its customers to provide better value for money. If you have any queries related to technology and labs you can simply ask our technical team for assistance via Live Chat or Email.

Our Products

Technology Workbooks

IPSpecialist Technology workbooks are the ideal guides to developing the hands-on skills necessary to pass the exam. Our workbook covers official exam blueprint and explains the technology with real life case study based labs. The content covered in each workbook consists of individually focused technology topics presented in an easy-to-follow, goal-oriented, step-by-step approach. Every scenario features detailed breakdowns and thorough verifications to help you completely understand the task and associated technology.

We extensively used mind maps in our workbooks to visually explain the technology. Our workbooks have become a widely used tool to learn and remember the information effectively.

Quick Reference Sheets

Our quick reference sheets are a concise bundling of condensed notes of the complete exam blueprint for AWS Certified Cloud Practitioner. It's an ideal handy document to help you remember the most important technology concepts related to Cloud Practitioner exam.

Practice Questions

IP Specialists' Practice Questions are dedicatedly designed for certification exam perspective. The collection of these questions from our technology workbooks are prepared to keep the exam blueprint in mind covering not only important but necessary topics as well. It's an ideal document to practice and revise your certification.

Content at a glance

Chapter 1: Cloud Concepts 20

Chapter 2: Security 37

Chapter 3: Technology 79

Chapter 4: Billing and Pricing 224

References 253

Acronyms 255

About Our Products 257

Contents

About this Workbook 13

AWS Cloud Certifications 13

    Role-Based Certifications 14
    Specialty Certifications 14

AWS Certified Cloud Practitioner 15

    Pricing 17
    Exam Length 17
    Exam Content 17
    Exam Results 17
    Exam Validity 17

How to become an AWS Certified Cloud Practitioner? 18

Chapter 1: Cloud Concepts 20

What is Cloud Computing? 20

    Advantages of Cloud Computing 20
    Types of Cloud Computing 21
    Cloud Computing Deployments Models 21

Amazon Web Services Cloud Platform 22

    The Cloud Computing Difference 23

AWS Cloud Economics 23

    AWS Virtuous Cycle 25

AWS Cloud Architecture Design Principles 26

Databases 30

    Relational Databases 30
    Non-Relational Databases 31
    Data Warehouse 32

Chapter 2: Security 37

Introduction to AWS Cloud Security 37

    Benefits of AWS Security 37

AWS Shared Responsibility Model 37
    AWS Security Responsibilities 38
    Customer Security Responsibilities 39

AWS Global Infrastructure Security 40

AWS Compliance Program 40
    Certifications / Attestations: 41
    Laws, Regulations, and Privacy: 42
    Alignments / Frameworks: 42

AWS Access Management 42
    Access Methods 42
    Getting Started with AWS 43

Lab 2-1: Creating a Billing Alarm 44
    Setting Up On Mac 47
    Setting Up On Windows 48
    Identity Access Management (IAM) 48

Lab 2-2: Creating IAM Users 54

Security Support 67
    AWS WAF 67
    AWS Shield 68

Lab 2-3: AWS Shield 70
    AWS Inspector 72

Lab 2-4: AWS Inspector 73
    AWS Trusted Advisor 75

Lab 2-04: AWS Trusted Advisor 77

Chapter 3: Technology 79

Introduction 79

AWS Cloud Deployment and Management Services 79
    AWS Elastic Beanstalk 80

Lab 3-1: AWS Elastic Beanstalk 81

AWS CloudFormation	86
Lab 3-2: AWS Cloud Formation	86
AWS Quick Starts	95
Lab 3-3: AWS Quick Start	96
AWS Global Infrastructure	98
What is a Region?	98
What is an Availability Zone?	98
What is an Edge Location?	99
AWS Compute	101
Amazon Elastic Compute Cloud (Amazon EC2)	101
Lab 3-4: AWS EC2 Instance	105
AWS Storage	120
Amazon Simple Storage Service (Amazon S3)	121
Lab 3-5: AWS S3 Transfer Acceleration	128
Lab 3-6: Static Website hosting on S3	147
Amazon Glacier	155
Amazon Elastic Block Store (Amazon EBS)	156
Lab 3-7: Using AWS Command Line	159
Lab 3-8: Using Roles	165
Lab 3-9: Building a Web Server	175
AWS Database	180
Amazon Relational Database Service (Amazon RDS)	181
Amazon Aurora	184
Amazon DynamoDB	184
Amazon Redshift	185
AWS Networking & Content Delivery	186
Amazon Virtual Private Cloud (Amazon VPC)	187
Amazon CloudFront	190
Lab 3-10: Create CloudFront Distribution for Large Files	194

  Elastic Load Balancing 201

 Lab 3-11: Using a Load Balancer 202

  Amazon Route 53 216

 Resource Groups and Tagging 217

  Resource Groups 217

 Lab 3-12: Creating Resource Groups 217

  Tags 220

 Lab 3-13: Using Tag Editor 220

Chapter 4: Billing and Pricing 224

 Introduction 224

 AWS Pricing Policy 224

 AWS Free Tier 226

  Free Services 226

 Fundamental Pricing Characteristics 228

  Amazon Elastic Compute Cloud (Amazon EC2) 228

  Amazon Simple Storage Service (Amazon S3) 230

  Amazon Relational Database Service (Amazon RDS) 231

  Amazon CloudFront 232

  Amazon Elastic Block Store (Amazon EBS) 233

 Saving Further Costs 233

  On-Demand Instance 234

  Reserved Instance 234

  Spot Instance 234

 AWS Support Plans 234

  Features of AWS Support Plans 235

  Comparison of Support Plans 237

 AWS Organizations 239

  Key Features of AWS Organizations 240

  Consolidated Billing 241

AWS Cost Calculators..244
    AWS Simple Monthly Calculator 244
Lab 4-1: AWS Simple Monthly Calculator...245
    AWS TCO (Total Cost of Ownership) Calculator...247
Lab 4-2: AWS Total Cost of Ownership Calculator.. 248
    Cost Management Using Tags 252

References 253
Acronyms...255
About Our Products 257

About this Workbook

This Workbook provides in-depth understanding and complete course material to pass the AWS Certified Cloud Practitioner Exam (CLF-C01). The workbook is designed to take a practical approach to learning with real-life examples and case studies.

- Covers complete CLF-C01 Exam Blueprint
- Summarized content
- Case study based approach
- Ready to practice labs
- Exam tips
- Mind maps
- 100% pass guarantee

AWS Cloud Certifications

AWS Certifications are industry-recognized credentials that validate your technical cloud skills and expertise while assisting you in your career growth. These are the most valuable IT certifications right now since AWS has established an overwhelming lead in the public cloud market. Even with the presence of several tough competitors such as Microsoft Azure, Google Cloud Engine, and Rackspace, AWS is by far the dominant public cloud platform today, with an astounding collection of proprietary services that continues to grow.

The two key reasons as to why AWS certifications are prevailing in the current cloud-oriented job market are as follows;

- There is a dire need of skilled cloud engineers, developers, and architects – the current shortage of experts is expected to continue into the near future.
- AWS certifications stand out for their thoroughness, rigor, consistency, and appropriateness for critical cloud engineering positions.

Value of AWS Certifications

AWS places equal emphasis on sound conceptual knowledge of its entire platform, as well as on hands-on experience with the AWS infrastructure and its many unique and complex components and services.

For Individuals

- Demonstrate your expertise on design, deploy, and operate highly available, cost-effective, and secured applications on AWS.
- Gain recognition and visibility for your proven skills and proficiency with AWS.
- Earn tangible benefits such as access to the AWS Certified LinkedIn Community, invite to AWS Certification Appreciation Receptions and Lounges, AWS Certification Practice Exam Voucher, Digital Badge for certification validation, AWS Certified Logo usage, access to AWS Certified Store.
- Foster credibility with your employers and peers.

For Employers

- Identify skilled professionals to lead IT initiatives with AWS technologies.
- Reduce risks and costs to implement your workloads and projects on the AWS platform.
- Increase customer satisfaction.

Types of Certification

Role-Based Certifications:

- *Foundational* - Validates overall understanding of the AWS Cloud. Prerequisite to achieving the Specialty certification or an optional start towards the Associate certification.
- *Associate* - Technical role-based certifications. No prerequisite.
- *Professional* - Highest level of technical role-based certification. Relevant Associate certification required.

Specialty Certifications:

- Validate advanced skills in specific technical areas.
- Require one active role-based certification.

Certification Roadmap

AWS Certified Cloud Practitioner is a new entry-level certification. Furthermore, there are five different AWS certification offerings in three different tracks. These include Solutions Architect, Developer and SysOps Administrator. AWS also offers two specialty certifications in technical areas which are Big Data and Advanced Networking.

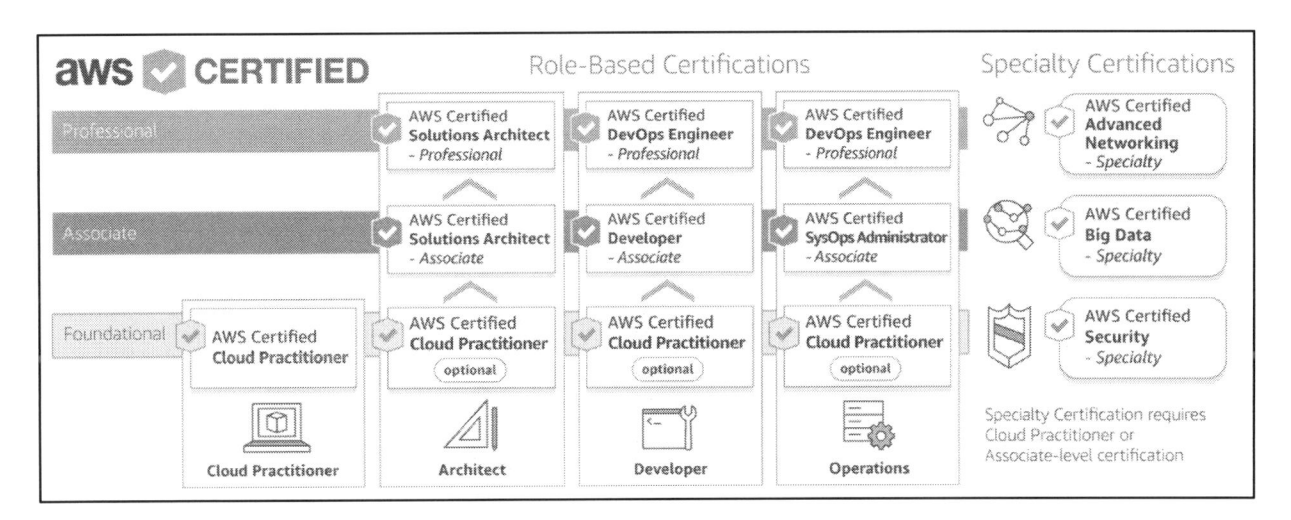

Figure 1: Certification Roadmap

AWS Certified Cloud Practitioner

The AWS Certified Cloud Practitioner (CLF-C01) examination is intended for individuals who have the knowledge and skills necessary to effectively demonstrate an overall understanding of the AWS Cloud. Those who are independent of specific technical roles addressed by other AWS certifications (e.g., Solutions Architect - Associate, Developer - Associate, or SysOps Administrator - Associate). This exam enables individuals to validate their knowledge of the AWS Cloud with an industry-recognized credential.

Overview of AWS Cloud Practitioner Certification

This exam certifies an individual's ability & understanding of the followings;

- AWS Cloud and its basic global infrastructure
- Basic AWS Cloud architectural principles
- AWS Cloud value proposition
- Key services on the AWS platform and their common use cases (e.g. compute analytics, etc.)
- Basic security and compliance aspects of the AWS platform and the shared security model
- Billing, account management, and pricing models
- Identify sources of documentation or technical assistance (example, white papers or support tickets)
- Basic/Core characteristics of deploying and operating in the AWS Cloud

Intended Audience

Candidates may be business analysts, project managers, chief experience officers, AWS Academy students, and other IT-related professionals. They may be serving in sales, marketing, finance, and legal roles.

Course Outline

The table below lists the main content domains and their weightings on the exam.

	Domain	% of Examination
Domain 1	Cloud Concepts	28%
Domain 2	Security	24%
Domain 3	Technology	36%
Domain 4	Billing and Pricing	12%
Total		100%

Following is the outline of the topics included in this examination; however, the list is not comprehensive.

Domain 1: Cloud Concepts

    1.1 Define the AWS Cloud and its value proposition
    1.2 Identify aspects of AWS Cloud economics
    1.3 List the different cloud architecture design principles

Domain 2: Security

    2.1 Define the AWS Shared Responsibility model
    2.2 Define AWS Cloud security and compliance concepts
    2.3 Identify AWS access management capabilities
    2.4 Identify resources for security support

Domain 3: Technology

    3.1 Define methods of deploying and operating in the AWS Cloud
    3.2 Define the AWS global infrastructure
    3.3 Identify the core AWS services
    3.4 Identify resources for technology support

Domain 4: Billing and Pricing

    4.1 Compare and contrast the various pricing models for AWS

    4.2 Recognize the various account structures in relation to AWS billing and pricing

    4.3 Identify resources available for billing support

Exam Details

Pricing: USD 100

Exam Length: 90 minutes

Exam Content: There are two types of questions on the examination;

- Multiple-choice: Has one correct response and three incorrect responses (distracters).
- Multiple-response: Has two correct responses out of five options.

Always choose the best response(s). Incorrect responses will be plausible and are designed to be attractive to candidates who do not know the correct response. Unanswered questions are scored as incorrect. There is no penalty for guessing.

Exam Results:

The AWS Certified Cloud Practitioner (CLF-C01) examination is a pass or fail exam. The examination is scored against a minimum standard established by AWS professionals who are guided by the certification industry's best practices and guidelines.

The results of the examination are reported as a scaled score from 100 through 1000, with a minimum passing score of 700. The score shows how you performed on the examination as a whole and whether or not you passed.

Exam Validity: 2 years; Recertification is required every 2 years for all AWS Certifications.

How to become an AWS Certified Cloud Practitioner?

Prerequisites

No prerequisite exam is required. Although, it is recommended to have at least six months of AWS cloud experience in any role, including technical, managerial, sales, purchasing, or financial. Also, the candidates should have a basic understanding of IT services and their uses in the AWS Cloud platform.

Exam Preparation Guide

Exam preparation can be accomplished through self-study with textbooks, practice exams, and on-site classroom programs. This workbook provides you with all the information and knowledge to help you pass the AWS Certified Cloud Practitioner Exam. IPSpecialist provides full support to the candidates in order for them to pass the exam.

Step 1: Take AWS Training Class

These training courses and materials will help with the exam preparations:

AWS Training (aws.amazon.com/training)

- AWS Cloud Practitioner Essentials course
- AWS Technical Essentials course
- AWS Business Essentials course

Step 2: Review the Exam Guide and Sample Questions

Review the Exam Blue Print and study the Sample Questions available at AWS website

Step 3: Practice with Self-Paced Labs and Study Official Documentations

Register for an AWS Free Tier accounts to use limited free services and practice Labs. Additionally, you can study official documentation on the website

Step 4: Study AWS Whitepapers

Broaden your technical understanding with whitepapers written by the AWS team.

AWS Whitepapers (aws.amazon.com/whitepapers) Kindle, .pdf and other materials

- Overview of Amazon Web Services whitepaper, April 2017
- Architecting for the Cloud: AWS Best Practices whitepaper, Feb 2016
- How AWS Pricing Works whitepaper, March 2016

- The Total Cost of (Non) Ownership of Web Applications in the Cloud whitepaper, Aug 2012
- Compare AWS Support Plans webpage

Step 5: Review AWS FAQs

Browse through these FAQs to find answers to commonly raised questions.

Step 6: Take a Practice Exam

Test your knowledge online in a timed environment by registering at aws.training.

Step 7: Schedule Your Exam and Get Certified

Schedule your exam at a testing center near you at aws.training.

Chapter 1: Cloud Concepts

What is Cloud Computing?

Cloud Computing is the practice of using a network of remote servers hosted on the internet to store, manage and process data rather than using a local server or personal computer. It is the on-demand delivery of computing resources through a cloud service platform with pay-as-you-go pricing.

Advantages of Cloud Computing

1. **Trade capital expense for variable expense**

   Pay only for the resources consumed instead of heavily investing in data centers and servers before knowing your requirements.

2. **Benefit from massive economies of scale**

   Achieve lower variable costs than you can get on your own. Cloud computing providers, such as Amazon, build their own data centers and achieve higher economies of scale that results in lower prices.

3. **Stop guessing capacity**

   Access as much or as little resources needed instead of buying too much or too little resources by guessing your needs. Scale up and down as required with no long-term contracts.

4. **Increase speed and agility**

   New IT resources are readily available so that you can scale up infinitely with demand. The result is a dramatic increase in agility for the organizations.

5. **Stop spending money on running and maintaining data centers**

   Eliminates the traditional need for spending money on running and maintaining data centers which are managed by the cloud provider.

6. **Go global in minutes**

   Provide lower latency at minimal cost by easily deploying your application in multiple regions around the world.

Chapter 1: Cloud Concepts

Types of Cloud Computing

Infrastructure as a Service (IaaS): Provides basic building blocks for cloud IT by offering access to networking features, computers, and data storage space.

Platform as a Service (PaaS): Manages its own underlying infrastructure, usually hardware and operating systems, and provides application development platform.

Software as a Service (SaaS): Offers a complete product as a web service that is run and maintained by the service provider along with the management of the underlying infrastructure.

Figure 1-01. Types of Cloud Computing

Cloud Computing Deployments Models

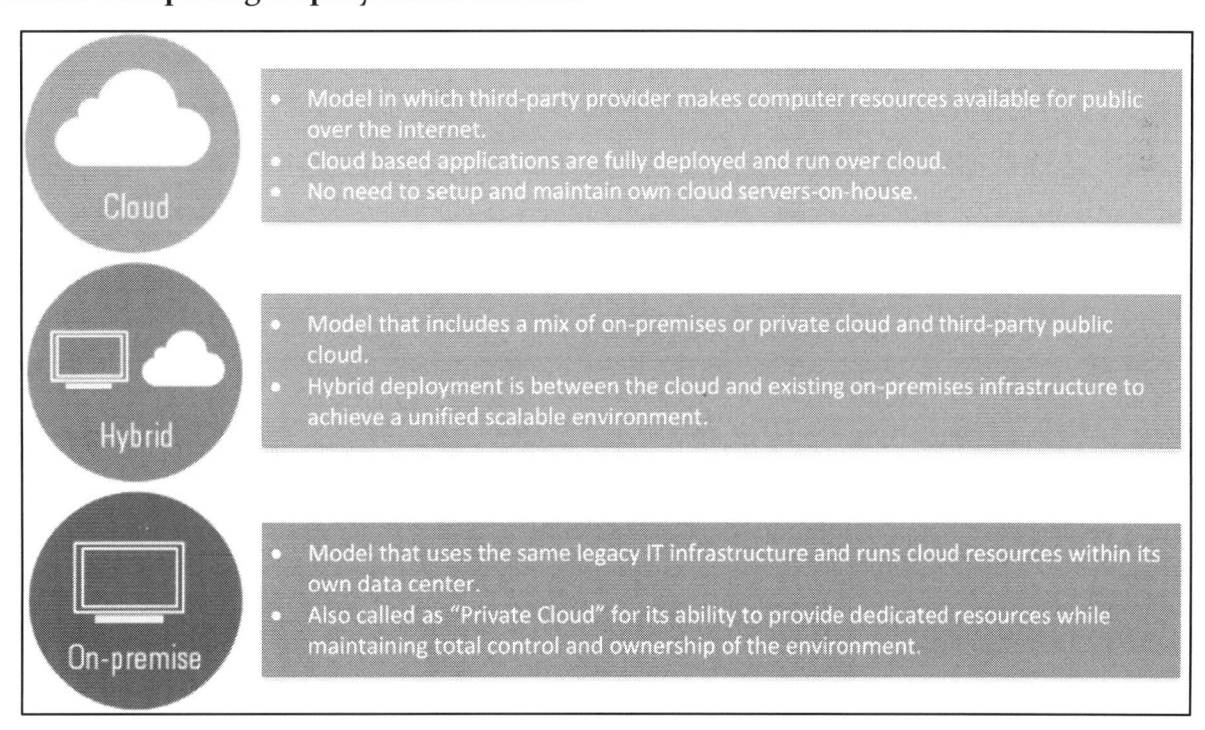

Cloud:
- Model in which third-party provider makes computer resources available for public over the internet.
- Cloud based applications are fully deployed and run over cloud.
- No need to setup and maintain own cloud servers-on-house.

Hybrid:
- Model that includes a mix of on-premises or private cloud and third-party public cloud.
- Hybrid deployment is between the cloud and existing on-premises infrastructure to achieve a unified scalable environment.

On-premise:
- Model that uses the same legacy IT infrastructure and runs cloud resources within its own data center.
- Also called as "Private Cloud" for its ability to provide dedicated resources while maintaining total control and ownership of the environment.

Figure 1-02. Cloud Computing Deployment Model

Amazon Web Services Cloud Platform

Amazon Web Services (AWS) is a secured cloud services platform, offering computing power, database storage, content delivery and other functionality on-demand to help businesses scale and grow. AWS cloud products and solutions can be used to build sophisticated applications with increased flexibility, scalability and reliability.

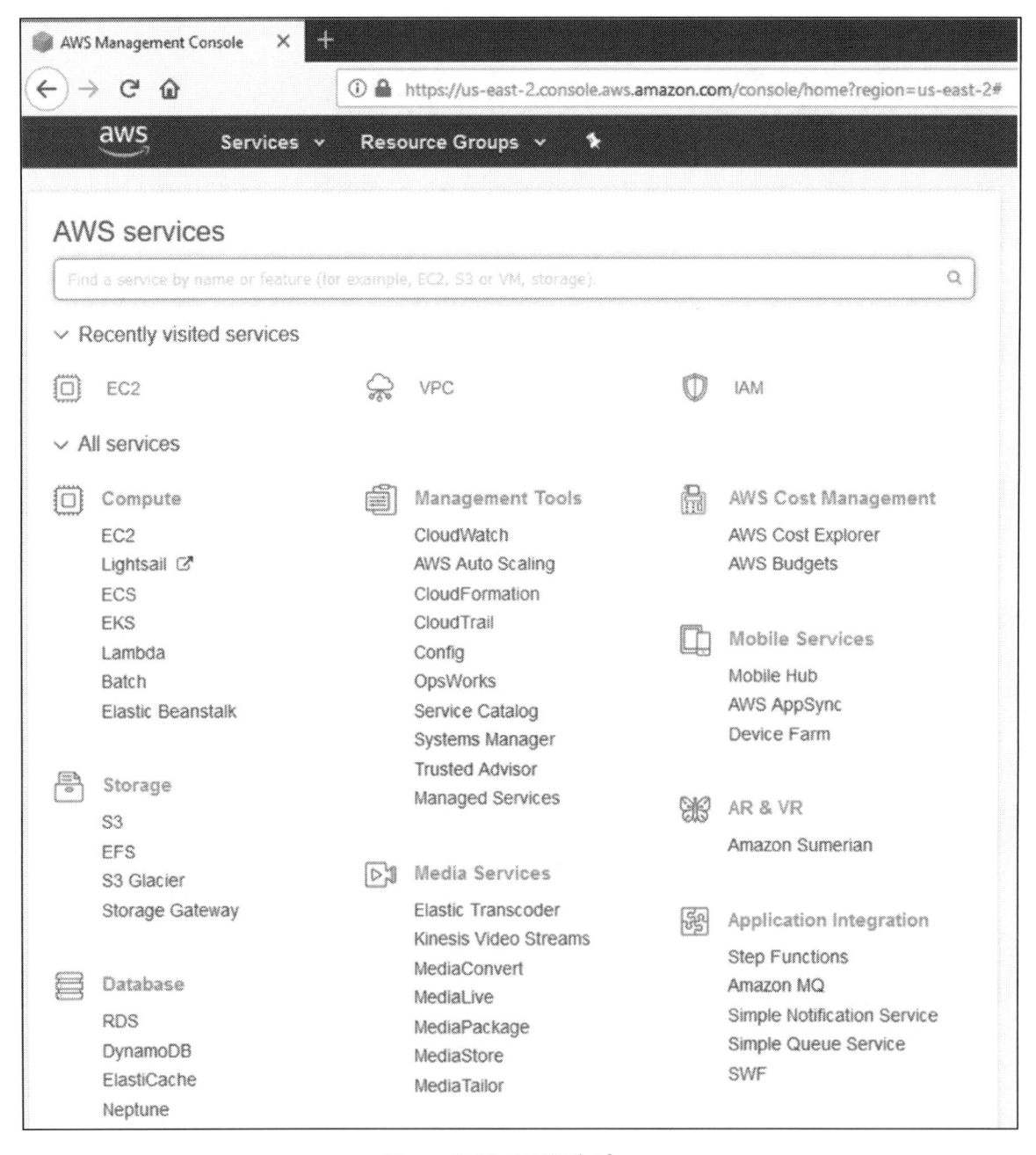

Figure 1-03. AWS Platform

The Cloud Computing Difference

This section compares cloud computing with the traditional environment, it reviews and provides the information to why these new better practices have emerged.

IT Assets Become Programmable Resources: In a traditional environment, it would take days to weeks depending on the complexity of the environment to setup IT resources such as servers and networking hardware, etc. On AWS, servers, databases, storage, and higher-level application components can be instantiated within seconds. These instances can be used as temporary and disposable resources to meet the actual demand, while only paying for what you have used.

Global, Available, and Unlimited Capacity: With AWS cloud platform you can deploy your infrastructure into different AWS regions around the world. Virtually unlimited on-demand capacity is available to enable future expansion of your IT architecture. The global infrastructure ensures high availability and fault tolerance.

Higher Level Managed Services: Apart from computing resources in the cloud, AWS also provides other higher-level managed services such as storage, database, analytics, application, and deployment services. These services are instantly available to developers, consequently reducing dependency on in-house specialized skills.

Security Built-in: In a non-cloud environment, security auditing would be a periodic and manual process. The AWS cloud provides plenty of security and encryption features with governance capabilities that enable continuous monitoring of your IT resources. Your security policy can be embedded in the design of your infrastructure.

AWS Cloud Economics

Weighing financial aspects of a traditional environment versus the cloud infrastructure is not as simple as comparing hardware, storage, and compute costs. You have to manage other investments, such as:

- Capital expenditures
- Operational expenditures
- Staffing
- Opportunity costs
- Licensing
- Facilities overhead

Chapter 1: Cloud Concepts

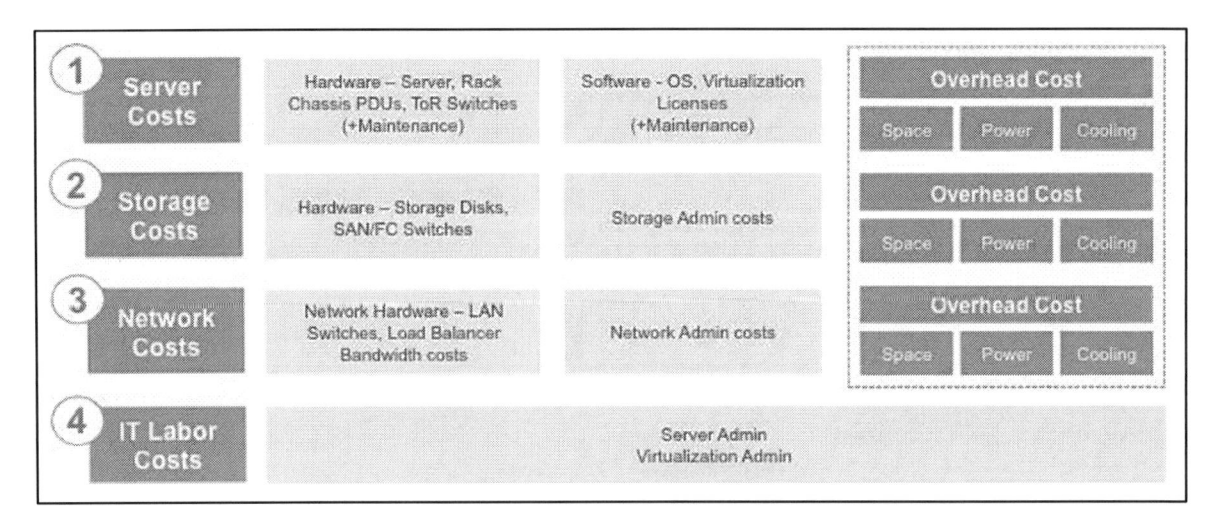

Figure 1-04. Typical Data Center Costs

On the other hand, a cloud environment provides scalable and powerful computing solutions, reliable storage, and database technologies at lower costs with reduced complexity, and increased flexibility. When you decouple from the data center, you are able to;

- **Decrease your TCO**: Eliminate the costs related to building and maintaining data centers or co-location deployment. Pay for only the resources that you have consumed.
- **Reduce complexity**: Reduce the need to manage infrastructure, investigate licensing issues, or divert resources.
- **Adjust capacity on the fly**: Scale resources up and down depending on the business needs using secure, reliable, and broadly accessible infrastructure.
- **Reduce time to market**: Design and develop new IT projects faster.
- **Deploy quickly, even worldwide**: Deploy applications across multiple geographic areas.
- **Increase efficiencies**: Use automation to reduce or eliminate IT management activities that waste time and resources.
- **Innovate more**: Try out new ideas as the cloud makes it faster and cheaper to deploy, test, and launch new products and services.
- **Spend your resources strategically**: Free your IT staff from handling operations and maintenance by switching to a DevOps model.
- **Enhance security**: Cloud providers have teams of people who focus on security, offering best practices to ensure you are compliant.

Chapter 1: Cloud Concepts

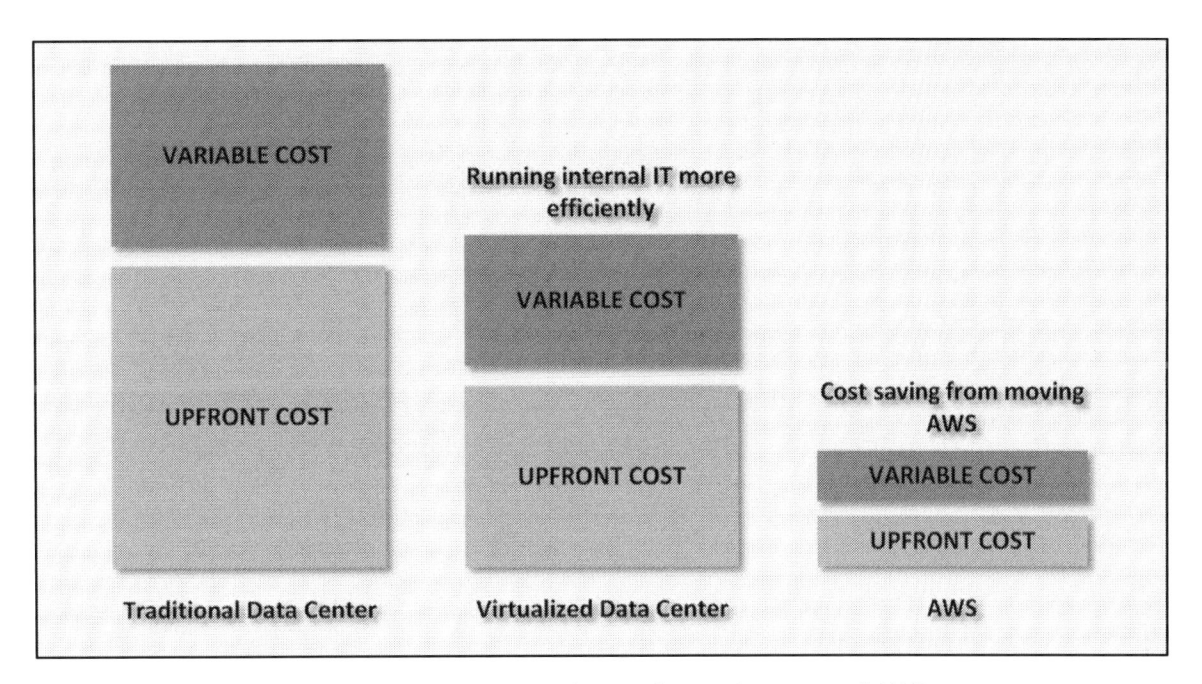

Figure 1-05. Cost Comparisons of Data Centers and AWS

AWS Virtuous Cycle

The AWS pricing philosophy is driven by a virtuous cycle. Lower prices mean more customers are taking advantage of the platform, which in turn results in driving the costs down further.

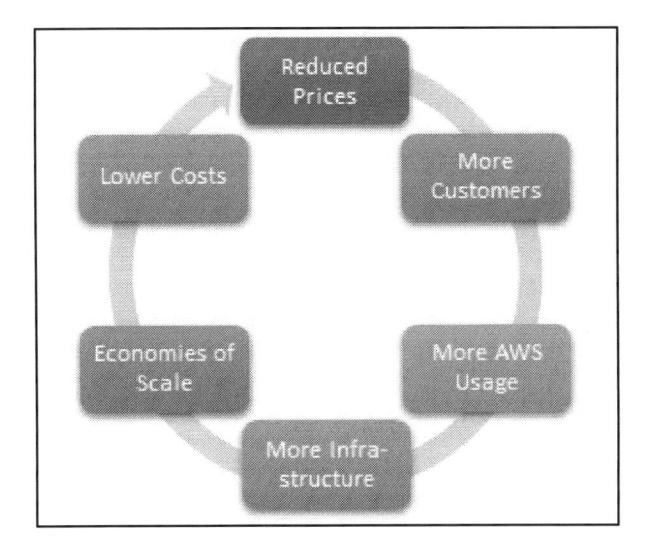

Figure 1-06. AWS Virtuous Cycle

AWS Cloud Architecture Design Principles

Good architectural design should take advantage of the inherent strengths of the AWS cloud computing platform. Below are the key design principles that need to be taken into consideration while designing.

Scalability

Systems need to be designed in such a way that they are capable of growing and expanding over time with no drop in performance. The architecture needs to be able to take advantage of the virtually unlimited on-demand capacity of the cloud platform and scale in a manner where adding extra resources results in an increase in the ability to serve additional load.

There are generally two ways to scale an IT architecture; vertically and horizontally.

Scale Vertically- Increase specifications such as RAM, CPU, IO, or networking capabilities of an individual resource.

Scale Horizontally- Increase the number of resources such as adding more hard drives to a storage array or adding more servers to support an application.

- Stateless Applications– An application that needs no knowledge of previous interactions and stores no sessions. It could be an application that when given the same input, provides the same response to an end user. A stateless application can scale horizontally since any request can be serviced by any of the available compute resources (e.g., Amazon EC2 instances, AWS Lambda functions). With no session data to be shared, you can simply add more compute resources as needed and terminate them when the capacity is no longer required.

- Stateless Components- Most applications need to maintain some kind of state information, for example, web applications need to track previous activities such as whether a user is signed in or not etc. A portion of these architectures can be made stateless by storing state in the client's browser using cookies. This can make servers relatively stateless because the sessions are stored in the user's browser.

- Stateful Components – Some layers of the architecture are stateful, such as the database. You need databases that can scale. Amazon RDS DB can scale up, and by adding read replicas, it can also scale out. Whereas, Amazon DynamoDB scales automatically and is a better choice. It requires the consistent addition of Read Replicas.

- Distributed Processing – Processing of very large data requires a distributed processing approach where big data is broken down into pieces and have computing instances work on them separately in parallel. On AWS, the core service that handles this is Amazon Elastic Map Reduce (EMR). It manages a fleet of EC2 instances that work on the fragments of data simultaneously.

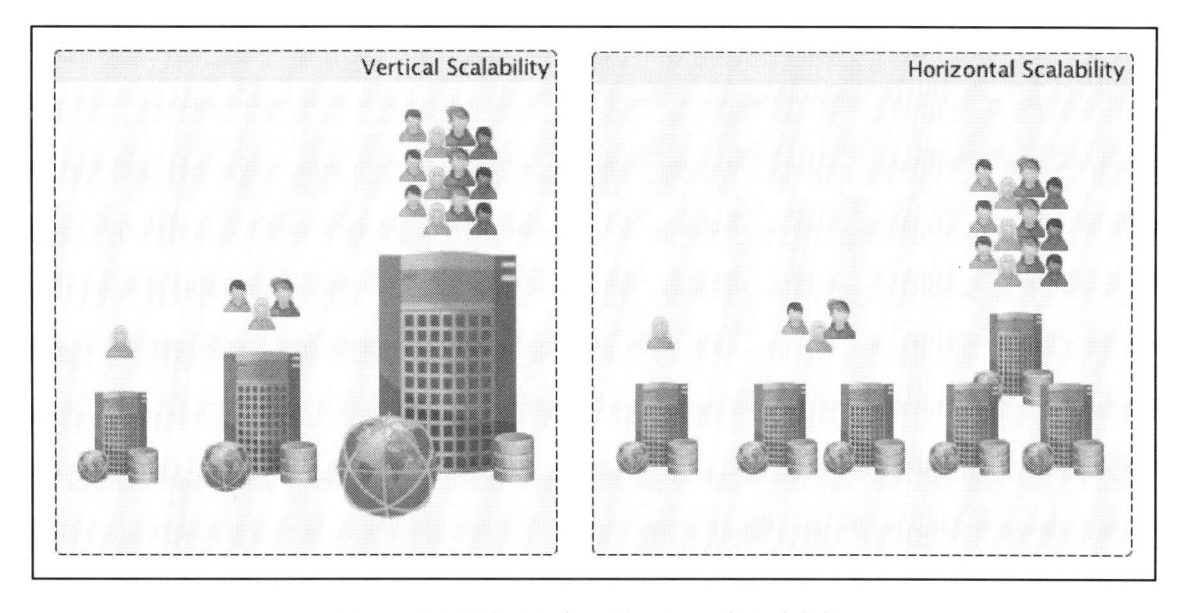

Figure 1-07. Vertical vs. Horizontal Scalability

Disposable Resources Instead of Fixed Servers

In a cloud computing environment, you can treat your servers and other components as temporary disposable resources instead of fixed components. Launch as many as needed and use as long as you need them. If a server goes down or needs a configuration update, it can be replaced with the latest configuration server instead of updating the old one.

Instantiating Compute Resources - When deploying resources for a new environment or increasing the capacity of the existing system, it is important to keep the process of configuration and coding as an automated and repeatable process to avoid human errors and long lead times.

- Bootstrapping– Executing bootstrapping after launching a resource with the default configuration, enables you to reuse the same scripts without modifications.
- Golden Image– Certain resource types such as Amazon EC2 instances, Amazon RDS DB instances, Amazon Elastic Block Store (Amazon EBS) volumes, etc., can be launched from a golden image, which is a snapshot of a particular state of that

resource. This is used in auto-scaling, for example, by creating an Amazon Machine Image (AMI) of a customized EC2 instance; you can launch as many instances as needed with the same customized configurations.

- Hybrid– Using a combination of both approaches, where some parts of the configuration are captured in a golden image, while others are configured dynamically through a bootstrapping action. AWS Elastic Beanstalk follows the hybrid model.

Infrastructure as Code– AWS assets are programmable, allowing you to treat your infrastructure as code. This lets you repeatedly deploy the infrastructure across multiple regions without the need to go and provision everything manually. AWS Cloud Formation and AWS Elastic Beanstalk are the two such provisioning resources.

Automation

One of the design's best practices is to automate whenever possible to improve the system's stability and efficiency of the organization using various AWS automation technologies. These include AWS Elastic Beanstalk, Amazon EC2 Auto recovery, Auto Scaling, Amazon Cloud Watch Alarms, Amazon Cloud Watch Events, AWS Ops Works Lifecycle events and AWS Lambda Scheduled events.

Loose Coupling

IT systems can ideally be designed with reduced interdependency. As applications become more complex, you need to break them down into smaller loosely coupled components so that the failure of any one component does not cascade down to other parts of the application. The more loosely coupled a system is, the more resilient it is.

Well-Defined Interfaces– Using technology-specific interfaces such as RESTful APIs, components can interact with each other to reduce inter-dependability. This hides the technical implementation detail allowing teams to modify any underlying operations without affecting other components. Amazon API Gateway service makes it easier to create, publish, maintain and monitor thousands of concurrent API calls while handling all the tasks involved in accepting and processing including traffic management, authorization, and accessing control.

Service Discovery– Applications deployed as a set of smaller services require the ability to interact with each other since the services may be running across multiple resources. Implementing Service Discovery allows smaller services to be used irrespective of their network topology details through the loose coupling. In AWS platform service discovery can be achieved through Amazon's Elastic Load Balancer that uses DNS end points; so if your RDS instance goes down and you have Multi-AZ enabled on that RDS database, the Elastic Load Balancer will redirect the request to the copy of the database in the other Availability Zone.

***Asynchronous Integration*-** Asynchronous Integration is a form of loose coupling where an immediate response between the services is not needed, and an acknowledgment of the request is sufficient. One component generates events while the other consumes. Both components interact through an intermediate durable storage layer, not through point-to-point interaction. An example is an Amazon SQS Queue. If a process fails while reading messages from the queue, messages can still be added to the queue for processing once the system recovers.

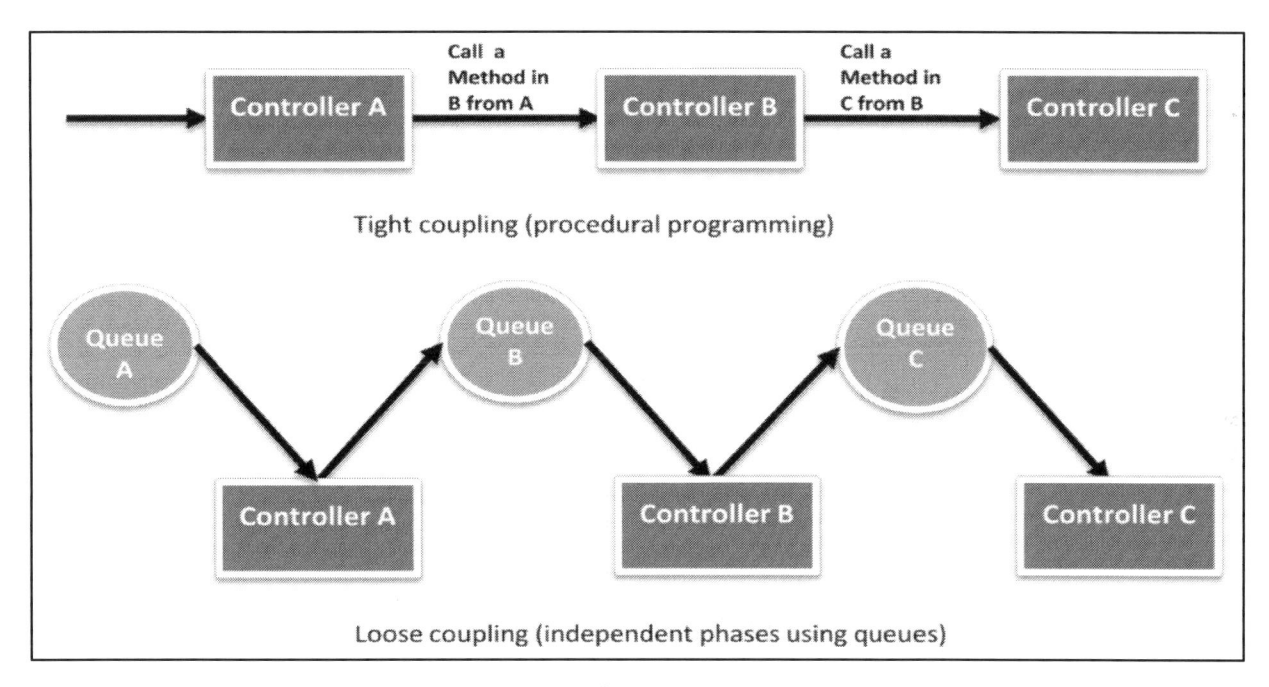

Figure 1-08. Tight and Loose Coupling

***Graceful Failure*–** Increases loose coupling by building applications that handle component failure in a graceful manner. In the event of component failure, this helps to reduce the impact on the end users and increase the ability to progress on offline procedures.

Services, Not Servers

Developing large-scale applications requires a variety of underlying technology components. Best design practice would be to leverage the broad set of computing, storage, database, analytics, application, and deployment services of AWS to increase developer productivity and operational efficiency.

Managed Services- Always rely on services, not severs. Developers can power their applications by using AWS managed services that include databases, machine learning, analytics, queuing, search, email, notifications, and many more. For example, Amazon S3 can be used to store data without having to think about capacity, hard disk configurations, replication, etc. Amazon S3 also provides a highly available static web hosting solution that can scale automatically to meet traffic demand.

> EXAM TIP: Amazon S3 is great for static website hosting.

Serverless Architectures - Serverless architectures reduce the operational complexity of running applications. Event-driven and synchronous services can both be built without managing any server infrastructure. For example, your code can be uploaded to AWS lambda compute service that runs the code on your behalf. Develop scalable synchronous APIs powered by AWS Lambda using Amazon API Gateway. Lastly combining this with Amazon S3 for serving static content, a complete web application can be produced.

> EXAM TIP: For event-driven managed service/serverless architecture, use AWS Lambda. If you want to customize to your own needs, then Amazon EC2 offers flexibility and full control.

Databases

AWS managed database services remove constraints that come with licensing costs and the ability to support diverse database engines. While designing system architecture, keep in mind these different kinds of database technologies:

Relational Databases

- Often called RDBS or SQL databases.
- Consist of normalized data in well-defined tabular structures known as tables, consisting of rows and columns.
- Provide powerful query language, flexible indexing capabilities, strong integrity controls, and ability to combine data from multiple tables fast and efficiently.

Chapter 1: Cloud Concepts

- Amazon Relational Database Service (Amazon RDS) and Amazon Aurora.
- *Scalability:* Can scale vertically by upgrading to a larger Amazon RDS DB instance or adding more and faster storage. For read-heavy applications, use Amazon Aurora to horizontally scale by creating one or more read replicas.
- *High Availability:* using Amazon RDS Multi-AZ deployment feature creates synchronously replicated standby instance in a different Availability Zone (AZ). In case of failure of the primary node, Amazon RDS performs an automatic fail over to the standby without manual administrative intervention.
- *Anti-Patterns:* If your application does not need joins or complex transactions, consider a NoSQL database instead. Store large binary files (audio, video, and image) in Amazon S3 and only hold the metadata for the files in the database.

Non-Relational Databases

- Often called NoSQL databases
- The trade off query and transaction capabilities of relational databases for a more flexible data model
- Utilize a variety of data models, including graphs, key-value pairs, and JSON documents
- Amazon DynamoDB
- *Scalability:* Automatically scales horizontally by data partitioning and replication
- *High Availability:* Synchronously replicates data across three facilities in an AWS region to provide fault tolerance in case of a server failure or Availability Zone disruption
- *Anti-Patterns:* If your schema cannot be de-normalized and requires joins or complex transactions, consider a relational database instead. Store large binary files (audio, video, and image) in Amazon S3 and only hold the metadata for the files in the database

> 💡 **EXAM TIP**: In any kind of given scenario, if you have to work on complex transactions or using JOINs, then you should use Amazon Aurora, Amazon RDS, MySQL or any other relational database. However, if you are not, then you should use a non-relational database like Amazon DynamoDB.

31

Chapter 1: Cloud Concepts

Data Warehouse

- A special type of relational data base optimized for analysis and reporting of large amounts of data.

- Used to combine transactional data from disparate sources making them available for analysis and decision-making.

- Running complex transactions and queries on the production database create massive overhead and require immense processing power, hence the need for data warehousing arises.

- Amazon Redshift

- *Scalability:* Amazon Redshift uses a combination of massively parallel processing (MPP), columnar data storage and targeted data compression encoding to achieve efficient storage and optimum query performance. It increases performance by increasing the number of nodes in data warehouse cluster.

- *High Availability:* By deploying production workloads in multi-node clusters, it enables the data written to a node to be automatically replicated to other nodes within the cluster. Data is also continuously backed up to Amazon S3. Amazon Redshift automatically re-replicates data from failed drives and replaces nodes when necessary.

- *Anti-Patterns:* It is not meant to be used for online transaction processing (OLTP) functions as Amazon Redshift is a SQL-based relational database management system (RDBMS). For high concurrency workload or a production database, consider using Amazon RDS or Amazon DynamoDB instead.

Search

- Search service is used to index and search, it is in both structured and free text format.

- Sophisticated search functionality typically outgrows the capabilities of relational or NO SQL databases. Therefore a search service is required.

- AWS provides two services, Amazon CloudSearch and Amazon ElasticSearch Service (Amazon ES).

- Amazon CloudSearch is a managed search service that requires little configuration and scales automatically; whereas Amazon ES offers an open source API offering more control over the configuration details.

- *Scalability:* Both uses data partitioning and replication to scale horizontally.

- *High-Availability:* Both services store data redundantly across Availability Zones.

Removing Single Points of Failure

A system needs to be highly available to withstand any failure of the individual or multiple components (e.g., hard disks, servers, network links, etc.).You should have resiliency built across multiple services as well as multiple availability zones to automate recovery and reduce disruption at every layer of your architecture.

Introducing Redundancy - Have multiple resources for the same task. Redundancy can be implemented in either standby or active mode. In standby mode, functionality is recovered through secondary resource while the initial resource remains unavailable. In active mode, requests are distributed to multiple redundant compute resources when one of them fails.

Detect Failure - Detection, and reaction to failure should both be automated as much as possible. Configure health checks and mask failure by routing traffic to healthy endpoints using services like ELB and Amazon Route53. Auto Scaling can be configured to replace unhealthy nodes using the Amazon EC2 autorecovery feature or services such as AWS OpsWorks and AWS Elastic Beanstalk.

Durable Data Storage – Durable data storage is vital for data availability and integrity. Data replication can be achieved by introducing redundant copies of data. The three modes of replication that can be used are; asynchronous replication, synchronous replication, and Quorum-based replication.

- **Synchronous replication** only acknowledges a transaction after it has been durably stored in both the primary location and its replicas.

- **Asynchronous replication** decouples the primary node from its replicas at the expense of introducing replication lag.

- **Quorum-based replication** combines synchronous and asynchronous replication to overcome the challenges of large-scale distributed database systems.

Automated Multi-Data Center Resilience – This is achieved by using the multiple availability zones offered by the AWS global infrastructure. Availability zones are designed to be isolated from failures of the other availability zones. For example, a fleet of application servers distributed across multiple Availability Zones can be attached to the Elastic Load Balancing service (ELB). When health checks of the EC2 instances of a particular Availability Zone fail, ELB will stop sending traffic to those nodes. Amazon RDS provides automatic failover support for DB instances using Multi-AZ deployments, while Amazon S3 and Amazon DynamoDB stores data redundantly across multiple facilities.

Fault Isolation and Traditional Horizontal Scaling – Fault isolation can be attained through sharding. Sharding is a method of grouping instances into groups called shards. Each customer is assigned to a specific shard instead of spreading traffic from all customers across every node. Shuffle sharding technique allows the client to try every endpoint in a set of shared resources until one succeeds.

Optimize for Cost

Reduce capital expenses by benefiting from the AWS economies of scale. Main principles of optimizing for cost include:

Right-Sizing – AWS offers a broad set of options for instance types. Selecting the right configurations, resource types and storage solutions that suit your workload requirements can reduce cost.

Elasticity – Implement Auto Scaling to horizontally scale up and down automatically depending upon your need to reduce cost. Automate turning off non-production workloads when not in use. Use AWS managed services wherever possible that helps in taking capacity decisions as and when needed.

Take Advantage of the Variety of Purchasing Options – AWS provides flexible purchasing options with no long-term commitments. These purchasing options can reduce cost while paying for instances. Two ways to pay for Amazon EC2 instances are:

- Reserved Capacity – Reserved instances enable you to get a significantly discounted hourly rate when reserving computing capacity as oppose to On-Demand instance pricing. Ideal for applications with predictable capacity requirements.
- Spot Instances – Available at discounted pricing compared to On-Demand pricing. Ideal for workloads that have flexible start and end times. Spot instances allow you to bid on spare computing capacity. When your bid exceeds the current Spot

market price, your instance is launched. If the Spot market price increases above your bid price, your instance will be terminated automatically.

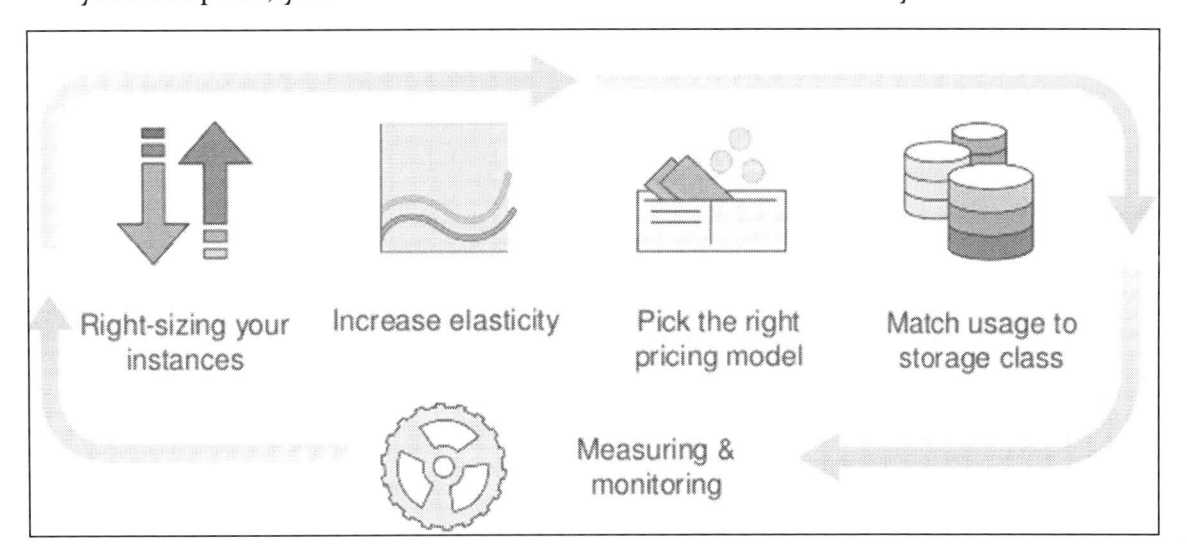

Figure 1-09. Cost Optimization Pillars

Caching

Caching is used to store previously calculated data for future use. This improves application performance and increases the cost efficiency of implementation. A good practice is to implement caching in the IT architecture whenever possible.

***Application Data Caching*–** Application data can be stored in the cache for subsequent requests to improve latency for end users and reduce the load on back-end systems. Amazon ElastiCache makes it easy to deploy, operate, and scale an in-memory cache in the cloud.

***Edge Caching*–** Both static and dynamic content can be cached at multiple edge locations around the world using Amazon CloudFront. This allows content to be served by infrastructure that is closer to viewers, lowering latency and providing high, sustained data transfer rates to deliver large popular objects to end users at scale.

Security

AWS allows you to improve your security in a variety of ways, plus also letting the use of security tools and techniques that traditional IT infrastructures implement.

***Utilize AWS Features for Defense in Depth*–**Isolate parts of the infrastructure by building a VPC network topology using subnets, security groups, and routing controls. Setup web application firewall for protection using AWS WAF.

Offload Security Responsibility to AWS- Security of the underlying cloud infrastructure is managed by AWS; you are only responsible for securing the workloads you deploy in AWS.

Reduce Privileged Access– To avoid a breach of security, reduce privileged access to the programmable resources and servers. For example, defining IAM roles to restrict root level access.

Security as Code -AWS Cloud Formation scripts can be used that incorporates your security policy and reliably deploys it. Security scripts can be reused among multiple projects as part of your continuous integration pipeline.

Real-Time Auditing– AWS allows you to continuously monitor and automate controls to minimize security risk exposures. Services like AWS Config, Amazon Inspector, and AWS Trusted Advisor continually monitor IT resources for compliance and vulnerabilities. Testing and auditing in real-time are essential for keeping the environment fast and safe.

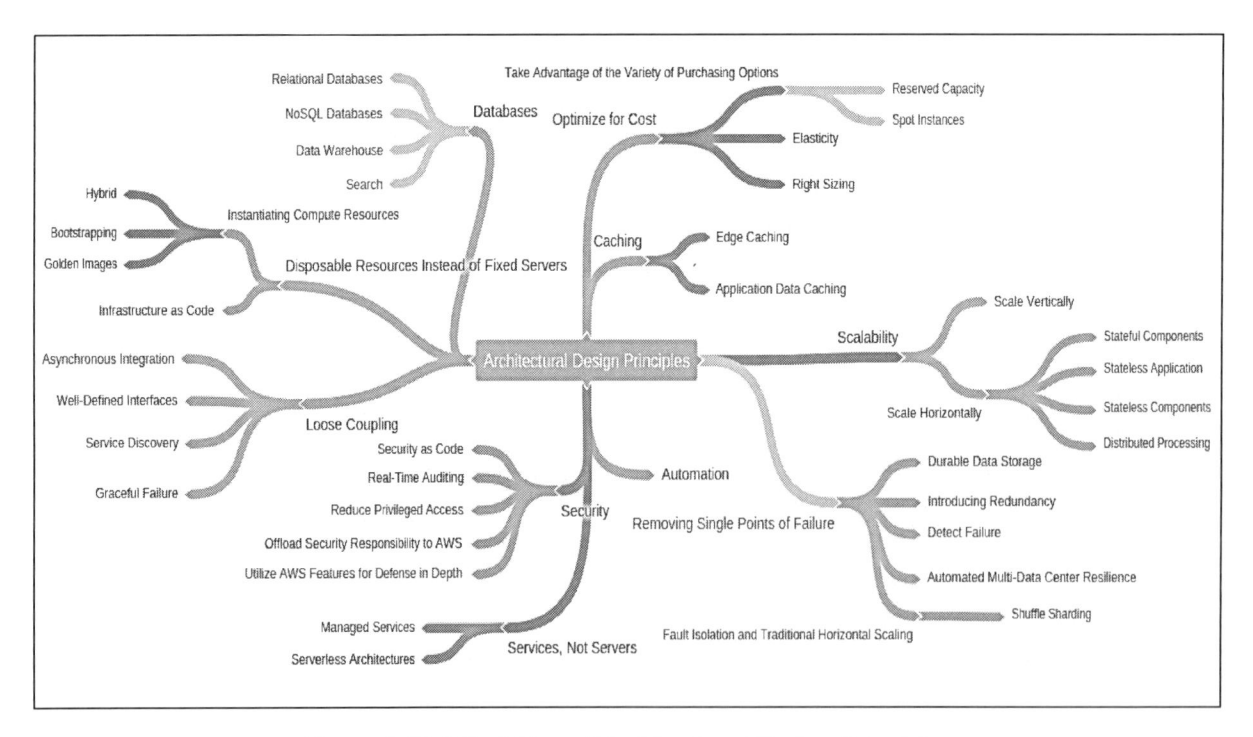

Figure 1-10. Mind Map of Architectural Design Principles

Chapter 2: Security

Introduction to AWS Cloud Security

Security in the cloud is much like security in traditional IT on-premises data centers, only without the costs of maintaining facilities and hardware. This includes protecting critical information from theft, data leakage, integrity, and deletion. In the cloud scenario, the cloud provider handles management of physical servers or storage devices while the customer uses software-based security tools to monitor and protect the flow of information going in and out of the cloud resources.

Benefits of AWS Security

- *Keep your data safe*- With strongly safeguarded AWS infrastructure; data is stored in highly secured AWS data centers.

- *Meet compliance requirements* -AWS infrastructure incorporates dozens of compliance programs. This means that segments of user compliance have already been completed.

- *Save money* - While using the highly secured AWS data centers, pay only for the services without the upfront expenses at a lower cost than in an on-premises environment.

- *Scale quickly* -AWS allows customers to scale and innovate the environment while maintaining the security of the environment. Infrastructure is designed to keep data safe no matter what the size of your system is.

AWS Shared Responsibility Model

The management of the security in the cloud is slightly different from the security in the on-premises data center. Migrating computer systems and data to the cloud requires AWS and customers to work together towards security objectives. The security responsibilities are shared between the user and the cloud service provider. Under this shared responsibility model, AWS is responsible for securing the underlying infrastructure that supports the cloud, and the user is responsible for anything deployed in the cloud or connects to the cloud.

While AWS manages the security of the cloud, security in the cloud is the responsibility of the customer. The control of security implementation for protecting the content, platform, applications systems, and networks, retains with the customer, it is no different than it would be in an on-site datacenter.

Following is the shared security responsibility model that describes what AWS and the customer is responsible for in this cloud-computing domain.

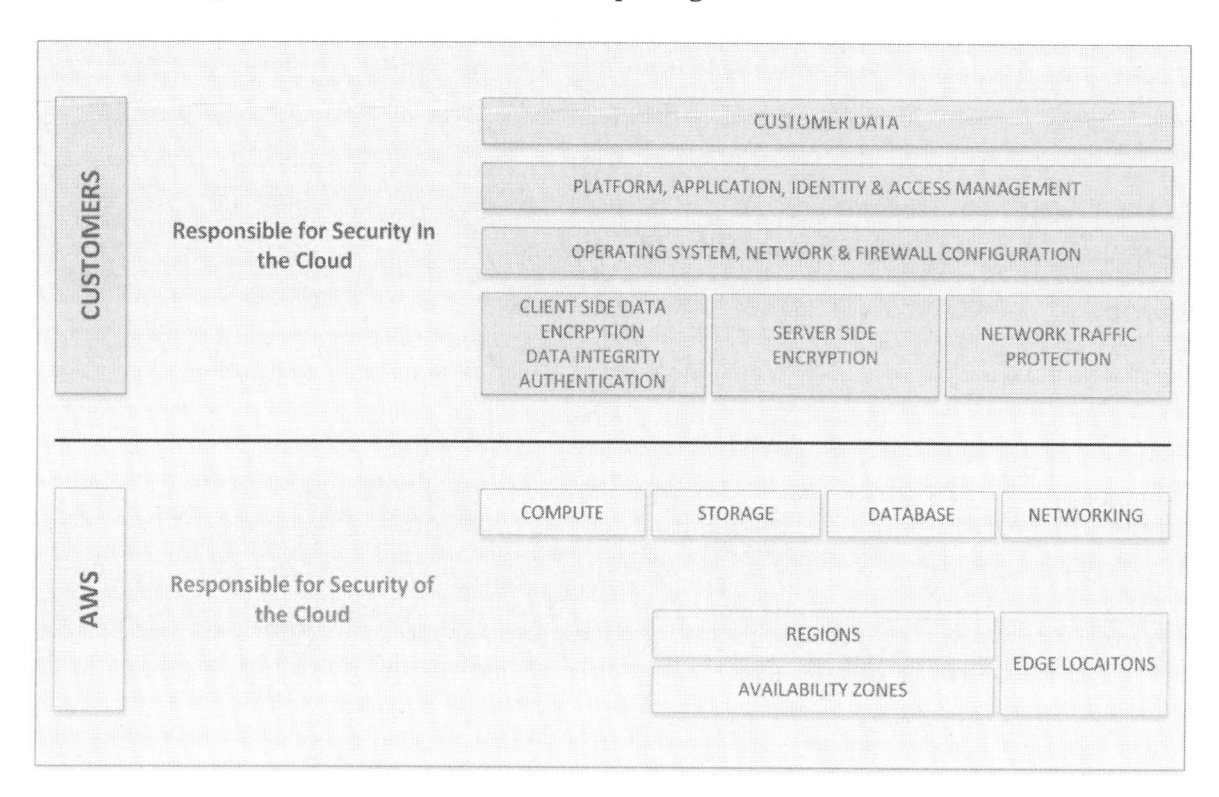

Figure 2-01. AWS Shared Security Responsibility Model

AWS Security Responsibilities

AWS operates, manages, and controls the components of the host operating system and virtualization layer down to the physical security of the facilities in which the services operate. Therefore, AWS is responsible for securing their complete global infrastructure including foundational compute, storage, networking and database services, as well as higher-level services.

In addition to the above, AWS is also responsible for the security configuration of its products that are considered managed services. Examples of these types of services include Amazon DynamoDB, Amazon RDS, Amazon Redshift, Amazon Elastic MapReduce, Amazon WorkSpaces, and several other services. For these services, AWS handles basic security tasks like guest operating system (OS) and database patching, firewall configuration, and disaster recovery.

Customer Security Responsibilities

As AWS customers retain control over their data, they consequently hold the responsibilities relating to that content as part of the AWS "shared responsibility" model. Their responsibility is to protect the confidentiality, integrity, and availability of their data in the cloud. They undertake responsibility for the management of their operating system (including updates and security patches), other associated application software, as well as the configuration of the AWS-provided security group firewall. AWS provides a range of security services and features that AWS customers can use to secure their assets.

The responsibilities and the amount of security configuration work the customer needs to take care of depends on the type of AWS services selected and sensitivity of the data. If the services fall under the category of Infrastructure as a service (IaaS), such as Amazon EC2 and Amazon VPC, then all the necessary security configuration and management tasks need to be handled completely by the customer. Whereas for AWS managed services such as Amazon RDS or Amazon Redshift, there is no need to worry about the configuration work as AWS handles it for you.

Irrespective of the AWS services used, you should always configure security by using AWS Account credentials and setting up individual user accounts with Amazon Identity and Access Management (IAM) so that each of the users has their own credentials. Other security features such as using multi-factor authentication (MFA) with each account, requiring the use of SSL/TLS to communicate with your AWS resources, setting up API/user activity logging with AWS CloudTrail, leveraging technology such as host-based firewalls, host-based intrusion detection/ prevention, and encryption are some of the AWS assistive tools provided to the customers to enhance security.

> EXAM TIP: A way to remember the shared responsibility model is to analyze what is it that you have control over and what you do not. When given a specific scenario, consider whether you have control over that particular task, service or resource, if not, then its Amazon's responsibility. Security 'in' the cloud is your responsibility and security 'of' the cloud is Amazon's share.

AWS Global Infrastructure Security

The AWS global infrastructure is one of the most flexible and secure cloud computing platform present today. It is designed to offer an exceptionally scalable, highly reliable platform that facilitates customers in deploying applications and data swiftly and securely. The infrastructure includes the services, network, hardware, and operational software (e.g., host OS, virtualization software, etc.) that support the provisioning and use of computing resources.

AWS runs under a shared security responsibility model, where AWS is in-charge of the cloud infrastructure security and the user is responsible for securing workloads deployed in the cloud. This provides the flexibility and agility to implement appropriate security controls such as strongly restricting access to locations that process sensitive data, or setting up less rigid controls for data admissible to the public.

The AWS global infrastructure utilizes the security's best practices along with a range of security compliance standards. AWS monitors and protects the underlying infrastructure 24x7 using redundant and layered controls, continuous validation and testing, and extensive automation. AWS ensures the replication of these controls in each new data center or service.

AWS Compliance Program

AWS computing environments are continuously audited with certifications from accreditation bodies across geographies and verticals, including ISO 27001, FedRAMP, DoD CSM, and PCI DSS. By operating in an accredited environment, customers reduce the scope and cost of audits they need to perform. AWS continuously undergoes assessments of its underlying infrastructure including the physical and environmental security of its hardware and data centers so customers can take advantage of those certifications and simply inherent those controls. Following are the programs that AWS have in terms of Compliance. These are divided into three areas;

1. Certifications / Attestation
2. Laws, Regulations and Privacy
3. Alignments / Framework

Chapter 2: Security

Certifications/Attestation

DoD SRG - FedRAMP - FIPS - IRAP - ISO 9001 - ISO 27001
ISO 27017 - ISO 27018 - MTCS - PCI DSS Level 1 - SEC Rule
17-a-4(f) - SOC 1 - SOC 2 - SOC 3

Laws, Regulations, and Privacy

EAR - EU Model Clauses - FERPA GLBA - HIPAA - HITECH - IRS
1075 - ITAR - My Number Act (Japan) - U.K. DPA 1988 VPAT/-
Section 508 - EU Data Protection Directive
Privacy Act (Australia) - PDPA - 2010 (Malaysia) - PDPA - 2012
(Singapore)

Alignments/Frameworks

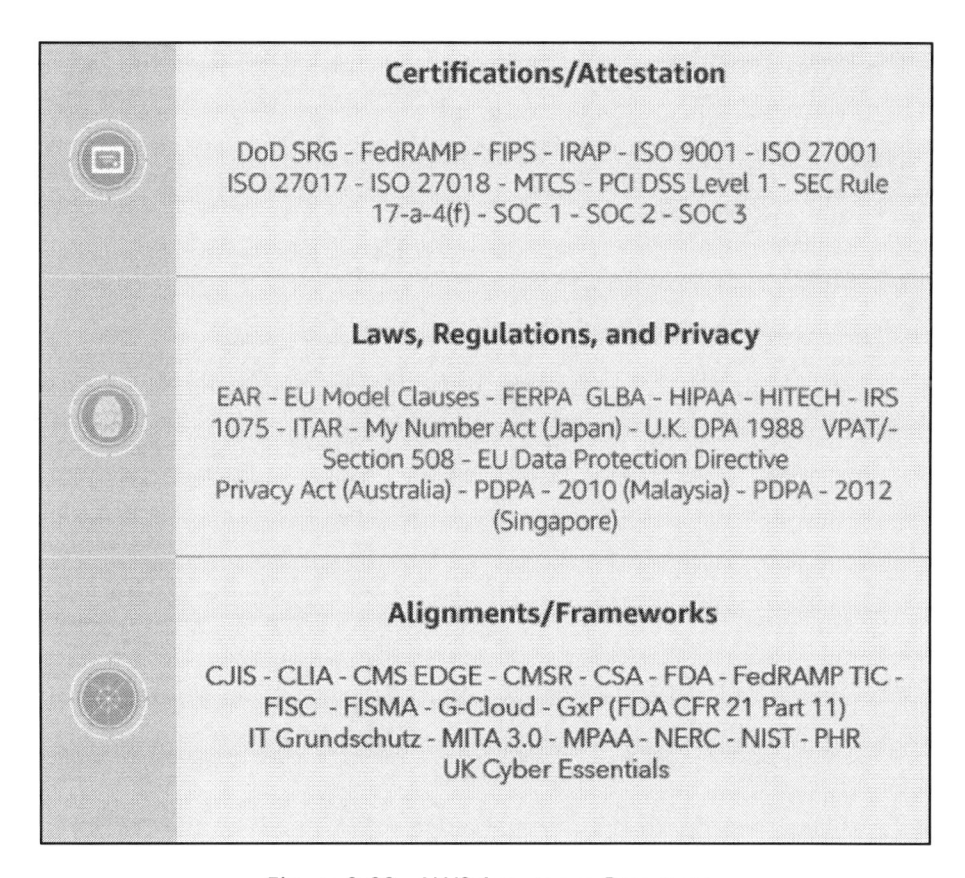

CJIS - CLIA - CMS EDGE - CMSR - CSA - FDA - FedRAMP TIC -
FISC - FISMA - G-Cloud - GxP (FDA CFR 21 Part 11)
IT Grundschutz - MITA 3.0 - MPAA - NERC - NIST - PHR
UK Cyber Essentials

Figure 2-02. AWS Assurance Programs

Certifications / Attestations:

Compliance certifications and attestations are assessed by a third party, independent auditor and result in a certification, audit report, or attestation of compliance. Major ones that you need to be aware of for this course are ISO 27001, PCI DSS Level 1, SOC 1, SOC 2, and SOC 3.

- *ISO 27001* - ISO 27001 is a security management standard that specifies security management's best practices and comprehensive security controls.
- *PCI DSS Level 1*- The Payment Card Industry Data Security Standard (PCI DSS) is a proprietary information security standard (means protected by copyright or trademark) administered by the PCI Security Standards Council. All entities that deal with online payments by means of credit cards that involve storing, processing or transmitting cardholder's data, need to be PCI DSS Level 1 compliant.

- **SOC** - AWS System & Organization Control (SOC) Reports are independent third-party examination reports that demonstrate how AWS achieves key compliance controls and objectives. AWS platform is compatible with SOC 1, SOC 2, & SOC3.

Laws, Regulations, and Privacy:

AWS customers remain responsible for complying with applicable compliance laws and regulations. The main one you should be aware of is HIPAA.

- **HIPAA** - U.S. Health Insurance Portability and Accountability Act (HIPAA) is a set of federal standards intended to protect the security and privacy of PHI Protected Health Information (PHI). AWS enables covered entities and their business associates subject to HIPAA to leverage the secure AWS environment for processing, maintaining, and storing protected health information.

Alignments / Frameworks:

Compliance alignments and frameworks include published security or compliance requirements for a specific purpose, such as a specific industry or function. The one to be looked at is G-Cloud [UK].

- **G-Cloud [UK]** -The G-Cloud framework is an agreement between the UK government and cloud-based service providers. The framework enables public bodies to procure commodity-based, pay-as-you-go cloud services on government-approved short-term contracts. Hence, in order to host on AWS, they need to meet the G-Cloud [UK] requirements.

AWS Access Management

AWS contains numerous cloud services that can be accessed and used in combination depending on your business or organizational requirements.

Access Methods

There are three ways of accessing these services;

- **The AWS Management Console**– AWS offers web access to services by using the AWS Management Console. This is a simple and intuitive user interface to easily access and manage Amazon Web Services. There is also a mobile app version, AWS Console Mobile App, to view resources swiftly on the move.
- **The Command Line Interface**- The AWS Command Line Interface (CLI) is an integrated tool that manages the AWS services by controlling them from the

command line and provides programmatic access by automating them through scripts.

- *Software Development Kits (SDKs)* - Software Development Kits (SDKs) that contain libraries and sample code for numerous programming languages and platforms (Java, Python, Ruby, .NET, iOS, Android, etc.), provide programmatic access to AWS services in your applications through Application Program Interface (API), are personalized for your programming language or platform.

> **EXAM TIP:** Remember these three access methods i.e AWS Management console, SDK and CLI.

Getting Started with AWS

Go to 'aws.amazon.com/free' to create an account. A Free Tier account gives you the benefit of getting free, hands-on experience with the AWS platform, products, and services. You will get some of the services free for 12 months while some are always free. For compute capacity and database service, you get 750 hours/month of Amazon EC2 and Amazon RDS respectively and 5 GB of Amazon S3 for storage.

Create a billing alarm

After creating your Free Tier account, sign in to the Management Console to setup billing alarms. Creating a billing alarm will save you from any unnecessary cost and will alert you if you are being charged over a certain amount.

Chapter 2: Security

Lab 2-1: Creating a Billing Alarm

1. Log in to the 'AWS Console'.
2. Click on your account name at the top right corner for the drop down menu. Select 'My Billing Dashboard'.

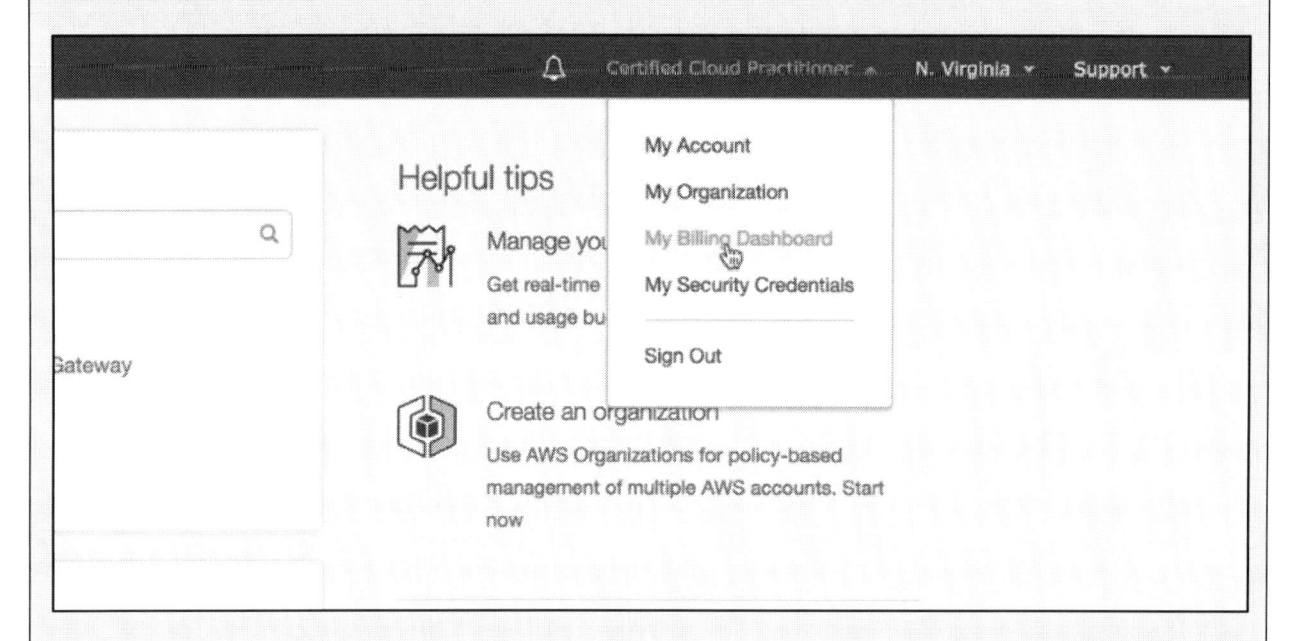

3. Scroll down to the 'Alerts & Notifications' section. Click 'Enable Now' for 'Monitor your estimated charges' option.

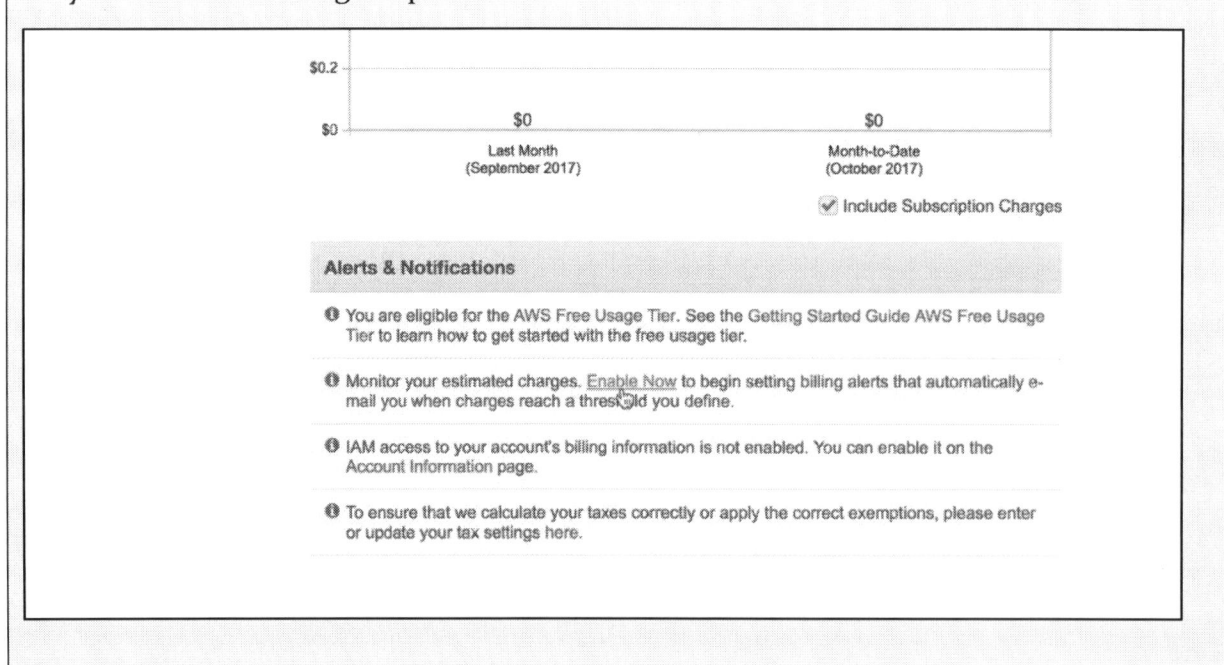

4. Select the checkbox for 'Receive Billing Alerts' and click 'Save preferences'.

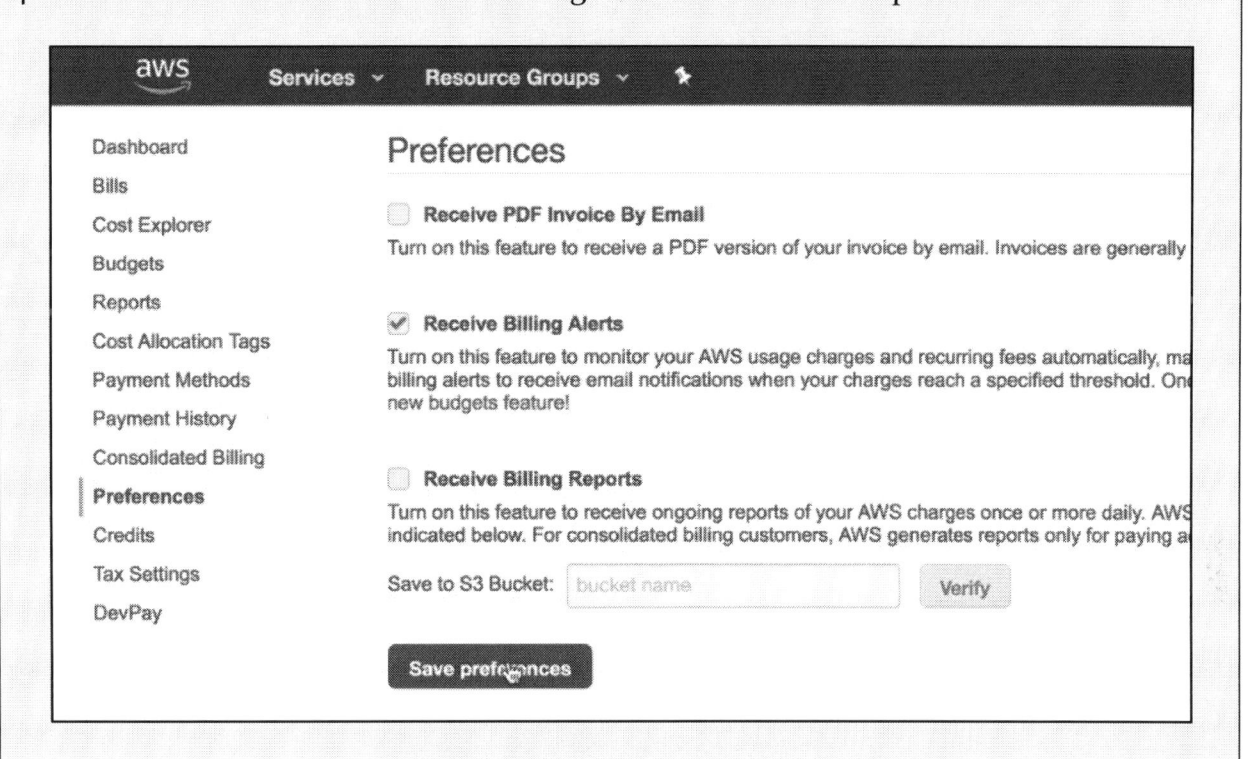

5. Once that is done, go on to select 'Manage Billing Alerts' in the 'Receive Billing Alert' option. In the 'Alarm Summary' section, select 'Create a billing alarm'.

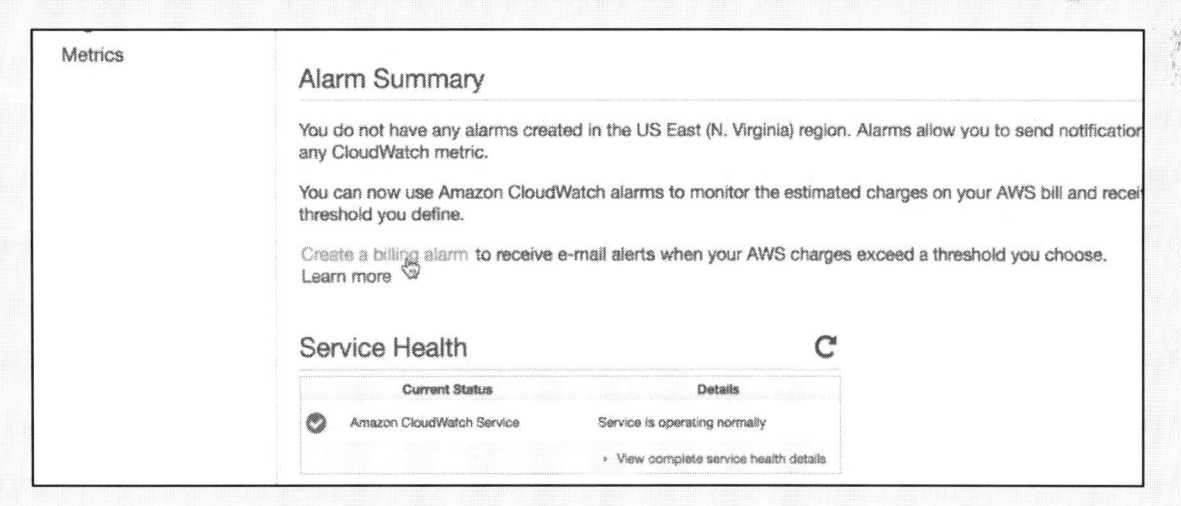

6. Enter the threshold amount for which you want Amazon to alert you and the email address where you want to be notified. Click 'Create Alarm' when done.

Chapter 2: Security

> **Create Alarm**
>
> **Billing Alarm**
> You can create a billing alarm to receive e-mail alerts when your AWS charges exceed a threshold you choose. Simply:
> 1. Enter a spending threshold
> 2. Provide an email address
> 3. Check your inbox for a confirmation email and click the link provided
>
> When my total AWS charges for the month
> exceed: $ 10 USD
> send a notification to: [type your email address]
>
> **Reminder:** for each address you add, you will receive an email from AWS with the subject "*AWS Notification - Subscription Confirmation*". Click the link provided in the message to confirm that AWS may deliver alerts to that address.
>
> **Additional settings**
> Provide additional configuration for your alarm.
>
> Treat missing data as: missing
>
> showing simple options | show advanced
>
> **Alarm Preview**
> This alarm will trigger when the blue line goes above the red line
>
> EstimatedCharges > 10
>
> **More resources**
> AWS Billing console
> Getting started with billing alarms
> More help with billing alarms
> AWS Billing FAQs
>
> Cancel   Previous   Next   **Create Alarm**

7. You will need to check your inbox for an email confirmation. Once you have finished the email verification process, you will be able to see your alarm.

Chapter 2: Security

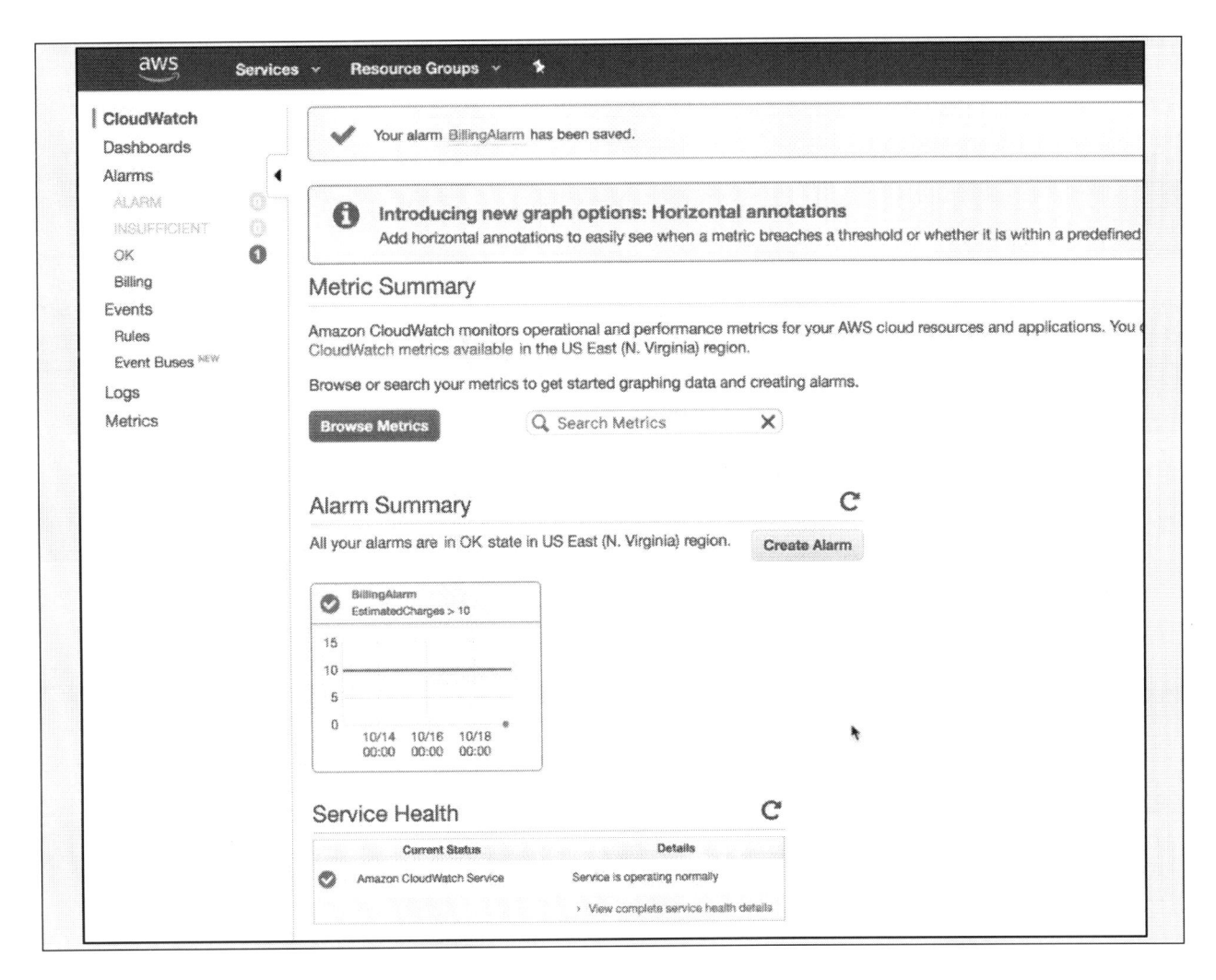

Setting Up On Mac

- For Code Editing
    - Download TextWrangler from the App Store.
    - This will make it easy for us to look at our code when we start building and working with webpages.
- For connecting to Windows instances
    - Download Microsoft Remote Desktop from the App Store.
    - This RDP (Remote Desktop Protocol) client will enable us to connect to Windows servers.
- For connecting to Linux instances
    - Go to Finder; under the Applications tab select Utilities. Select the Terminal app from the list.

Chapter 2: Security

- o Apple's Terminal app will enable us to connect to Linux instances via SSH protocol.

Setting Up On Windows

- For Code Editing
    - o Download Notepad++ from 'notepad-plus-plus.org'.
    - o This text editor will make it easy to edit your code.
- For connecting to remote instances
    - o Download PuTTY from 'chiark.greenend.org.uk'.
    - o This open-source terminal emulator will enable us to connect to remote instances via SSH protocol.
- For generating an access key
    - o Log in to the AWS console to Create Key Pair and download it.
    - o Open PuTTYgen and use the downloaded Key Pair to generate and save your access key.
    - o This key will be used to log in to the web servers.

Identity Access Management (IAM)

AWS Identity and Access Management (IAM) is a web service that provides secured control access to AWS resources such as compute, storage, database and application services in the AWS Cloud. IAM manages authentication and authorization by controlling who is signed-in and has permissions to utilize the resources. IAM uses access control concepts such as Users, Groups, Roles and Policies to control which users can access specific services, the kinds of actions they can perform, and which resources are available to them. The IAM service is free of any additional charge. However, your account will be charged upon usage of other AWS services by your users.

When you first create an AWS account, you begin with a single sign-in identity that has complete access to all AWS services and resources in the account. This identity is called the AWS account root user and is accessed by signing in with the email address and password that you used to create the account. Since these credentials have complete access to the AWS account, it is highly recommended to adopt the best practice of using the Root User only to create other Users for individuals within your organization. Make sure the credentials for the Root User account are kept safe and used only for a few account and service management tasks.

Chapter 2: Security

> **EXAM TIP**: Understand what the Root User is and know its privileges. It always has full administrator access, and for this reason, you should not give these account credentials away to anyone. Instead, you should create a user for each individual within your organization and always secure this root account using multi-factor authentication.

IAM Features

The IAM service is the component of the AWS secure global infrastructure. With IAM, you can create and manage users and groups, security credentials such as passwords, access keys, and permission policies to allow and deny access to the AWS resources.

Figure 2-03. IAM Features

What is an IAM user?

An IAM user is a unique identity that has limited access to an AWS account and its resources, as defined by their IAM permissions and policies. IAM users can represent a person, system, or application. IAM policies assigned to a user must grant explicit permissions to services or resources before the user can view or use them.

IAM lets you create individual users within your AWS account and give them each their own username, password, and access keys. Individual users can then log into the console using a URL that is specific to your account. You can also create access keys for individual users so that they can make programmatic calls to access AWS resources. You can permit a user to access any or all of the AWS services that have been integrated with IAM or use IAM in conjunction with external identity sources, such as Microsoft Active Directory, AWS Directory Service, or Login with Amazon.

If the users in your organization already have a way to be authenticated, such as by signing in to your corporate network, you do not have to create separate IAM users for them. Instead, you can federate those user identities into AWS. As a best practice, it is recommended that you create an IAM user even for yourself and that you do not use your AWS account credentials for everyday access to AWS.

What is a Group?

A group is a collection of IAM users. You can use groups to specify permissions for a collection of users, which makes it easier to manage permissions for them. For example, you can have a group called Admins and give that group the types of permissions that administrators typically need. Any user in that group automatically has the permissions that are assigned to the group. If a new user joins your organization and needs to have administrator privileges, you can assign the appropriate permissions by adding the user to that group. Similarly, if a person changes jobs in your organization, instead of editing that user's permissions, you can remove him or her from the old groups and add him or her to the appropriate new groups.

Some key aspects of Groups:

- A user can be added or removed from a group.
- A user can belong to multiple groups.
- A group cannot belong to other groups.
- Groups can be granted permissions using access control policies. This makes it easier to manage permissions for a collection of users, rather than having to manage permissions for each individual user.
- Groups do not have security credentials, and cannot access web services directly; they exist solely to make it easier to manage user permissions.

> EXAM TIP: A group is simply a collection of IAM users. The users will inherit all permissions that the group has.

What is an IAM role?

An IAM role is an IAM entity that lets you define a set of permissions to access the resources that a user or service needs, but the permissions are not attached to a specific IAM user or group. Instead, IAM users, mobile, and EC2-based applications, or AWS services (like Amazon EC2) can programmatically assume a role. Assuming the role returns temporary security credentials that the user or application can use to make

Chapter 2: Security

programmatic requests to AWS. These temporary security credentials have a configurable expiration and are automatically rotated.

Using IAM roles and temporary security credentials mean you do not always have to manage long-term credentials and IAM users for each entity that requires access to a resource. Therefore, roles are much more secured than using access key ids and secret access keys and are easier to manage. You cannot attach multiple IAM roles to a single instance, but you can attach a single IAM role to multiple instances.

Roles are universal just like everything else in identity access management. You do not need to specify what region they are in, similar to users.

> **EXAM TIP**: IAM resources are global. You can use the IAM Roles across regions.

What are Policies?

An IAM policy is a rule or set of rules defining the operations allowed/denied to be performed on an AWS resource. Permissions are granted through policies. A policy when attached to an identity or resource defines their permissions. AWS evaluates these policies when a user makes a request. Permissions in the policies determine whether the request is allowed or denied. Policies are stored in AWS as JSON documents as identity-based policies, or as resource-based policies.

Policies can be granted in a number of ways:

- Attaching a managed policy. AWS provides a list of pre-defined policies such as AmazonS3 Read Only Access.
- Attaching an inline policy; An inline policy is a custom policy created by hand.
- Adding the user to a group that has appropriate permission policies attached.
- Cloning the permission of an existing IAM user.

By default, IAM users, groups, and roles have no permissions. To set permissions, you can create and attach policies using the AWS Management Console, the IAM API, or the AWS CLI. Users who have been granted the necessary permissions can create policies and assign them to IAM users, groups, and roles.

Managed policies are IAM resources that express permissions using the IAM policy language. You can create, edit, and manage separately from the IAM users, groups, and roles to which they are attached. After you attach a managed policy to multiple IAM users, groups, or roles, you can update that policy in one place, and the permissions automatically extend to all attached entities. Managed policies are policies that are managed either by customers (Customer managed policies) or by AWS (AWS managed policies).

Use IAM groups to collect IAM users and define common permissions for them. Use managed policies to share permissions across IAM users, groups, and roles. For example, if you want a group of users to be able to launch an Amazon EC2 instance, and you also want the role on that instance to have the same permissions as the users in the group, you can create a managed policy and assign it to the group of users and the role on to the Amazon EC2 instance.

> **EXAM TIP**: To set permissions in a group you need to apply a policy to that group. Policies consist of JavaScript Object Notation (JSON).

Key Differences between IAM user, IAM group, and IAM role

- An IAM user has permanent long-term credentials and is used to directly interact with AWS services.
- An IAM group is primarily a management convenience to manage the same set of permissions for a set of IAM users.
- An IAM role is an entity with permissions to make AWS service requests. An IAM role does not have any credentials and cannot make direct requests to AWS services. They are meant to be assumed by authorized entities, such as IAM users, applications, or AWS services such as EC2. Use IAM roles to delegate access within or between AWS accounts.

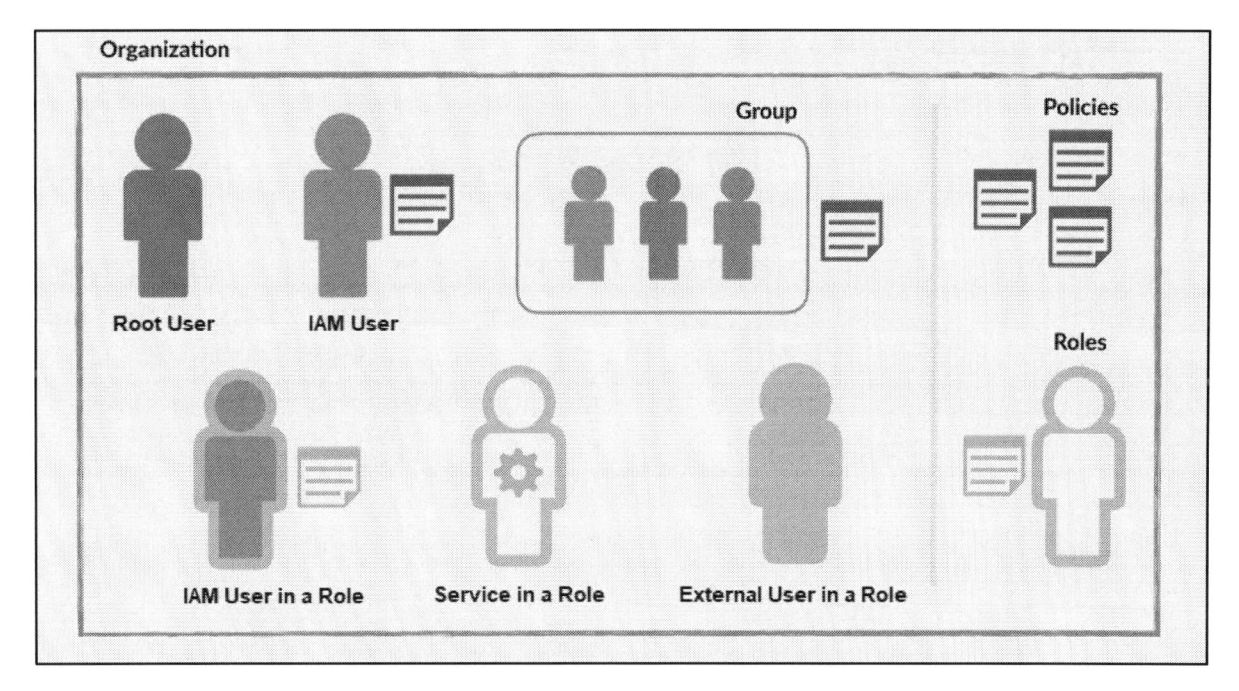

Figure 2-04. IAM Concepts

IAM Functionality

IAM assists in creating roles and permissions. AWS IAM allows you to:

- Manage IAM users, and their access – You can create users in IAM, assign them individual security credentials (in other words, access keys, passwords, and multi-factor authentication devices), or request temporary security credentials to provide users access to AWS services and resources. You can manage permissions in order to control which operations a user can perform.

- Manage IAM roles and their permissions – You can create roles in IAM and manage permissions to control which operations can be performed by the entity, or AWS service, that assumes the role. You can also define which entity is allowed to assume the role.

- Manage federated users, and their permissions– Federated users (external identities) are users you manage outside of AWS in your corporate directory, but to whom you grant access to your AWS account using temporary security credentials without the need to create an IAM user for each identity. They differ from IAM users, which are created and maintained in your AWS account.

Chapter 2: Security

IAM Best Practices

AWS has a list of best practices to help IT professionals and developers manage access to AWS resources.

- Users – Create individual IAM users.
- Groups – Use Groups to assign permissions to IAM users.
- Permissions – Use AWS defined policies to assign permissions whenever possible and granting least privileges. Review IAM Permissions using access levels.
- Auditing – Turn on AWS CloudTrail to monitor activity in your AWS account.
- Password – Configure a strong password policy for your users.
- MFA – Enable MFA for privileged users.
- Roles – Use Roles for applications that run on Amazon EC2 instances.
- Sharing – Use IAM roles to share access instead of sharing credentials.
- Rotate – Rotate security credentials regularly and remove unnecessary credentials.
- Conditions – Restrict privileged access further by using policy conditions for extra security.
- Root – Lock away your AWS Account Root User access keys and reduce or remove the use of root.

Lab 2-2: Creating IAM Users

1. Log in to the 'AWS Console'.
2. Click on 'Services'.
3. Scroll down to 'Security, Identity & Compliance'.
4. Select 'IAM'.

Chapter 2: Security

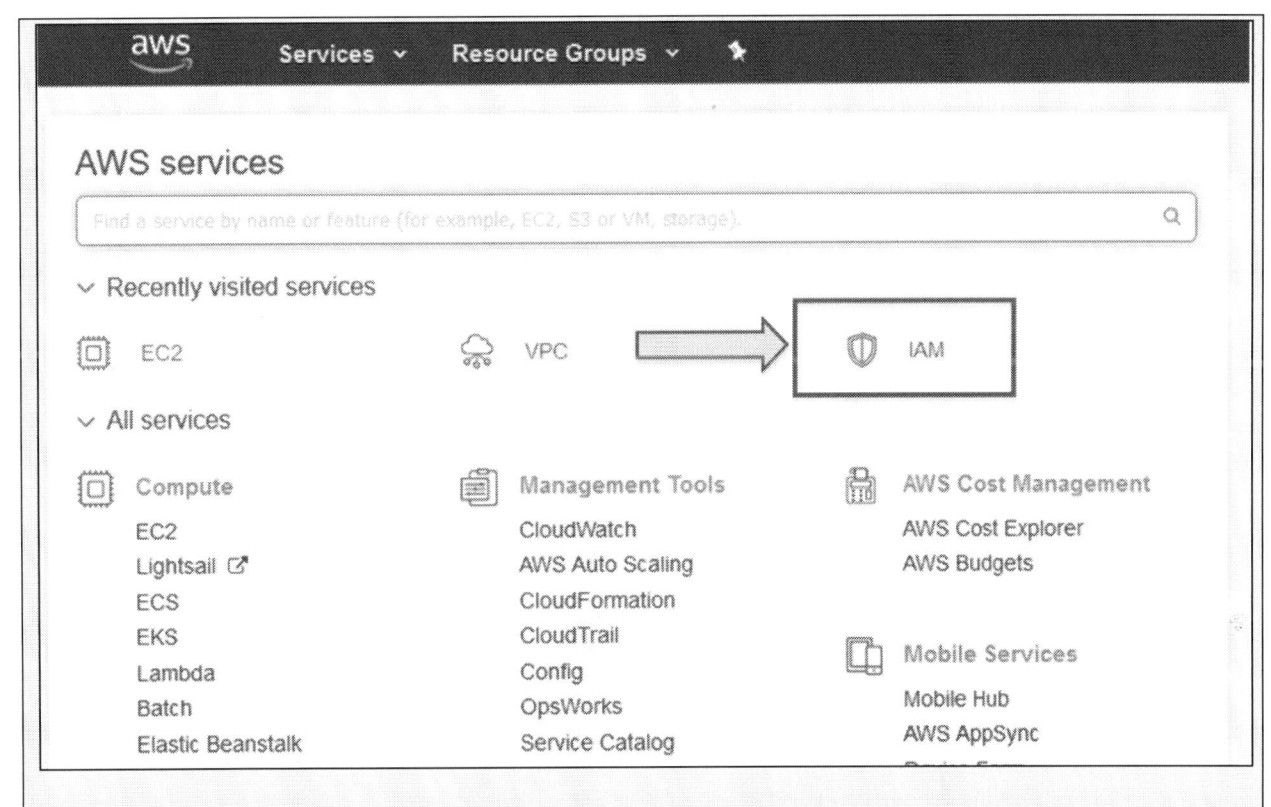

5. You will see IAM user's sign-in link at the top. This is a custom link where your users can sign-in. The greyed-out portion of the link contains your account number. For security reasons, you should use an alias name instead. Click on 'Customize' to enter an alias.

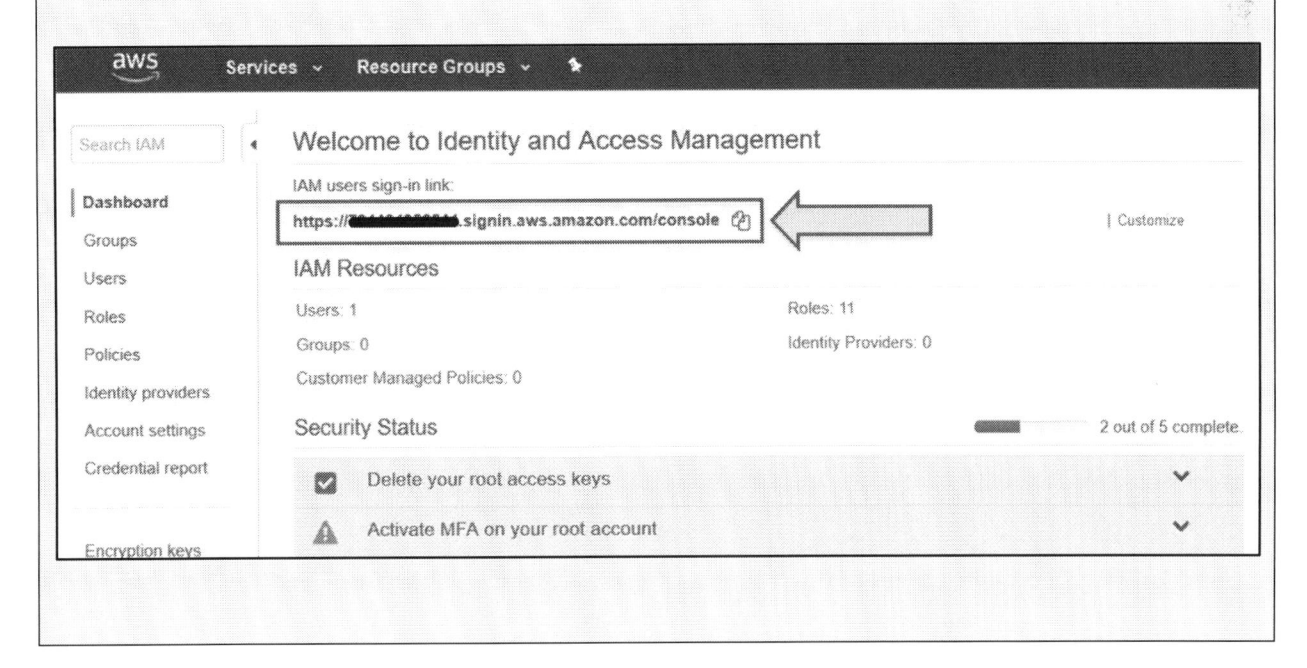

Chapter 2: Security

6. Click 'Yes, Create' to create an account alias.

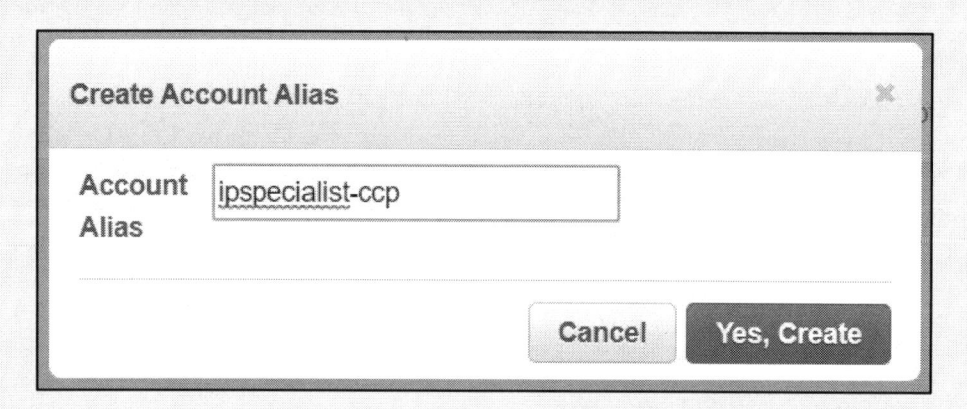

7. Next, you need to activate multi-factor authentication on your root account. Select 'Activate MFA on your root account' and click 'Manage MFA'.

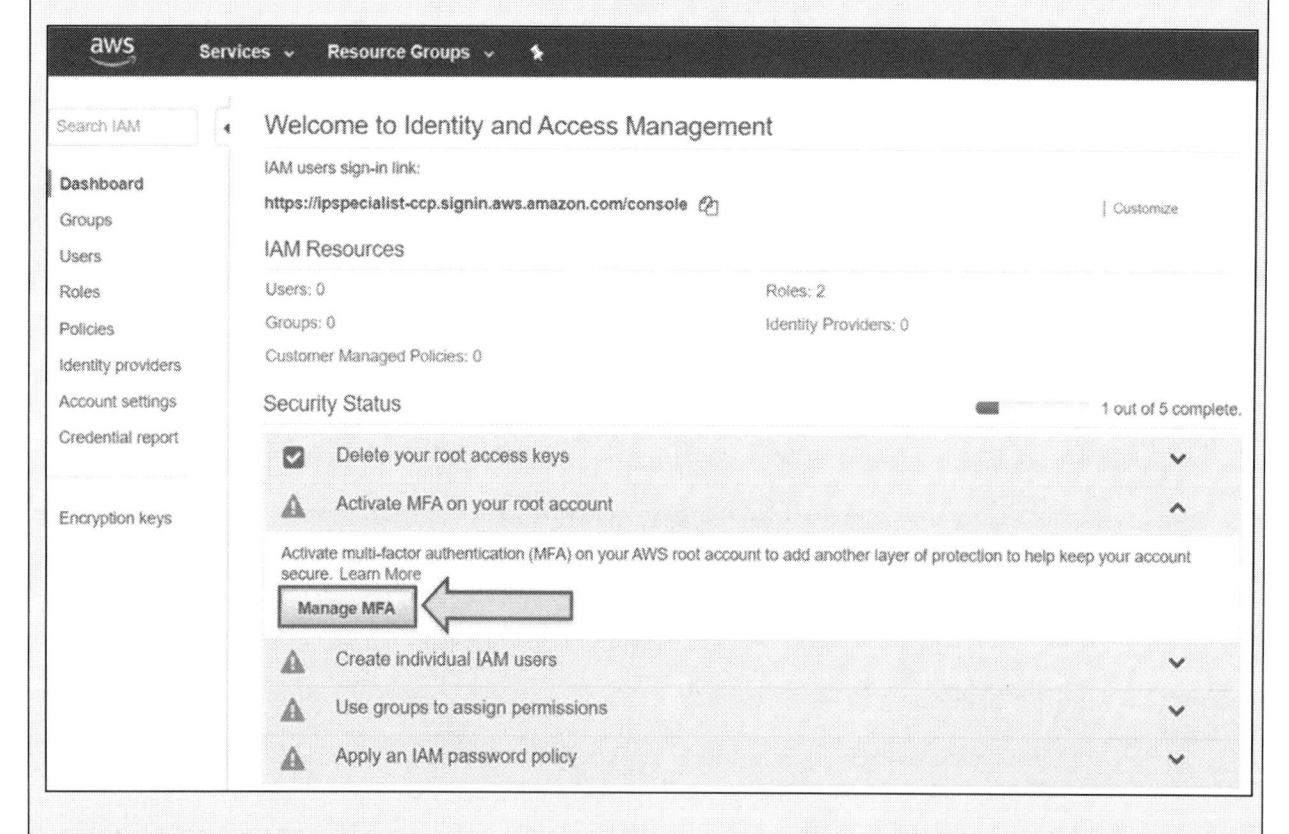

8. You need a physical device to enable hardware MFA. Use your smartphone and Google Authenticator to enable virtual MFA. You can download Google authenticator from the Google Play Store or iTunes on your smartphone.

Chapter 2: Security

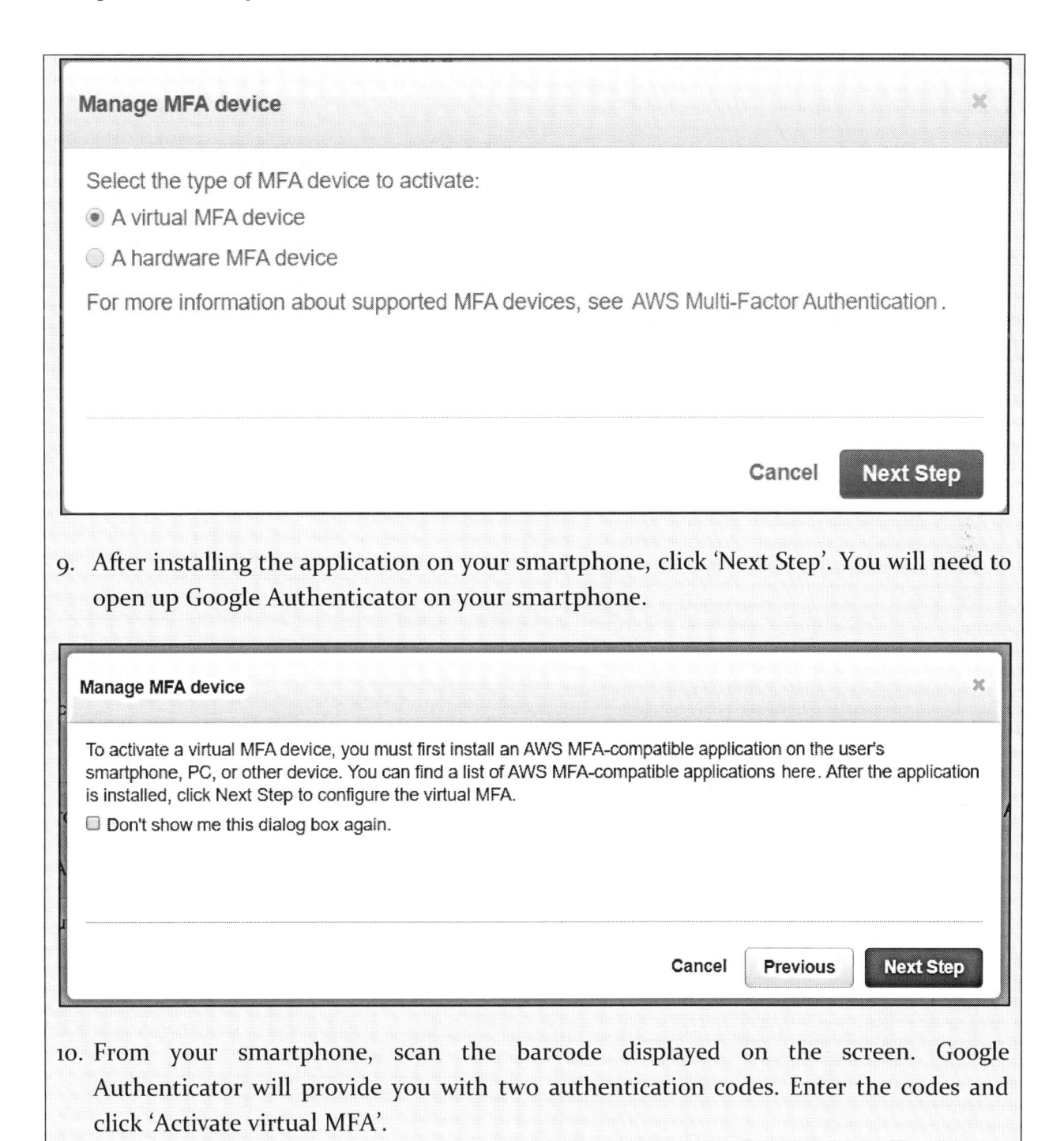

> **Manage MFA device**
>
> Select the type of MFA device to activate:
>
> ● A virtual MFA device
> ○ A hardware MFA device
>
> For more information about supported MFA devices, see AWS Multi-Factor Authentication.
>
> Cancel | **Next Step**

9. After installing the application on your smartphone, click 'Next Step'. You will need to open up Google Authenticator on your smartphone.

> **Manage MFA device**
>
> To activate a virtual MFA device, you must first install an AWS MFA-compatible application on the user's smartphone, PC, or other device. You can find a list of AWS MFA-compatible applications here. After the application is installed, click Next Step to configure the virtual MFA.
>
> ☐ Don't show me this dialog box again.
>
> Cancel | Previous | **Next Step**

10. From your smartphone, scan the barcode displayed on the screen. Google Authenticator will provide you with two authentication codes. Enter the codes and click 'Activate virtual MFA'.

Chapter 2: Security

Manage MFA device

If your virtual MFA application supports scanning QR codes, scan the following QR code with your smartphone's camera.

▸ Show secret key for manual configuration

After the application is configured, enter two consecutive authentication codes in the boxes below and choose **Activate virtual MFA**.

Authentication code 1: 370834

Authentication code 2: 292960

Cancel | Previous | **Activate virtual MFA**

11. A pop up will display MFA was successful. Click 'Finish' and refresh your browser. You will be able to see a green tick mark before the MFA activation tab.

Manage MFA device

The MFA device was successfully associated with your account.

Finish

Chapter 2: Security

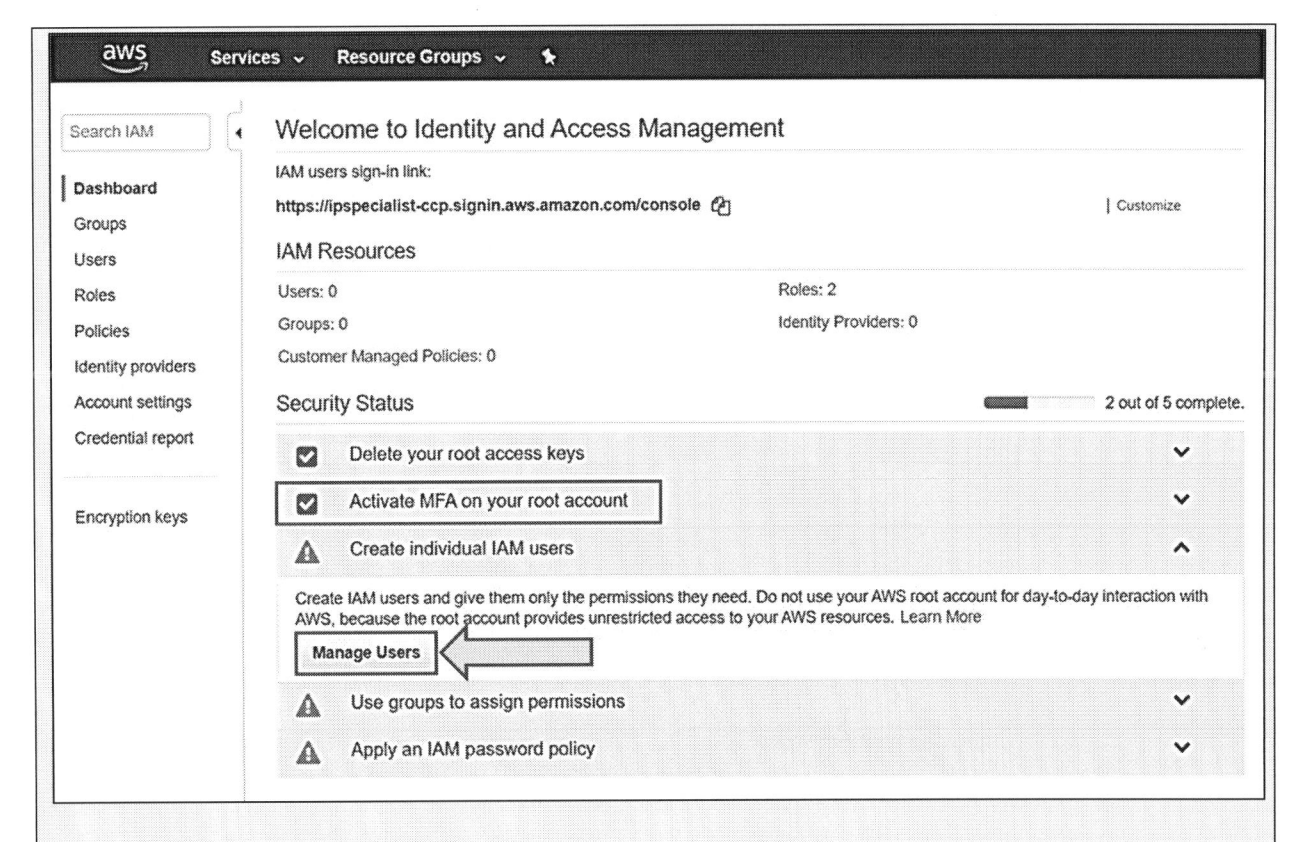

12. Next step is to create users within your root account. Select 'Create individual IAM users' tab and click 'Manage Users'. Click 'Add user' button at the top to add users.

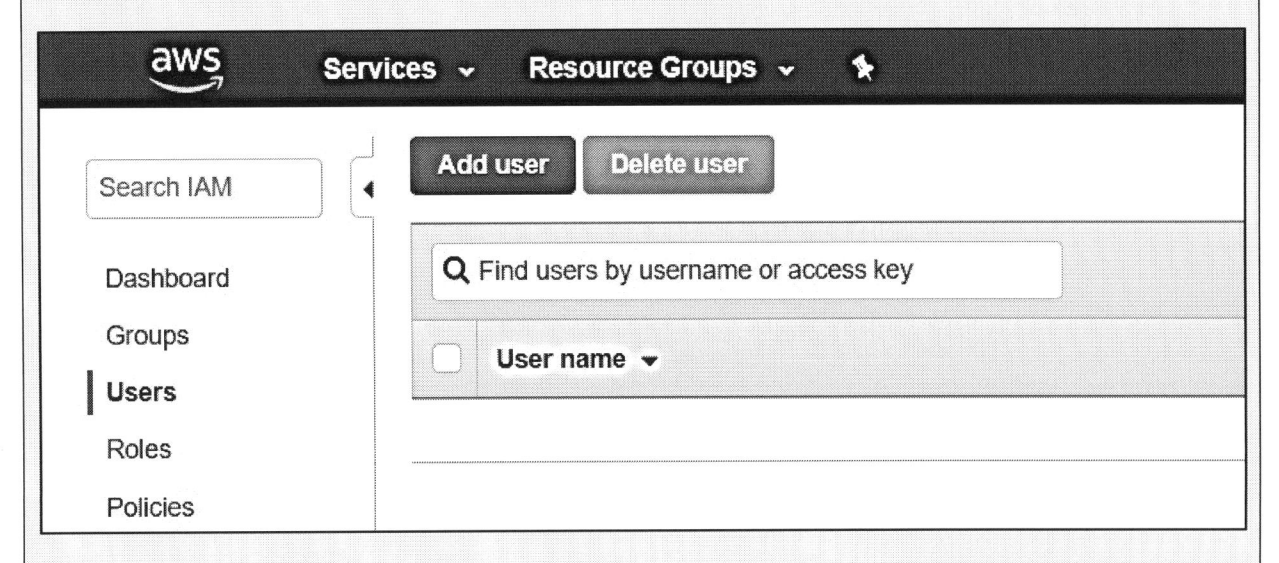

13. Enter a Username and select the access type for the user. Programmatic access will generate access key ID and secret access key for the user. Accessing AWS via the management console will require a password for which you can select 'Auto generated

Chapter 2: Security

password' or provide your custom password. Lastly, you have the option to enable password reset, which will let the user create a new password when signing in for the first time. Click 'Next: Permissions'.

Add user ① ② ③ ④

Set user details

You can add multiple users at once with the same access type and permissions. Learn more

User name* [   ]

● Add another user

Select AWS access type

Select how these users will access AWS. Access keys and autogenerated passwords are provided in the last step. Learn more

Access type* ☑ **Programmatic access**
Enables an **access key ID** and **secret access key** for the AWS API, CLI, SDK, and other development tools.

☑ **AWS Management Console access**
Enables a **password** that allows users to sign-in to the AWS Management Console.

Console password* ● Autogenerated password
○ Custom password

[   ]

Require password reset ☑ Users must create a new password at next sign-in
Users automatically get the IAMUserChangePassword policy to allow them to change their own password.

* Required   Cancel   **Next: Permissions**

14. To set permissions for the new user, you can either add a user to a group or copy permissions from existing user, or you can attach existing policies directly. For this tutorial, we will add a user to a group by creating a group first. Select 'Create group'.

Chapter 2: Security

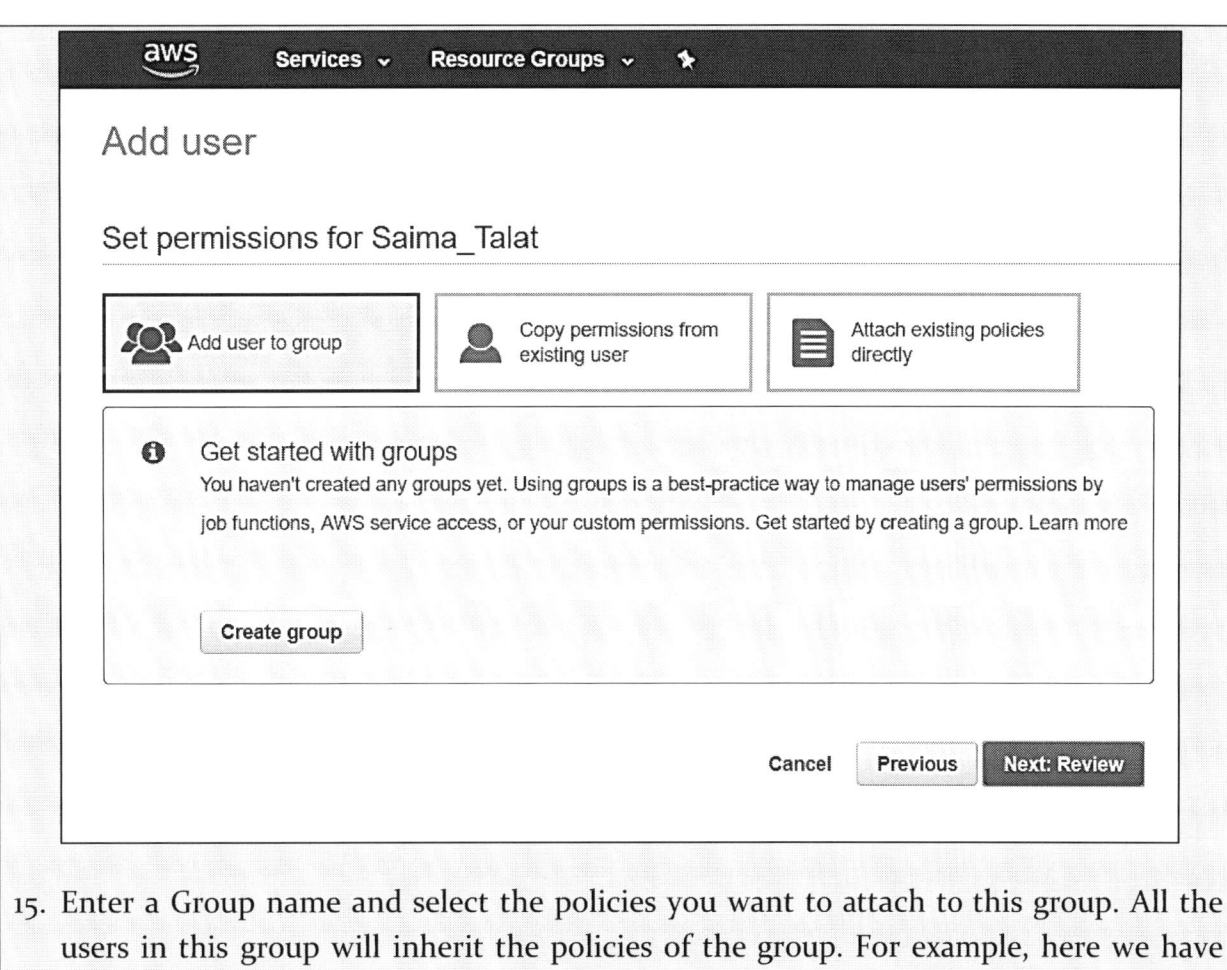

15. Enter a Group name and select the policies you want to attach to this group. All the users in this group will inherit the policies of the group. For example, here we have selected Administrator Access policy for our group named 'Administrators_Group,' which provides full access to AWS services and resources. Click 'Create group'.

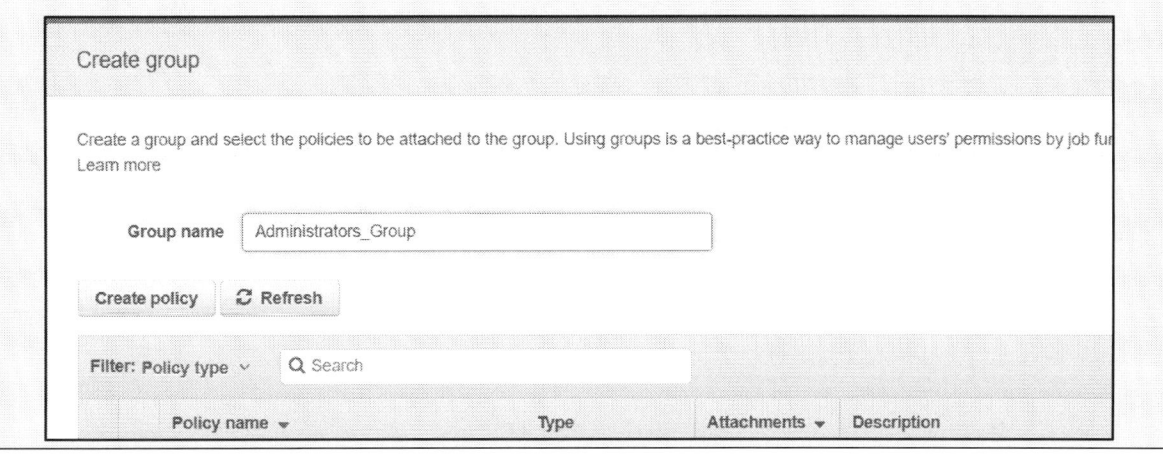

Chapter 2: Security

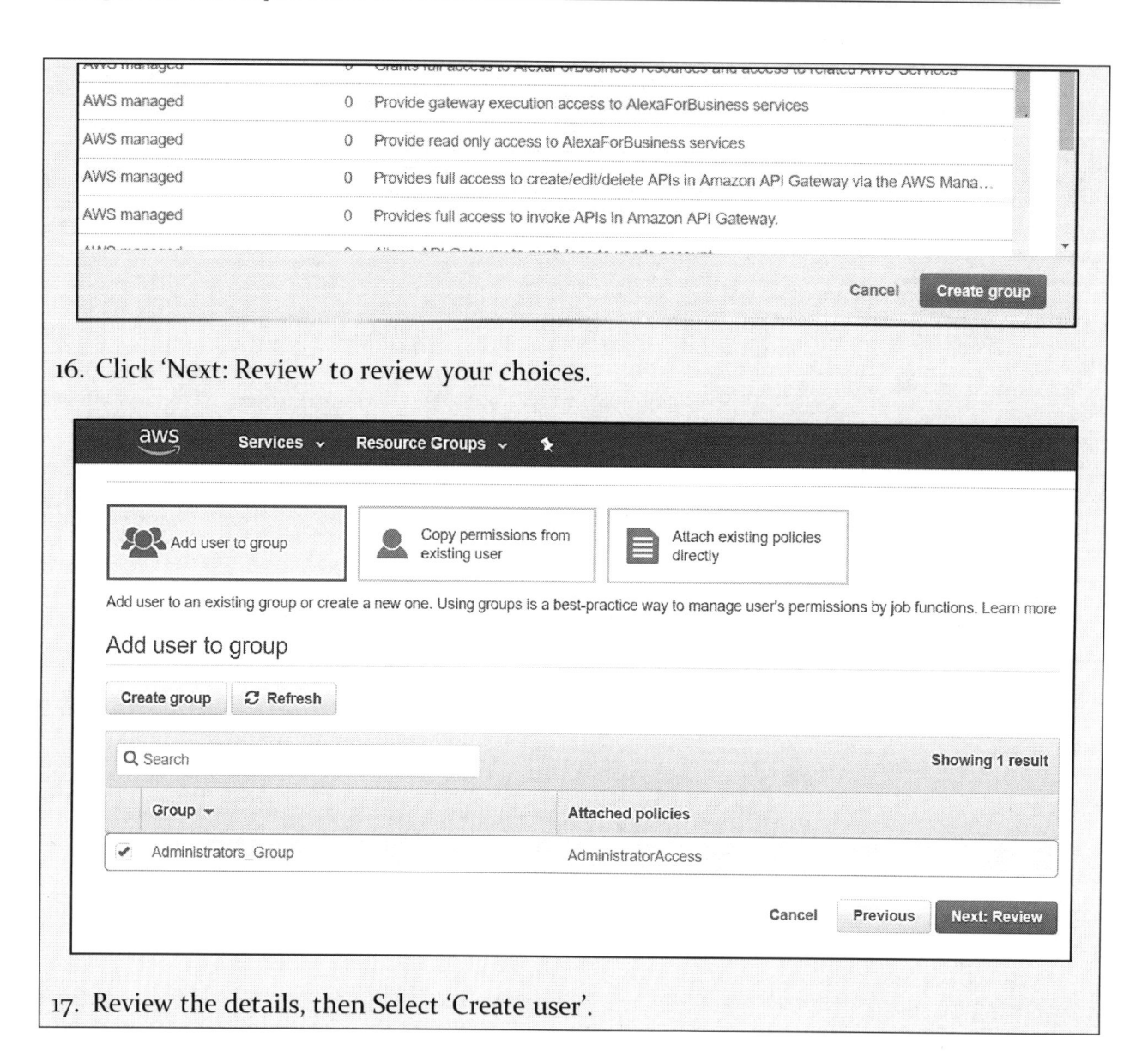

16. Click 'Next: Review' to review your choices.

17. Review the details, then Select 'Create user'.

Chapter 2: Security

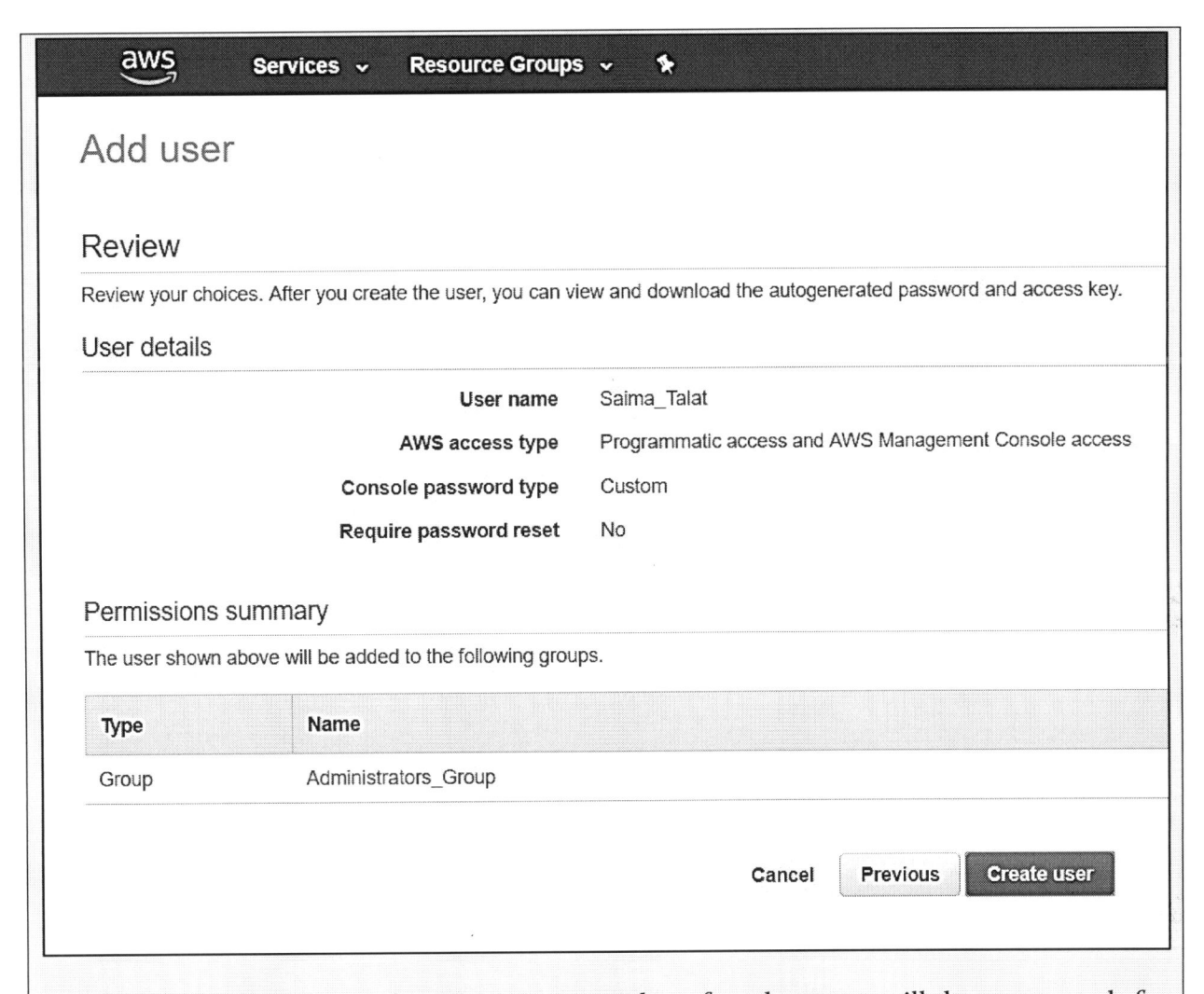

![AWS Add User Review Screen]

Add user

Review

Review your choices. After you create the user, you can view and download the autogenerated password and access key.

User details

User name	Saima_Talat
AWS access type	Programmatic access and AWS Management Console access
Console password type	Custom
Require password reset	No

Permissions summary

The user shown above will be added to the following groups.

Type	Name
Group	Administrators_Group

Cancel | Previous | **Create user**

18. An Access key ID and a Secret access key for the user will be generated for programmatic access to the AWS. These security credentials must always be kept secured. Click 'Download .csv' button to download user security credentials and then click 'Close'.

63

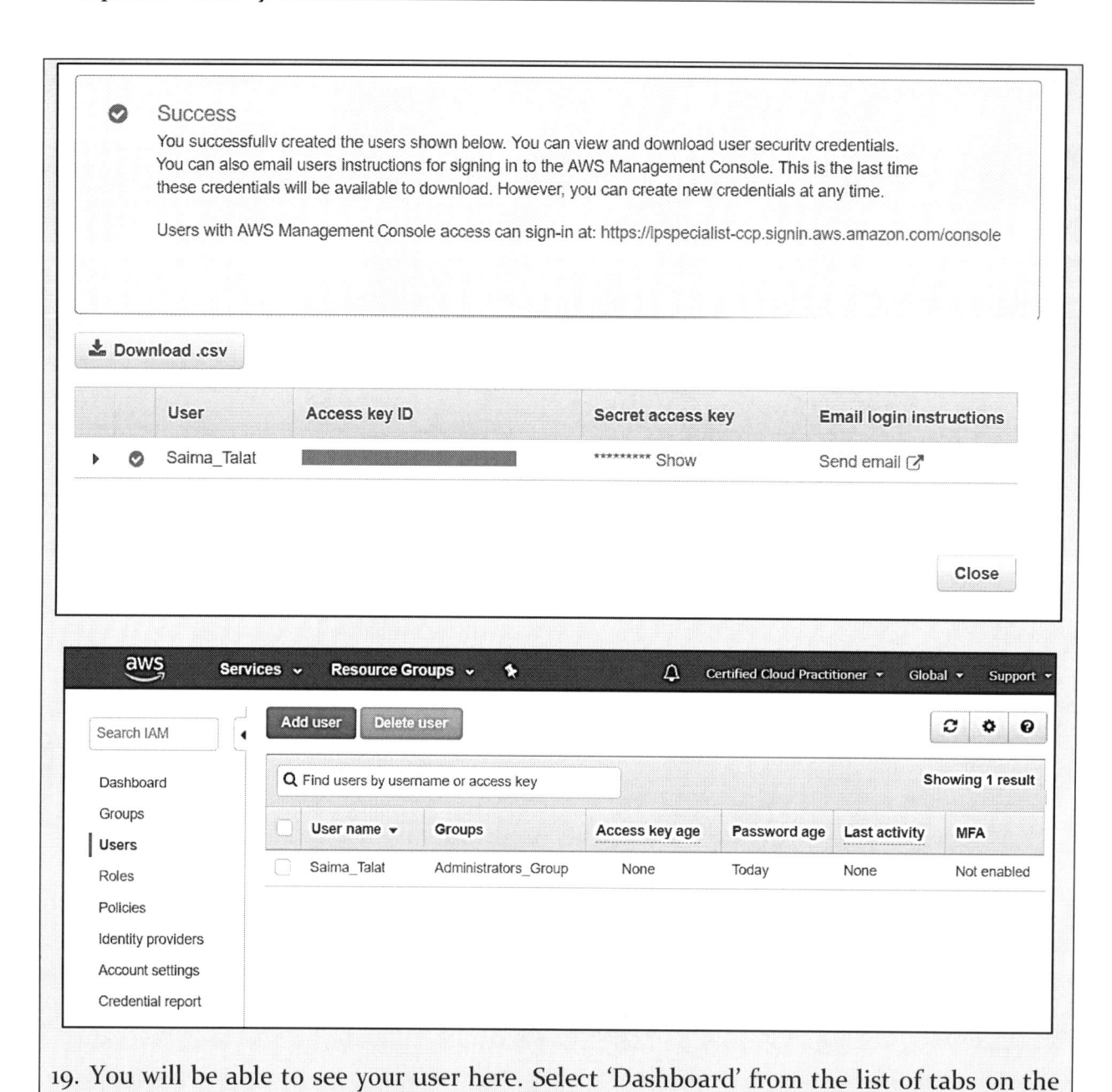

Chapter 2: Security

> **Success**
> You successfully created the users shown below. You can view and download user security credentials. You can also email users instructions for signing in to the AWS Management Console. This is the last time these credentials will be available to download. However, you can create new credentials at any time.
>
> Users with AWS Management Console access can sign-in at: https://ipspecialist-ccp.signin.aws.amazon.com/console

Download .csv

User	Access key ID	Secret access key	Email login instructions
Saima_Talat		********* Show	Send email

Close

User name	Groups	Access key age	Password age	Last activity	MFA
Saima_Talat	Administrators_Group	None	Today	None	Not enabled

Search IAM:
- Dashboard
- Groups
- Users
- Roles
- Policies
- Identity providers
- Account settings
- Credential report

19. You will be able to see your user here. Select 'Dashboard' from the list of tabs on the left to go back to the main IAM window.

Chapter 2: Security

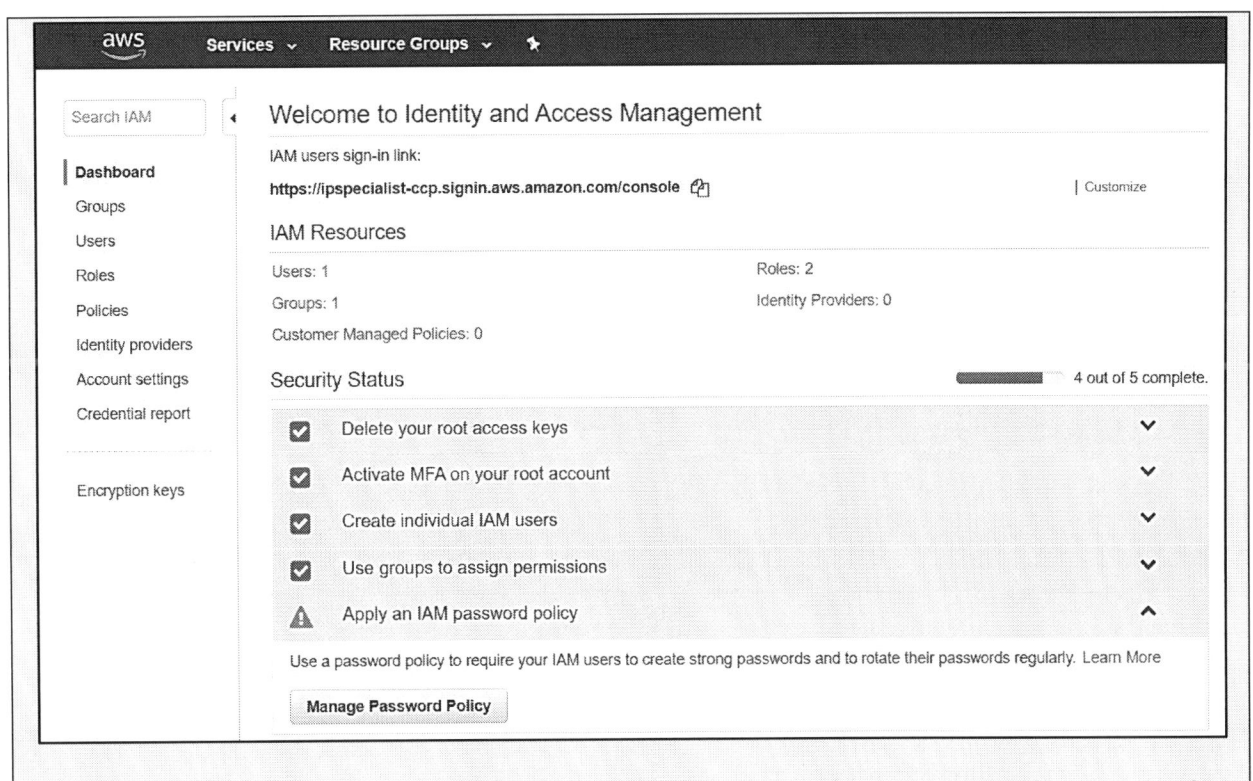

20. After creating a user and assigning permissions using groups, you now have to apply a password policy. This policy defines what passwords your users can create. Select 'Apply an IAM password policy' tab and click 'Manage Password Policy'.

Chapter 2: Security

21. Specify the password policy by selecting options for your preferred password criteria. Click 'Apply password policy'. Once done, select 'Dashboard' to go back to the main IAM window.

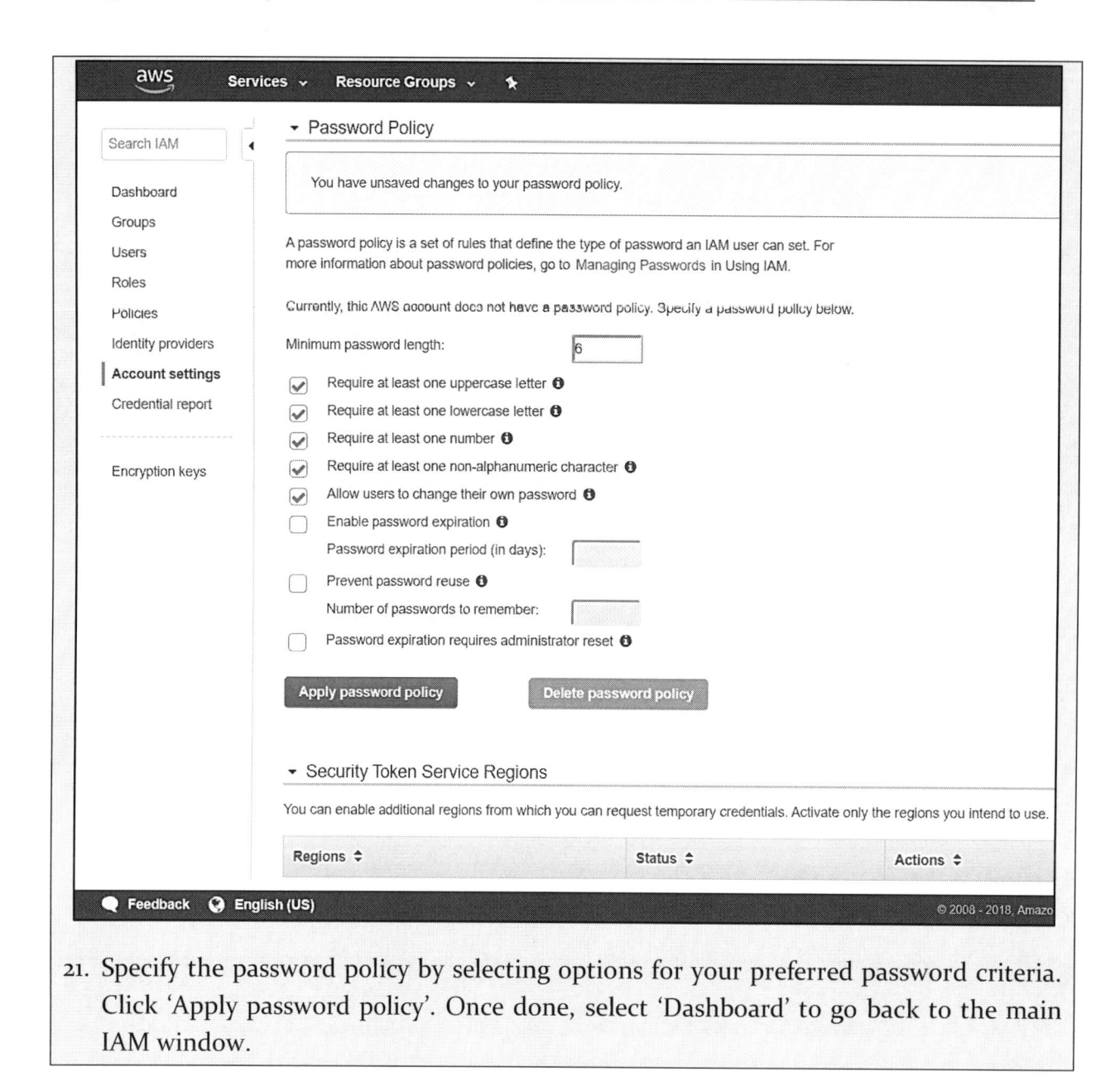

Chapter 2: Security

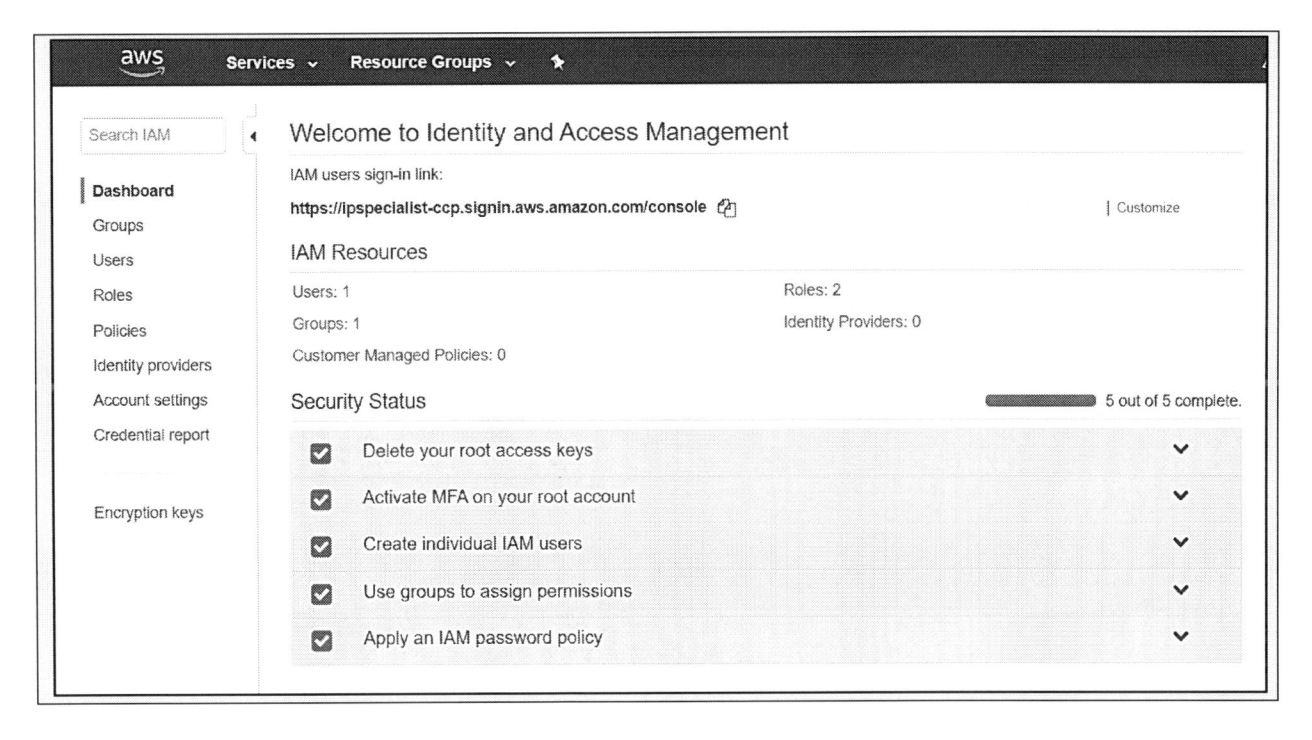

[screenshot of AWS IAM dashboard showing Welcome to Identity and Access Management, IAM users sign-in link https://ipspecialist-ccp.signin.aws.amazon.com/console, IAM Resources: Users: 1, Groups: 1, Customer Managed Policies: 0, Roles: 2, Identity Providers: 0, Security Status 5 out of 5 complete with all items checked: Delete your root access keys, Activate MFA on your root account, Create individual IAM users, Use groups to assign permissions, Apply an IAM password policy]

Security Support

AWS provides its customers a variety of tools and features to assist them in achieving security objectives and maintaining an optimized environment. Following are the four major ones covered in this course.

AWS WAF

AWS Web Application Firewall (WAF) provides protection to web applications against common web exploits that disrupt application accessibility, compromise security, or consume undue resources. AWS WAF lets you create and define custom web security rules for your specific applications that offer you control over the web traffic, whether to allow, block, or monitor (count web requests) based on conditions you define. Those conditions can be IP addresses, HTTP headers, HTTP body, URI strings, SQL injection and cross-site scripting. Furthermore, security rules can also be created to block attacks from specific user-agents, bad bots, or content scrapers.

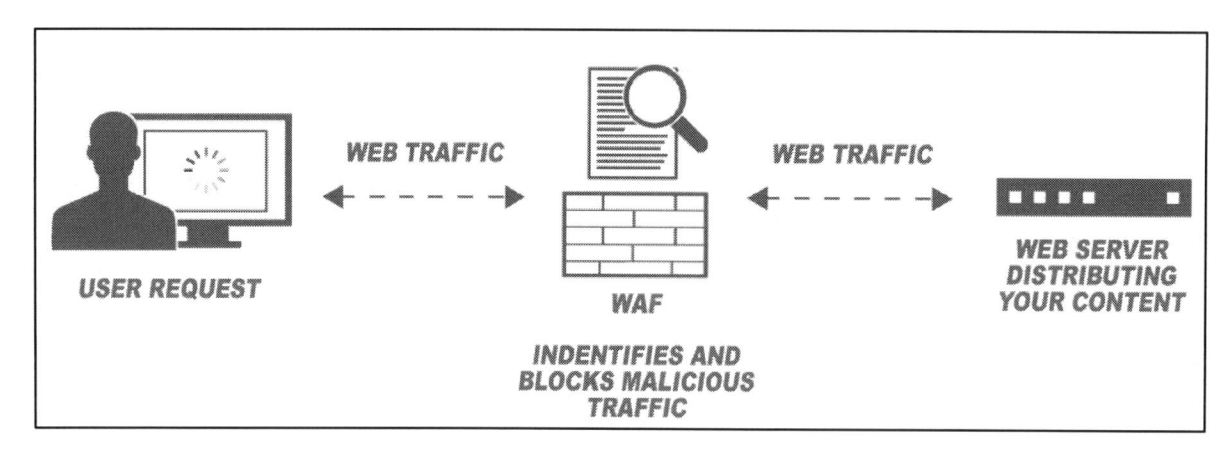

Figure 2-05. Web Application Firewall

AWS WAF contains a full-featured API to automate the creation, deployment, and maintenance of web security rules as and when required, depending on the change in traffic patterns. AWS WAF can be deployed on either Amazon CloudFront as part of CDN to protect resources and content at Edge locations before they reach the web servers, or as a part of the Application Load Balancer (ALB) to protect origin web servers running behind the ALBs or the internet-facing servers.

An example scenario of this can be a hacker sending a cross-site scripting attack using an SQL injection. WAF can go down to layer seven of the OSI (Open Systems Interconnection) model and analyze network traffic at the application layer. It can inspect the data the hacker is sending and intervene by blocking that traffic in case of cross-site attack or SQL injection.

AWS WAF also follows the 'pay only for what you use' model with no upfront commitments. The pricing depends upon the number of rules you deploy, and the number of web requests your web application receives.

> **EXAM TIP:** The best way to remember WAF is to think of it as an intelligent Security Group. AWS WAF prevents common attack patterns like SQL injection and Cross-Site Scripting (XSS) efficiently by monitoring the HTTP and HTTPS requests.

AWS Shield

AWS Shield is a managed protection service that safeguards web applications running on AWS against Distributed Denial of Service (DDoS) attacks. It delivers always-on detection with automatic inline mitigations that reduce application downtime and latency. A Denial of Service (DoS) attack is a malicious attempt to disrupt the availability of a targeted system by flooding it with packets or requests, causing the system to crash due to the overwhelming traffic volume. For a Distributed Denial of Service (DDoS) attack, the attacker has to use several compromised systems or controlled sources to generate the attack.

There are two tiers of Aws Shield. These two tiers are as follows;

- AWS Shield- Standard
- AWS Shield Advanced
    - AWS Shield Standard is offered to all AWS customers with no additional charges.
    - AWS Shield Advanced is an optional paid service accessible to AWS Business Support and AWS Enterprise Support customers with a monthly fee of $3,000.

AWS Shield Standard protects against commonly occurring Infrastructure (OSI layer 3 and layer 4) attacks such as SYN/UDP Floods, Reflection attacks, and others to maintain high availability of applications on AWS.

AWS Shield Advanced delivers enhanced protection against larger and more sophisticated attacks by flow-based monitoring of network traffic and active application scrutiny to notify of DDoS attacks in near real-time. Customers can take immediate actions using the highly flexible controls over attack mitigations.

Chapter 2: Security

Lab 2-3: AWS Shield

1. Log in to the 'AWS Console'.
2. Click on 'Services'.
3. Scroll down to 'Security, Identity & Compliance'.
4. Select 'WAF & Shield'.

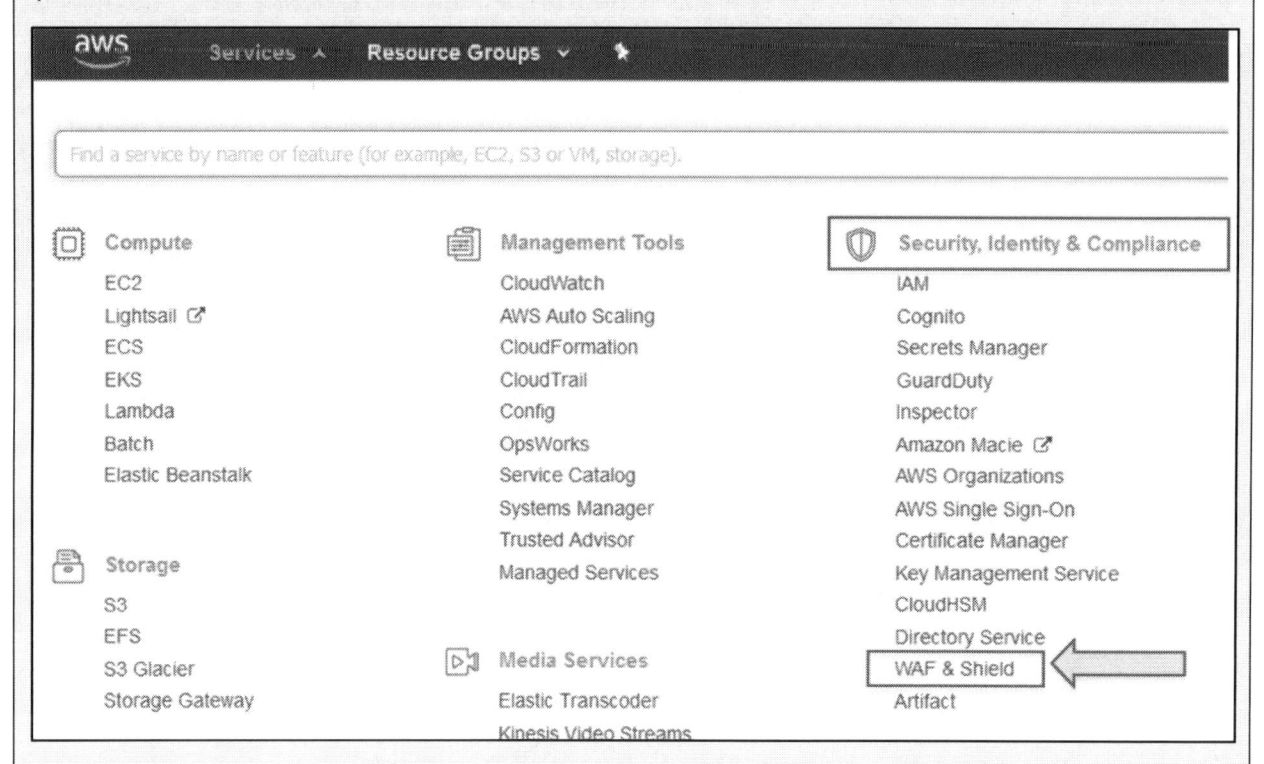

5. Click on 'Go to AWS WAF' to configure web application firewall services or Select 'Go to AWS Shield' to determine Standard and Advance version options.

Chapter 2: Security

AWS WAF and AWS Shield

AWS WAF and AWS Shield help protect your AWS resources from web exploits and DDoS attacks

AWS WAF

AWS WAF is a web application firewall service that helps protect your web apps from common exploits that could affect app availability, compromise security, or consume excessive resources.

AWS Shield

AWS Shield provides expanded DDoS attack protection for your AWS resources. Get 24/7 support from our DDoS response team and detailed visibility into DDoS events.

AWS Firewall Manager

AWS Firewall Manager simplifies your AWS WAF administration and maintenance tasks across multiple accounts and resources.

AWS WAF

AWS WAF is a web application firewall service that helps protect the websites and web apps that you deliver with Amazon CloudFront and ELB Application Load Balancers. Create web access control lists (web ACLS) that define which HTTP and HTTPS requests to allow, block, or count. Learn more

[Configure web ACL]

Web traffic filtering with custom rules

Create custom rules that can allow, block, or count web requests based on originating IP addresses or strings that appear in web requests.

Block malicious requests

Configure AWS WAF to recognize and block common web application security risks like SQL injection (SQLi) and cross-site scripting (XSS).

Tune your rules and monitor traffic

Review details about the web requests that AWS WAF allows, blocks, or counts, and update rules to thwart new attacks.

Chapter 2: Security

AWS Shield

As an AWS customer, you automatically have basic DDoS protection with the AWS Shield Standard plan, at no additional cost beyond what you already pay for AWS WAF and your other AWS services. For an additional cost, you can get advanced DDoS protection by activating the AWS Shield Advanced plan. The following table shows a comparison of the two plans.

Features	AWS Shield Standard	AWS Shield Advanced
Active monitoring		
Network flow monitoring	✓	✓
Automated application (layer 7) traffic monitoring	-	✓
DDoS mitigations		
Helps protect from common DDoS attacks, such as SYN floods and UDP reflection attacks	✓	✓
Access to additional DDoS mitigation capacity	-	✓
Visibility and reporting		
Layer 3/4 attack notification and attack forensic reports	-	✓
Layer 3/4/7 attack historical report	-	✓
DDoS response team support		
Incident management during high severity	-	✓

> **EXAM TIP:** You only need to know the general overview of AWS WAF and AWS Shield. Remember AWS Shield Standard is free of charge and is activated by default; but for the AWS Shield Advanced version, you will have to pay $3000/month. Similarly, AWS WAF also costs money.

AWS Inspector

Amazon Inspector is an automated security assessment service that assists in improving the security and compliance of the applications running on Amazon EC2.

Chapter 2: Security

It provides a thorough list of security findings, listed in order of severity after assessing applications for vulnerabilities or deviations from best practices. Amazon Inspector is API-driven service that makes it easy to deploy, manage, and automate.

While using Amazon Inspector, an assessment target is defined. This includes the collection of AWS resources to be monitored and then eventually a security assessment run of this target is launched. A complete detailed assessment report is then delivered via the Amazon Inspector console or API with a list of findings for potential security issues after analyzing and monitoring the network, process activity and file system of the specified target.

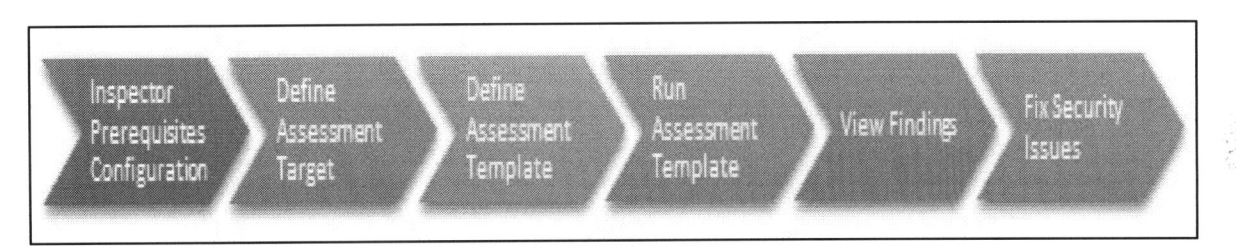

Figure 2-06. AWS Inspector

Lab 2-4: AWS Inspector

1. Log in to the 'AWS Console'.
2. Click on 'Services'.
3. Scroll down to 'Security, Identity & Compliance'.
4. Select 'Inspector'.

Chapter 2: Security

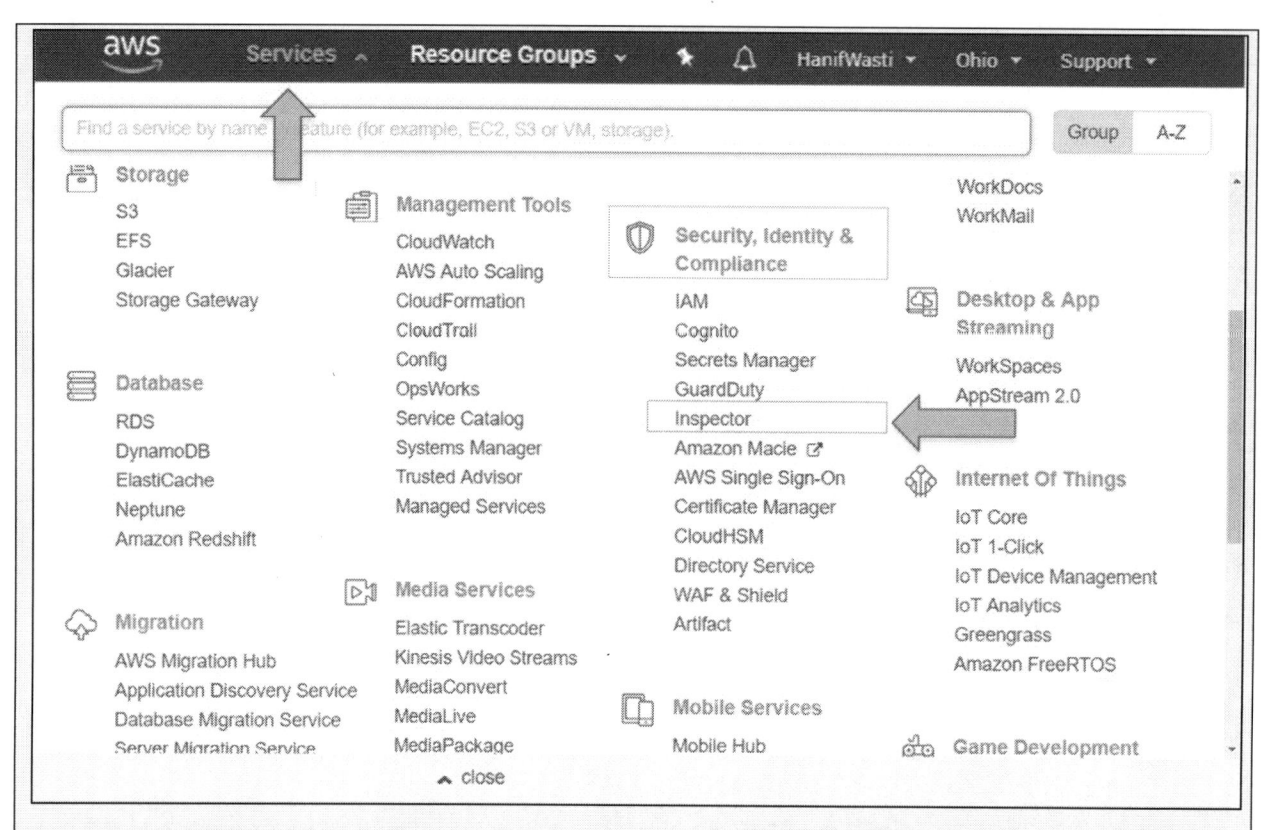

5. Click 'Get started' to configure Amazon Inspector by creating a role, tagging your EC2 instances, installing AWS agent and defining an assessment target.

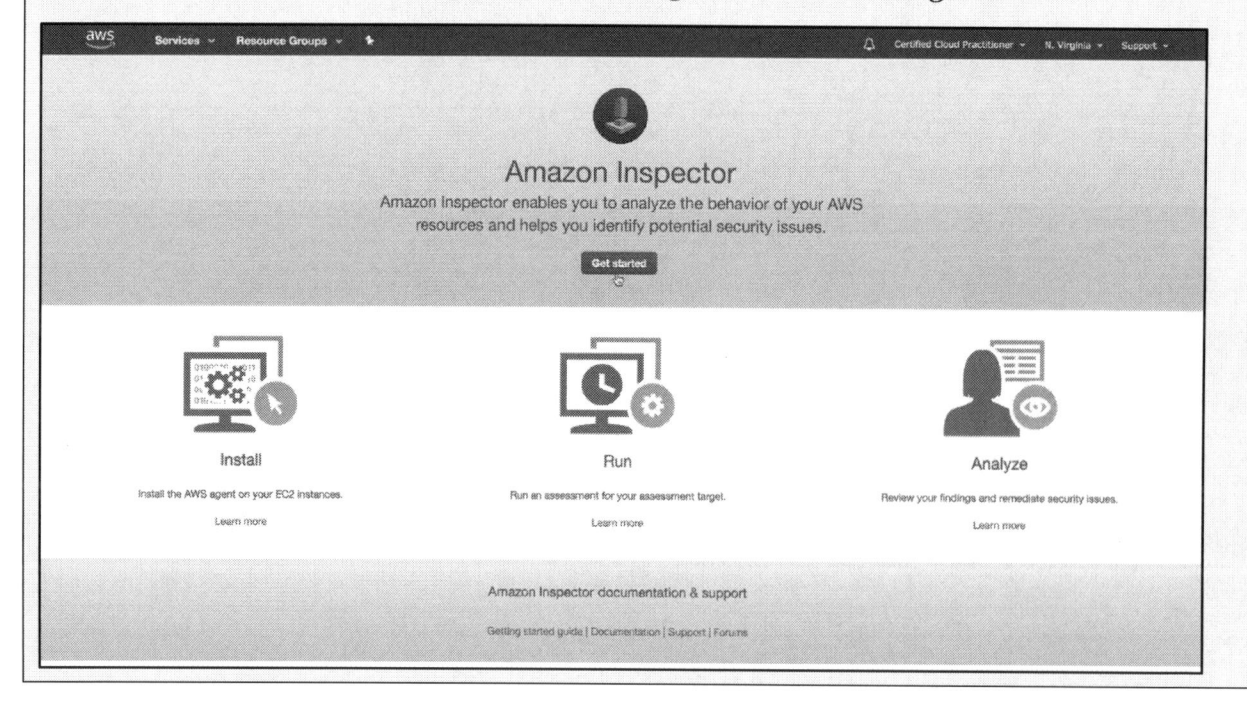

Chapter 2: Security

AWS Trusted Advisor

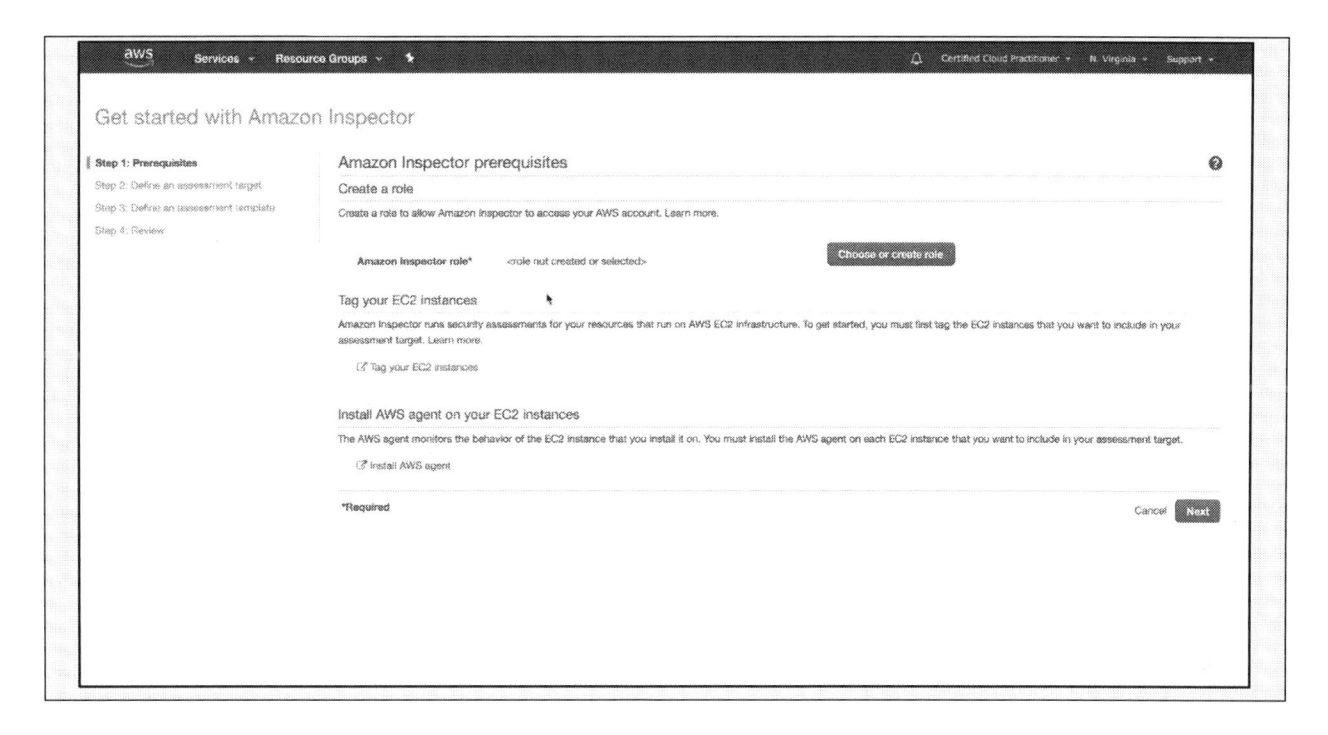

AWS Trusted Advisor is an online resource for optimizing your AWS environment by following AWS best practices. It helps you identify the resources you can configure to reduce cost, increase performance, and improve security. Trusted Advisor works as a customized cloud expert that inspects your AWS environment and provides real-time guidance. It is not just a security tool but also a complete analyzer that will inform you on how your infrastructure is performing and generates a report of recommended actions.

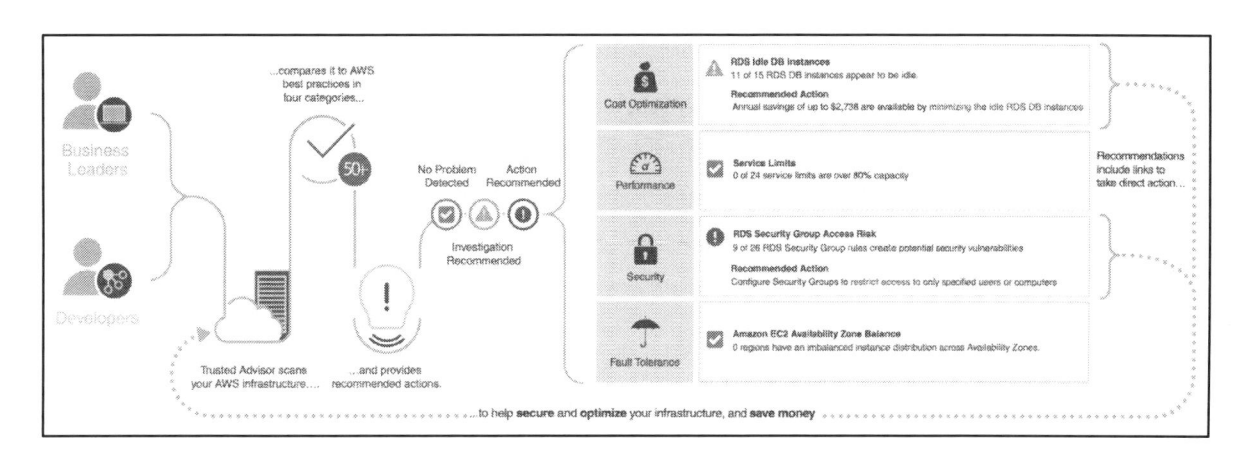

Figure 2-07. An Environment with Trusted Advisor

Trusted Advisor performs a list of checks in the following four categories:

- **Cost Optimization**– Recommendations on saving money by highlighting idle resources and prospects to cut down cost.
- **Security** – Identification of optimum security settings that can help close security gaps to make the environment more secure.
- **Fault Tolerance**– Recommendations that help increase the resiliency of AWS solutions by highlighting redundancy shortfalls, current service limits, and over-utilized resources.
- **Performance**– Recommendations for improving promptness and responsiveness of applications by detecting common security misconfigurations, suggestions for refining system performance and under-utilized resources.

AWS Trusted Advisor is available to the customers in two different forms:

Core Checks and Recommendations;

- Available to all AWS Customers at no additional cost
- Access to seven core checks to improve security and performance: S3 Bucket Permissions, Security Groups - Specific Ports Unrestricted, IAM Use, MFA on Root Account, EBS Public Snapshots, and RDS Public Snapshots
- Service Limits: checks for service usage that is more than 80% of the limit
- Upgrade to Business or Enterprise subscription to unlock all Trusted Advisor's Features

Full Trusted Advisor

- Available with Business and Enterprise Support Plans only
- Access to complete set of checks to help optimize your entire AWS infrastructure
- Additional Benefits include: Notifications to stay up-to-date and Programmatic Access to retrieve and refresh Trusted Advisor results

> **EXAM TIP**: Inspector is a security product that you install on your EC2 instances to look out for vulnerabilities whereas, Trusted Advisor gives recommendations on security as well as cost optimization, performance and fault tolerance. Trusted Advisor looks into a whole plethora of services and is not limited to EC2 instances only.

Lab 2-04: AWS Trusted Advisor

1. Log in to the 'AWS Console'.
2. Click on 'Services' and scroll down to 'Management Tools'. Select 'Trusted Advisor'.

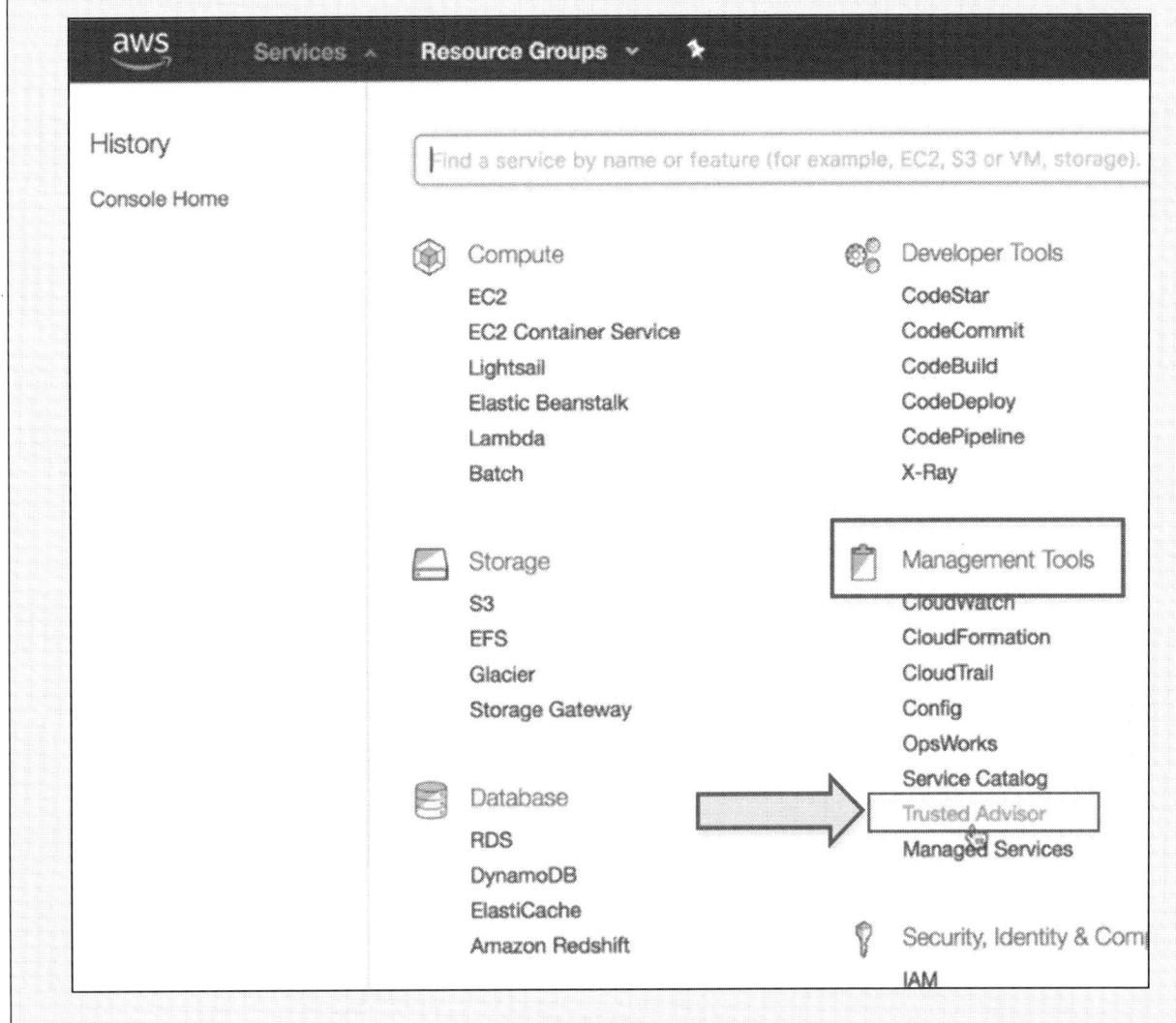

3. Click the 'refresh' logo at the top right corner to re-run all the Cost Optimization, Performance, Security and Fault Tolerance checks.

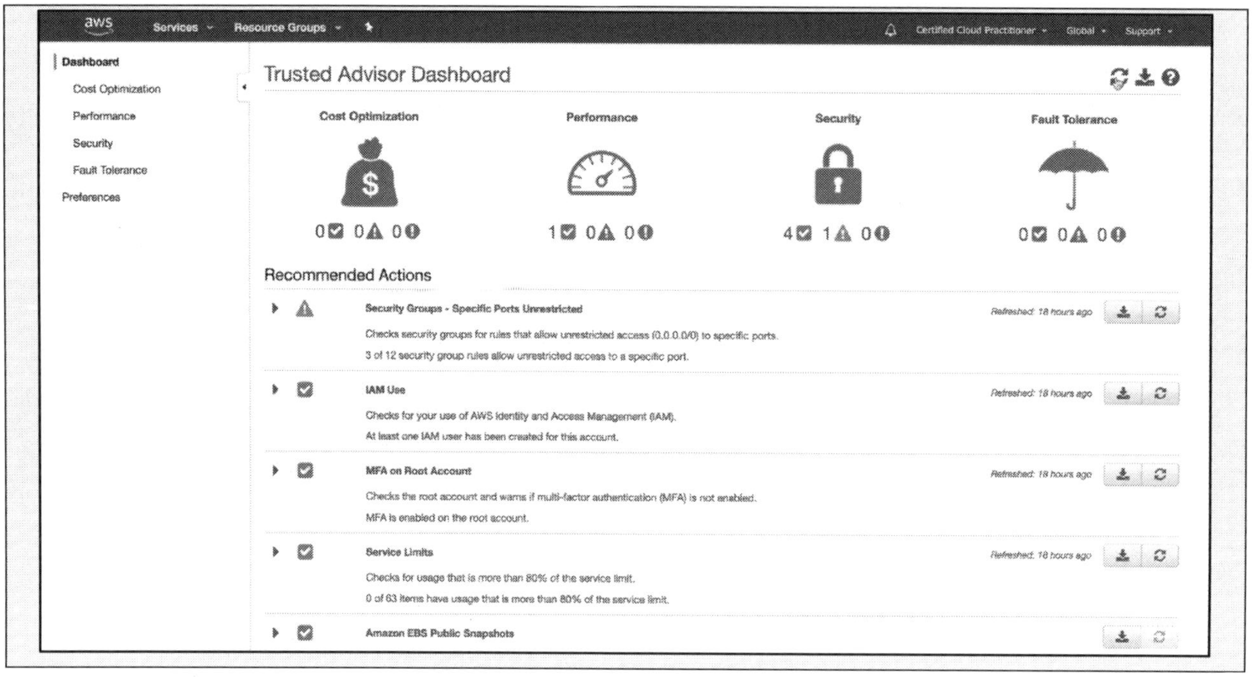
Services
Resource Groups
Certified Cloud Practitioner
Global
Support
Dashboard
Cost Optimization
Performance
Security
Fault Tolerance
Preferences
Trusted Advisor Dashboard
Cost Optimization
Performance
Security
Fault Tolerance
Recommended Actions
Security Groups - Specific Ports Unrestricted
Checks security groups for rules that allow unrestricted access (0.0.0.0/0) to specific ports.
3 of 12 security group rules allow unrestricted access to a specific port.
IAM Use
Checks for your use of AWS Identity and Access Management (IAM).
At least one IAM user has been created for this account.
MFA on Root Account
Checks the root account and warns if multi-factor authentication (MFA) is not enabled.
MFA is enabled on the root account.
Service Limits
Checks for usage that is more than 80% of the service limit.
0 of 63 items have usage that is more than 80% of the service limit.
Amazon EBS Public Snapshots
Refreshed: 18 hours ago

Chapter 3: Technology

Introduction

AWS offers a broad set of global cloud-based products and services that can be used as building blocks for setting up common cloud architectures. The products and services are divided into categories. Some of the categories and their services covered in this course include:

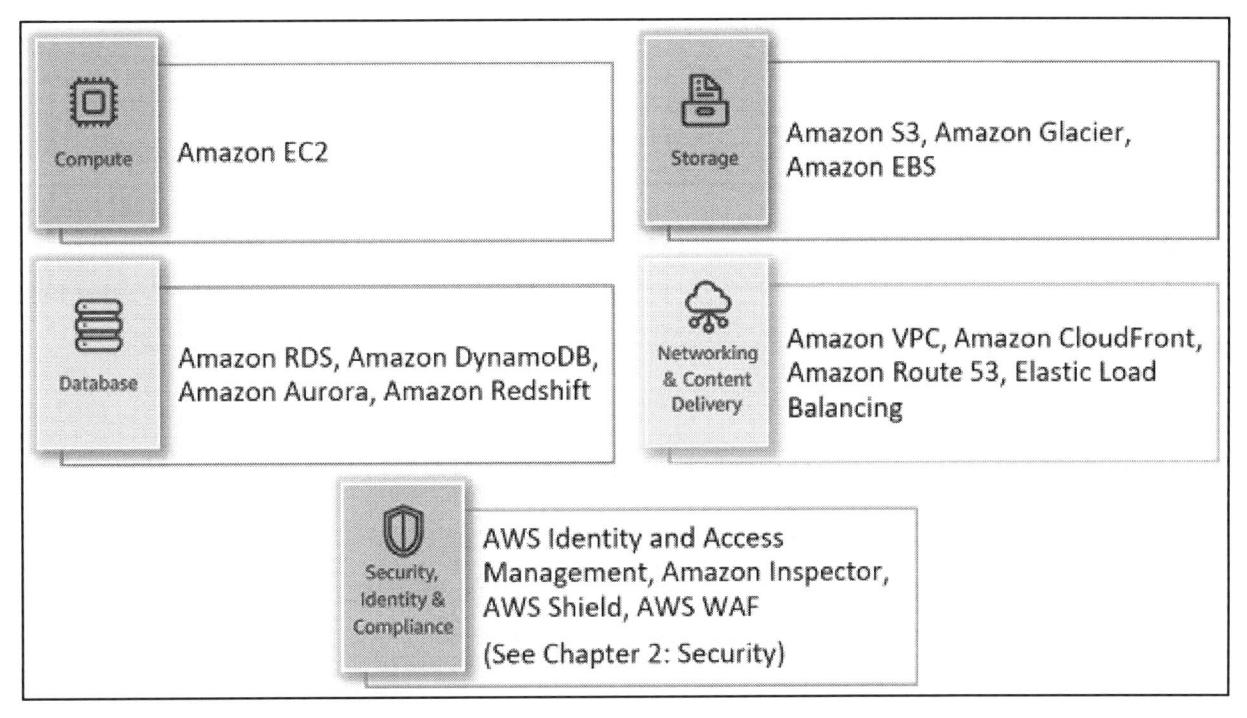

Category	Services
Compute	Amazon EC2
Storage	Amazon S3, Amazon Glacier, Amazon EBS
Database	Amazon RDS, Amazon DynamoDB, Amazon Aurora, Amazon Redshift
Networking & Content Delivery	Amazon VPC, Amazon CloudFront, Amazon Route 53, Elastic Load Balancing
Security, Identity & Compliance	AWS Identity and Access Management, Amazon Inspector, AWS Shield, AWS WAF (See Chapter 2: Security)

Figure 3-01. AWS

AWS Cloud Deployment and Management Services

AWS caters to various customers with distinctive requirements by offering several customization alternatives so it can serve a wide range of use cases. When it comes to deployment and management services, whether it is a simple application or a complex set of workloads, AWS offers multiple options for provisioning your IT infrastructure. As the deployment model differs from customer to customer, you can use the building blocks (Amazon EC2, Amazon EBS, Amazon S3, Amazon RDS) and leverage the integration provided by third-party tools to deploy your application or you can consider the automation provided by the AWS deployment services.

Chapter 3: Technology

The deployment services are easier ways to deploy your application on the underlying infrastructure. AWS deployment tool handles the complexity of provisioning the AWS resources required for your application to run.

Despite providing similar functionality in terms of deployment, each service has its own unique method for deploying and managing your application. For the Cloud Practitioner Exam, you need to study Elastic Beanstalk and CloudFormation services.

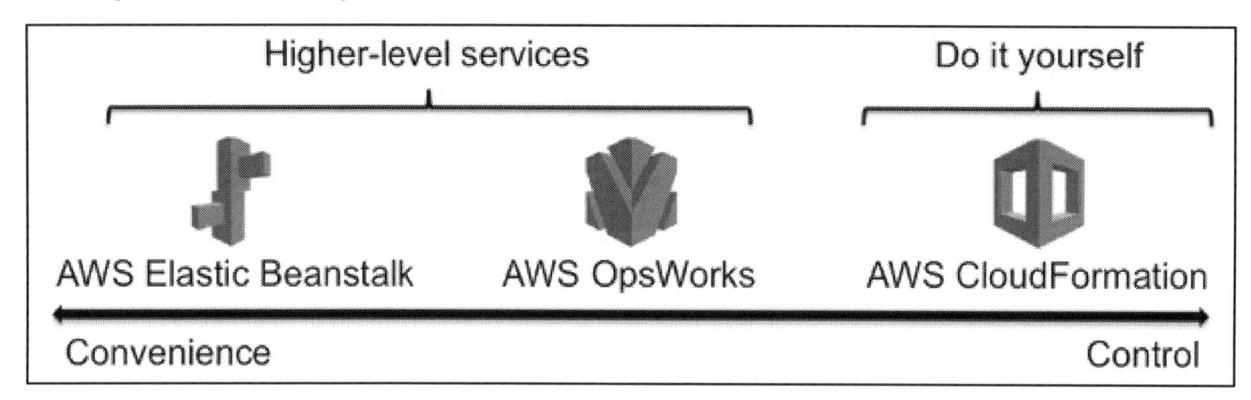

Figure 3-02. AWS Deployment & Management Services Overview

AWS Elastic Beanstalk

AWS Elastic Beanstalk allows us to deploy everything at a click of a button. It is the fastest and simplest way to get an application up and running on AWS without worrying about managing the underlying infrastructure. Developers only need to upload their code while the service automates the deployment of all resources.

Elastic Beanstalk works best with a standard three-tier PHP, Java, Python, Ruby, Node.js, NET, Go or Docker application running on an app server with a database. Common use cases include web apps, content management systems (CMS), and API backends.

Elastic Beanstalk uses Auto Scaling and Elastic Load Balancing to handle peaks in workload and automatically scales the application up and down based on the application's requirements while you retain full control over the AWS resources.

Lab 3-1: AWS Elastic Beanstalk

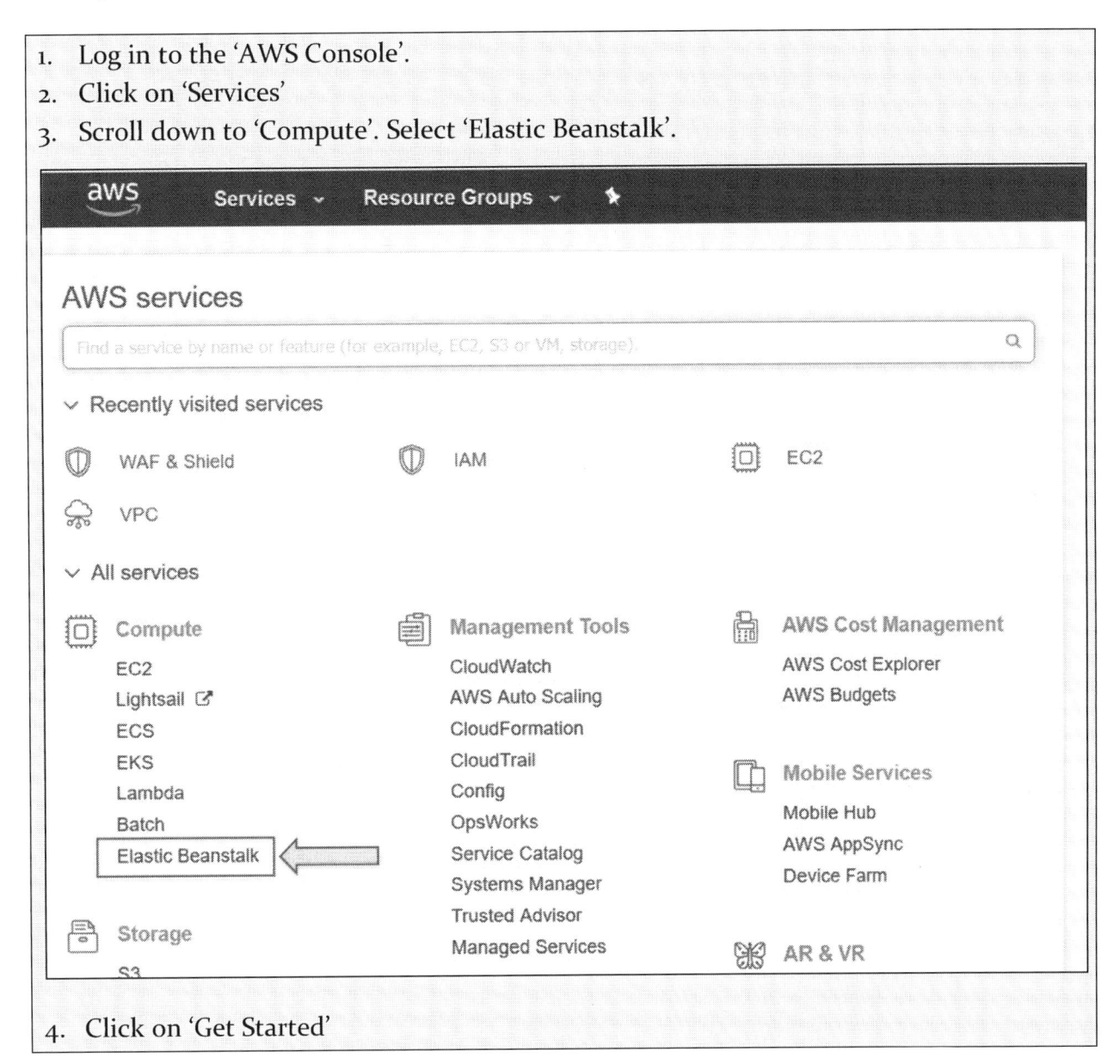

1. Log in to the 'AWS Console'.
2. Click on 'Services'
3. Scroll down to 'Compute'. Select 'Elastic Beanstalk'.

4. Click on 'Get Started'

Chapter 3: Technology

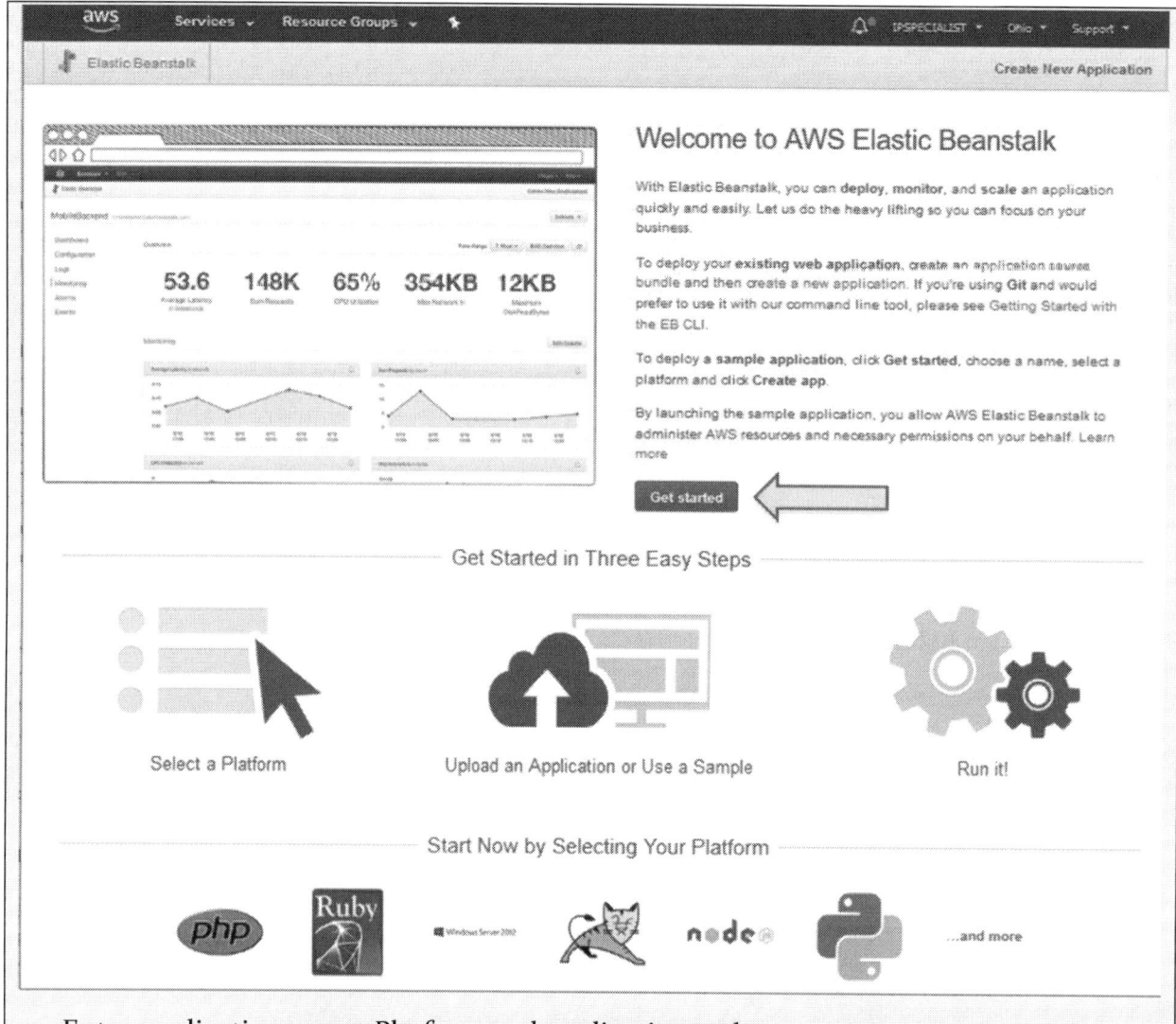

5. Enter application name, Platform and application code.
6. Here we select Platform "PHP," and we use the application code "sample application." Click "create application"

Chapter 3: Technology

> Create a new application and environment with a sample application or your own code. By creating an environment, you allow AWS Elastic Beanstalk to manage AWS resources and permissions on your behalf. Learn more

Application information

Application name: IPS-test
Up to 100 Unicode characters, not including forward slash (/).

Base configuration

Platform: PHP
Choose **Configure more options** for more platform configuration options.

Application code: ● Sample application
Get started right away with sample code

○ Upload your code
Upload a source bundle from your computer or copy one from Amazon S3.
⬆ Upload   ZIP or WAR

Cancel   Configure more options   **Create application**

7. Now the application starts creating.

All Applications > IPS-test > IpsTest-env-1 (Environment ID: e-zykks9tbhg)

ⓘ Creating IpsTest-env-1
This will take a few minutes..

2:25pm Using elasticbeanstalk-us-east-1-709714787087 as Amazon S3 storage bucket for environment data.
2:25pm createEnvironment is starting.

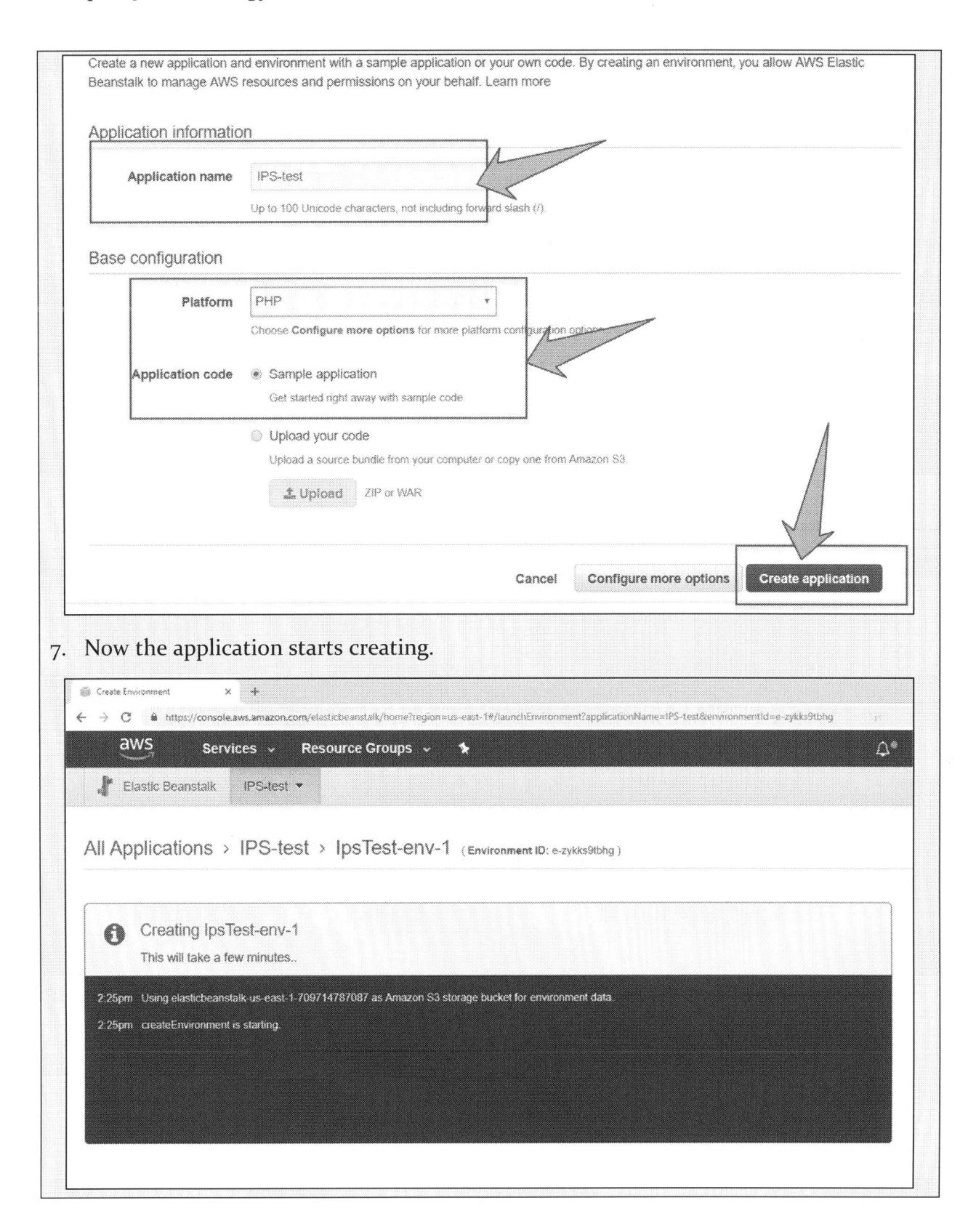

Chapter 3: Technology

8. Once the application is created, and its environment is also created. Now click on Application "IPS-test."

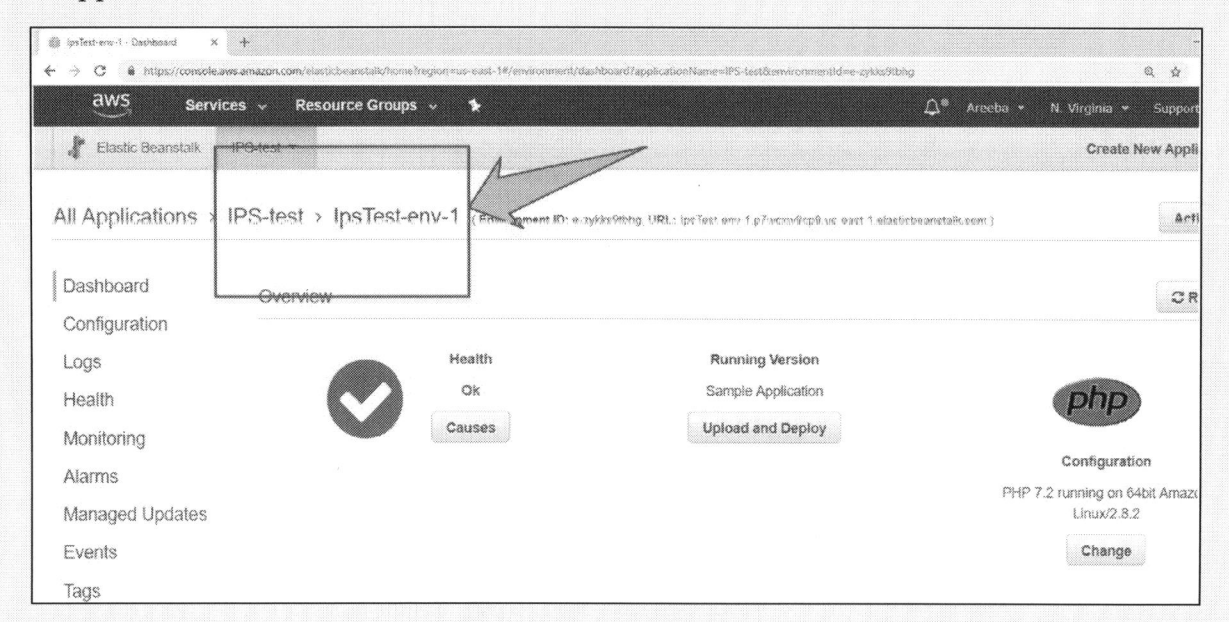

9. Now you can see information related to the environment. In the application, you can create multiple environments as well.

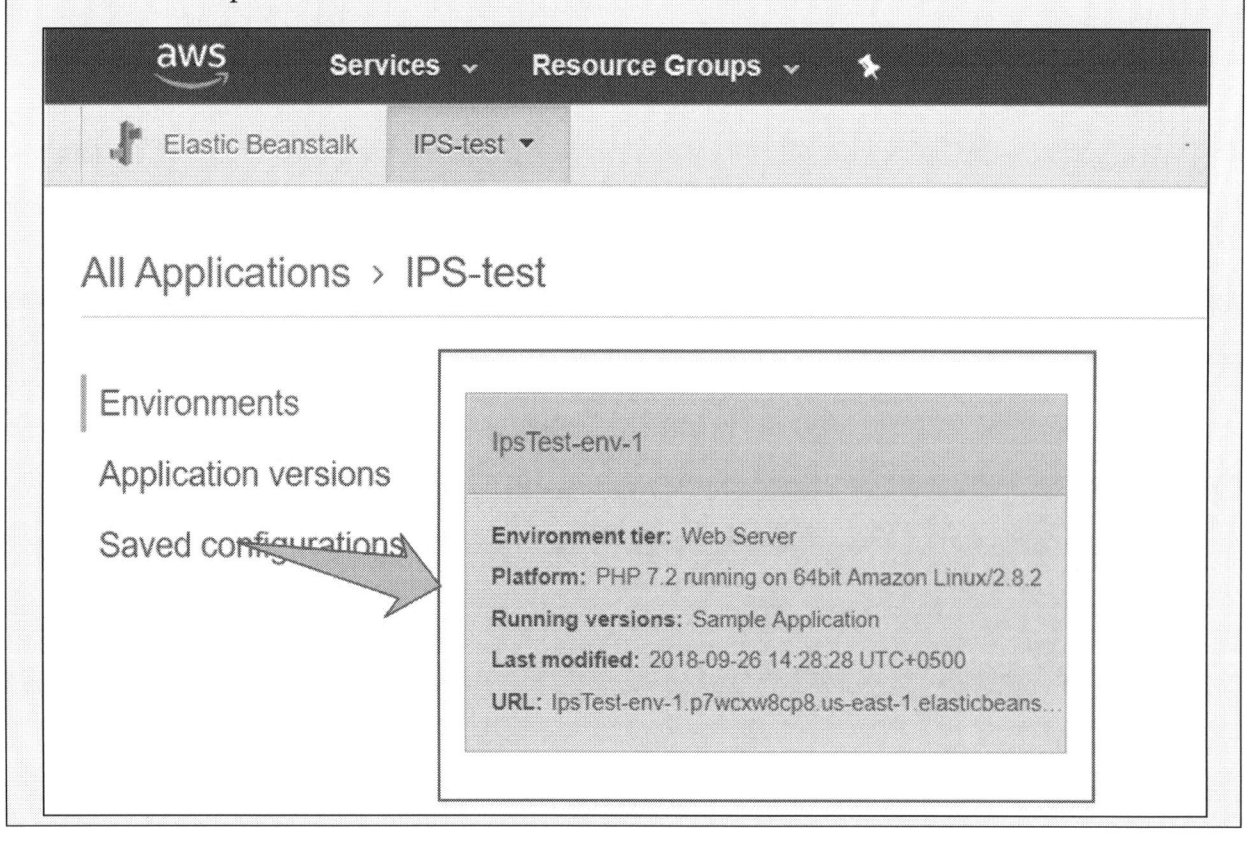

Chapter 3: Technology

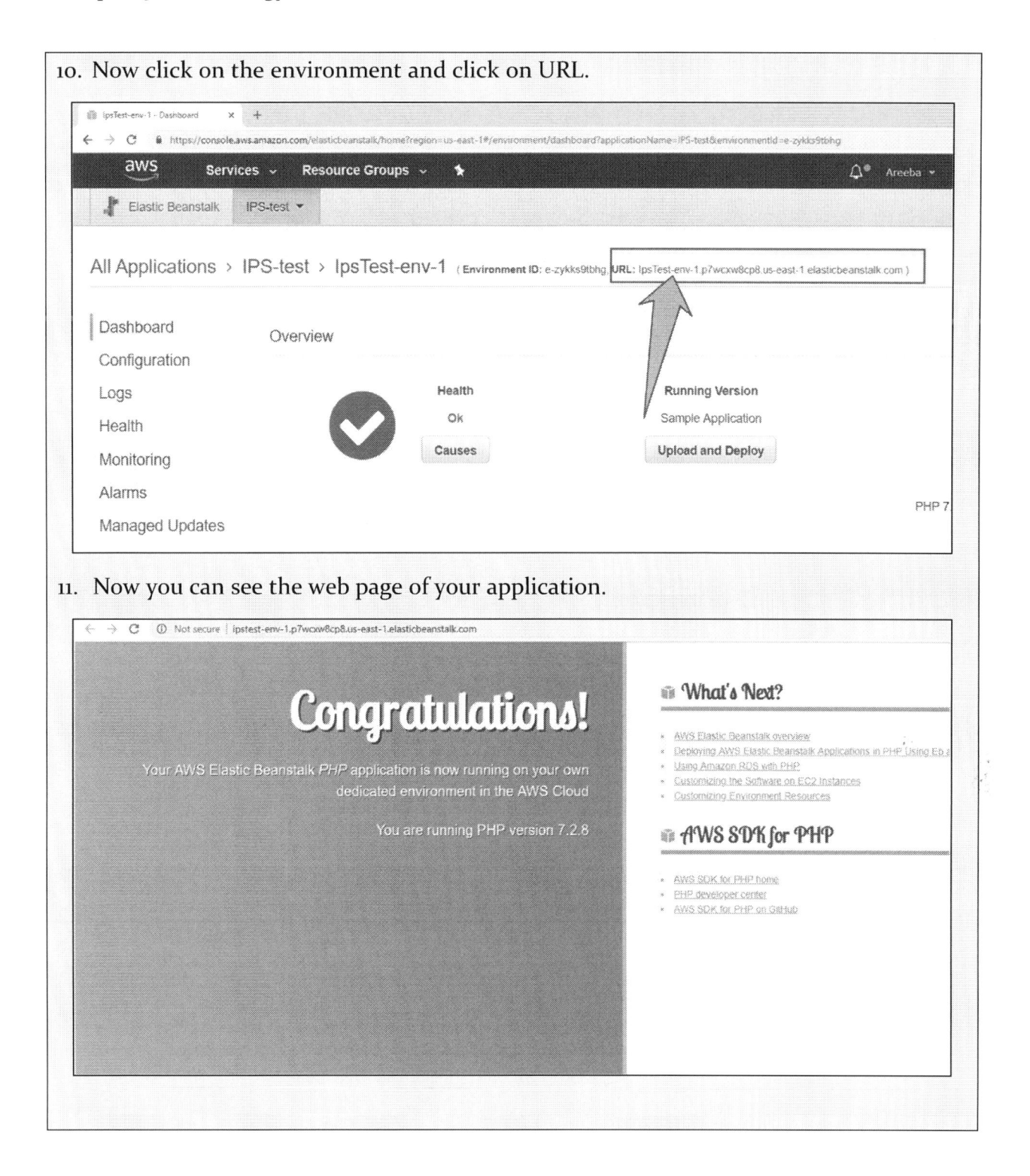

10. Now click on the environment and click on URL.

11. Now you can see the web page of your application.

AWS CloudFormation

AWS CloudFormation offers system administrators, developers and network architects, the facility to provision and manages a collection of related AWS resources by coding out the infrastructure. This is achieved by creating templates to model infrastructure, which in turn manages everything from a single Amazon EC2 instance to a complex multi-tier, multi-regional applications.

It is a powerful tool as it gives you the ability to script your infrastructure so that you can easily replicate your infrastructure stack quickly and as many times as you want. The stack is nothing but a collection of templates. Compared to Elastic Beanstalk and AWS OpsWorks, AWS CloudFormation gives you more granular control and flexibility over provisioning and management of resources.

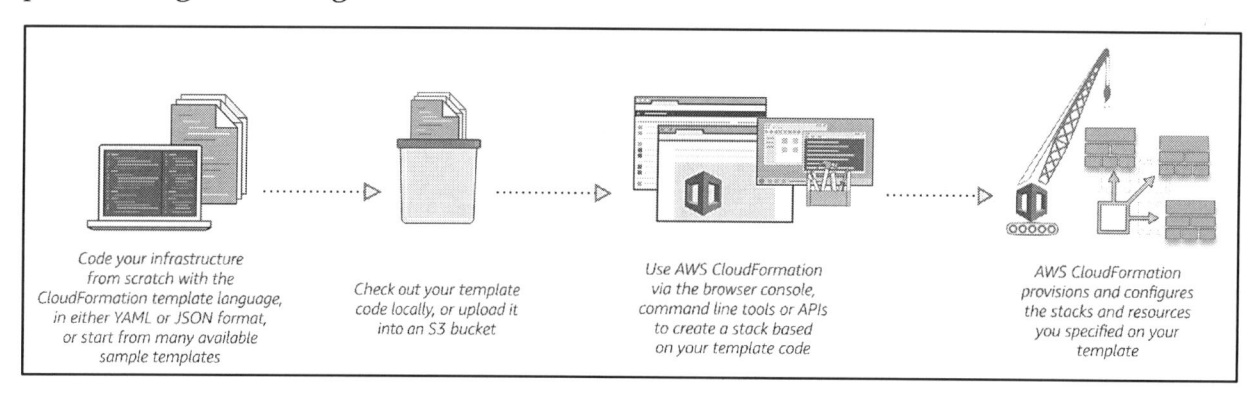

Figure 3-03. How AWS CloudFormation Works

> **EXAM TIP**: AWS CloudFormation and AWS Elastic BeanStalk are completely free services, but the resources they provisions, are not free. All the resources provisioned under these services whether the EC2 instances, the elastic load balancer, the RDS instances, etc., will cost money.

Lab 3-2: AWS Cloud Formation

1. Log in to the 'AWS Console'
2. Click on 'Services'.
3. Scroll down to 'Management Tools'. Select 'CloudFormation'.

Chapter 3: Technology

History	Find a service by name or feature (for example, EC2, S3 or VM, storage).
EC2	
OpsWorks	**Compute** **Developer Tools**
Console Home	EC2 CodeStar
Snowball	Lightsail CodeCommit
Trusted Advisor	Elastic Container Service CodeBuild
S3	EKS CodeDeploy
	Lambda CodePipeline
	Batch Cloud9
	Elastic Beanstalk X-Ray
	Storage **Management Tools**
	S3 CloudWatch
	EFS AWS Auto Scaling
	Glacier CloudFormation
	Storage Gateway CloudTrail
	Config
	OpsWorks
	Database Service Catalog
	RDS Systems Manager
	DynamoDB Trusted Advisor

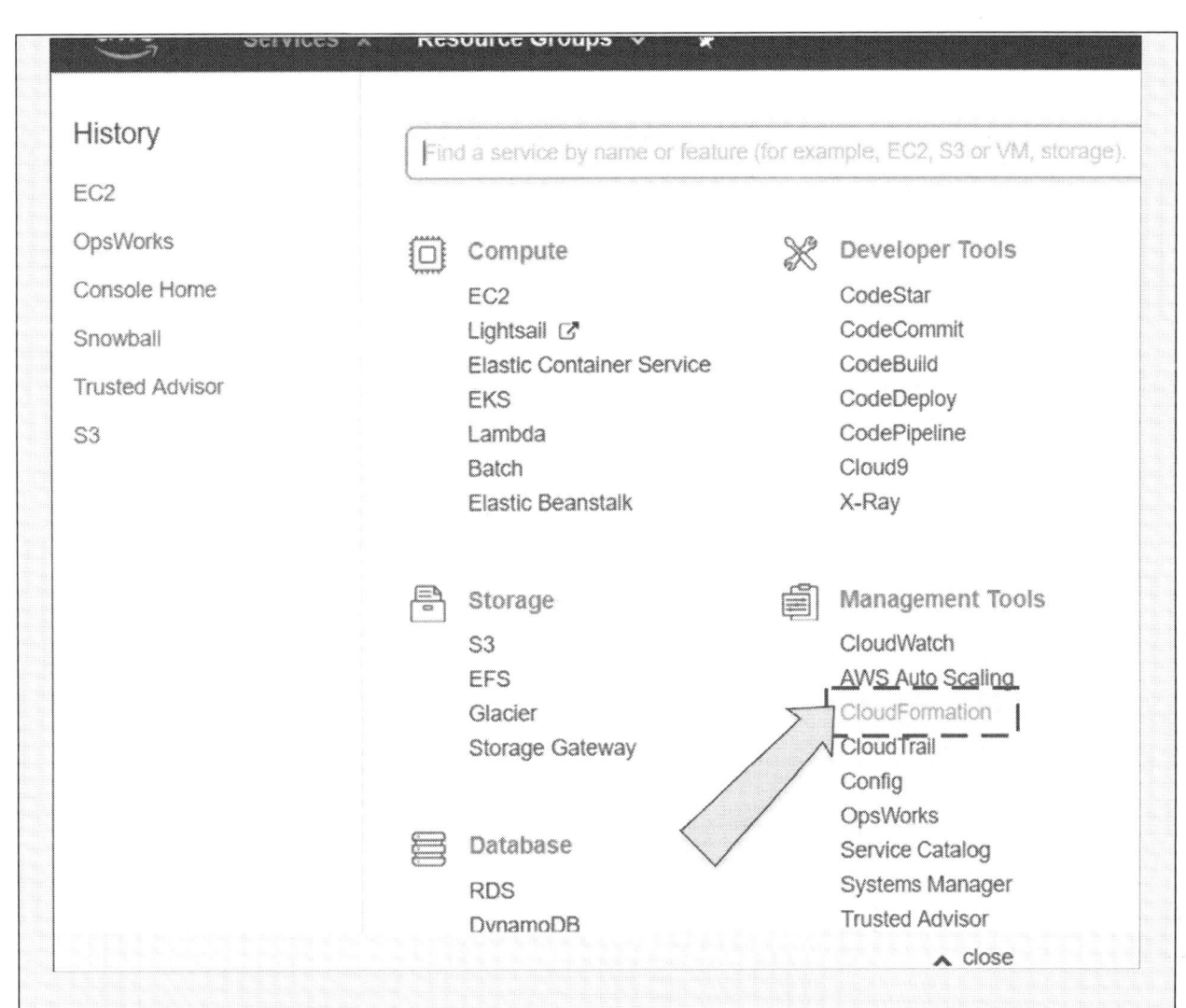

4. From the options given on the main dashboard, click on 'Create new stack'. The stack is a template that will provision resources for you. Alternately, you can also code your infrastructure in either YAML or JSON format. However, for this course, we will use one of the sample templates as an example.

Chapter 3: Technology

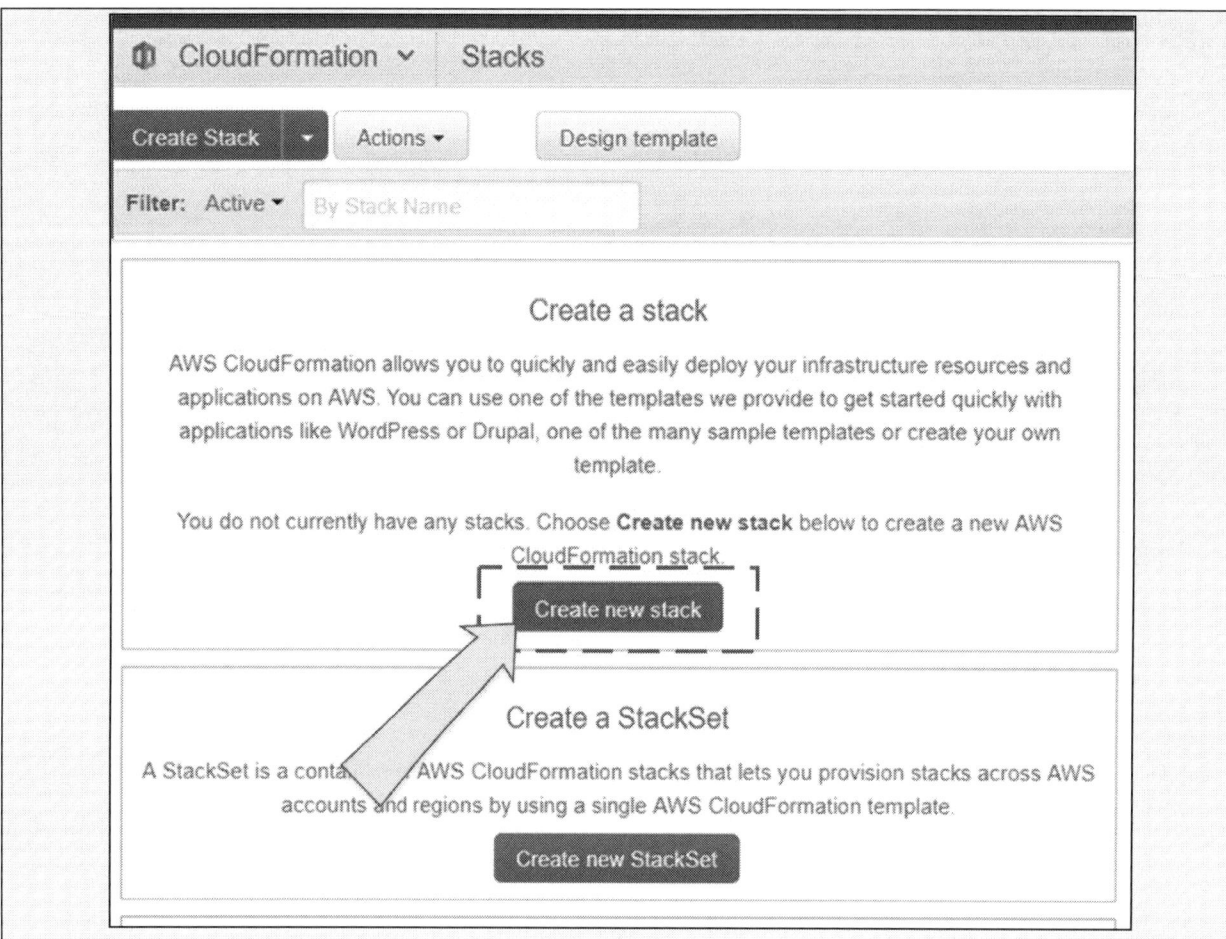

5. Choose a template from the list of drop-down menu. Here, we are selecting "WordPress" blog as an example. Click 'Next'.

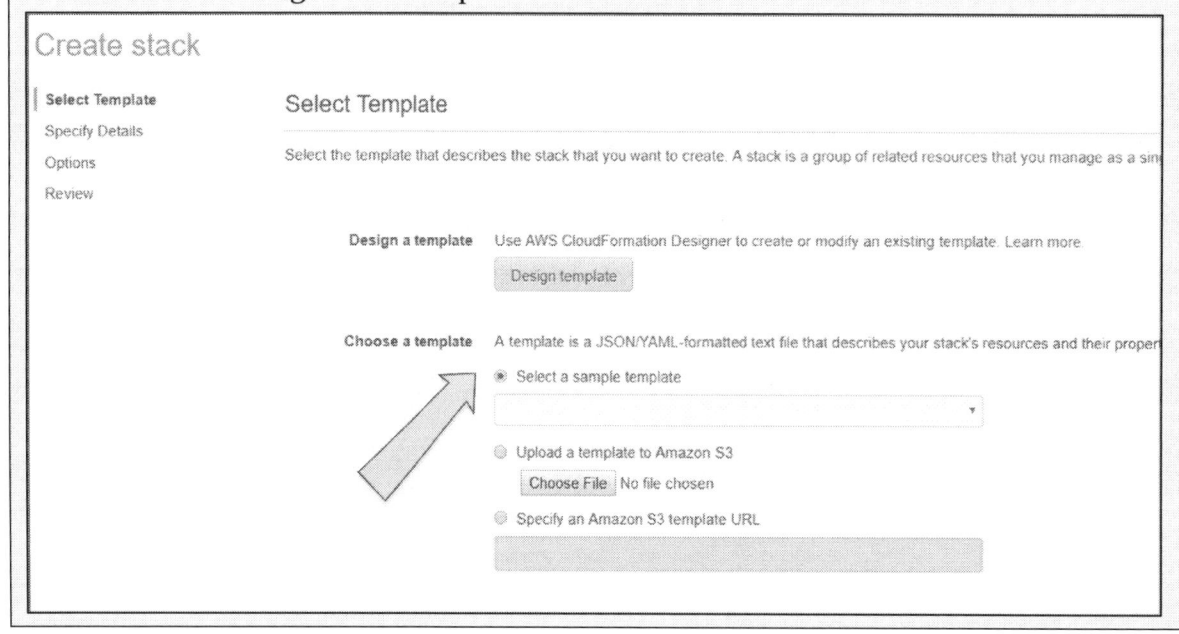

Chapter 3: Technology

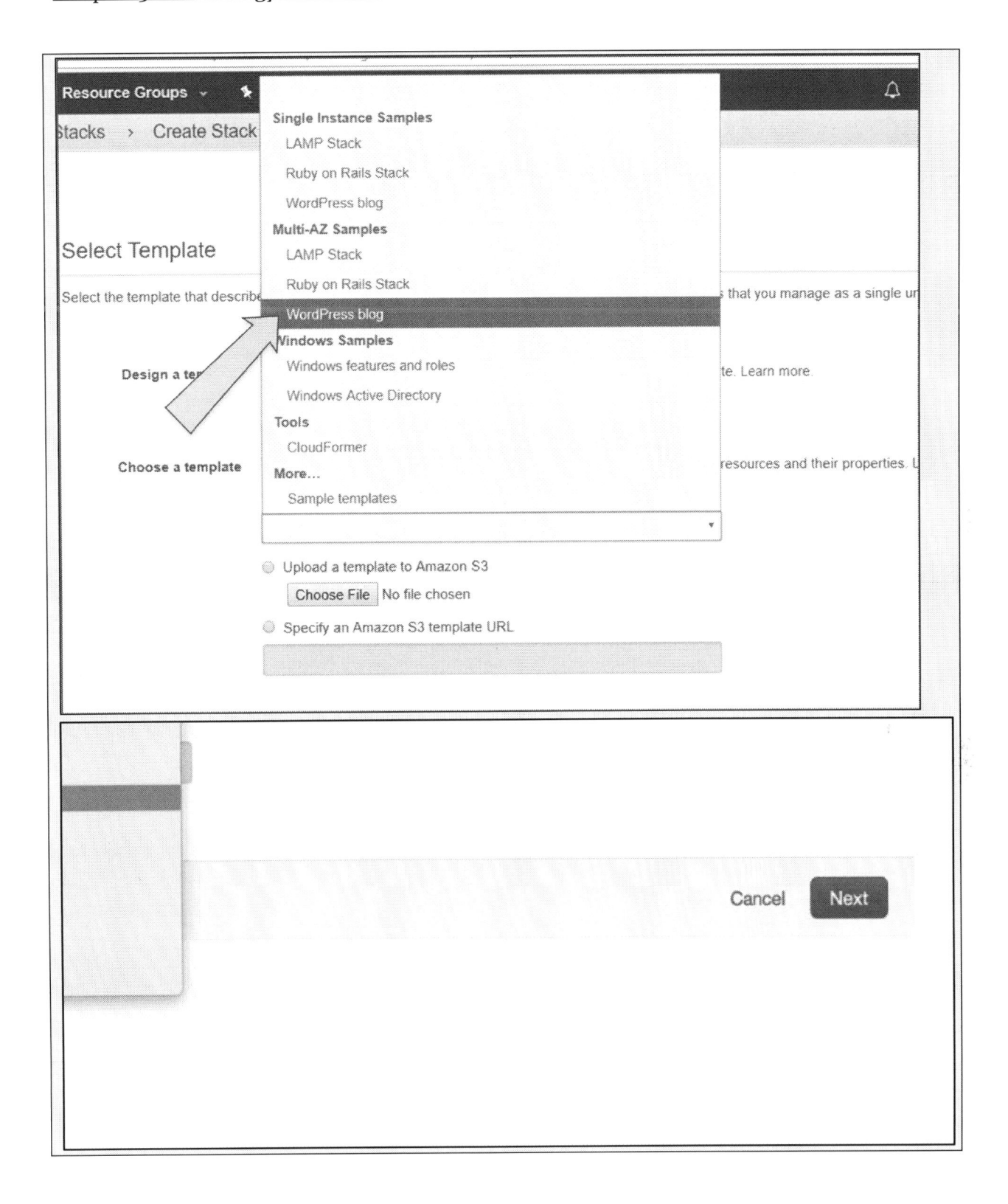

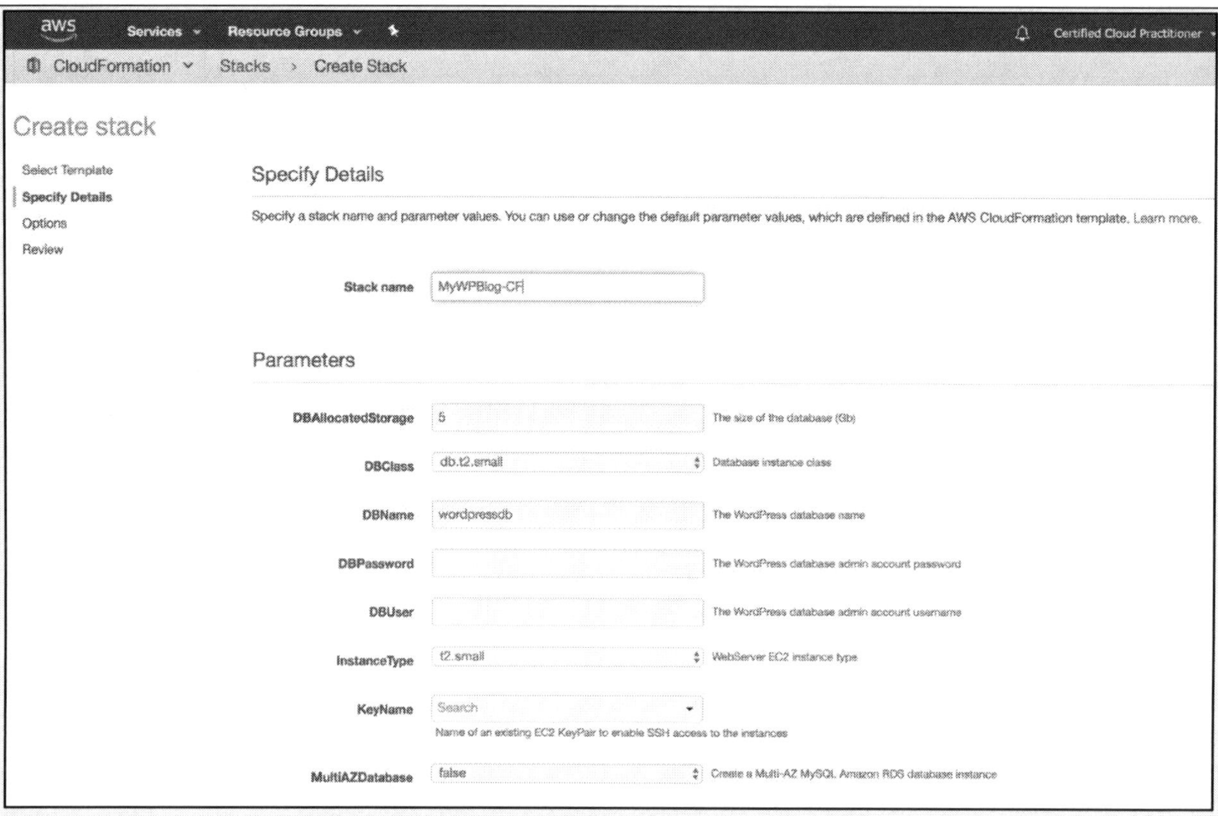
aws
Services
Resource Groups
Certified Cloud Practitioner
CloudFormation
Stacks
Create Stack
Create stack
Select Template
Specify Details
Options
Review
Specify Details
Specify a stack name and parameter values. You can use or change the default parameter values, which are defined in the AWS CloudFormation template. Learn more.
Stack name
MyWPBlog-CF
Parameters
DBAllocatedStorage
5
The size of the database (Gb)
DBClass
db.t2.small
Database instance class
DBName
wordpressdb
The WordPress database name
DBPassword
The WordPress database admin account password
DBUser
The WordPress database admin account username
InstanceType
t2.small
WebServer EC2 instance type
KeyName
Search
Name of an existing EC2 KeyPair to enable SSH access to the instances
MultiAZDatabase
false
Create a Multi-AZ MySQL Amazon RDS database instance

6. Enter the below details and click 'Next'.

- Your stack name
- Name, instance type, and size of your database
- Database admin username and password
- Webserver (EC2) instance type and number of webservers
- Key pair to enable SSH access and SSH location
- Subnets where you want to deploy your stack into and VPC ID

Chapter 3: Technology

DBAllocatedStorage	5	The size of the database (Gb)
DBClass	db.t2.micro	Database instance class
DBName	wordpressdb	The WordPress database name
DBPassword	••••••••••	The WordPress database admin account password
DBUser	••••••••••	The WordPress database admin account username
InstanceType	t2.micro	WebServer EC2 instance type
KeyName	myWPKP	Name of an existing EC2 KeyPair to enable SSH access to the instances
MultiAZDatabase	false	Create a Multi-AZ MySQL Amazon RDS database instance
SSHLocation	0.0.0.0/0	The IP address range that can be used to SSH to the EC2 instances
Subnets	subnet-331ffc1c (172.31.80.0/20) × subnet-ba882c85 (172.31.48.0/20) × subnet-c64f7eca (172.31.64.0/20) × subnet-f5812cbe (172.31.16.0/20) × subnet-f10ce8ac (172.31.32.0/20) × subnet-e7bb3b83 (172.31.0.0/20) ×	The list of SubnetIds in your Virtual Private Cloud (VPC)
VpcId	vpc-e56db29d (172.31.0.0/16)	VpcId of your existing Virtual Private Cloud (VPC)
WebServerCapacity	1	The initial number of WebServer instances

7. These parameters can also be configured inside the JSON document.
8. You can fill in the optional details, but for this example, you can leave it for now and click 'Next'.

Chapter 3: Technology

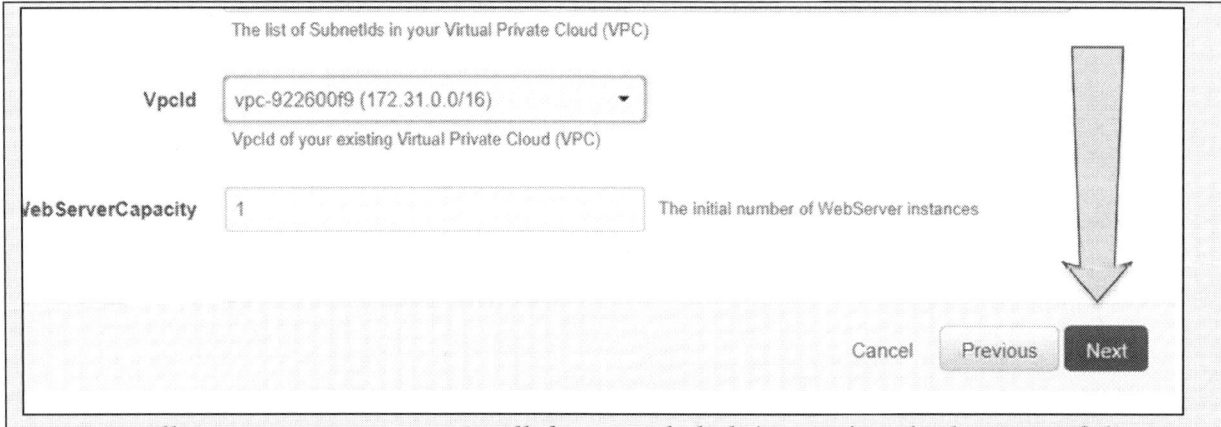

9. You will see a review screen. Scroll down and click 'Create' at the bottom of the screen to create the stack. This may take some time (5 to 20 minutes), depending on how complex the stack is.

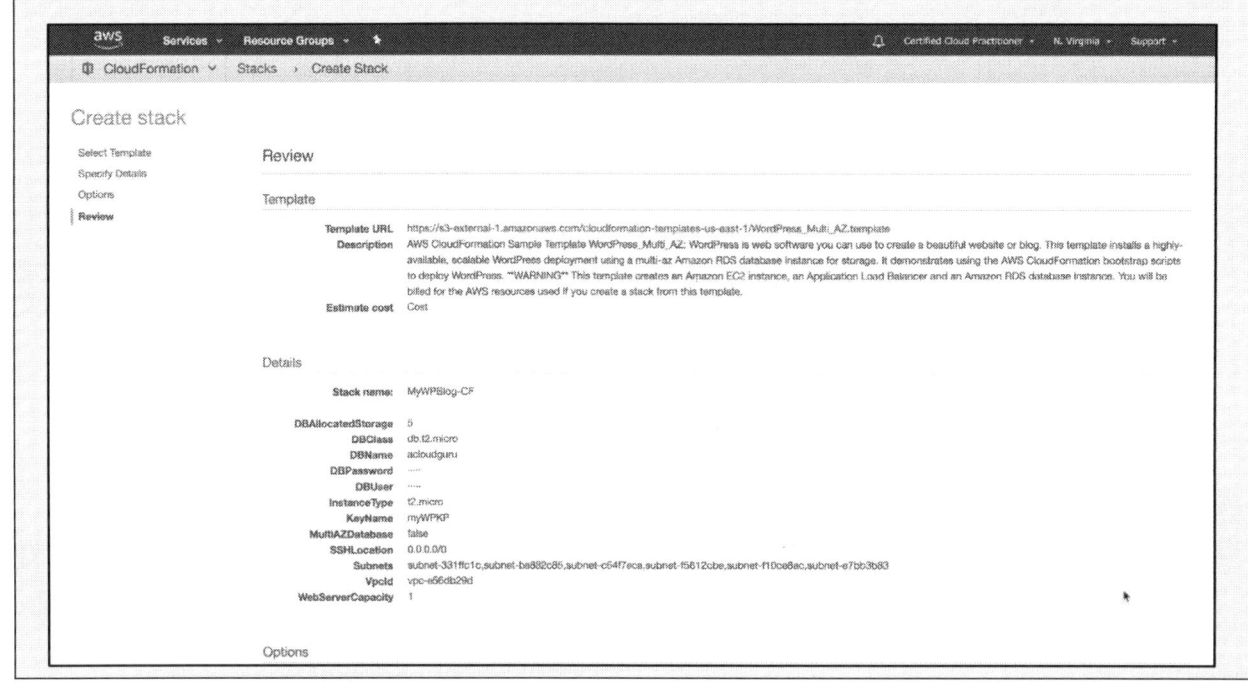

Chapter 3: Technology

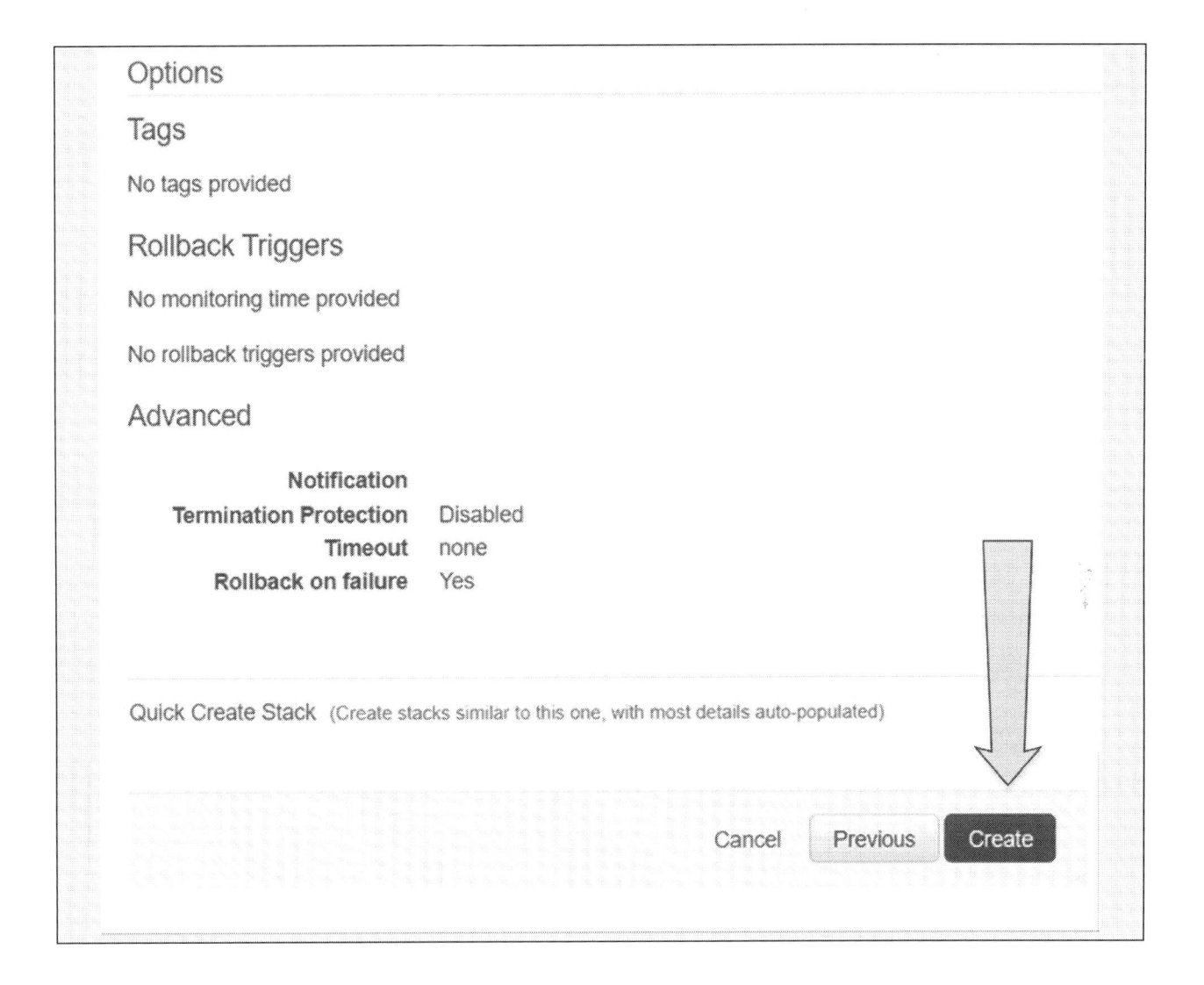

Options

Tags

No tags provided

Rollback Triggers

No monitoring time provided

No rollback triggers provided

Advanced

Notification	
Termination Protection	Disabled
Timeout	none
Rollback on failure	Yes

Quick Create Stack (Create stacks similar to this one, with most details auto-populated)

Cancel   Previous   **Create**

Chapter 3: Technology

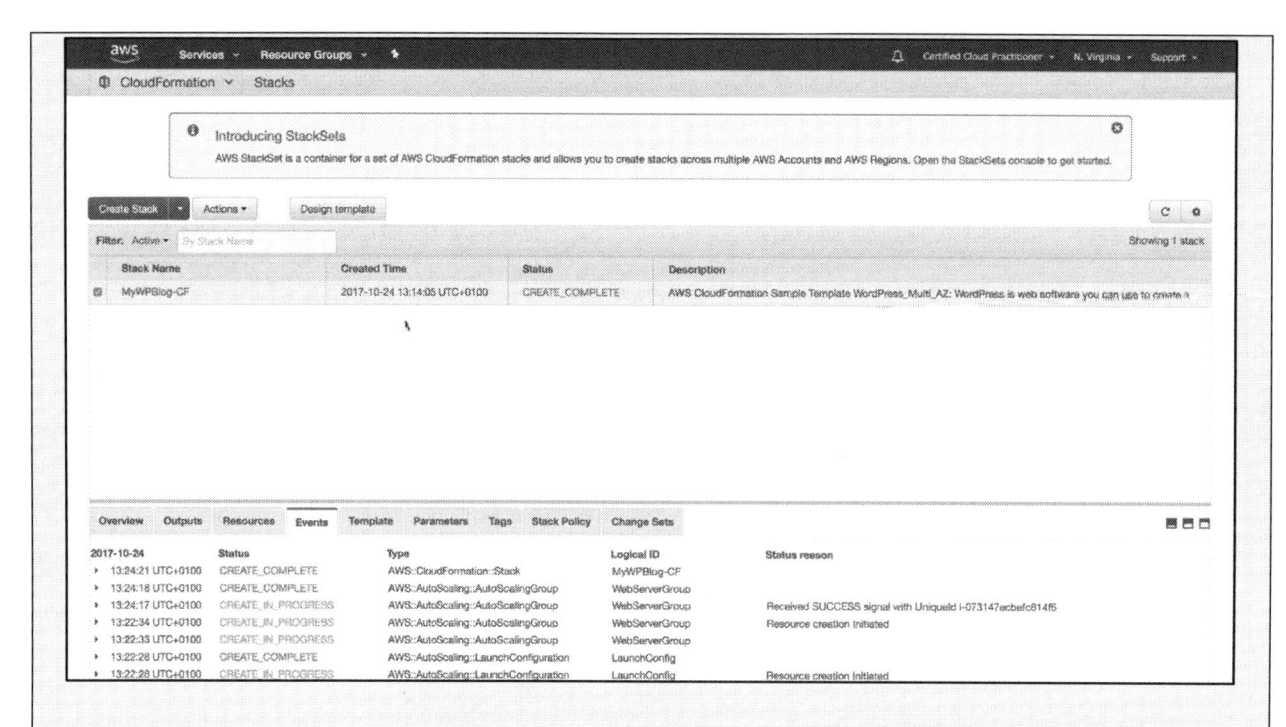

10. Once the stack is created, select the 'Outputs' tab. You will be able to see your website URL address.

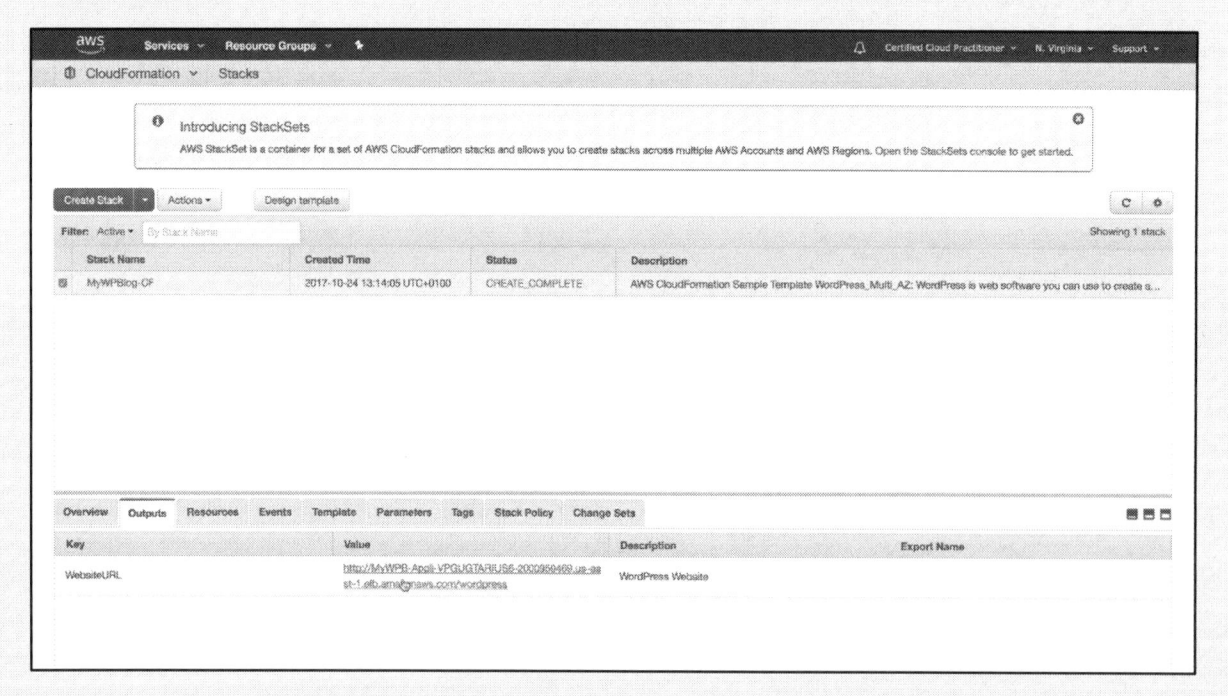

11. This is the Website URL of your WordPress site. Click on it to be directed to your WordPress site. You can also delete the entire CloudFormation Stack and its provisioned resources anytime.

AWS Quick Starts

If you are new to AWS and want to deploy any particular type of technology onto the AWS cloud, AWS Quick Starts is a simple and quick way of getting started. Quick Starts are automated reference deployments like templates, built by AWS solutions architects

Chapter 3: Technology

and partners to assist you in deploying popular solutions of key technologies on AWS cloud, using AWS best practices for security and high availability.

Each Quick Start launches configures and runs the AWS compute, network, storage, and other services required to deploy a specific workload on AWS. You can build your test or production environment in a few simple steps, and start using it immediately. Quick Starts saves time by eliminating hundreds of manual installation and configuration steps with a single click.

Quick Starts include:

1. A reference architecture for the deployment
2. AWS CloudFormation templates (JSON or YAML scripts) that automate and configure the deployment
3. A deployment guide, which explains the architecture and implementation in detail, and provides instructions for customizing the deployment

Lab 3-3: AWS Quick Start

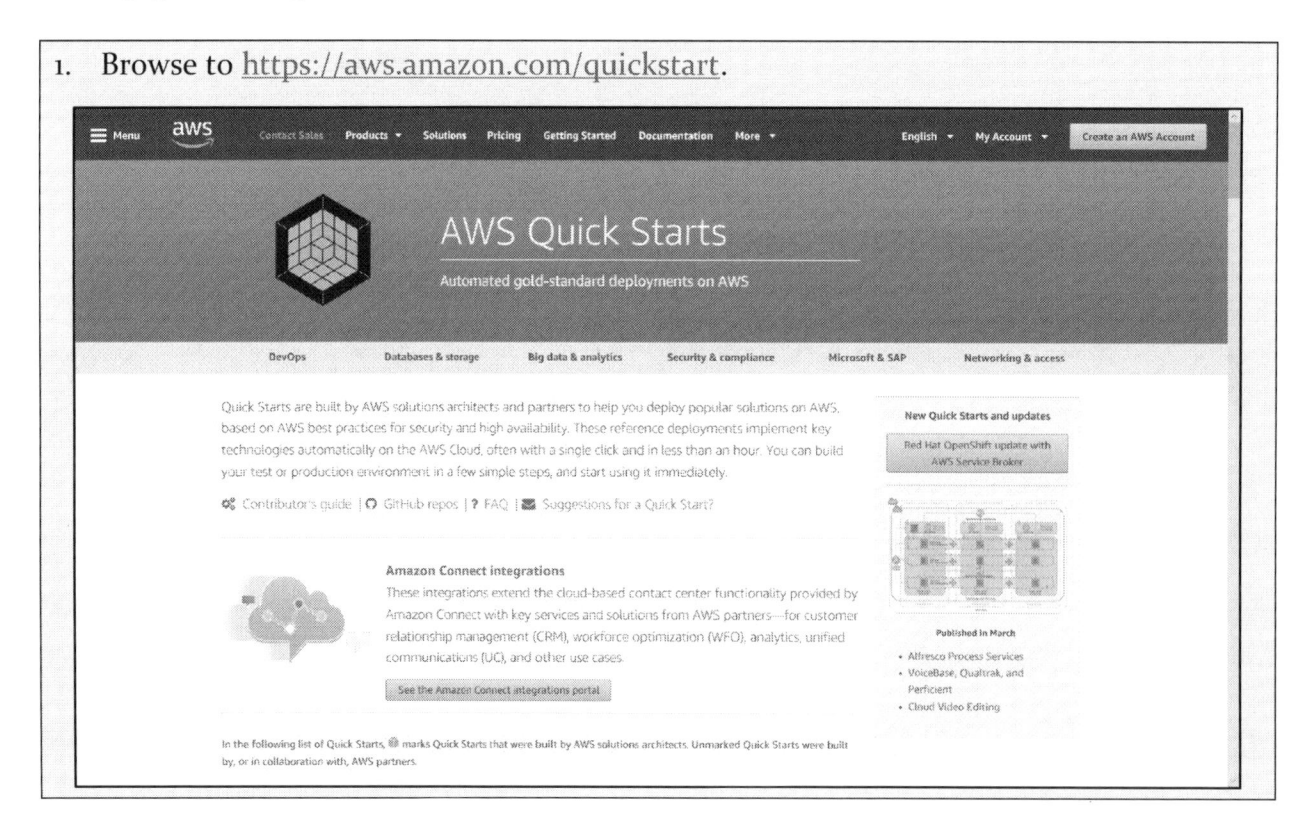

1. Browse to https://aws.amazon.com/quickstart.

Chapter 3: Technology

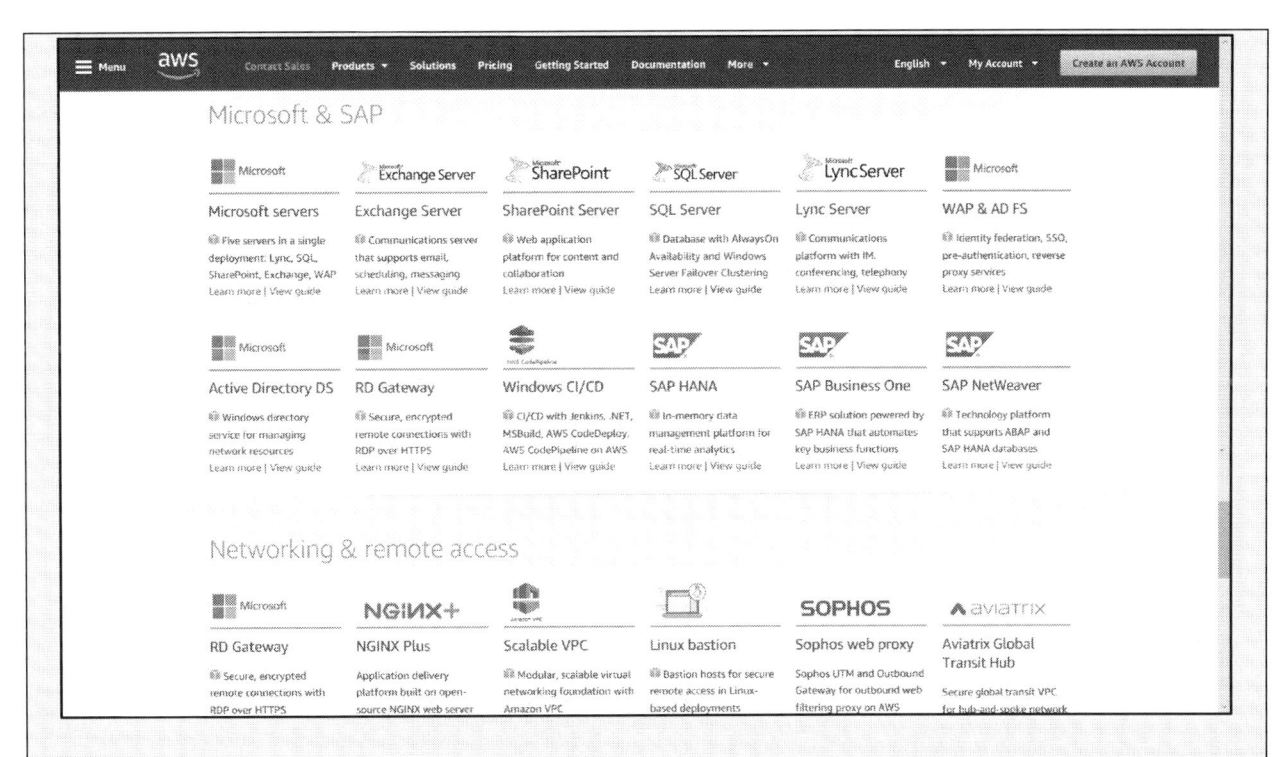

2. You will see a list of popular deployment models. Select the solution you need to deploy by clicking 'View guide'. For this example, we will deploy a SharePoint server.

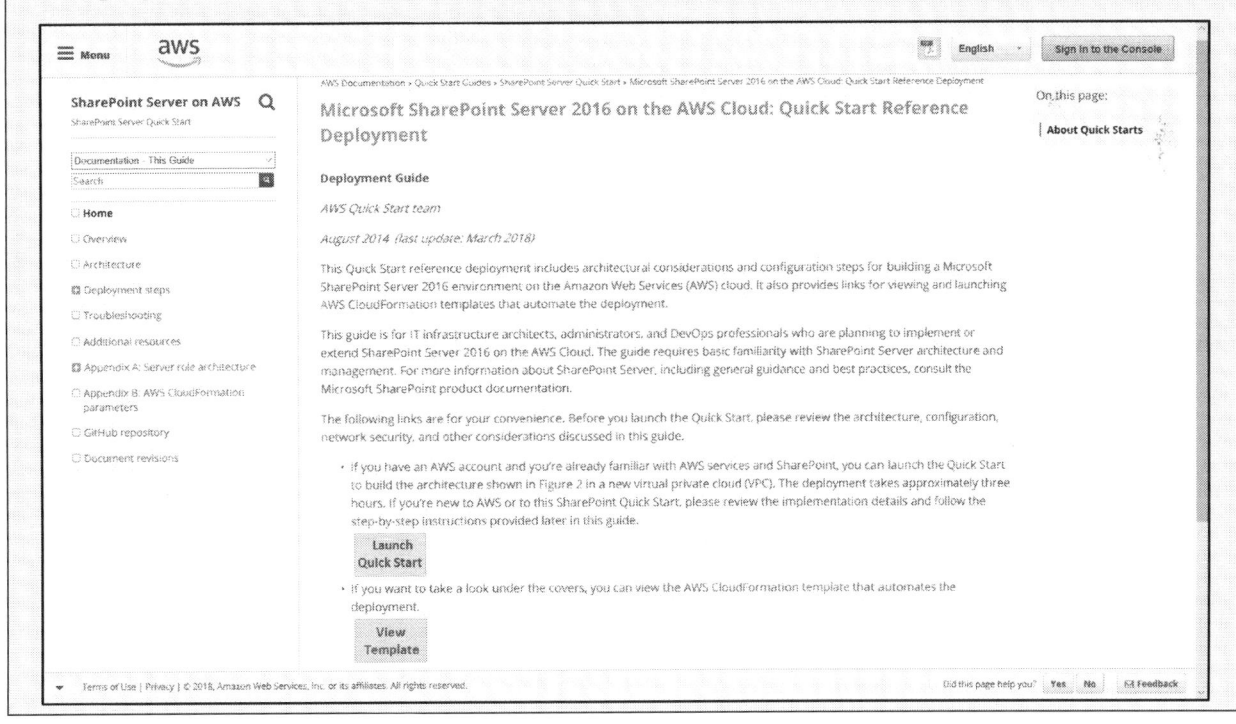

Chapter 3: Technology

3. You will see a complete guide to the deployment solution you selected. After reading the guide, go ahead and click 'Launch Quick Start.' This will open up the AWS console and launch AWS CloudFormation, which can be used to setup your SharePoint infrastructure without the need to manually configuring the resources.

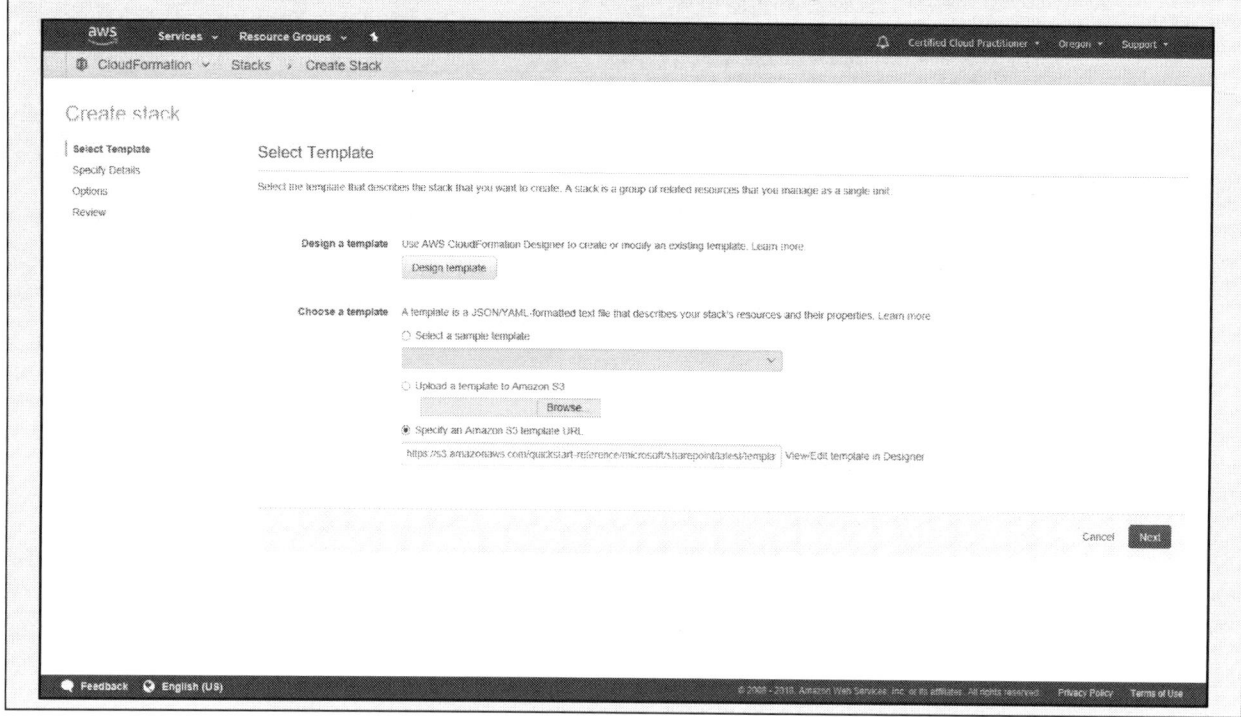

AWS Global Infrastructure

The AWS Cloud spans across 18 geographic Regions with 53 Availability Zones and 1 Local Region around the world, with further announced plans for 12 more Availability Zones and four more Regions in Bahrain, Hong Kong SAR, Sweden, and a second AWS GovCloud Region in the US.

What is a Region?

The region is a complete independent and separate geographical area. Each region has multiple, physically separated and isolated locations known as Availability Zones. Examples of Region include London, Dublin, Sydney, etc.

What is an Availability Zone?

Availability zone is simply a data center or a collection of data centers. Each Availability zone in a Region has separate powers, networking and connectivity to reduce the chances of two zones failing simultaneously. No two Availability zones share a data center; however, the data centers within a particular Availability zone are connected to each other over redundant low-latency private network links. Likewise, all zones in a region are linked by highly resilient and very low latency private fiber optic connections for communication. The Availability zones are at a certain length or distance apart from each other.

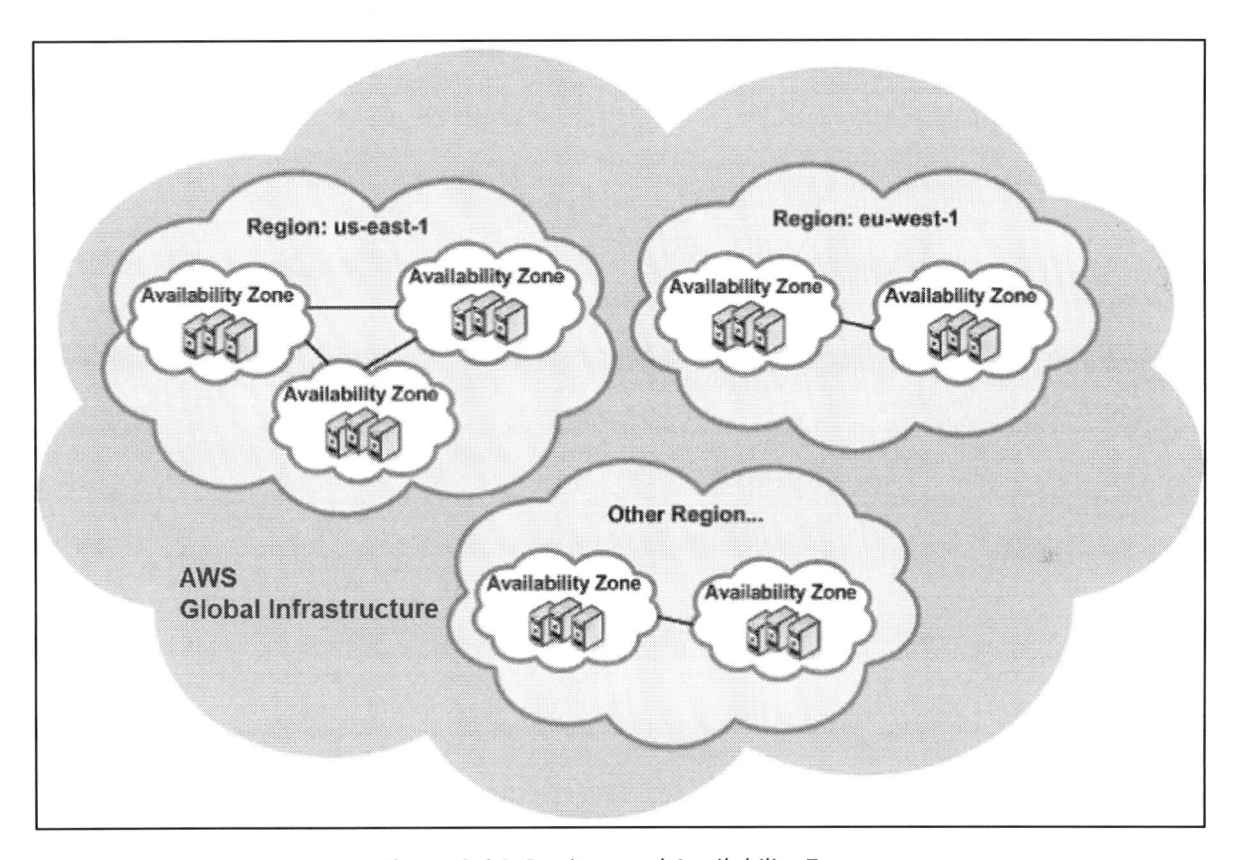

Figure 3-04. Regions and Availability Zones

What is an Edge Location?

Edge Locations are AWS sites deployed in major cities and highly populated areas across the globe. There are many more Edge locations than there are regions. Currently, there are over 102 edge locations. Edge Locations are used by AWS services such as AWS CloudFront to cache data and reduce latency for end-user access by using the Edge Locations as a global Content Delivery Network (CDN).

Therefore, Edge Locations are primarily used by end users who are accessing and using your services. For example, you may have your website hosted by the Ohio region with a configured CloudFront distribution associated. When a user accesses your website from Europe, they will be re-directed to their closest Edge Location (in Europe) where cached data could be read on your website, significantly reducing latency.

Regional Edge Cache

In November 2016, AWS announced a new type of Edge Location, called a Regional Edge Cache. This sits between your CloudFront Origin servers and the Edge Locations. A Regional Edge Cache has a larger cache-width than each of the individual Edge Locations and because data expires from the cache at the Edge Locations, the data is retained at the Regional Edge Caches.

Therefore, when a data is requested at the Edge Location that is no longer available, the Edge Location can retrieve the cached data from the Regional Edge Cache instead of the Origin servers, which would have a higher latency.

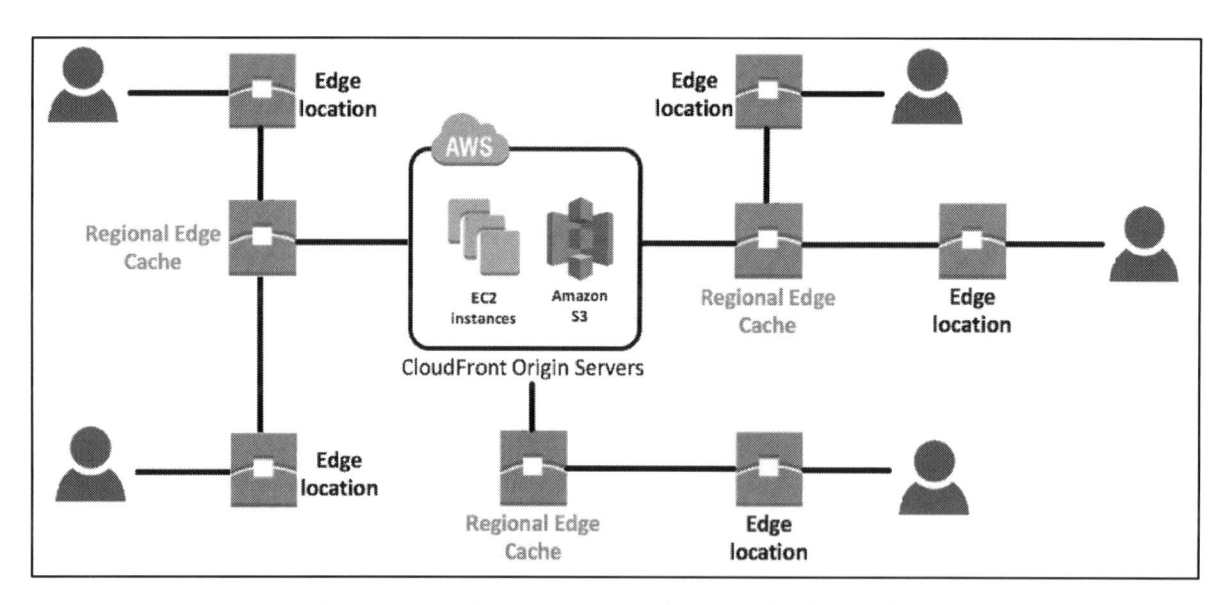

Figure 3-05. Edge Locations and Regional Edge Caches

EXAM TIP: Know the difference between these three: Region, Availability Zone, and Edge Location.

Chapter 3: Technology

AWS Compute

Provisioning of computing resources on demand is access to raw compute power or server capacity. This involves providing virtual or physical resources as a service. AWS offers a range of computing services that allow you to develop, deploy, run, and scale your applications and workloads in a cloud environment. AWS provides a robust and scalable platform for Virtual Server Hosting, Container Management, and Serverless Computing.

Amazon Elastic Compute Cloud (Amazon EC2)

Launched in 2006, Amazon Elastic Compute Cloud (Amazon EC2) is a web service that provides secure, resizable cloud-based compute capacity in the form of EC2 instances that are virtual servers in the cloud. Amazon EC2 enables any developer to leverage the compute capacity that Amazon offers to meet their business requirements with no up-front investment and performance compromises. Amazon EC2 provides a true virtual computing environment, where the web service interfaces can be used to launch instances with a variety of operating systems, load custom application environment, manage network's access permissions, and run image, consuming as many or few systems as desired.

Amazon EC2 offers the tools to build failure robust applications and isolate themselves from common failure scenarios. When designing a system, a good practice is to assume things will fail. In this way, you will always design, implement and deploy with an automated recovery and restore strategy. With Amazon EC2, you can provision multiple instances at once, so that even if one of them goes down, the system will still be up and running.

> **EXAM TIP**: EC2 is a compute-based service. It is not serverless. You are physically connecting to a virtual server. Always design for failure and provision at least one EC2 instance in each availability zone to avoid a system failure in case if any one instance goes down.

Benefits of Amazon EC2

- Quickly scales capacity both up and down by booting new server instances within minutes as your requirement changes
- Has complete control of the instances with root access
- Provides a wide range of Instance types optimized to fit different use cases

- Integrated with other AWS services to provide a complete solution for a wide range of applications
- A highly reliable environment with rapid replacement and provisioning of multiple instances simultaneously
- You pay only for the capacity you actually use
- Secure, inexpensive and easy to start-up

Pricing Models

There are four different pricing models for EC2 instances

On-Demand Instances: On-Demand Instances allows you to pay a fixed rate by the hour (or by the second, depending upon which instances you run) with no long-term commitments or upfront payments. Depending on your application demands, you can increase or decrease compute capacity and only pay the specified per hourly rates for the instance you use.

Reserved Instances: Reserved Instances offers significant discounts (up to 75%) compared to On-Demand instance pricing. It provides you with a capacity reservation over a 1-year or 3-years term. Reserving servers and paying all upfront for them entitles you to achieve massive discounted prices.

- Standard reserved instances give you up to 75% off on the On-Demand prices.
- Convertible RI's allows you to change the attributes of the reserved instances as long as the exchange results in the creation of Reserved Instances of equal or greater value. This gives up to 54% off on the On-Demand prices.
- Scheduled RI's lets you purchase capacity reservations that recur on a daily, weekly, or monthly basis, with a specified start time and duration, for a one-year term are available to launch within the time window you reserve.

Spot Instances: Spot Instances enables you to bid your preferred price on spare EC2 instance capacity, providing you with even greater savings. The moment spot price drops down below your bid amount, your instance is provisioned, and as soon as the spot price moves above your bid amount, your instance terminates. This allows you to grow your application's compute capacity and through put for the same budget and significantly reduce the cost of running your applications. If Amazon EC2 terminates your Spot instance, you will not be charged for a partial hour of usage. However, if you terminate the instance yourself, you will be charged for the hour in which the instance ran.

Dedicated Hosts: Dedicated Hosts are physical EC2 servers dedicated for your use. Dedicated hosts can help you reduce costs by allowing you to use your existing server-bound software licenses. They offer you more flexibility, visibility, and control over the placement of instances on dedicated hardware.

Recommended Uses Cases

On-Demand Instances:

- Users that require flexibility and low cost without any up-front payment or long-term commitment
- Applications being developed or tested on Amazon EC2 for the first time
- Applications having short-term, spiky, or unpredictable workloads that cannot be interrupted

Reserved Instances:

- Applications that require reserved capacity
- Applications with steady state or predictable usage, like webservers
- Users can commit to a 1-year or 3-year term contract to reduce their total computing costs even more

Spot Instances:

- Applications that have flexible start and end times
- Applications that are feasible at very low compute-price only
- Users have urgent computing needs for large amounts of additional capacity

Dedicated Hosts:

- Useful for regulatory requirements that may not support multi-tenant virtualization
- Great for licensing that does not support multi-tenancy or cloud deployment
- Can be purchased On-Demand (hourly)
- Can be purchased as a Reservation for up to 70% off the On-Demand price

> EXAM TIP: Understand the different pricing models; you will be questioned for the pricing model you use depending on the scenario mentioned.

EC2 Instance Types

Amazon EC2 offers an extensive variety of instance types optimized for different use cases. Instance types consist of varying combinations of CPU, memory, storage, and networking capacity with one or more instance sizes giving you the flexibility to select computational resources according to the requirements of your target workload.

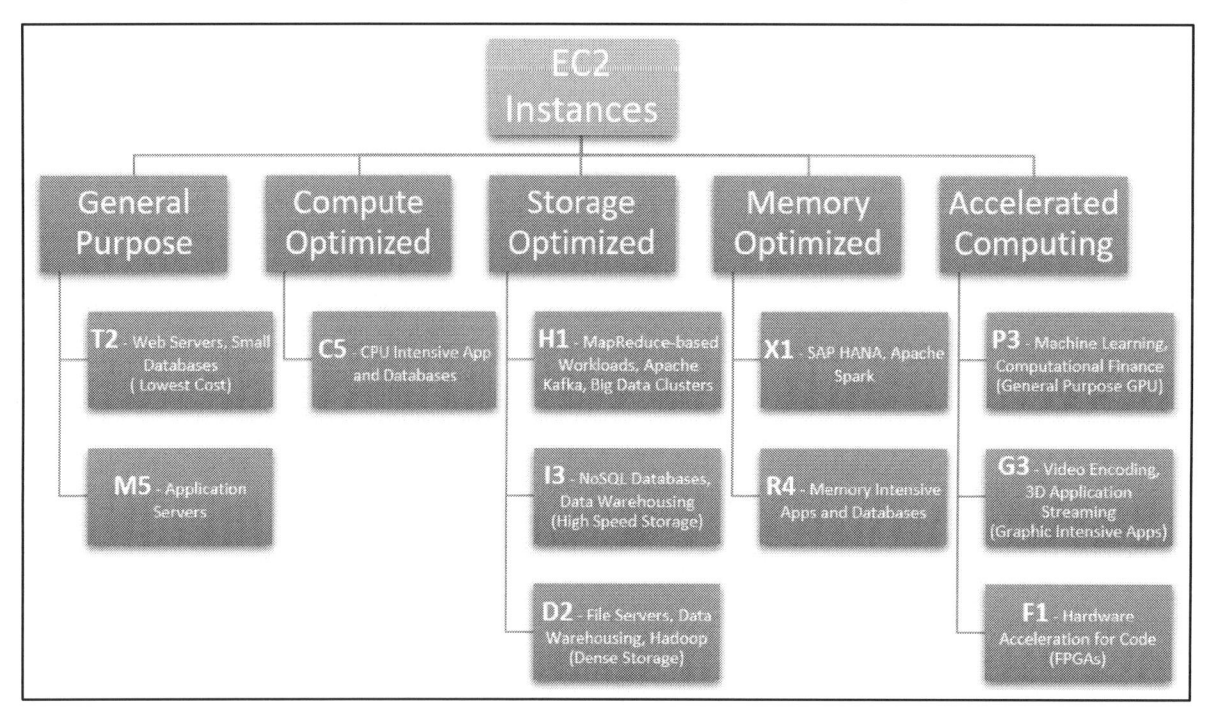

Figure 3-06. EC2 Instances

> **EXAM TIP**: Know that there are different types of EC2 instances for different use cases. For example, R4 for memory, C4 for computing, etc. You do not need to remember the instance types.

Lab 3-4: AWS EC2 Instance

1. Log in to the 'AWS Console'.
2. Click on 'Services'.
3. Select 'EC2' from Compute.

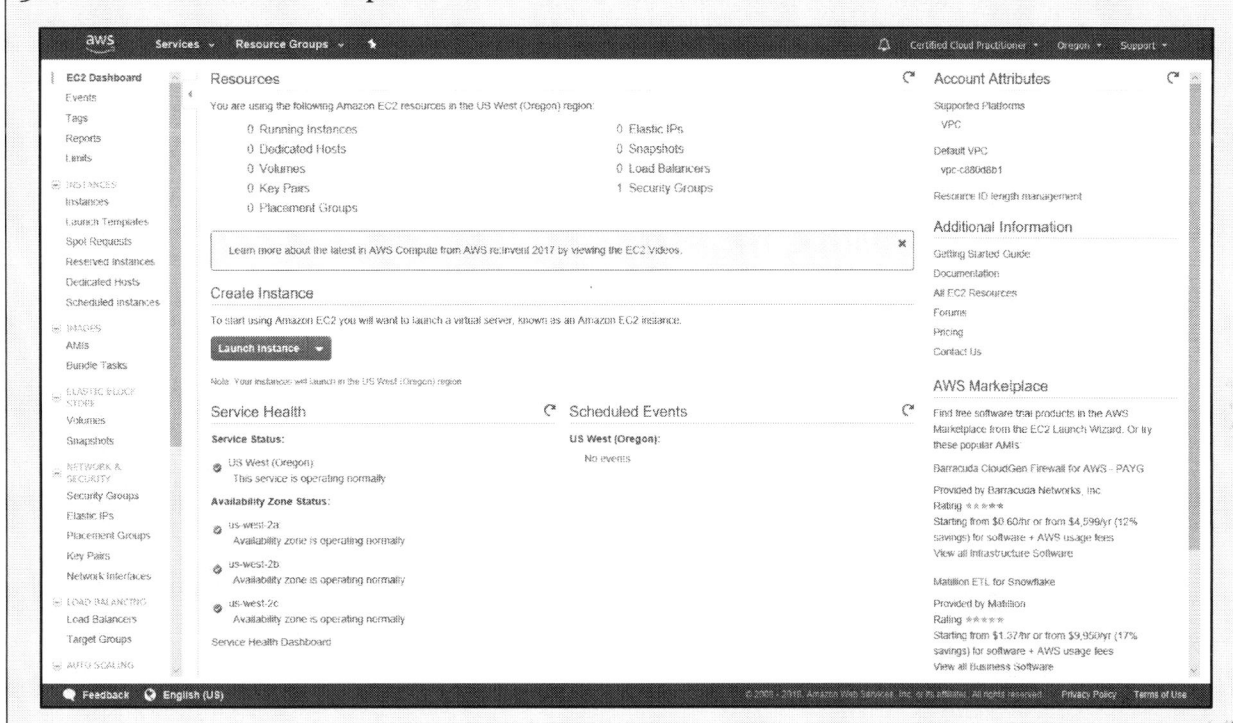

4. You will see one default Security Group and a default VPC. VPC is simply a virtual datacenter in the cloud where we will deploy our EC2 instance. Click 'Launch Instance' to get started.

Chapter 3: Technology

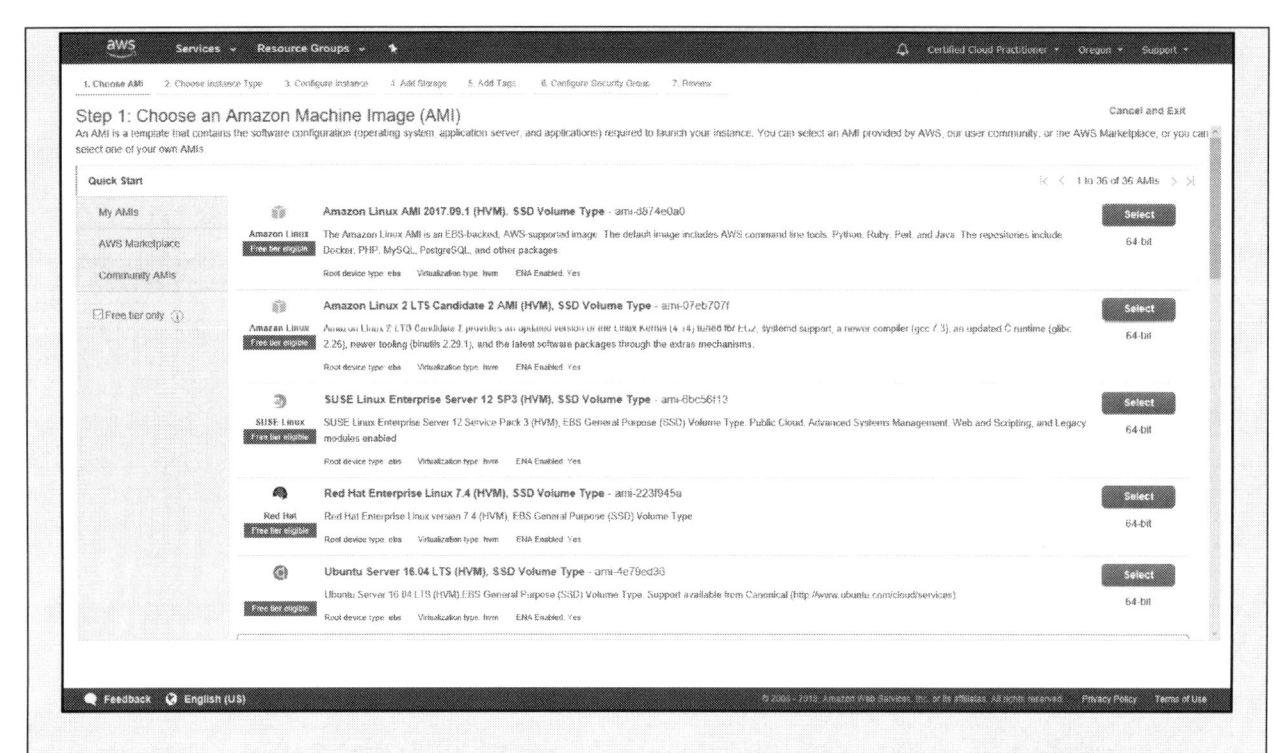

5. From the left tab, select checkbox for 'Free tier only.' This will only display a list of AMIs that are eligible for the free tier account. Click 'Select' for Amazon Linux AMI. We use this AMI because it comes with the AWS command line tools pre-installed.

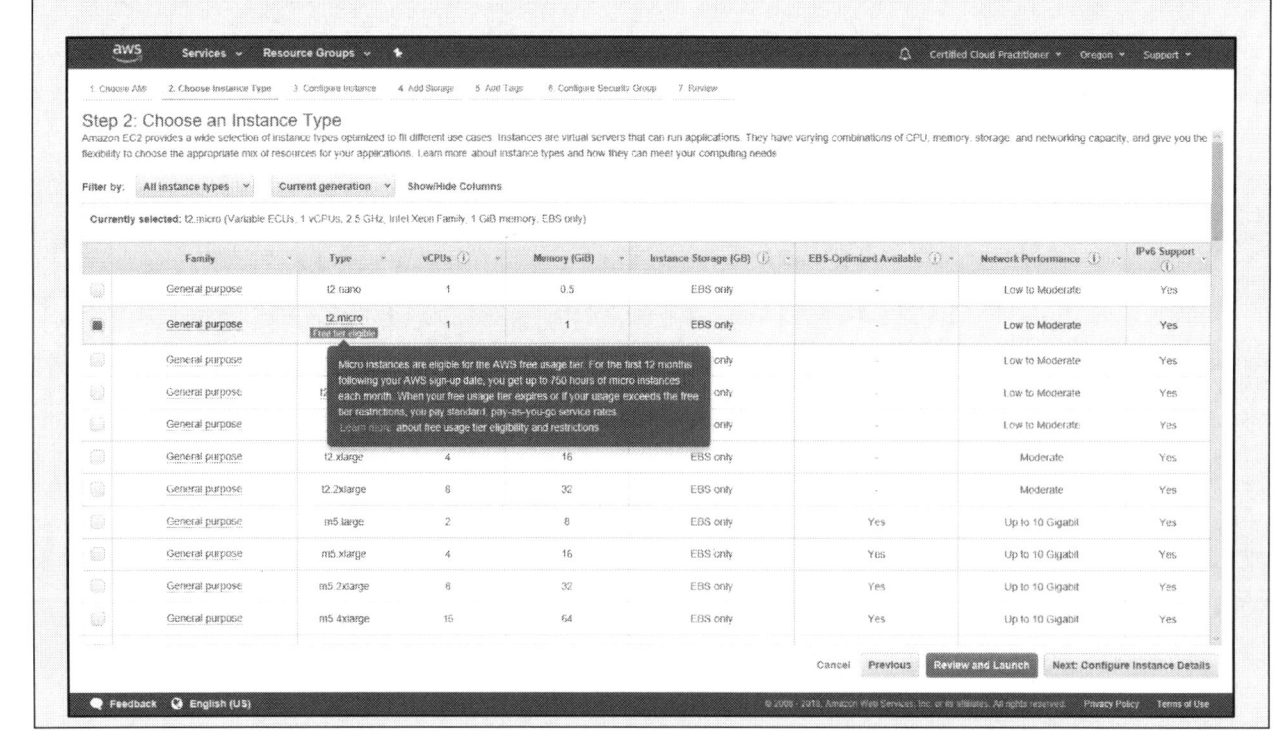

Chapter 3: Technology

6. Here you will see a list of different instance types. Select the general purpose 't2.micro' as it is eligible with a free tier. Click 'Next: Configure Instance Details'.

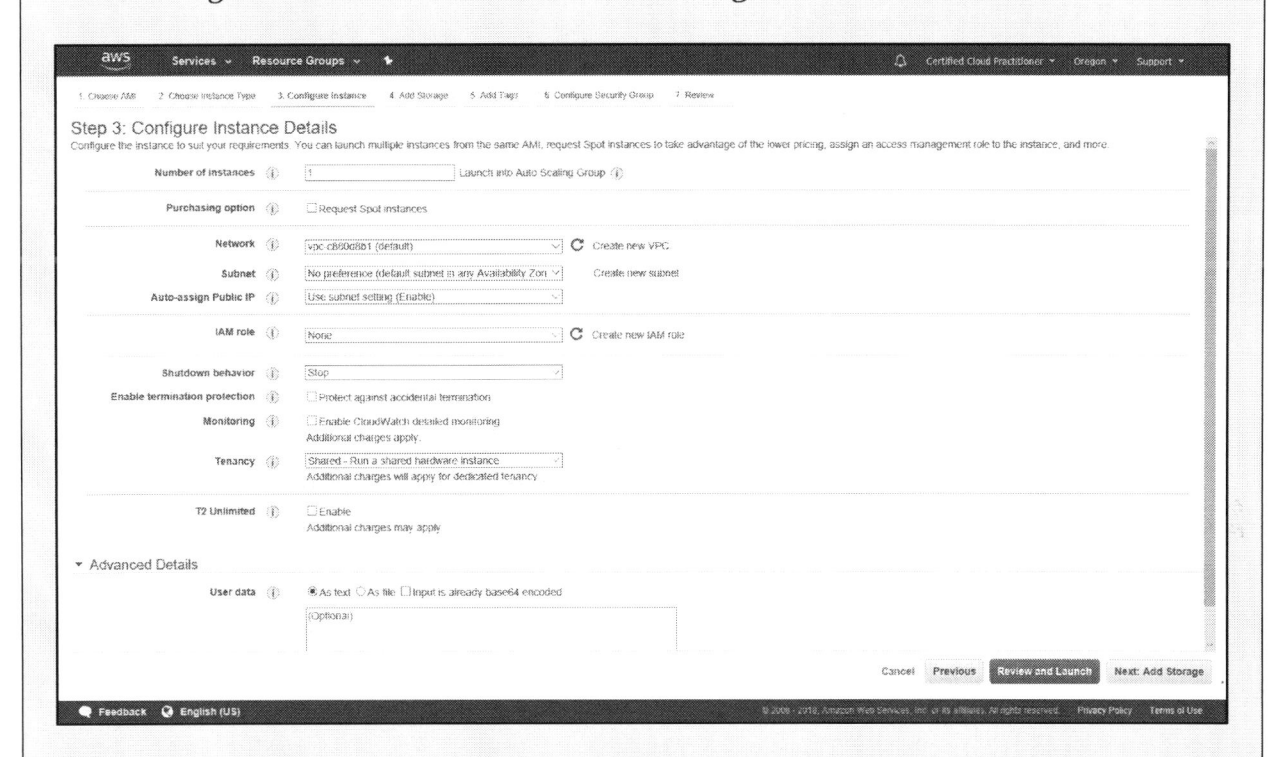

7. Configure instance details according to your requirements by defining number of instances; request for spot instances; selecting VPC; select particular Availability Zone for your subnet; enable Auto-assign Public IP for remote instance access; assign IAM role; define shutdown behaviour and termination protection; enable monitoring and run your instance on shared or dedicated host. For now, keep everything as default and click 'Next: Add Storage'.

Chapter 3: Technology

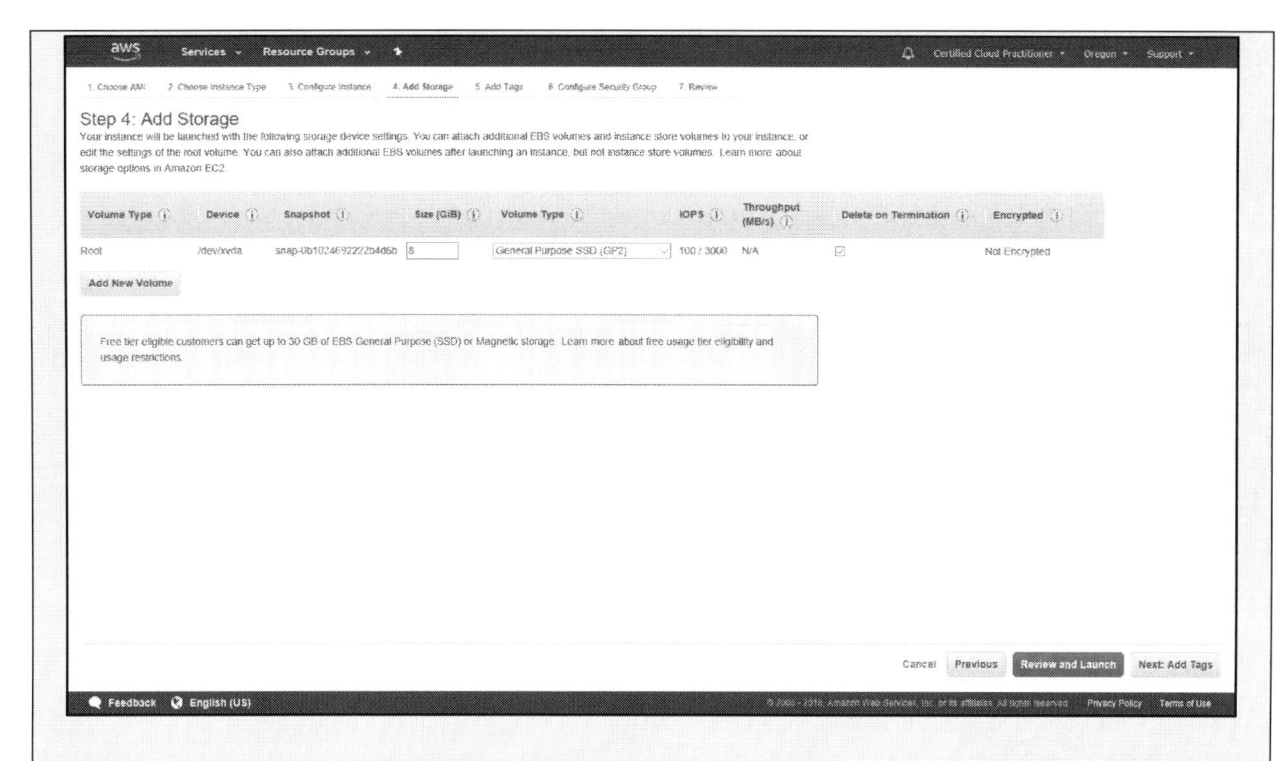

8. You now need to define EBS volume details such as size and type. This EBS volume will be attached to our EC2 instance. Keep everything as default and click 'Next: Add Tags'. For more details see Amazon Elastic Block Store (Amazon EBS).

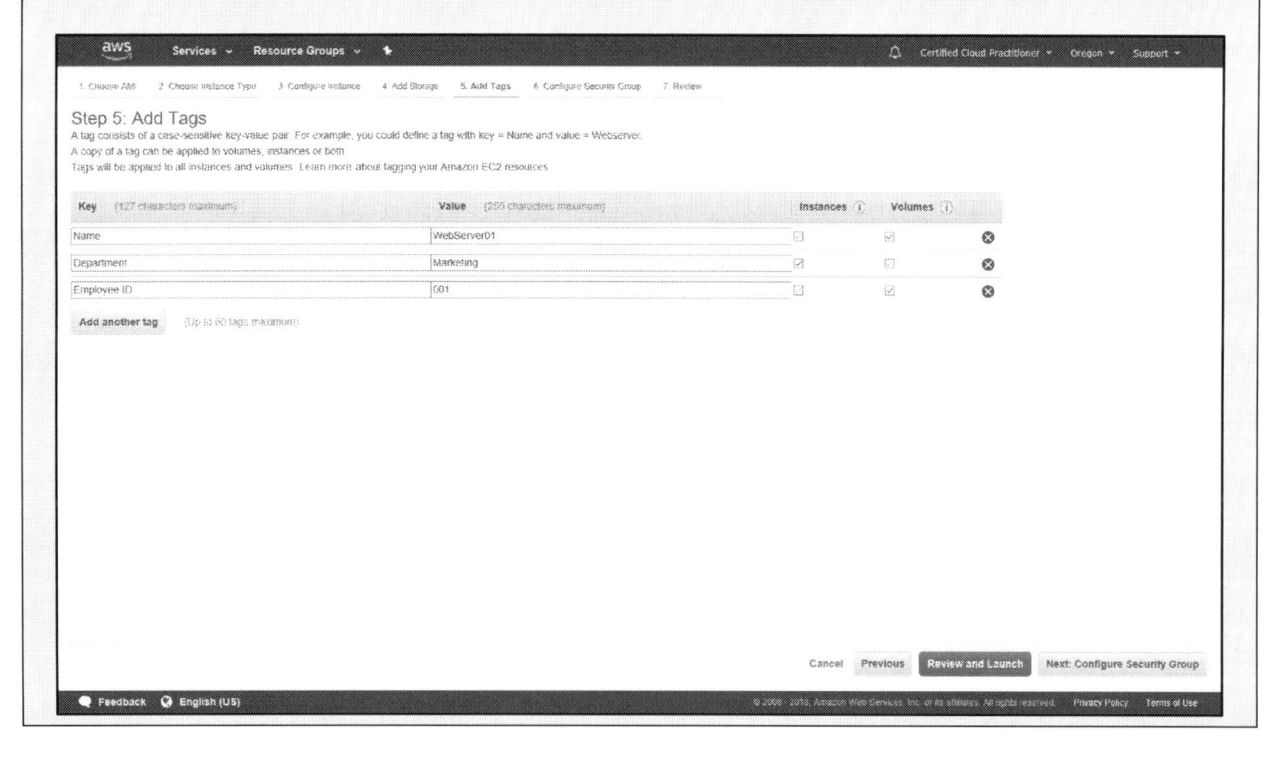

Chapter 3: Technology

9. Tags are labels you assign to AWS Resources. Add tags to this EC2 instances by defining a key-value pair. Here tags are added to Name, Department and Employee ID with their key values. Click 'Next: Configure Security Group.' For more details see Tags.

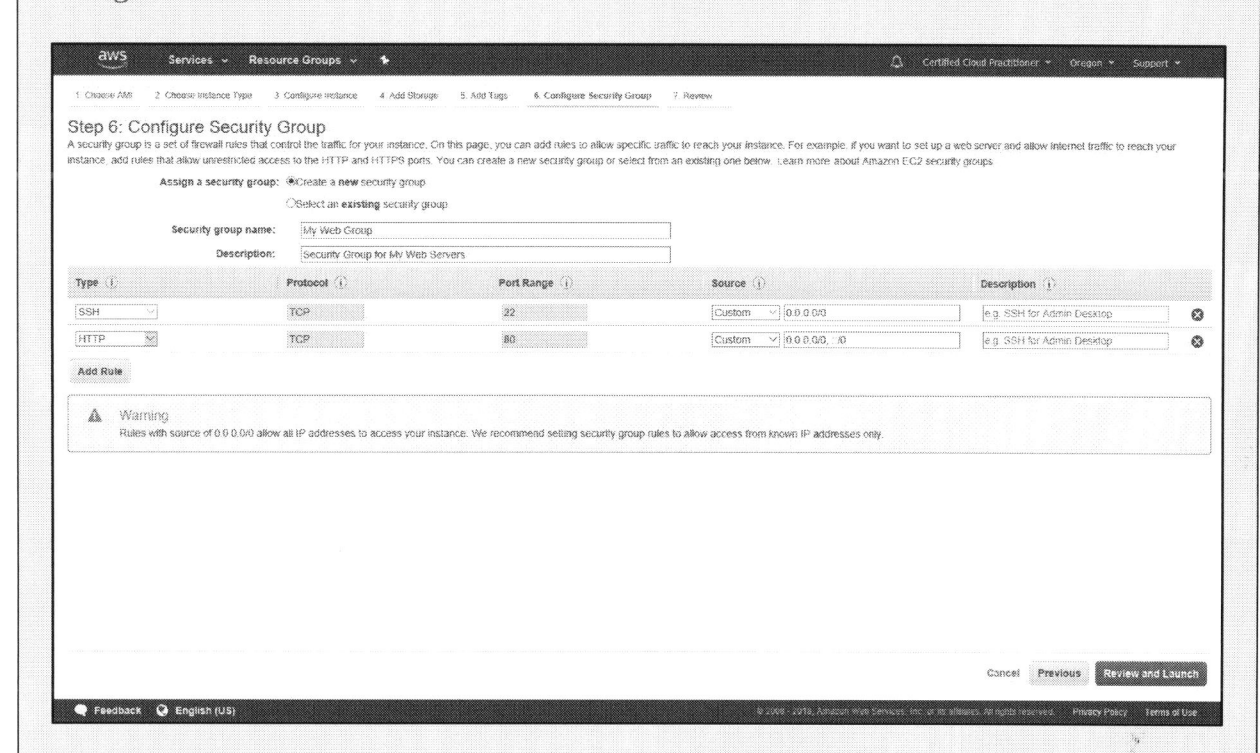

10. Security Groups are like the virtual firewall in the cloud. Create a new security group and enter a name. For example, we have named our group as 'My Web Group.' Since we are using a Linux machine, we need SSH protocol to log in our EC2 instance. We will use this EC2 instance as a webserver, so we need to allow in web traffic to the server. Click 'Add Rule' to add HTTP. After that click 'Review and Launch'.

Chapter 3: Technology

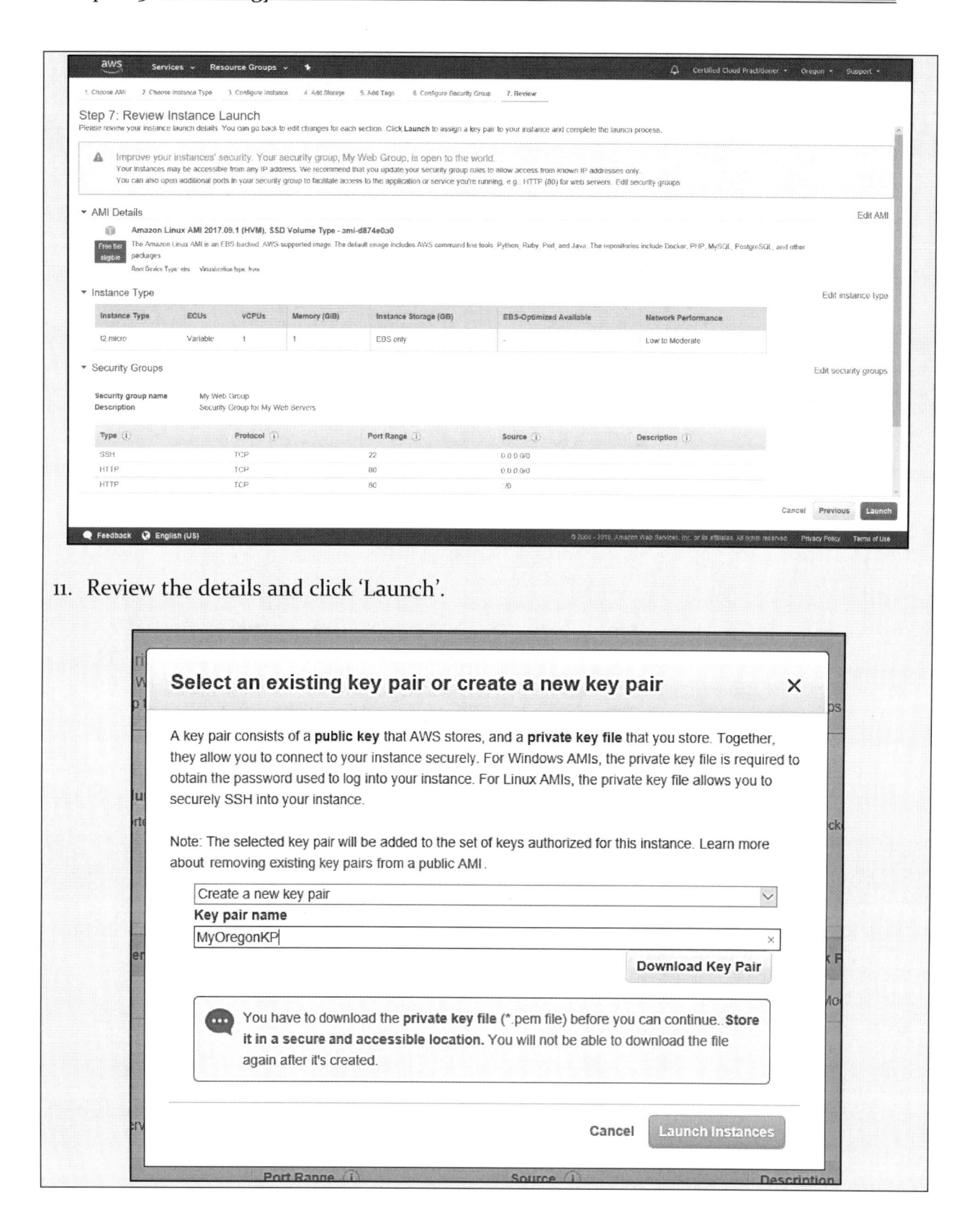

11. Review the details and click 'Launch'.

Chapter 3: Technology

12. You will need a key pair to SSH into your instance. Select 'Create a new key pair' and give it the name 'MyOregonKP'. Click 'Download Key Pair' to download it to your PC. Once downloaded, click 'Launch Instances'.

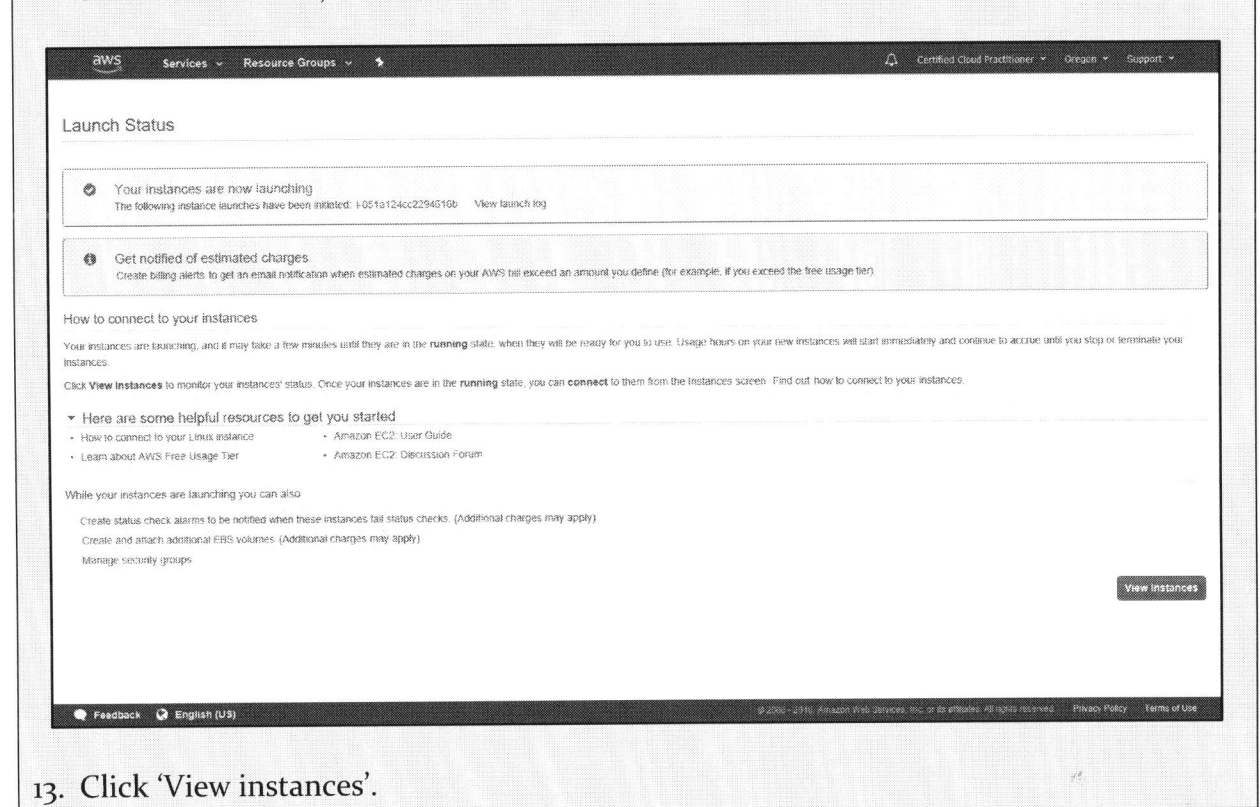

13. Click 'View instances'.

Chapter 3: Technology

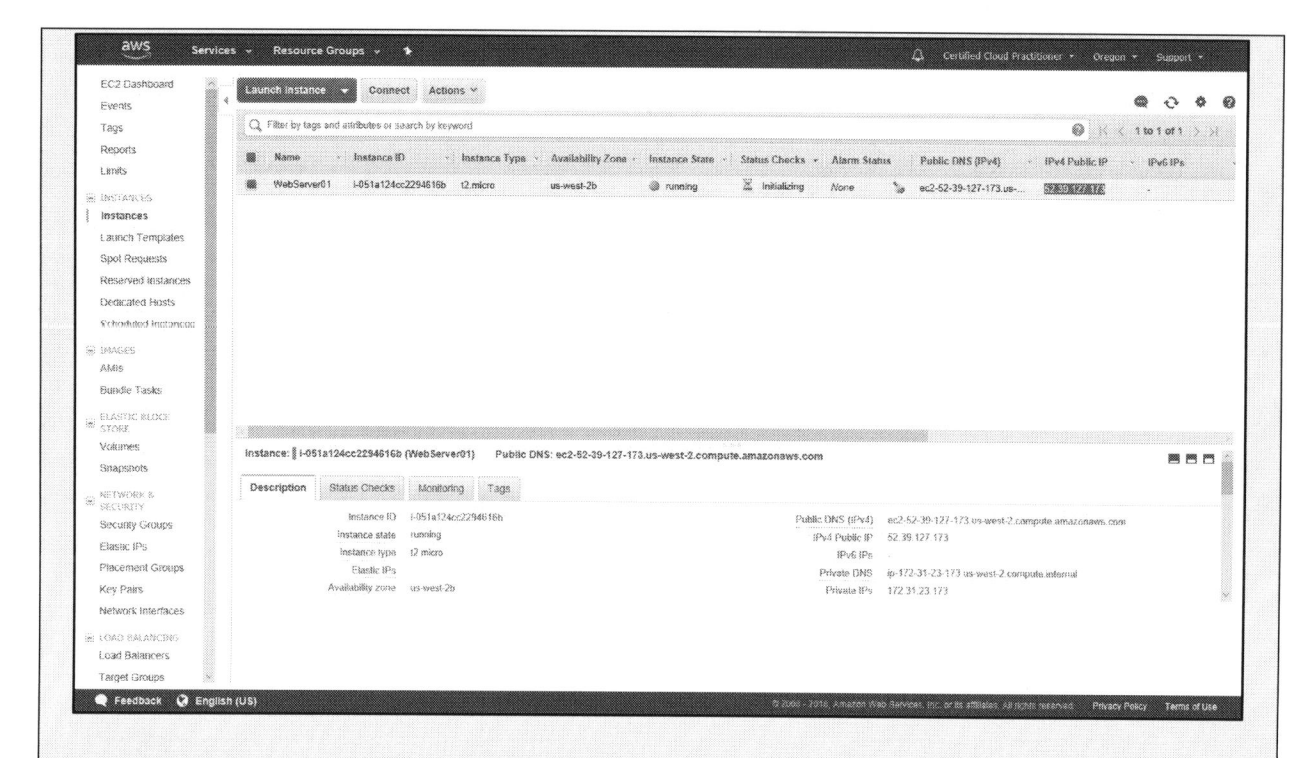

14. Once the instance is up and running, copy the public IP address of the instance somewhere on a notepad. You will need it in the future to log in to the instance.
15. Using the Key Pair you created, SSH into your EC2 instance. For Mac platform, follow the instructions on this link:

https://docs.aws.amazon.com/quickstarts/latest/vmlaunch/step-2-connect-to-instance.html

16. On windows platform, open PuTTYgen.

Chapter 3: Technology

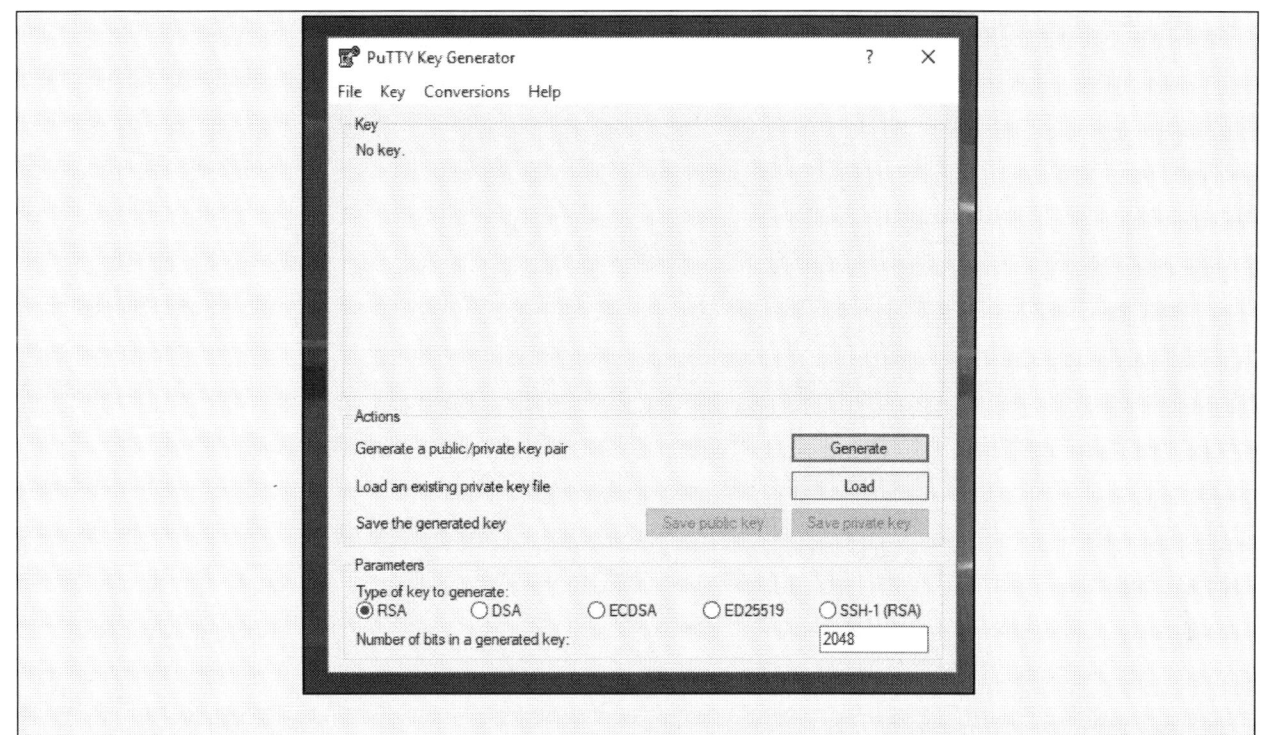

17. Click 'Load' to load the existing private key file 'MyOregonKP.pem' that you downloaded when creating the EC2 instance. With PuTTYgen convert '.pem.' file to '.ppk.' file.

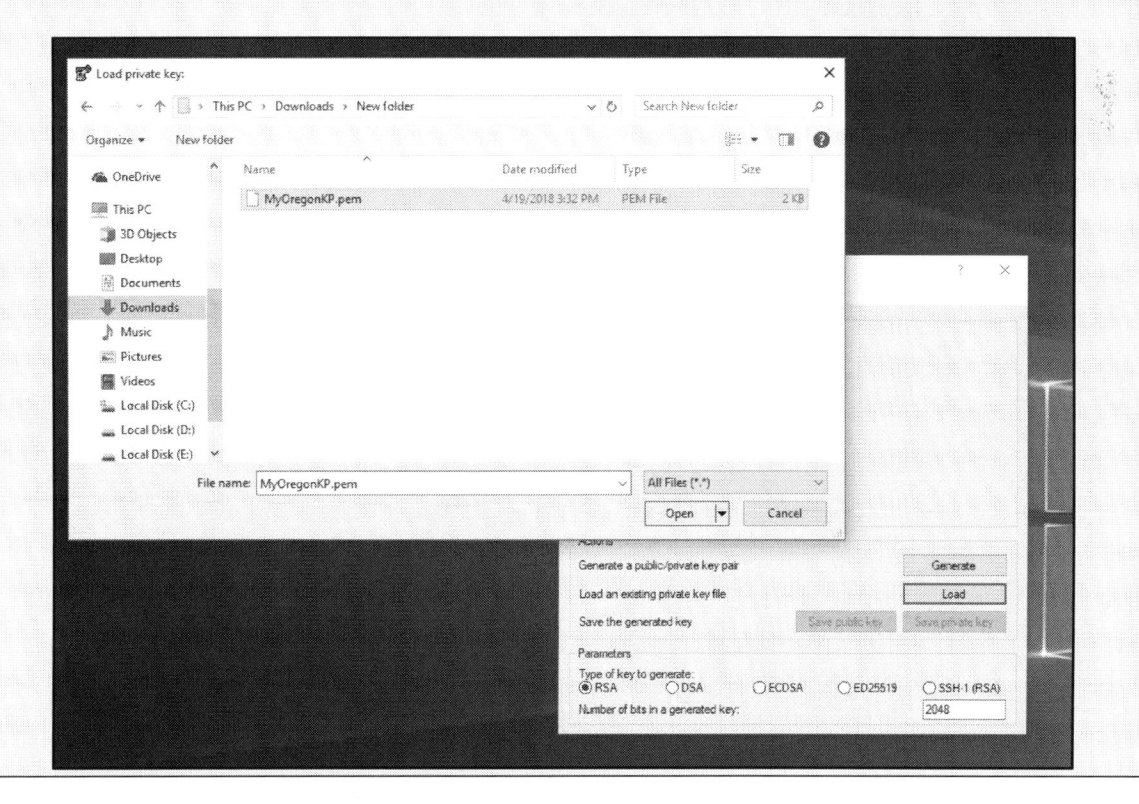

Chapter 3: Technology

18. Navigate to the folder where your key is, select it and click 'Open'.

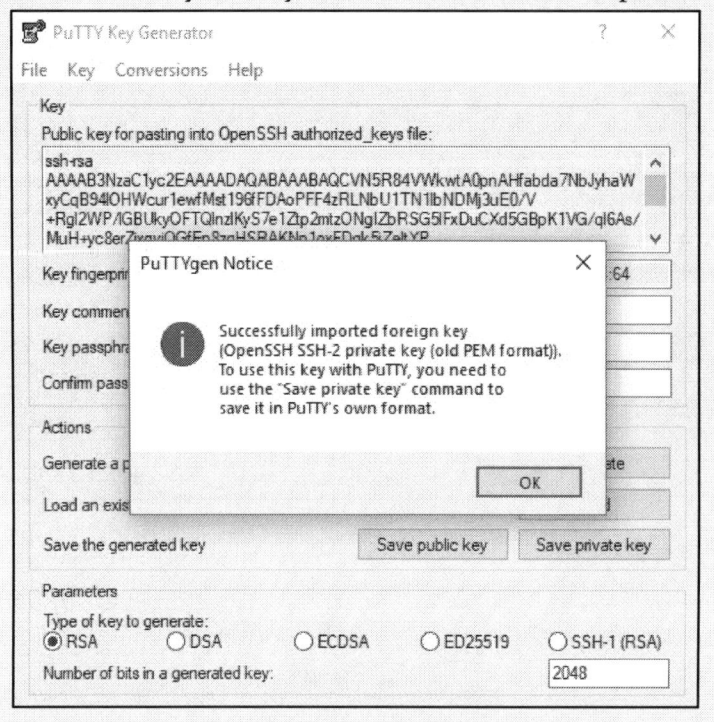

19. A dialogue box will be displayed 'Successfully imported foreign key'. Click 'OK'.

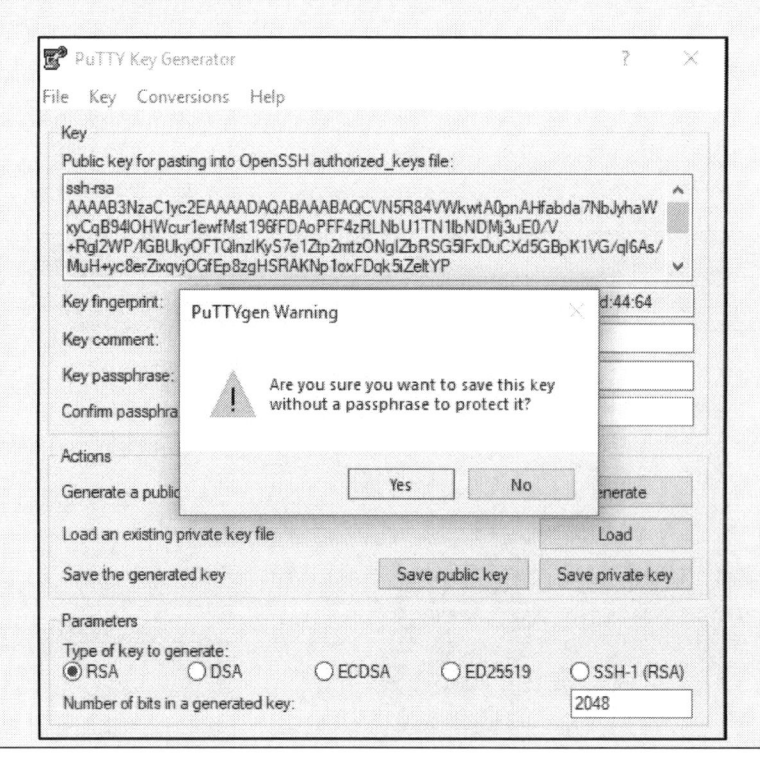

Chapter 3: Technology

20. Next, you will need to save this private key. Select 'Save private key' and click 'Yes'.

21. Enter the private key name and save it as 'MyOregonKP.ppk' file. Once you are done, close PuTTYgen and open PuTTY.

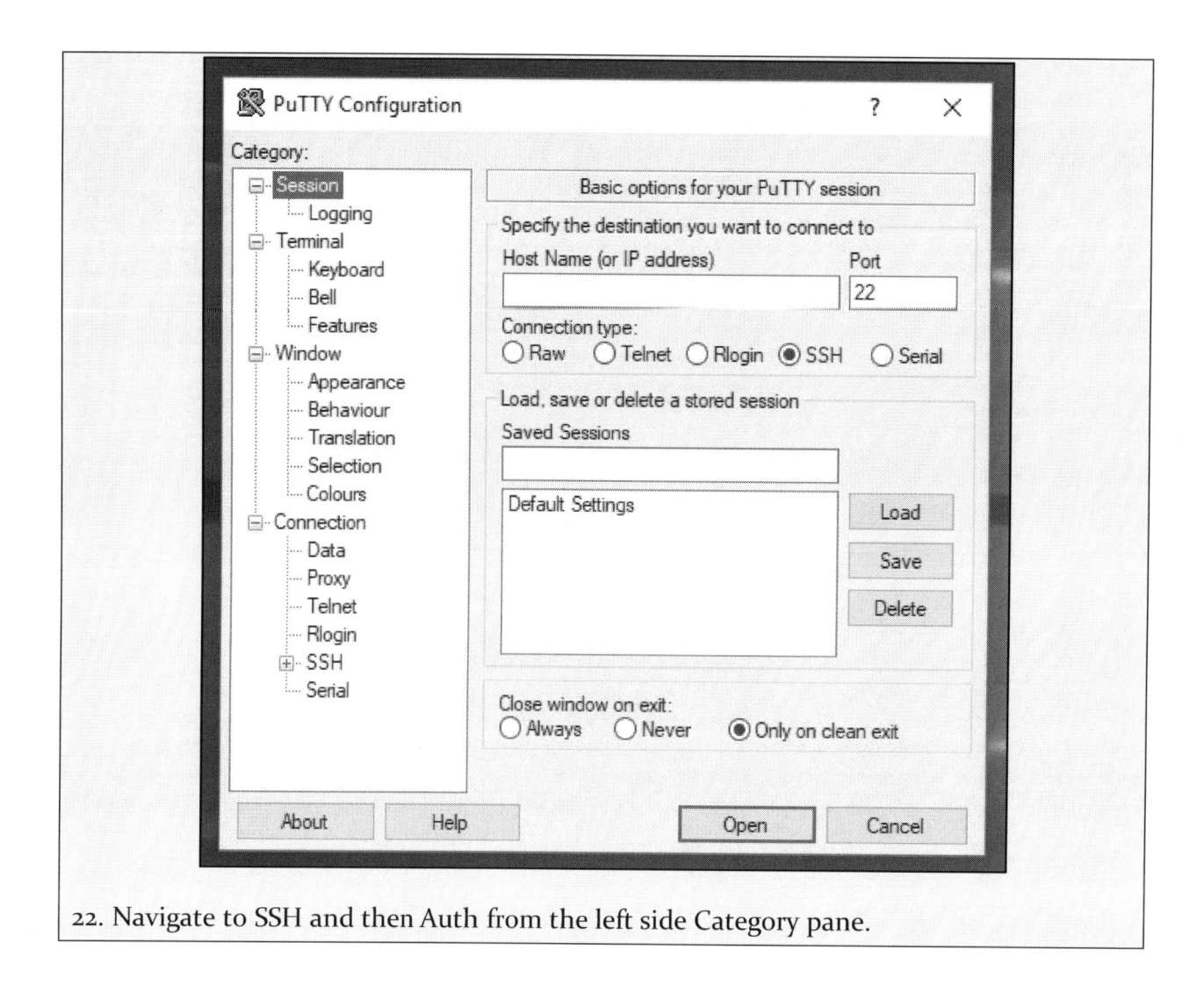

Chapter 3: Technology

22. Navigate to SSH and then Auth from the left side Category pane.

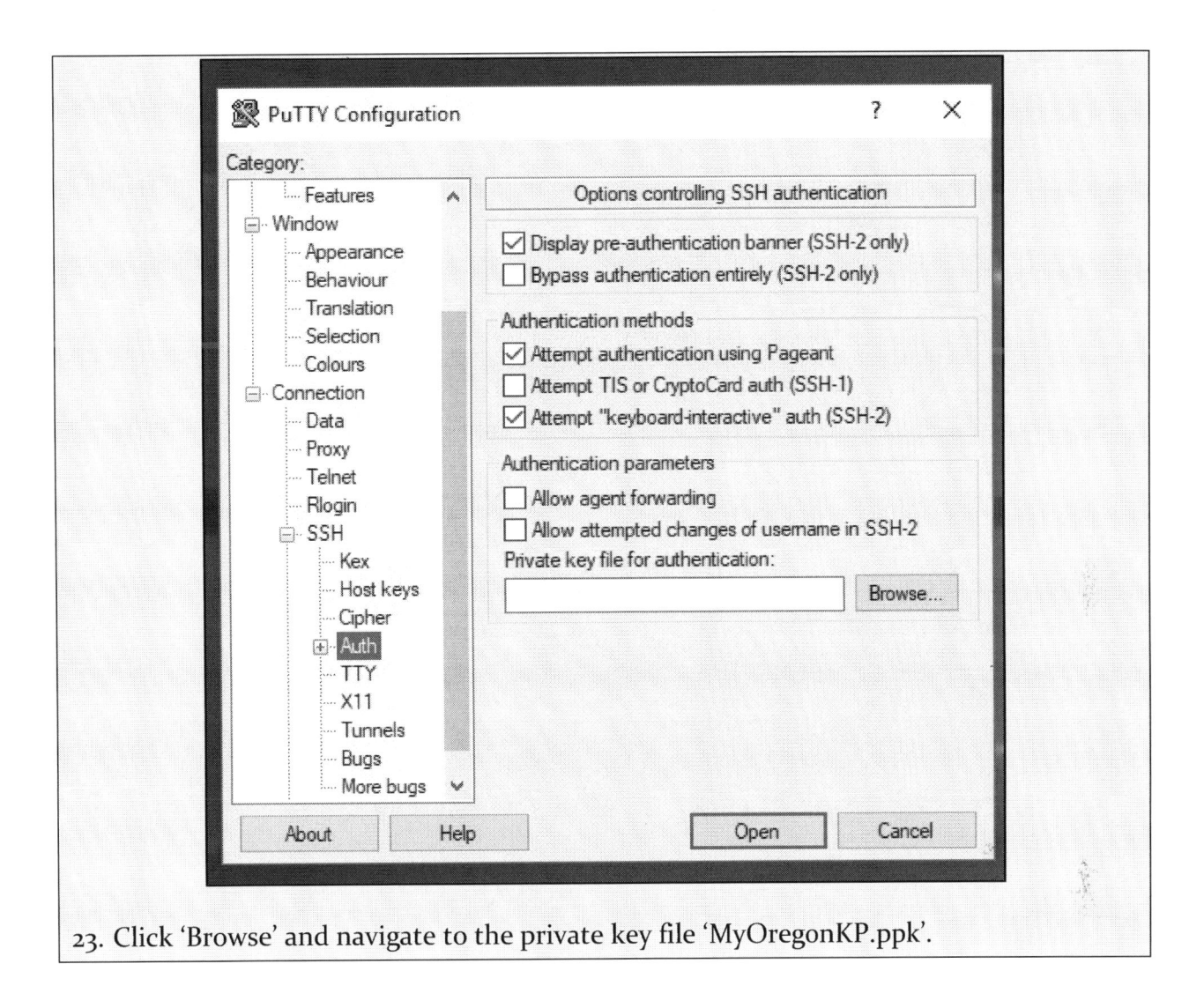

Chapter 3: Technology

23. Click 'Browse' and navigate to the private key file 'MyOregonKP.ppk'.

Chapter 3: Technology

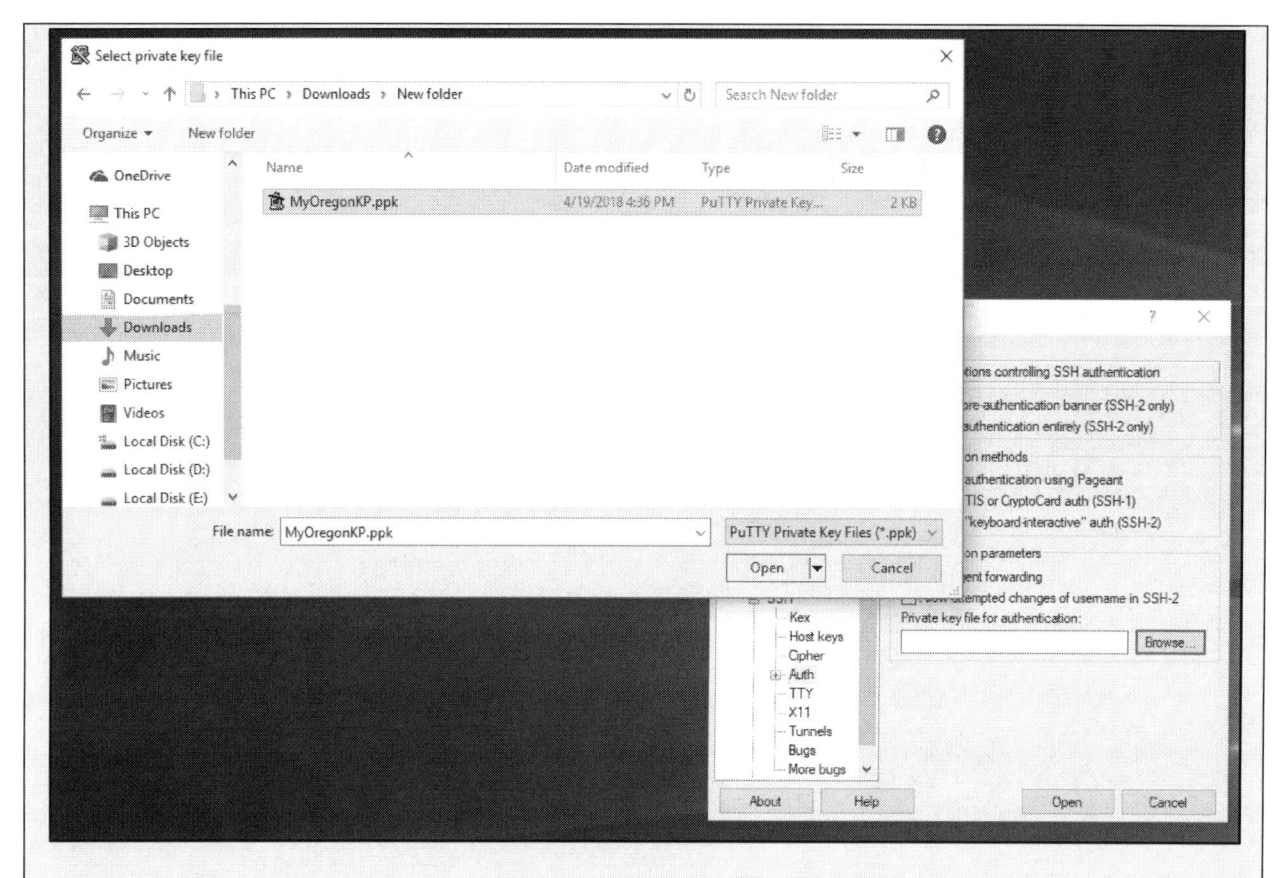

24. Select the key 'MyOregonKP.ppk' and click 'Open'. Now navigate to Session from the left side of the category pane.

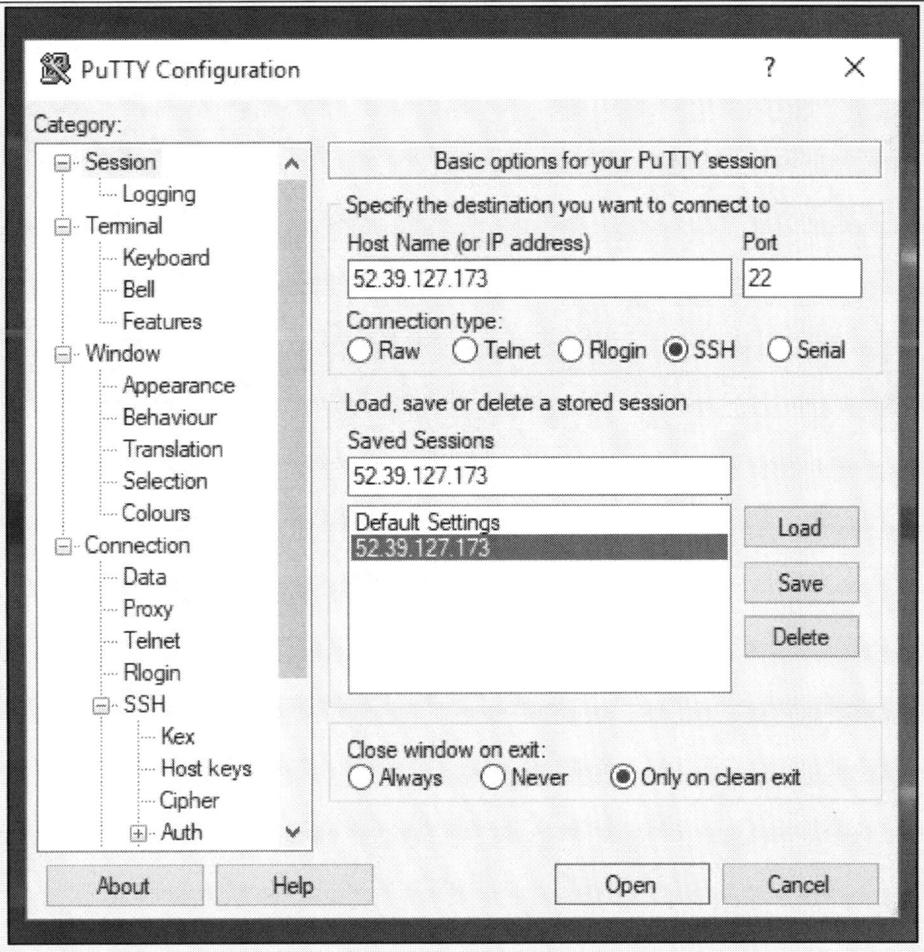

25. Copy the public IP address of the EC2 instance you previously saved in notepad and paste it in 'Host Name (or IP address)' and 'Saved Sessions' field. Click the 'Save' button, select the IP address and click 'Open'.

Chapter 3: Technology

```
login as: ec2-user
Authenticating with public key "imported-openssh-key"

       __|  __|_  )
       _|  (     /   Amazon Linux AMI
      ___|\___|___|

https://aws.amazon.com/amazon-linux-ami/2017.09-release-notes/
8 package(s) needed for security, out of 13 available
Run "sudo yum update" to apply all updates.
[ec2-user@ip-172-31-23-173 ~]$
```

26. It may prompt you for a username, type in 'ec2-user' and hit enter. You will be logged in to your Amazon Linux AMI on a windows machine.

EXAM TIPS:

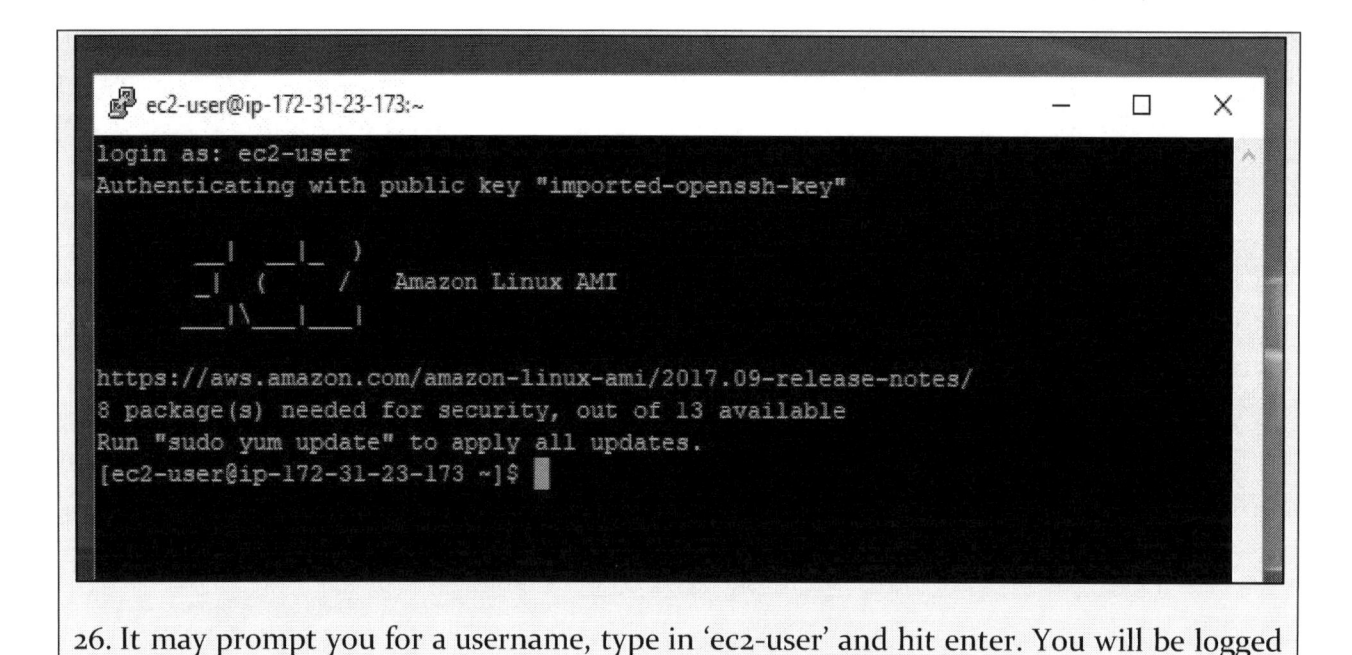

- Use a private key to connect to EC2 instance.
- Security Groups are virtual firewalls in the cloud.
- You need to open ports in order to use them. Popular ports are SSH(22) required for Linux instances and RDP(3389) for windows.
- HTTP(80) and HTTPS(443), is used when using the EC2 instance as a webserver.

AWS Storage

Cloud storage is a critical part of cloud computing as all the data used by the applications is stored there. All applications including databases, data warehouses, big data analytics, Internet of Things, backup and archive, etc depend heavily on some form of data storage architecture. Amazon Web Services (AWS) provides a variety of low-cost cloud storage services with high durability and availability. It offers object, file, and blocks storage choices to support application and archival requirements as well as disaster recovery use cases.

Chapter 3: Technology

Amazon Simple Storage Service (Amazon S3)

Amazon Simple Storage Service (Amazon S3) is an object storage designed to store, access and retrieve any type and amount of data over the internet through a simple web service interface. S3 provides a secure, highly durable and scalable platform for user-generated content (like photos, videos, music, and files), active archive, backup and recovery, data lakes for Big Data analytics and data warehouse platforms, or as a foundation for serverless computing.

Amazon S3 Features

- **Simple:** Simple to use with a web-based management console and mobile app.
- **Durable:** Provides durable infrastructure to store important data. Data is redundantly stored across multiple facilities and multiple devices in each facility.
- **Scalable:** Store as much data as you want and access it when needed while scaling up and down as required. It allows concurrent read or writes access to data by many separate clients or application threads.
- **Secure:** Supports data transfer over SSL and automatic encryption of data once it is uploaded. You can also configure bucket policies to manage object permissions and use access control lists to control access to your data.
- **Available:** Amazon S3 Standard is designed for up to 99.99% availability of objects over a given year and is backed by the Amazon S3 Service Level Agreement.
- **Low Cost:** Allows you to store large amounts of data at a very low cost. You can set policies to automatically migrate your data to Standard- Infrequent Access and Amazon Glacier for archiving to reduce costs further.
- **Simple Data Transfer:** Provides multiple options for cloud data migration, and makes it simple and cost-effective for you to move large volumes of data into or out of Amazon S3.
- **Integrated:** Amazon S3 is deeply integrated with other AWS services to make it easier to build solutions that use a range of AWS services.
- **Easy to Manage:** Amazon S3 Storage Management features allow you to take a data-driven approach to storage optimization, data security, and management efficiency by giving you information about your data, so you can manage your storage based on that personalized metadata.

Amazon S3 Basics

Amazon S3 is object-based storage where objects are simply files such as text files, images, videos, etc. It provides safe and secured storage as the data is spread across at least two or three Availability Zones, depending upon how many Availability Zones are present within that particular region.

Buckets:

A bucket is a container for objects stored in Amazon S3. To upload your data (photos, videos, documents, etc.), you first need to create a bucket in one of the AWS Regions. You can then upload any number of objects to the bucket. Each object can contain up to 5 TB of data. Amazon S3 bucket names are globally unique, regardless of the AWS Region in which you create the bucket. You cannot have the same bucket name as someone else. Amazon S3 creates buckets in a region you specify. You can choose any AWS Region that is geographically close to you to optimize latency, minimize costs, or address regulatory requirements.

Following is an example of an S3 Bucket URL:

```
                     Region
          https://s3-eu-west-1.amazonaws.com/test
           S3 Storage                  Bucket name
```

Figure 3-07. S3 Bucket URL

When you view your buckets, you view them globally irrespective of the regions. The actual console interface is at the global level similar to the Identity Access Management(IAM). You have to specify a particular region where you are going to deploy your buckets.

You can use Amazon S3 to host Static websites (such as .html). Deploying static websites on S3 is ideal when there are large numbers of requests to the site. Websites that are dynamic or require database connections such as WordPress cannot be hosted on S3. By default, all buckets are private with no public read access. You can use bucket policies to make entire S3 buckets public. Typically, you would do this while hosting a static website on S3.

Objects:

Objects are the fundamental entities stored in Amazon S3. Objects consist of object data and metadata. The metadata is a set of name-value pairs that describe the object. These include some default metadata, such as the date last modified, and standard HTTP metadata, such as Content-Type. An object is uniquely identified within a bucket by a key (name) and a version ID. You can change storage classes and encryption of your objects on the fly.

Keys:

A key is a unique identifier for an object within a bucket. Every object in a bucket has exactly one key. The combination of a bucket, key, and version ID uniquely identify each object

Amazon S3 Data Consistency Model:

Amazon S3 achieves high availability by replicating data across multiple servers within Amazon's data centers. If a PUT request is successful, your data is safely stored. When you upload a file to S3, you will receive an HTTP 200 code if the upload was successful. However, information about the changes must replicate across Amazon S3, which can take some time. Amazon S3 provides

- Read after Write consistency for PUTS of new Objects.

Eventual consistency for overwrite PUTS and DELETES can take some time to propagate. If you put up a new object in S3 for the very first time and immediately attempt to read it, you will be able to read it immediately. If the object is replaced or updated then accessed immediately, Amazon S3 might return the prior data until the change is fully propagated. The reason being this is that S3 is spread across multiple devices across multiple facilities, so if you try to read an object you just updated or after you deleted it, it can take some time for the changes to propagate across those devices and facilities.

Amazon S3 Storage Classes

1. ***Storage Classes for Frequently Accessed Objects:***
   - ***Standard S3:*** Best storage option for data that you frequently access. Amazon S3 delivers low latency and high throughput and is ideal for use cases such as cloud applications, dynamic websites, content distribution, gaming, and data analytics.
   - ***Reduced Redundancy Storage:*** This storage class is designed for noncritical, reproducible data that can be stored with less redundancy than the Standard storage class.
2. ***Storage Classes for Infrequently Accessed Objects:***

- **S3 Standard** – Infrequent Access: Ideal for data that is accessed less frequently, such as long-term backups and disaster recovery but at the same time requires rapid access when needed. Lower cost than S3 Standard but higher charges to retrieve or transfer data.

- **S3 One Zone** – Infrequent Access: It stores data in only one Availability Zone, which makes it less expensive than Standard- IA. However, the data is not resilient to the physical loss of the Availability Zone. Use it if you can recreate the data if the Availability Zone fails.

	S3 Standard	S3 Standard-Infrequent Access	Reduced Redundancy Storage
Durability	99.999999999%	99.999999999%	99.99%
Availability	99.99%	99.99%	99.99%
Concurrent Facility Fault Tolerance	2	2	1
SSL Support	Yes	Yes	Yes
First Byte Latency	Milliseconds	Milliseconds	Milliseconds
Lifecycle Management Policies	Yes	Yes	Yes

Table 3-1 Comparison S3 Standard, S3 Standard-IA, and Reduced Redundancy Storage

	S3 Standard	S3 Standard- IA	S3 One Zone - IA
Durability	99.999999999%	99.999999999%	99.999999999%
Availability	99.99%	99.9%	99.5%
Availability SLA	99.9%	99%	99%
Availability Zones	≥ 3	≥ 3	1
Min. Object Size	N/A	128 KB	128 KB
Min. Storage Duration	N/A	30 days	30 days
Retrieval Fee	N/A	per GB retrieved	per GB retrieved
First Byte Latency	milliseconds	milliseconds	milliseconds
Storage Type	Object level	Object level	Object level
Lifecycle Transitions	Yes	Yes	Yes

Table 3-2 Comparison S3 Standard, S3 Standard-IA, and S3 One Zone-IA

Amazon S3 Fundamental Characteristics

Security & Access Management:

A. *Flexible Access Control Mechanism*

Amazon S3 supports several mechanisms that give you the flexibility to control who can access your data, as well as how, when, and where they can access it. Amazon S3 provides four different access control mechanisms:

1. AWS Identity and Access Management (IAM) Policies: IAM enables organizations to create and manage multiple users under a single AWS account. With IAM policies, you can grant IAM users fine-grained control to your Amazon S3 bucket or objects.

2. Access Control Lists (ACLs): Allows you to control objects at an individual object level. You can use ACLs to add (grant) certain permissions on individual objects selectively.

3. Bucket Policies: Secure your data at a bucket level. Amazon S3 bucket policies can be used to add or deny permissions across some or all of the objects within a single bucket.

4. Query String Authentication: With Query String Authentication, you have the ability to share Amazon S3 objects through URLs that are valid for a specified period of time.

B. *Encryption*

You can securely upload or download your data to Amazon S3 via the SSL-encrypted endpoints using the HTTPS protocol. You can also choose to have Amazon S3 encrypt your data at rest with server-side encryption (SSE), Amazon S3 will automatically encrypt your data on write and decrypt your data on retrieval.

C. *Versioning*

Amazon S3 provides protection with versioning capability. You can use versioning to preserve, retrieve, and restore every version of every object stored in your Amazon S3 bucket. This allows you to recover from both unintended user actions and application failures easily. It is a great backup mechanism.

Storage Management

A. Object Tagging

S3 object tags are key-value pairs applied to S3 objects that can be created, updated, or deleted at any time during the lifetime of the object. With these, you have the ability to create Identity and Access Management (IAM) policies, setup S3 Lifecycle policies, and customize storage metrics.

A. Data Lifecycle Management

Create lifecycle policies for your objects within S3. Example, you can set S3 Lifecycle policies direct to Amazon S3 to automatically migrate your data to lower cost storage as your data ages.

B. Cross Region Replication

You can replicate the contents of one bucket to another bucket automatically by using cross-region replication. Cross-region replication (CRR) makes it simple to replicate new objects into any other AWS Region for reduced latency, compliance, security, disaster recovery, and a number of other use cases.

Data Transfer

Amazon S3 charges for the following:

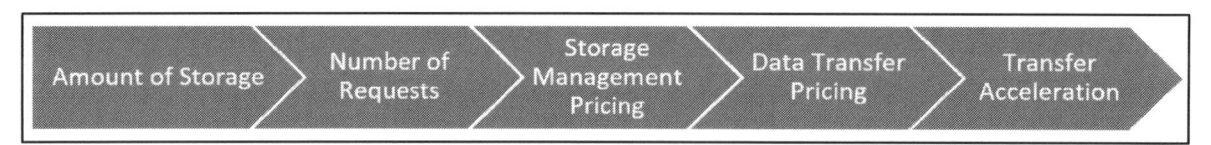

Amount of Storage → Number of Requests → Storage Management Pricing → Data Transfer Pricing → Transfer Acceleration

Figure 3-08. AWS S3 Charges

S3 Transfer Acceleration

Amazon S3 Transfer Acceleration enables fast, easy and secured transfer of files over long distances between your end users and an S3 bucket. Transfer acceleration takes advantage of Amazon CloudFront's globally distributed edge locations. As the data arrives at an edge location, the data is routed to Amazon S3 over an optimized network path.

Example, if users want to upload an object to a bucket at a particular location, with S3 transfer acceleration enabled, the users can upload it to an edge location nearest to them. When the edge location receives that object, it will then upload it to the particular storage location using Amazon's internal backbone network. This can dramatically increase the speed of uploads because the users no longer need to upload it directly to the storage location. Instead, they are uploading it to the server much closer to them.

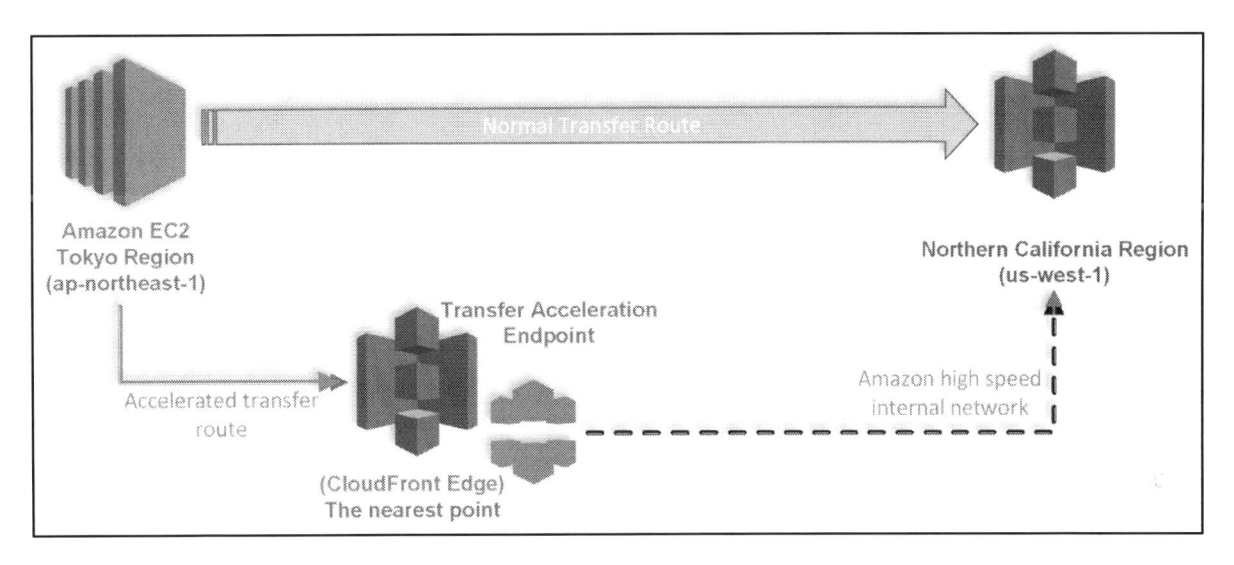

Figure 3-09. Amazon S3 Transfer Acceleration

> **EXAM TIPS:**
> - A bucket is simply a place to store your objects. Think of it as a directory on your computer, except you can access this from anywhere in the world using the AWS Console or using the command line.
> - Amazon S3 is a unique namespace so you cannot have the same bucket name as someone else.
> - When you view your buckets, you view them globally, but you can have buckets in individual regions.
> - S3 is object-based storage only for files. Not suitable to install on an operating system.
> - Successful uploads will generate an HTTP 200 status code.
> - You can encrypt objects in transit to S3 using SSL. You can also encrypt objects at rest on S3 using different encryption methods.
> - To restrict access to an entire bucket use Bucket Policies. To restrict access to an individual object (files) use Access Control Lists.
> - You can replicate the contents of one bucket to another bucket automatically using cross-region replication.

Chapter 3: Technology

> - You can change storage classes and encryption of your objects on the fly.
> - Understand what S3 transfer accelerator is.

Lab 3-5: AWS S3 Transfer Acceleration

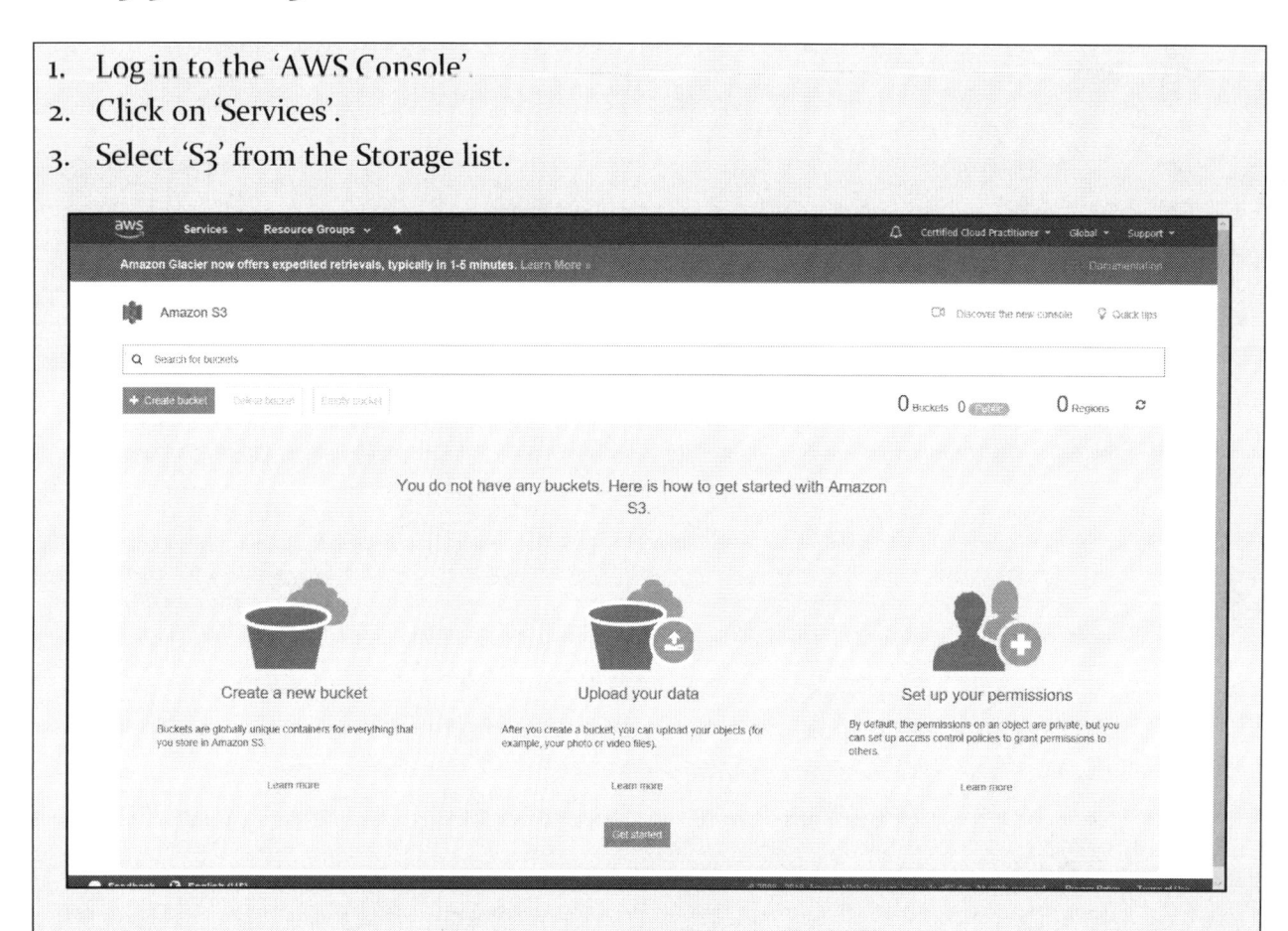

1. Log in to the 'AWS Console'.
2. Click on 'Services'.
3. Select 'S3' from the Storage list.

4. Similar to Identity Access Management, Amazon S3 interface is also global which you can see in the top right corner. You can select the region you would want to deploy your S3 bucket in while creating it. Click on 'Create bucket'.

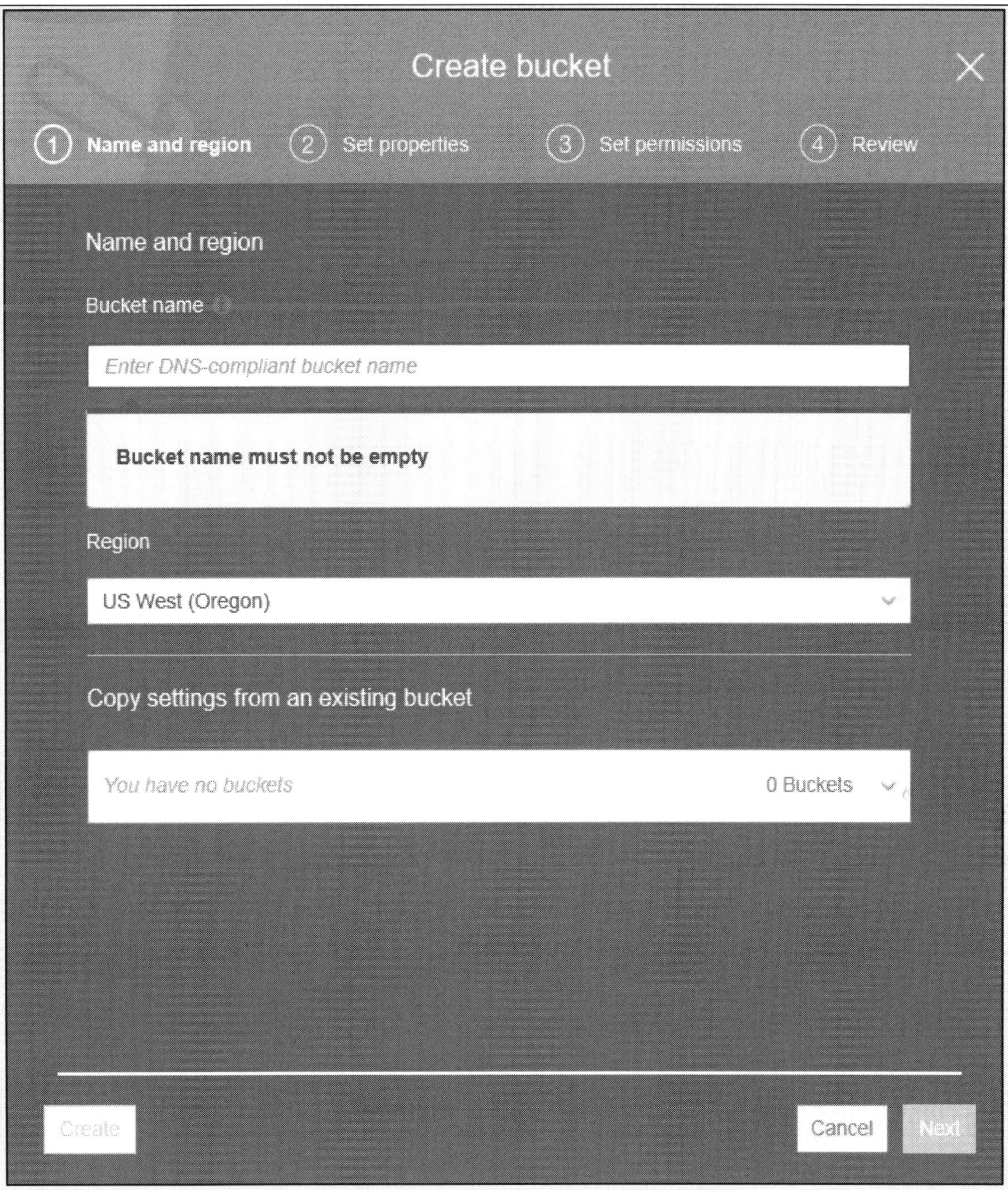
Create bucket
1 Name and region
2 Set properties
3 Set permissions
4 Review
Name and region
Bucket name
Enter DNS-compliant bucket name
Bucket name must not be empty
Region
US West (Oregon)
Copy settings from an existing bucket
You have no buckets
0 Buckets
Create
Cancel
Next

5. Enter a DNS-compliant bucket name. It should not contain uppercase characters and must start with a lowercase letter or number. Bucket name must be between 3 and 63 characters long and should not contain invalid characters.

Chapter 3: Technology

6. Select a Region where you want to deploy your bucket from the list of Regions.

Create bucket

① **Name and region** ② Set properties ③ Set permissions ④ Review

Name and region

Bucket name

    ccp.bucket

Region

    US West (Oregon)

Copy settings from an existing bucket

    You have no buckets   0 Buckets

Create   Cancel   Next

7. Click 'Next' to proceed to the properties section where you can enable Versioning, Server access logging, Object-level logging, automatic Encryption and add Tags.

Chapter 3: Technology

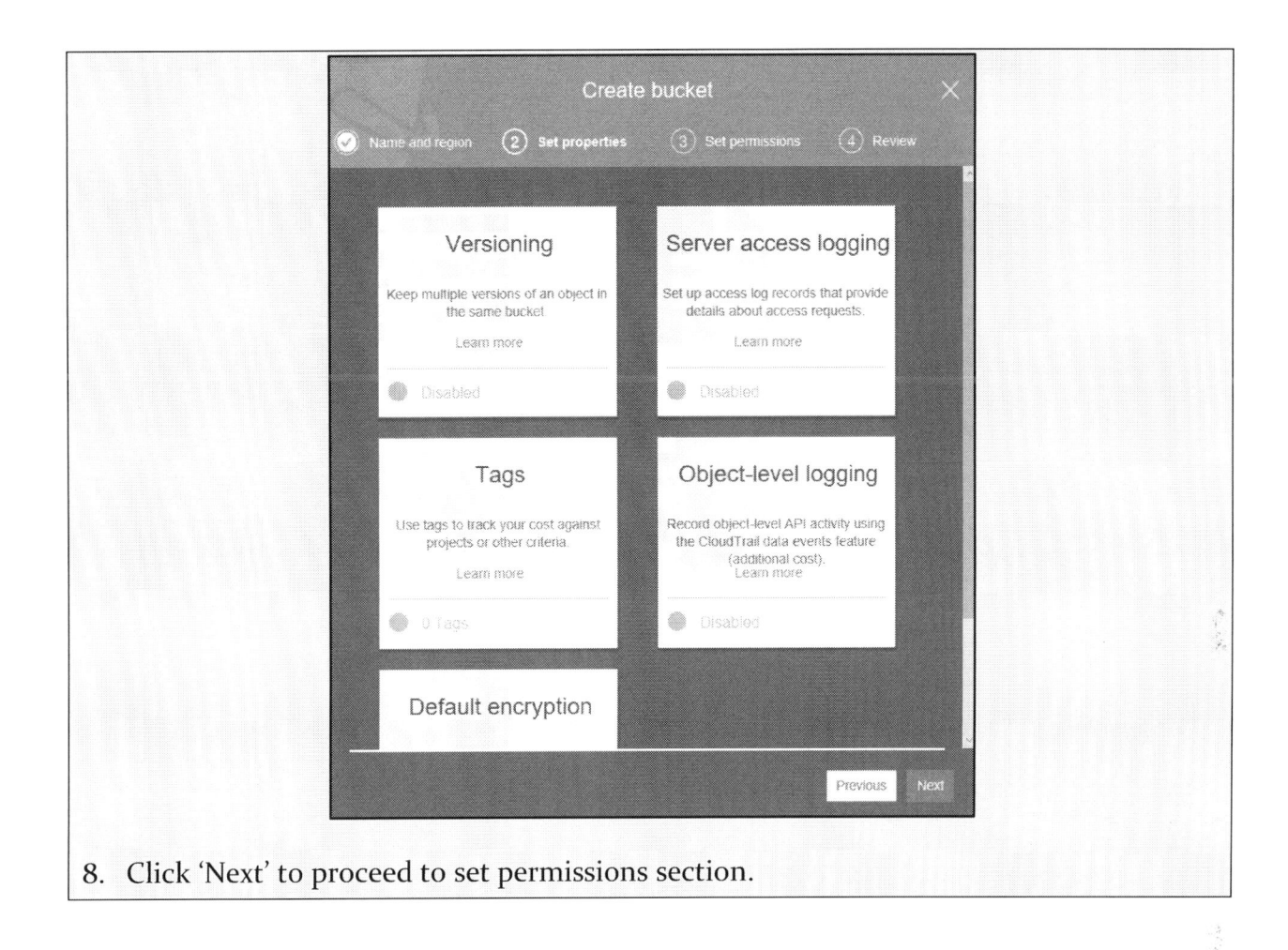

8. Click 'Next' to proceed to set permissions section.

Chapter 3: Technology

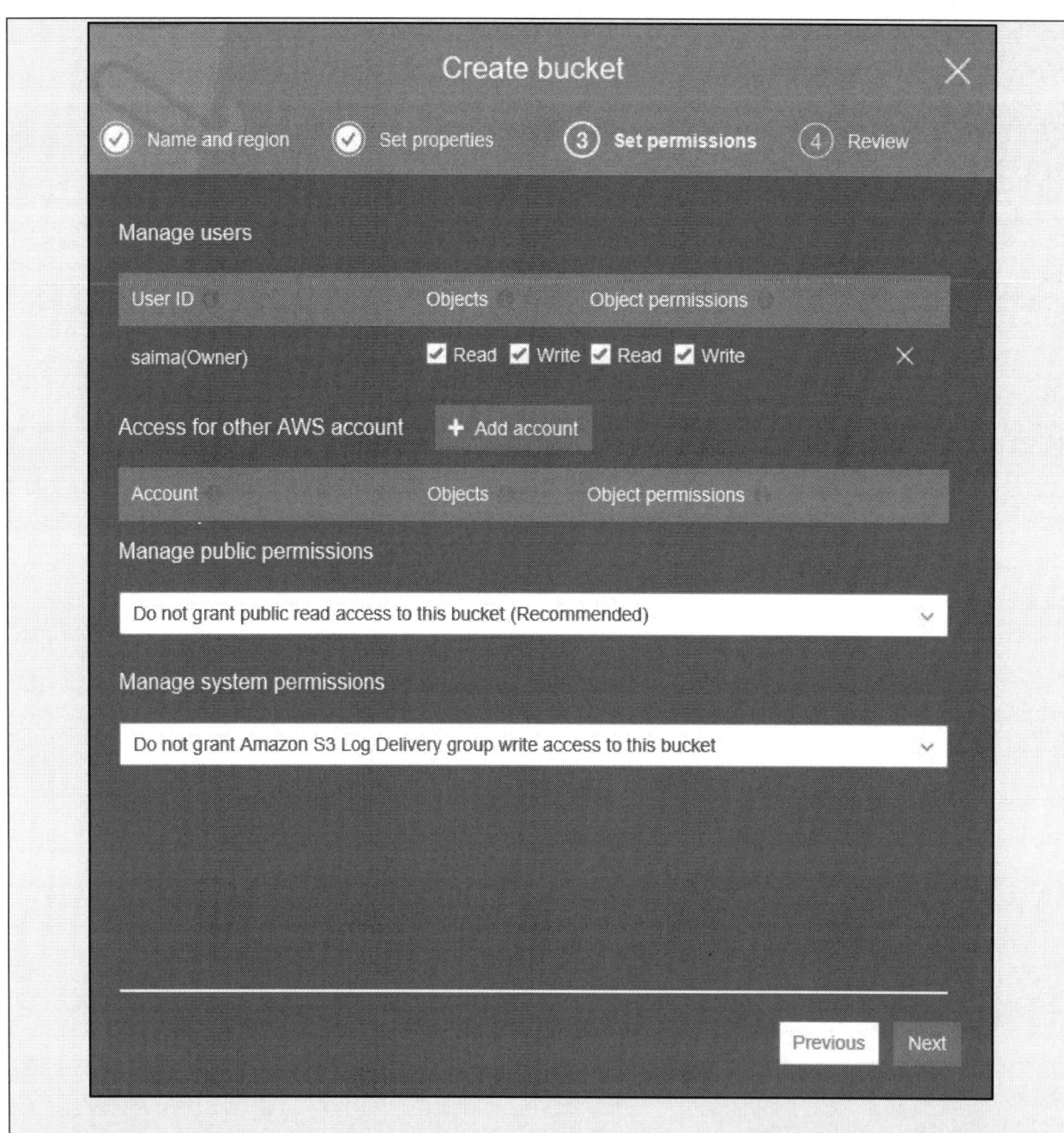

9. Here you can manage users and set permissions. You can allow public access to the bucket. By default, all buckets are private. Now, leave everything as it is and click 'Next'.

Chapter 3: Technology

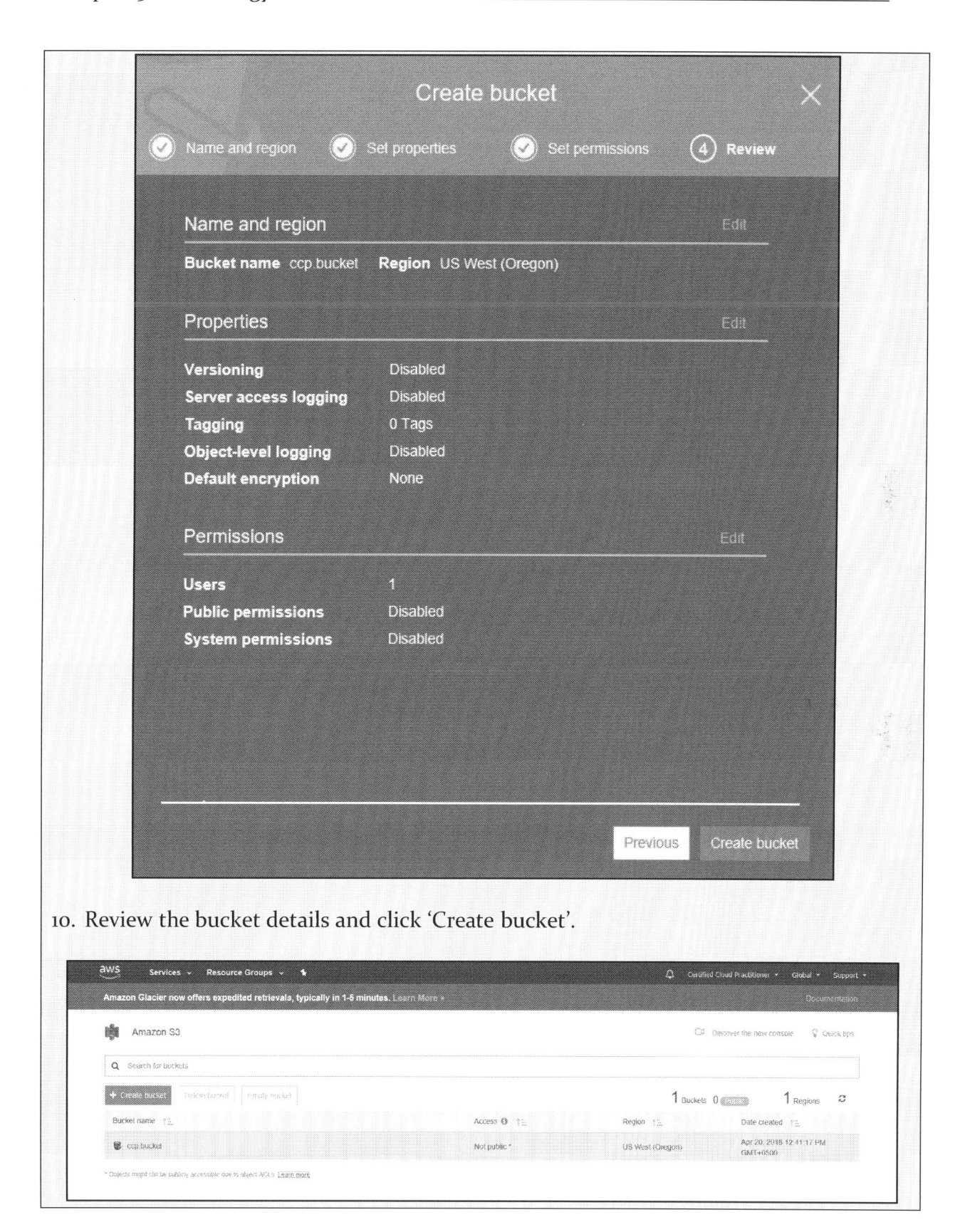

10. Review the bucket details and click 'Create bucket'.

Chapter 3: Technology

11. Click on the bucket name 'ccp.bucket' to open it and start adding files to it.

12. Click 'Create a folder' to add a new folder to the bucket.

Chapter 3: Technology

13. The folder will be added as an object in the bucket. You can select the encryption type for the object and click 'Save'.

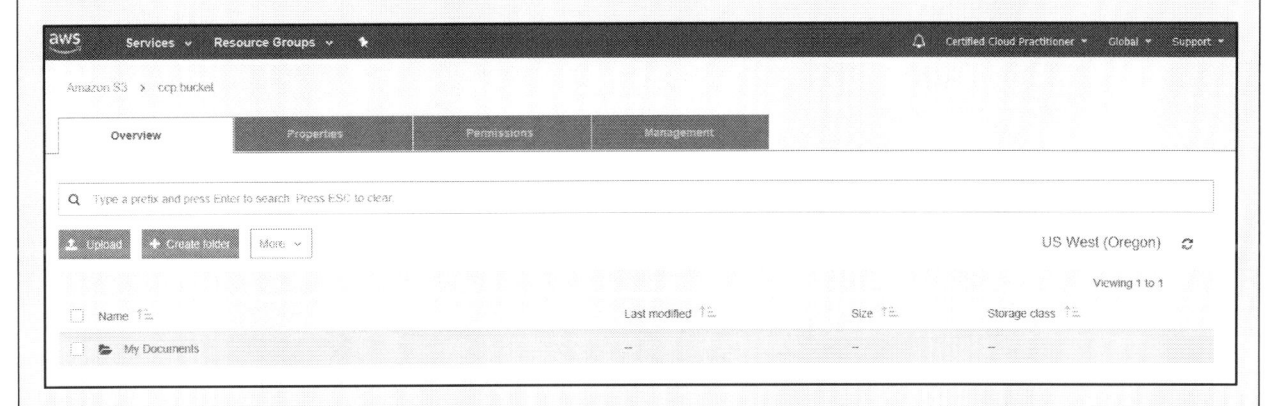

14. Add files to the bucket by clicking the 'Upload' button.

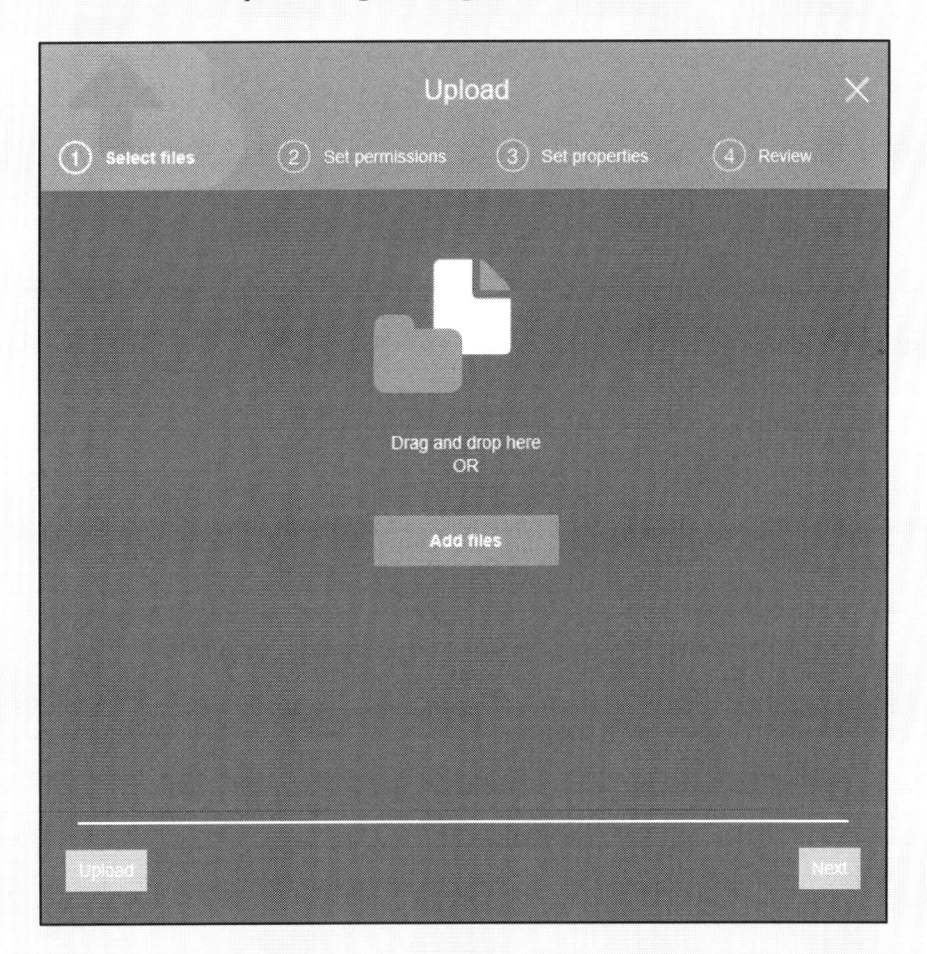

15. Click 'Add files' and select files to upload.

Chapter 3: Technology

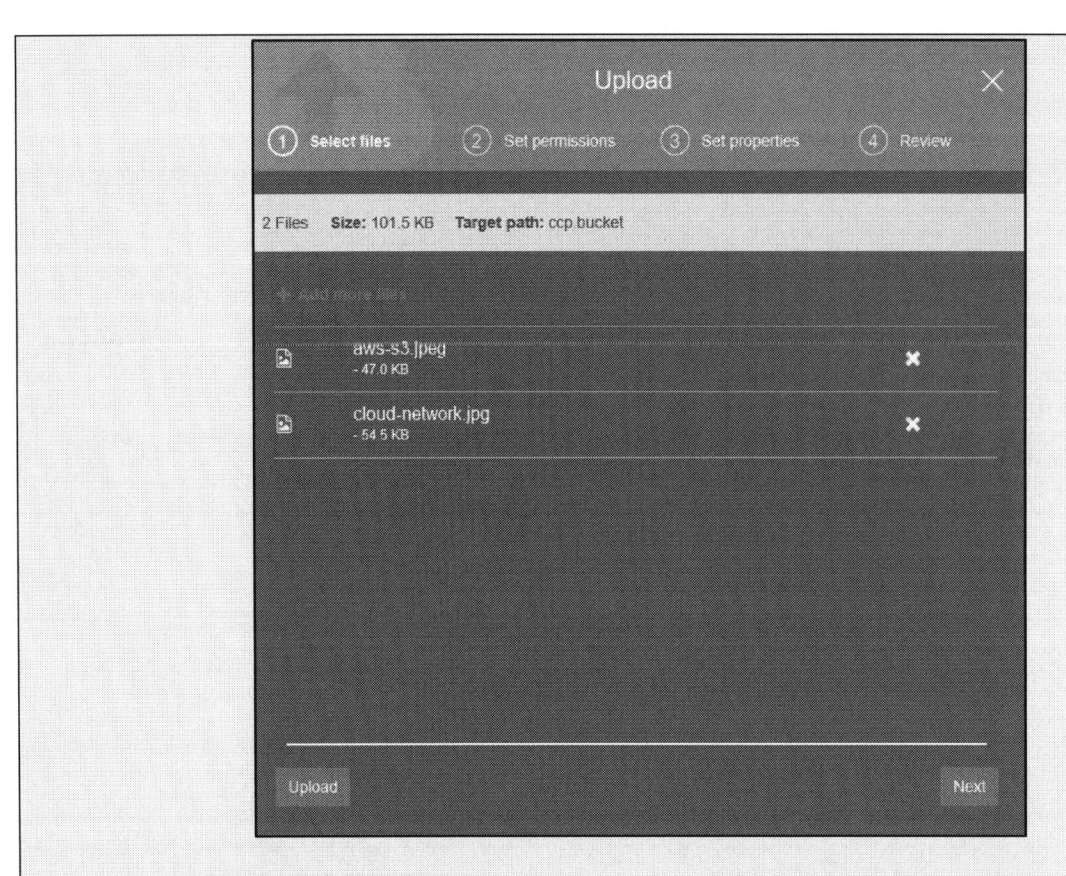

16. After selecting the files, you can click 'Upload' to upload them directly, or you can click 'Next' to set permissions and properties for the files.

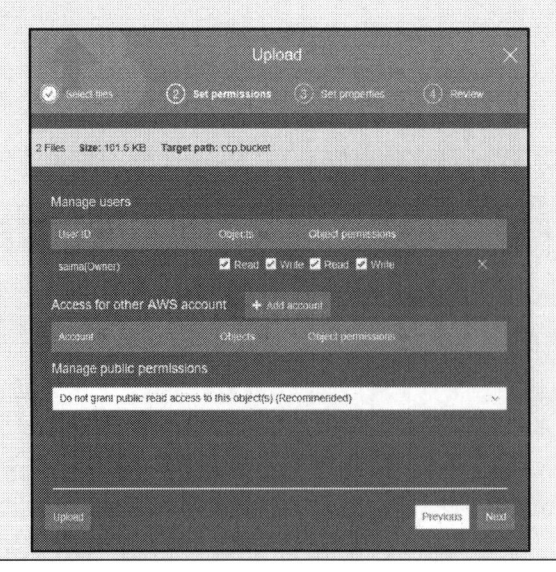

Chapter 3: Technology

17. In the 'Set permissions' section, you can manage users and their access permissions. You can also define whether you want to grant public access to the files. Once done, click 'Next'.

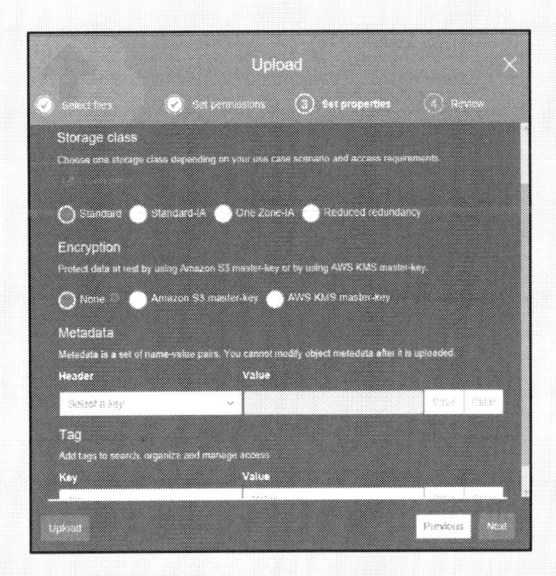

18. In the 'Set properties' section, you can select the storage class, encryption type for the files and add metadata and tags if you want. Click 'Next' when done.

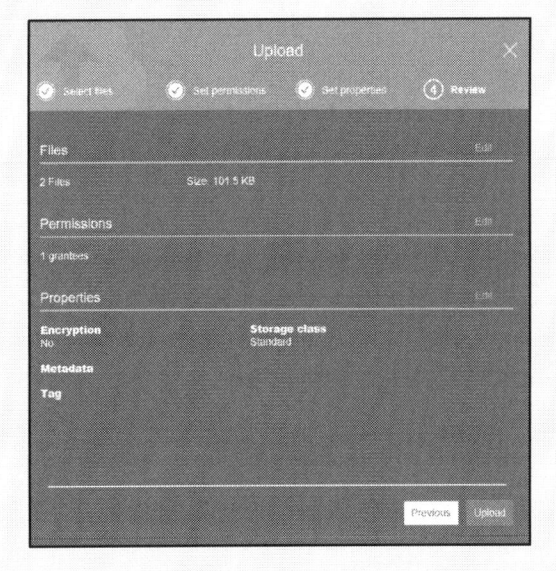

19. Review the details and click 'Upload' to upload your selected files to the bucket.

Chapter 3: Technology

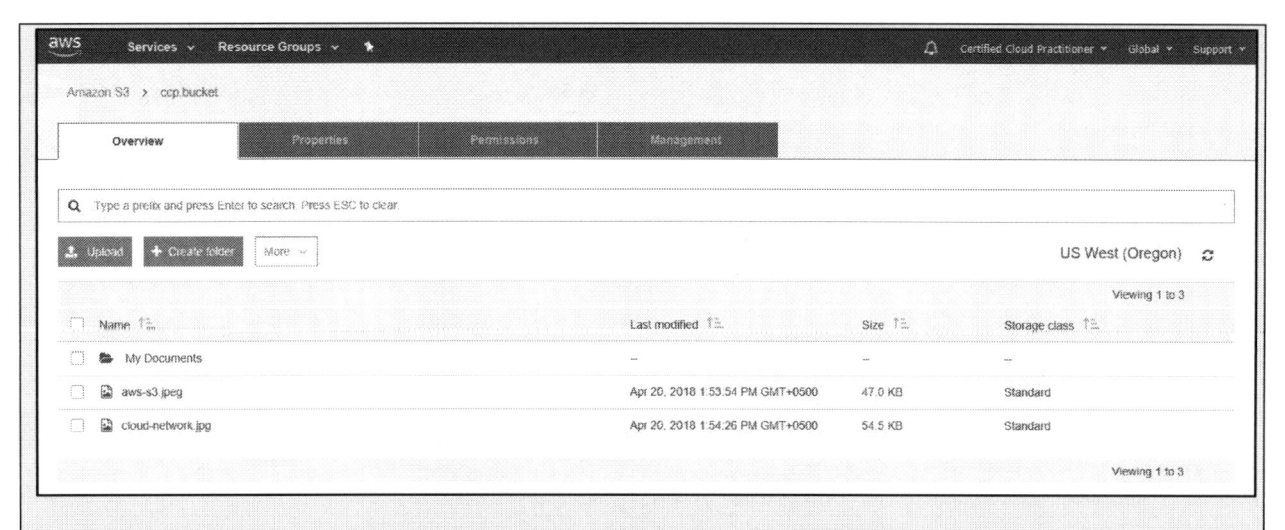

20. After the files are uploaded, you can still edit properties and permissions of the files. To do this, click on 'file' to navigate to its Overview tab.

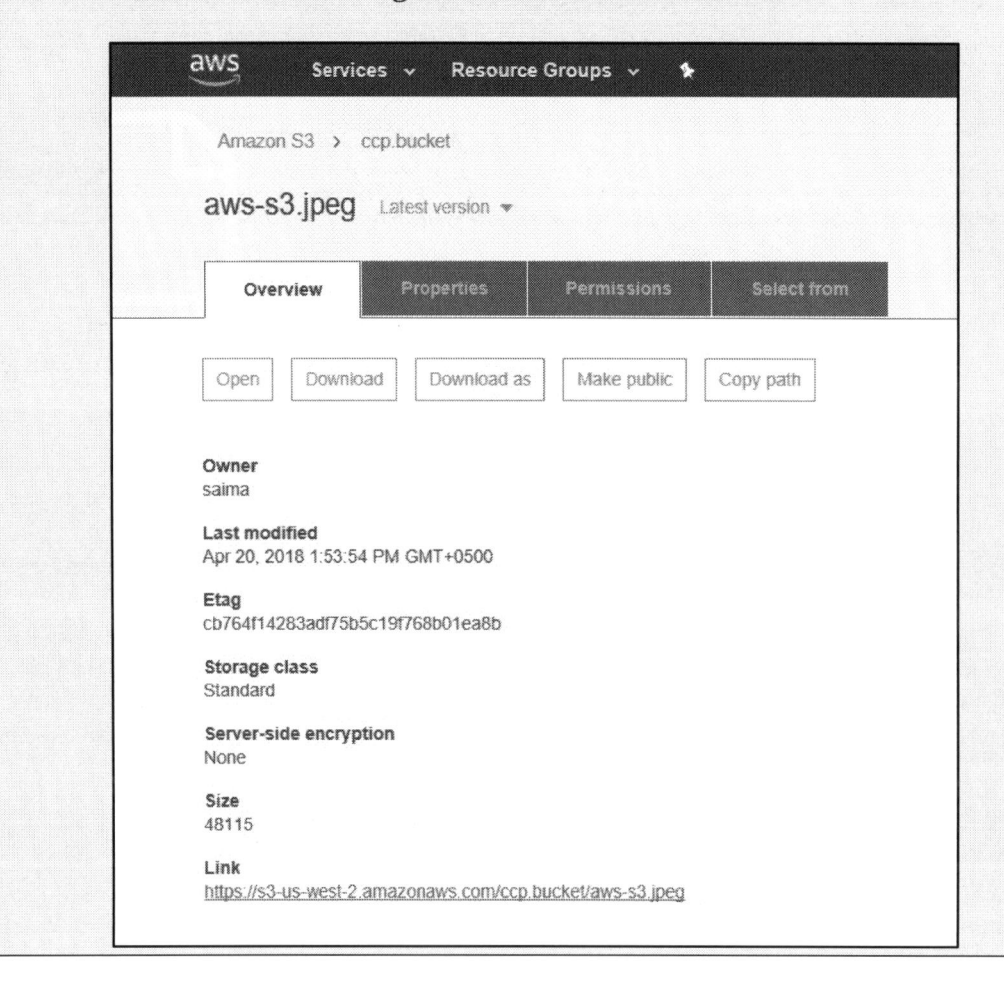

Chapter 3: Technology

21. Here you will see a URL link to the file. Since public access to the file is not granted, by clicking the link, you will be prompted to an error page.

```xml
<?xml version="1.0" encoding="UTF-8"?>
<Error>
    <Code>AccessDenied</Code>
    <Message>Access Denied</Message>
    <RequestId>BB25169CFEDA4D9D</RequestId>
    <HostId>pjeBY+CUvBNIJu6cJj1JhnTqzyIN3i9R6nzz6SfECIoZH81mQXiIpdG+lIxdD0LHWBeXzQcbOxs=</HostId>
</Error>
```

22. The reason for the error is that you are trying to access a private file via URL and you did not set public read permissions on this. To make this publicly accessible, click the 'back' button in your browser and select 'Permissions' tab.

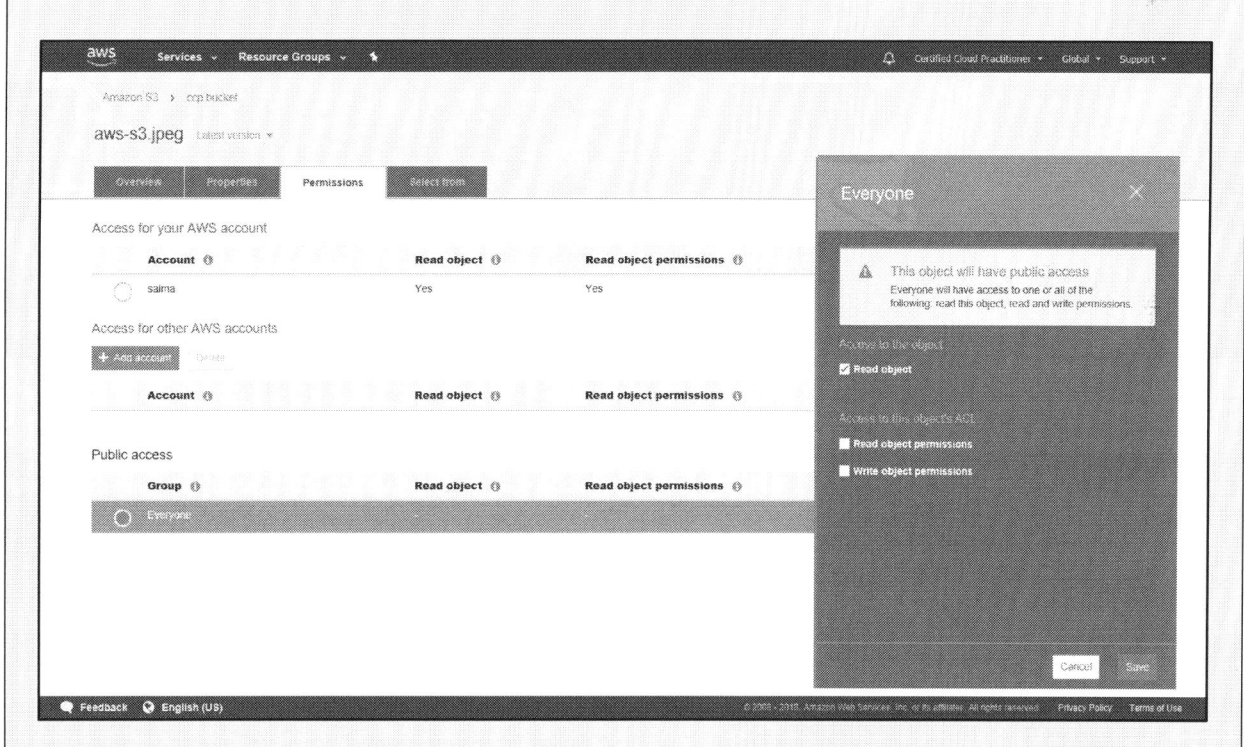

23. From the Public access, select 'Everyone'. This will open a pop-up window where you need to select 'Read object' under the Access to the object section then click 'Save'.

Chapter 3: Technology

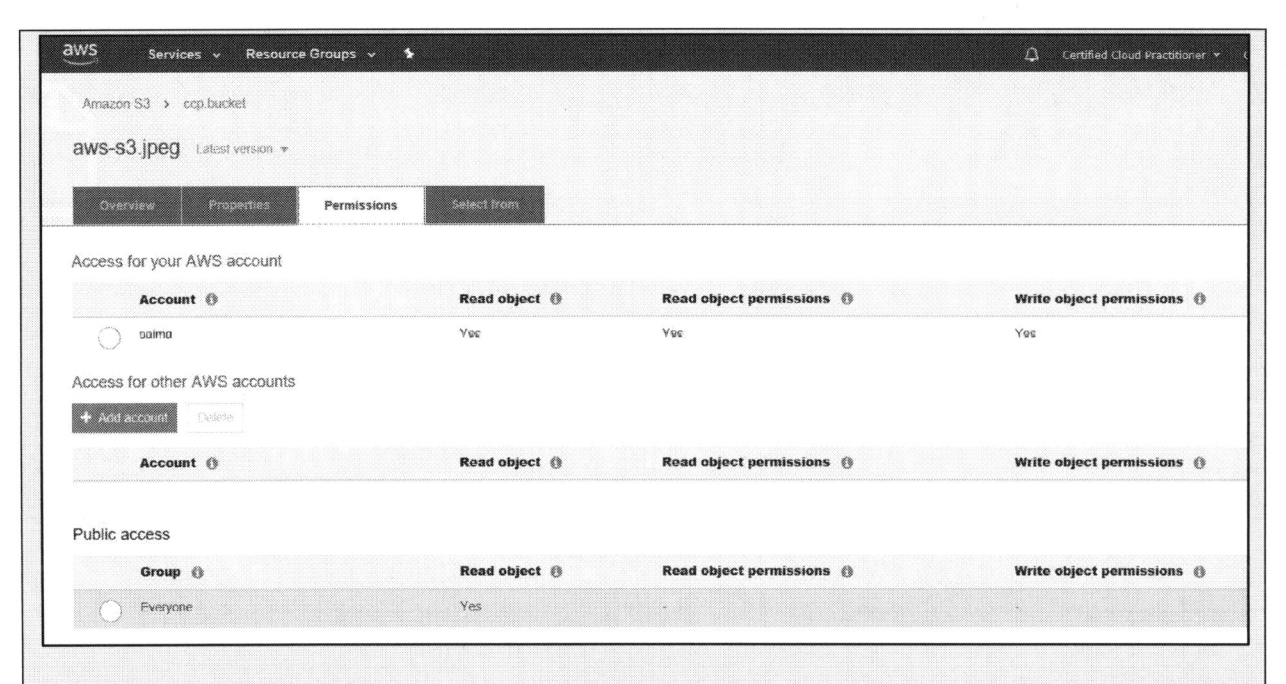

24. You will now be able to see 'Read object permission' under the Public access as 'Yes'. Go back to the Overview tab and click on the URL once again, and you will be able to see your file.
25. Another way of doing this is by enabling access from the bucket's main page.

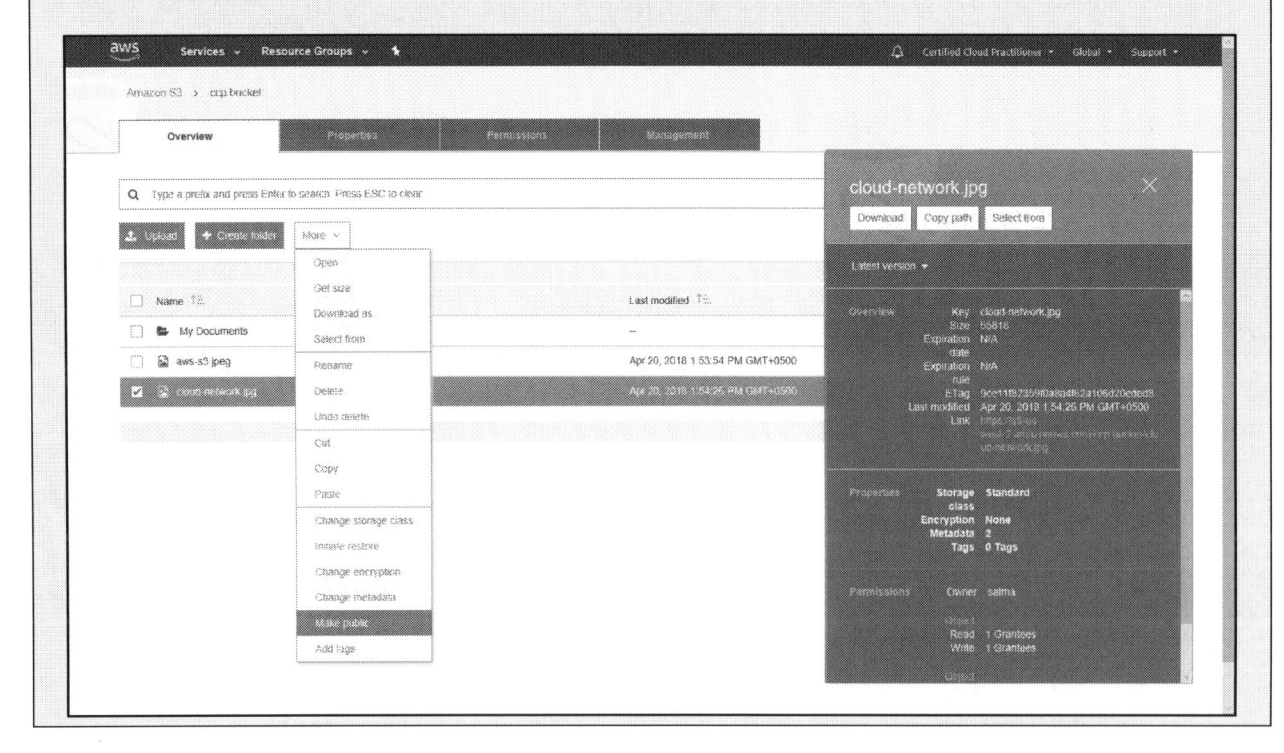

Chapter 3: Technology

26. Select the file, click on the 'More' button and select 'Make public' from the drop-down menu. This is an easier way of enabling public access to the file. If you now click on the URL of the file, you will be able to read it publicly via the browser.
27. The bucket's main window contains tabs of Overview, Properties, Permissions, and Management.

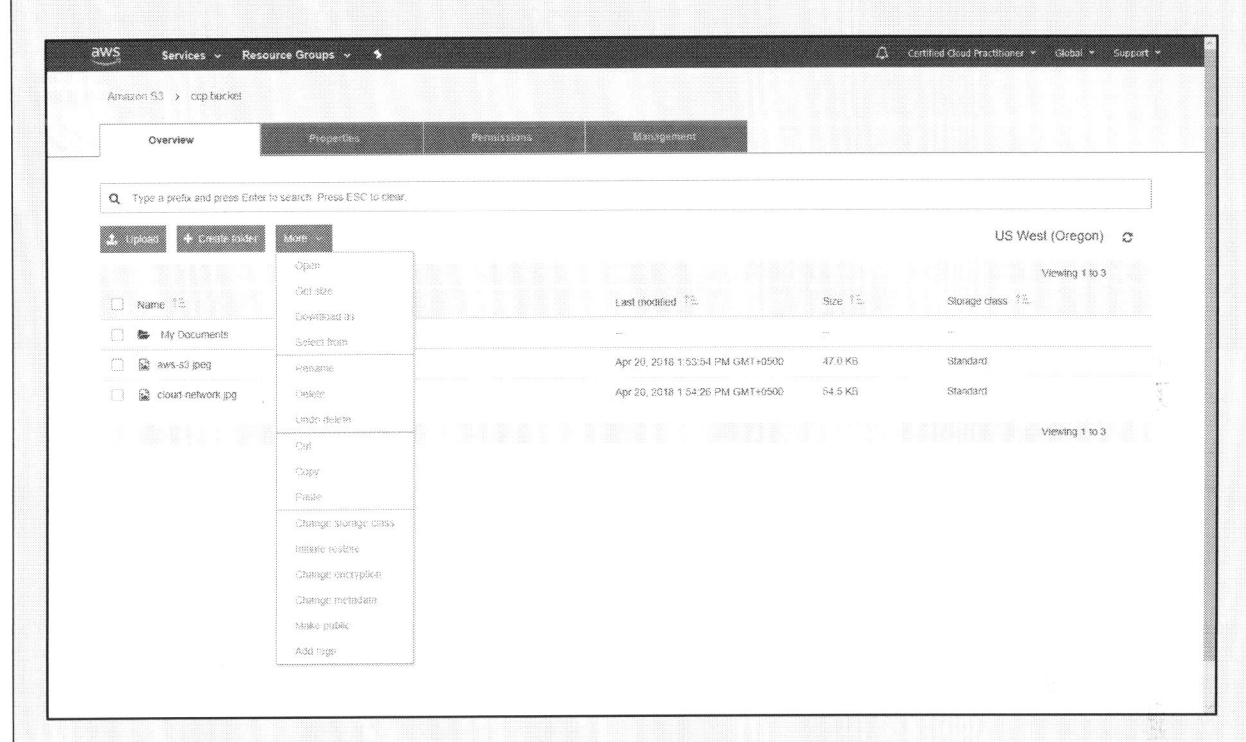

28. The Overview tab displays all the objects in the bucket and the options to upload files, create folders and a drop-down menu of file-specific actions.

Chapter 3: Technology

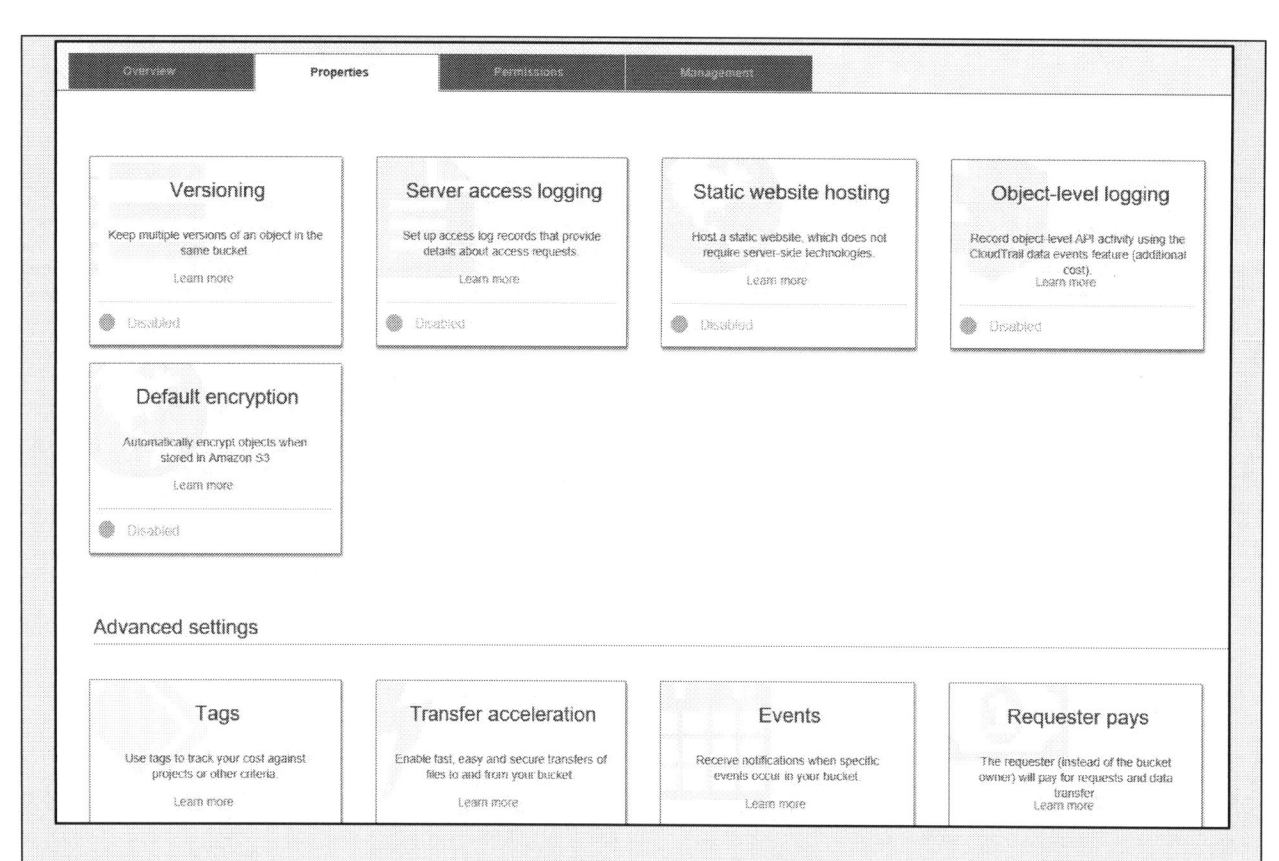

29. The Properties tab provides you different options, such as Versioning, Static website hosting, Default encryption, Tags and Transfer acceleration. Let us have a quick overview of Transfer acceleration by clicking on it.

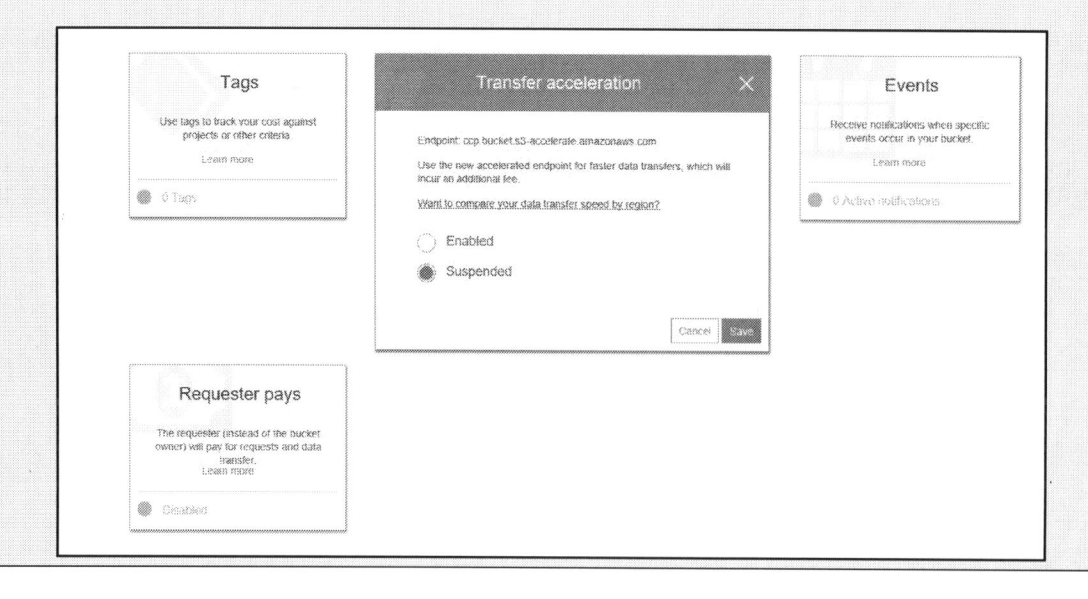

Chapter 3: Technology

30. This will open up a window asking whether to enable transfer acceleration. To get an idea how transfer acceleration will affect data transfers, click on the link 'Want to compare your data transfer speed by region?'

Amazon S3 Transfer Acceleration
Speed Comparison

Upload speed comparison in the selected region
(Based on the location of bucket: ccp.bucket)

Oregon
(US-WEST-2)   6% faster

S3 Direct Upload Speed
Upload complete

S3 Accelerated Transfer Upload Speed
Upload complete

This speed checker uses multipart uploads to transfer a file from your browser to various Amazon S3 regions with and without Amazon S3 Transfer Acceleration. It compares the speed results and shows the percentage difference for every region.

Note: In general, the farther away you are from an Amazon S3 region, the higher the speed improvement you can expect from using Amazon S3 Transfer Acceleration. If you see similar speed results with and without the acceleration, your upload bandwidth or a system constraint might be limiting your speed.

Chapter 3: Technology

Upload speed comparison in other regions

San Francisco (US-WEST-1)	3% slower
Virginia (US-EAST-1)	6% slower
Dublin (EU-WEST-1)	3756% faster
Frankfurt (EU-CENTRAL-1)	400% faster
Tokyo (AP-NORTHEAST-1)	388% faster
Seoul (AP-NORTHEAST-2)	100% slower
Singapore (AP-SOUTHEAST-1)	93% slower
Sydney (AP-SOUTHEAST-2)	293% faster
São Paulo (SA-EAST-1)	68% faster
Mumbai (AP-SOUTH-1)	31% faster
Ohio (US-EAST-2)	1% slower
Canada Central (CA-CENTRAL-1)	9% faster
London (EU-WEST-2)	7% faster

31. This speed checker simulates the transfer of a file from your browser to various Amazon S3 regions with and without Amazon S3 Transfer Acceleration. It compares the speed results and shows the percentage difference for every region.

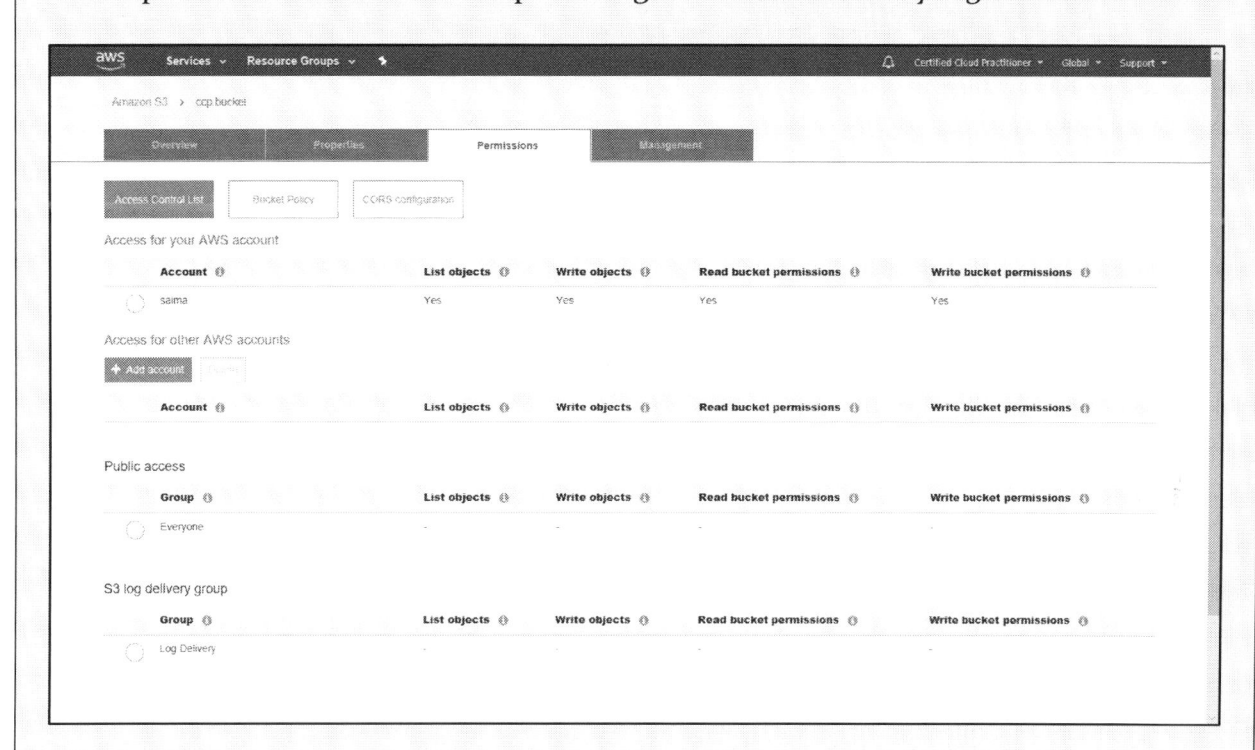

32. The Permissions tab provides access management options and allows you to write bucket policies.

Chapter 3: Technology

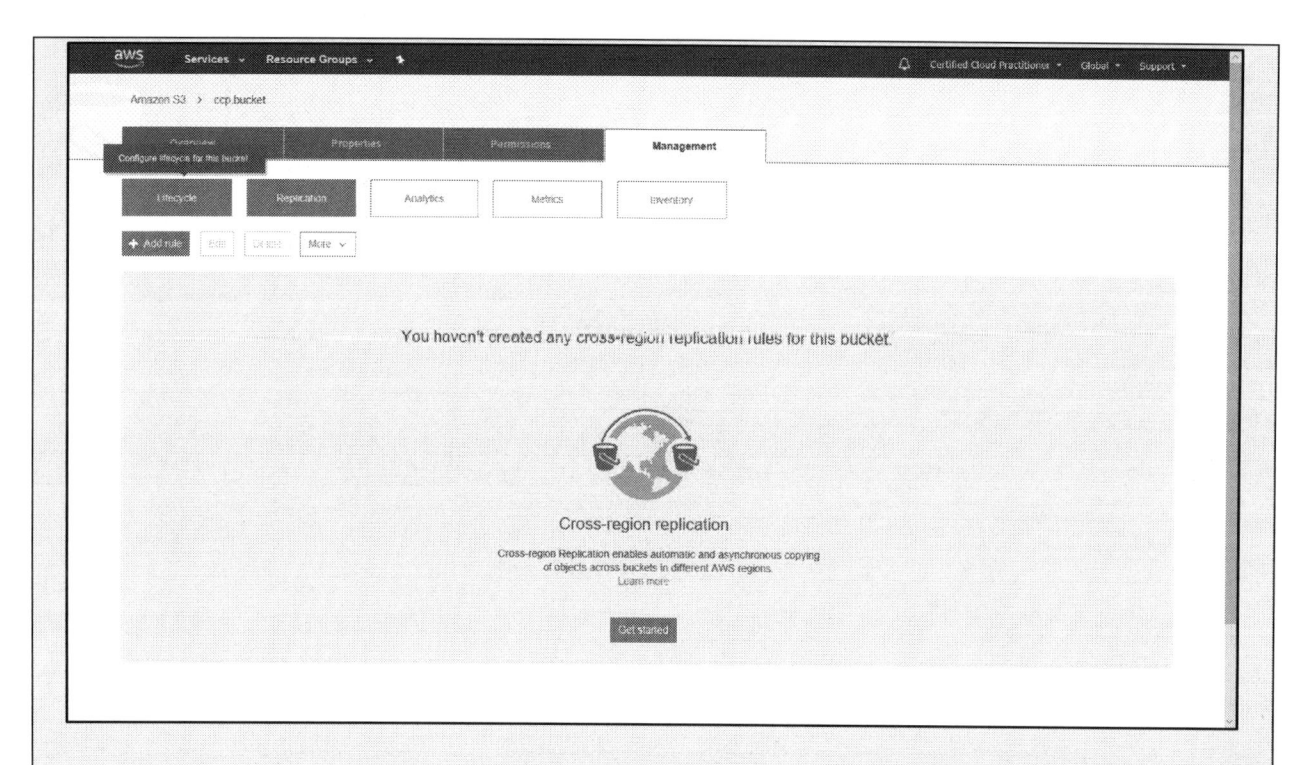

33. The management tab provides options for lifecycle configuration, analytics, metrics, inventory, and replication. Cross-region replication when configured, replicate the contents of one bucket to another. This can be used in the case of disaster recovery management.

Lab 3-6: Static Website hosting on S3

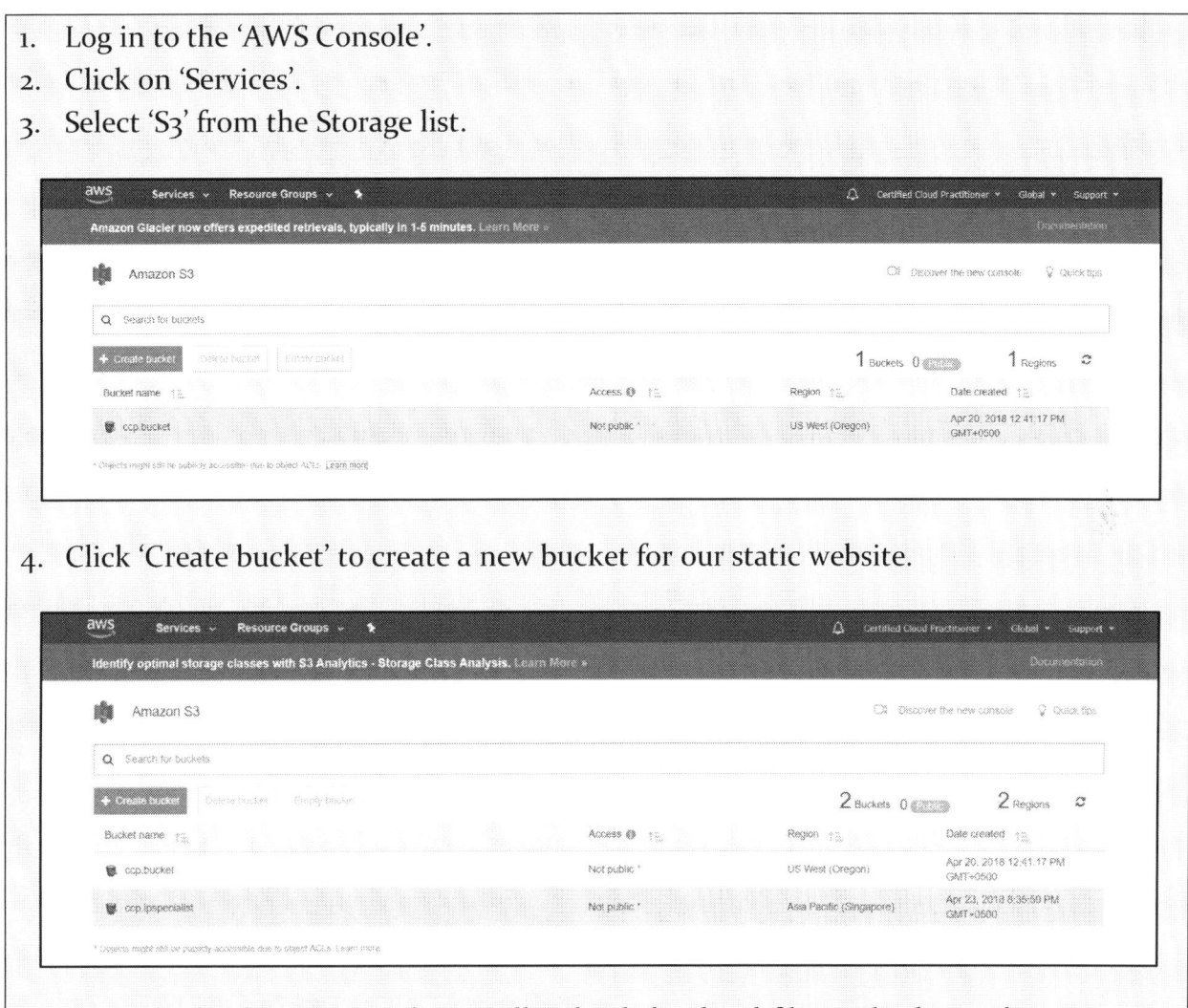

1. Log in to the 'AWS Console'.
2. Click on 'Services'.
3. Select 'S3' from the Storage list.

4. Click 'Create bucket' to create a new bucket for our static website.

5. Once the bucket is created, we will upload the .html files and other website content on to it. Click on the bucket to upload files.

Chapter 3: Technology

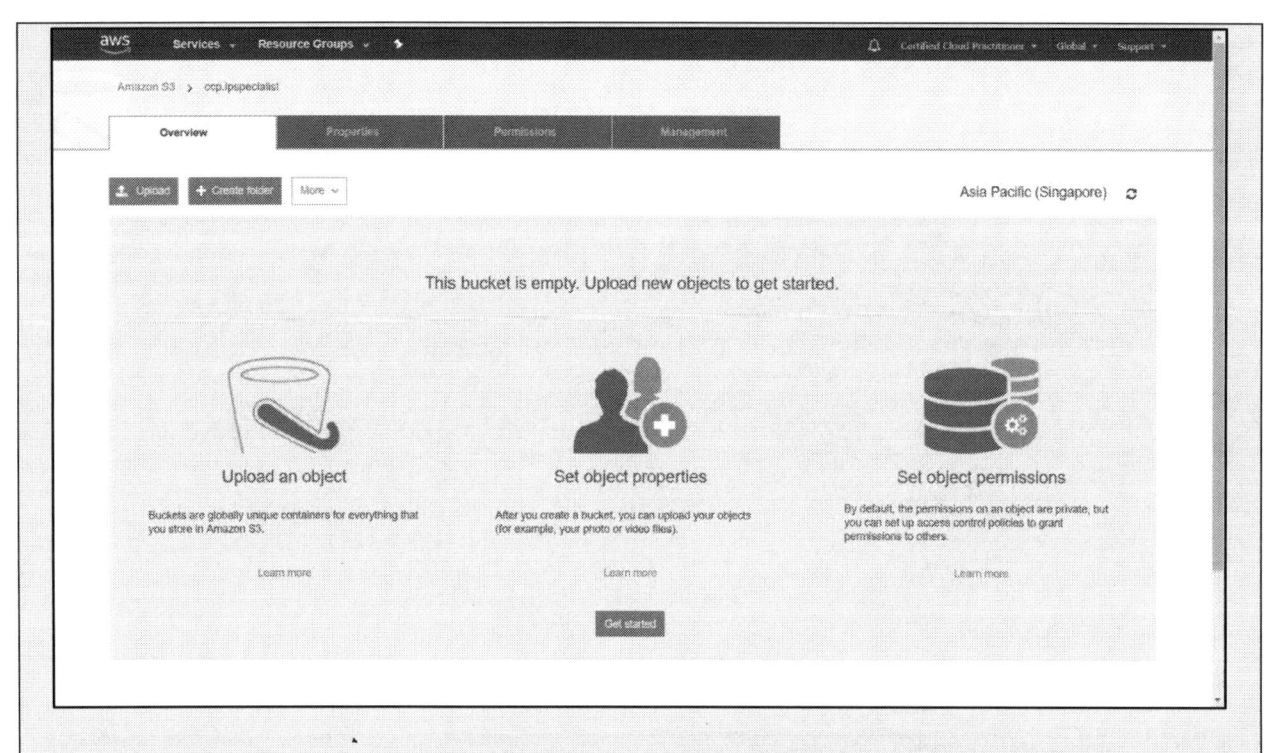

6. Click 'Upload'.

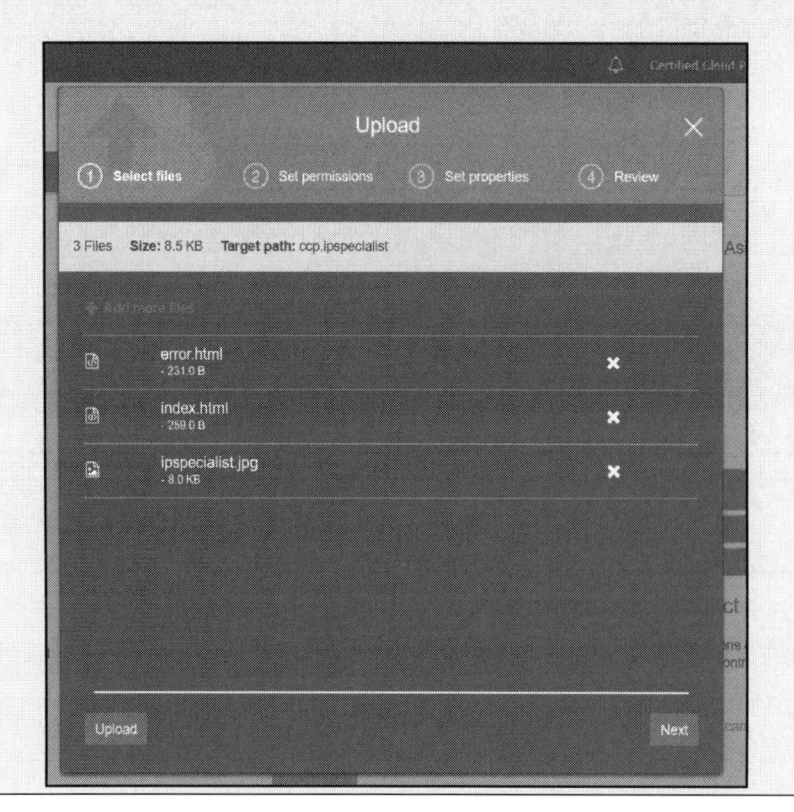

Chapter 3: Technology

7. Here, you are uploading 'index.html' and 'error.html' files for the landing and error page of your website respectively. 'ipspecialist.jpg' is an image file you will be using on your website.

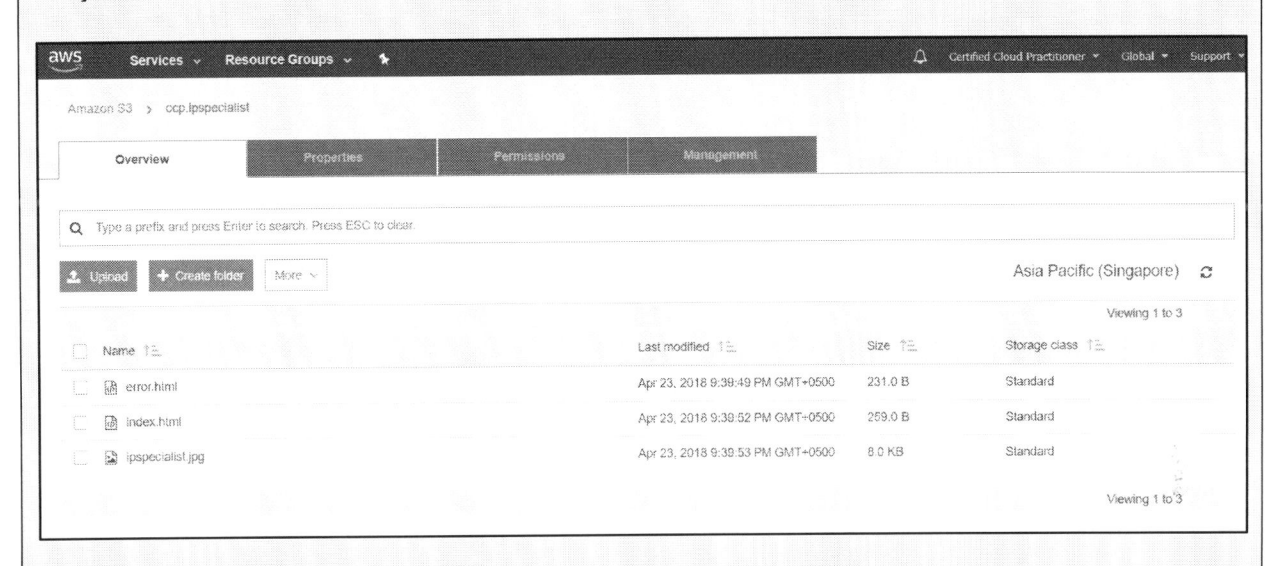

8. The 'index.html' and 'error.html' contain simple code as follows:

```html
<html>
    <title>
        Hello Cloud Specialists
    </title>
    <body>
        <div align="center">
            <h1>Welcome to IpSpecialist.net</h1>
            <h2>Let your career flow</h2>
            <img src="https://s3-us-west-2.amazonaws.com/ccp.bucket/ipspecialist.jpg">
        </div>
    </body>
</html>
```

```html
<html>
    <title>
        Error
    </title>
    <body>
        <div align="center">
            <h1>Sorry Cloud Specialists, there has been an error!</h1>
            <img src="https://s3-us-west-2.amazonaws.com/ccp.bucket/ipspecialist.jpg"">
        </div>
    </body>
</html>
```

Chapter 3: Technology

9. To make a website publicly accessible, all contents of the bucket must be granted public access. You can use bucket policy to make the entire bucket public. Click on the 'Permissions' tab.

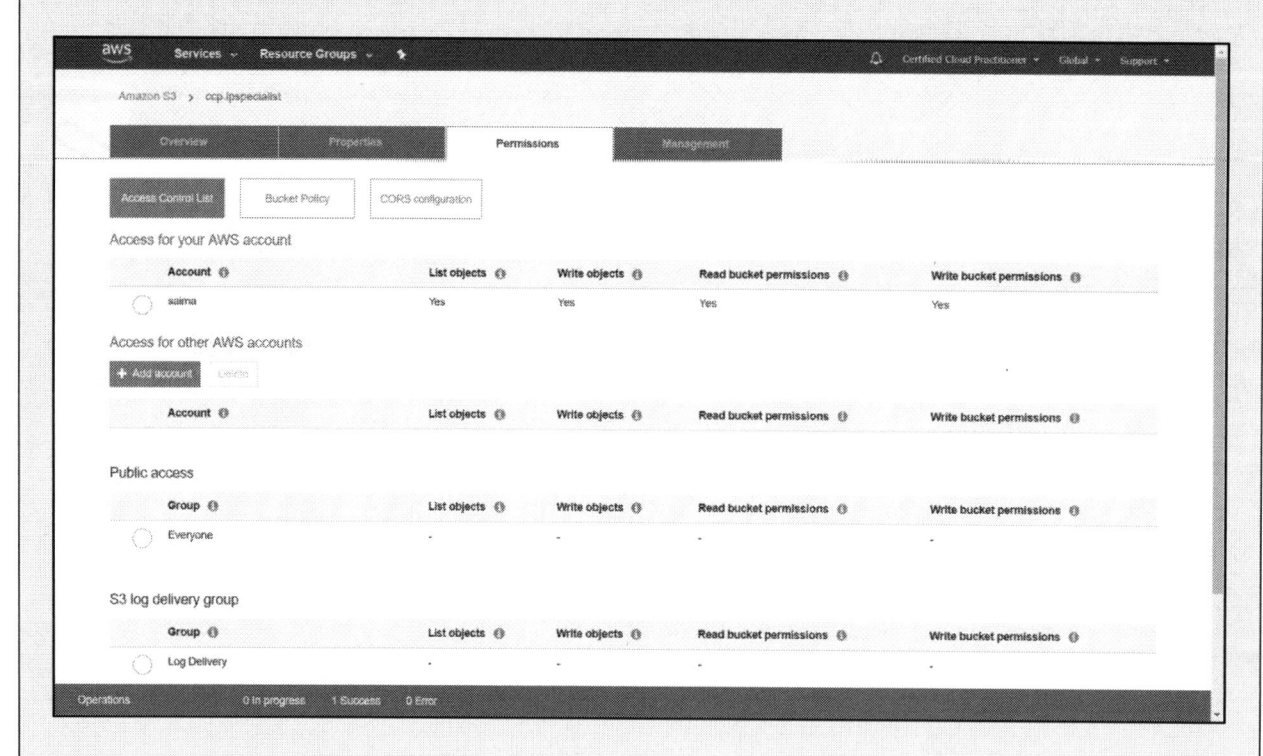

10. Click on 'Bucket Policy' to open its tab.

Chapter 3: Technology

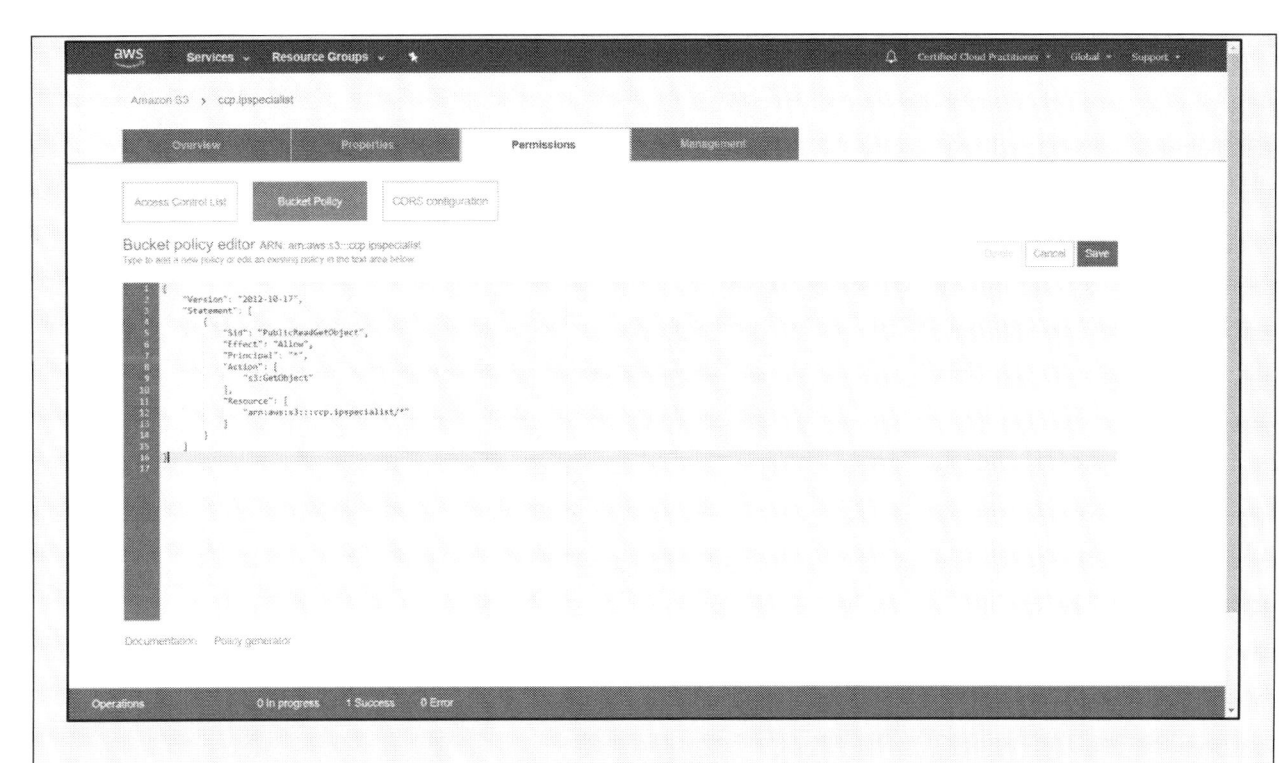

11. Copy paste the above .json code in the Bucket policy text area and click 'save'. Make sure line 12 of the code contains your bucket name.

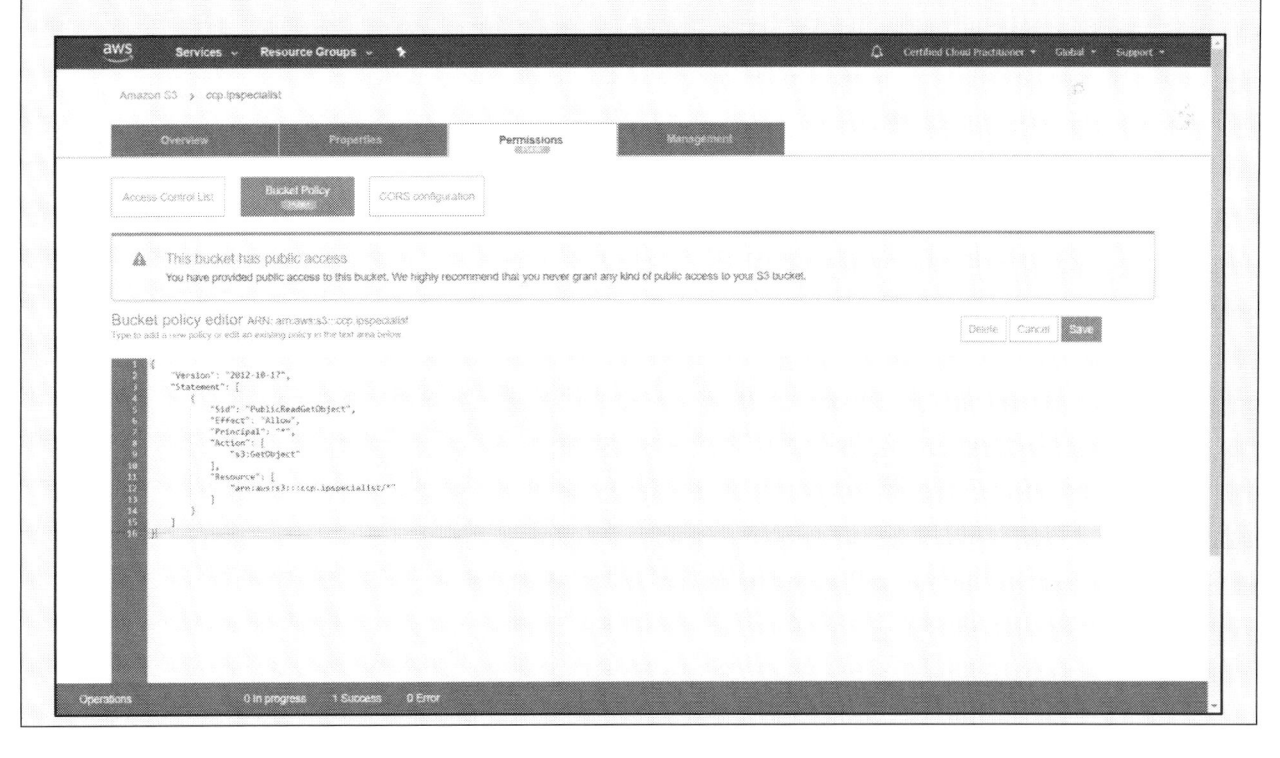

Chapter 3: Technology

12. Once you click save, you will see a notification alert that the bucket has public access. The above .json code is granting public access to your bucket. Now click on the 'Properties' tab.

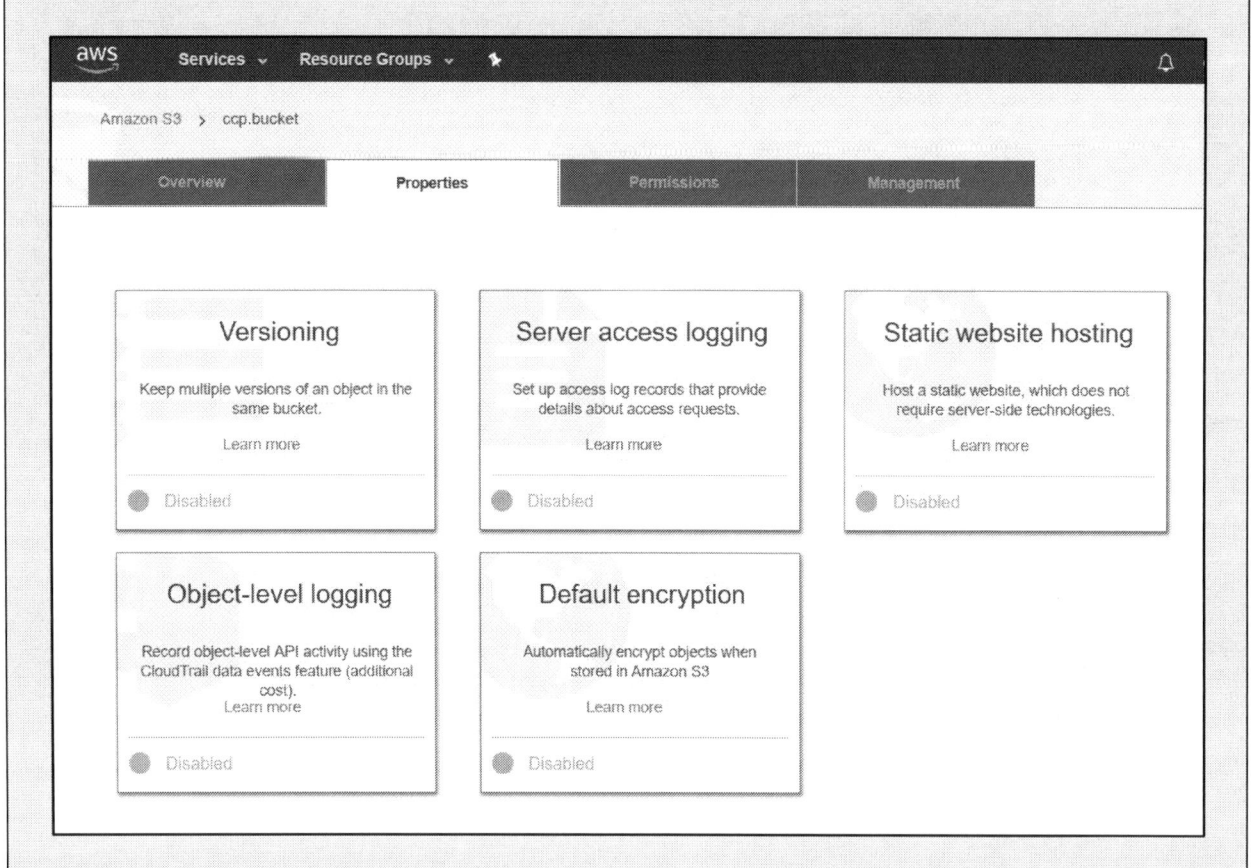

13. Select 'Static website hosting'.

Chapter 3: Technology

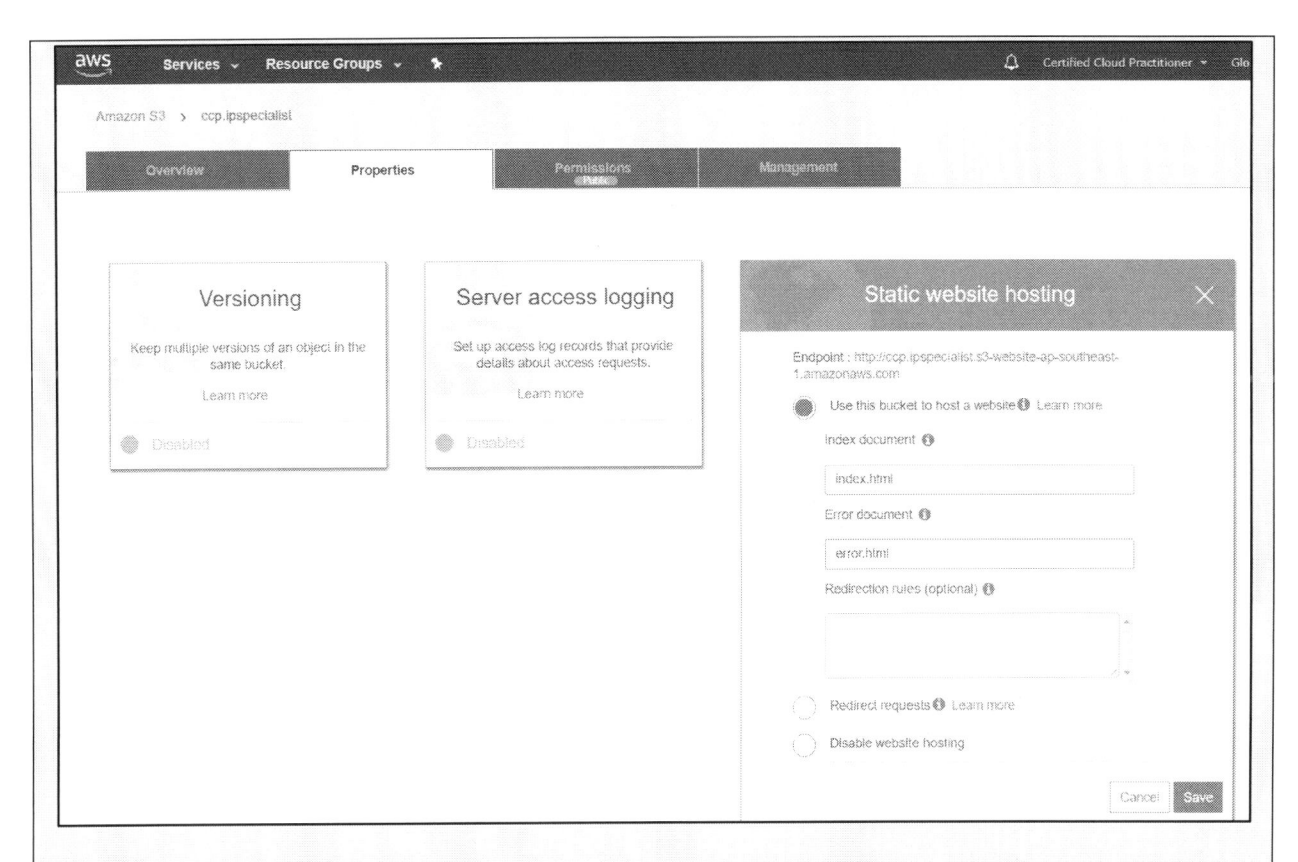

14. Select 'Use this bucket to host a website' and enter index and error document file names, which in your case are 'index.html' and 'error.html'. Click 'Save'.
15. Now click on the Endpoint link given at the top, which is your website URL, to open your website.

Chapter 3: Technology

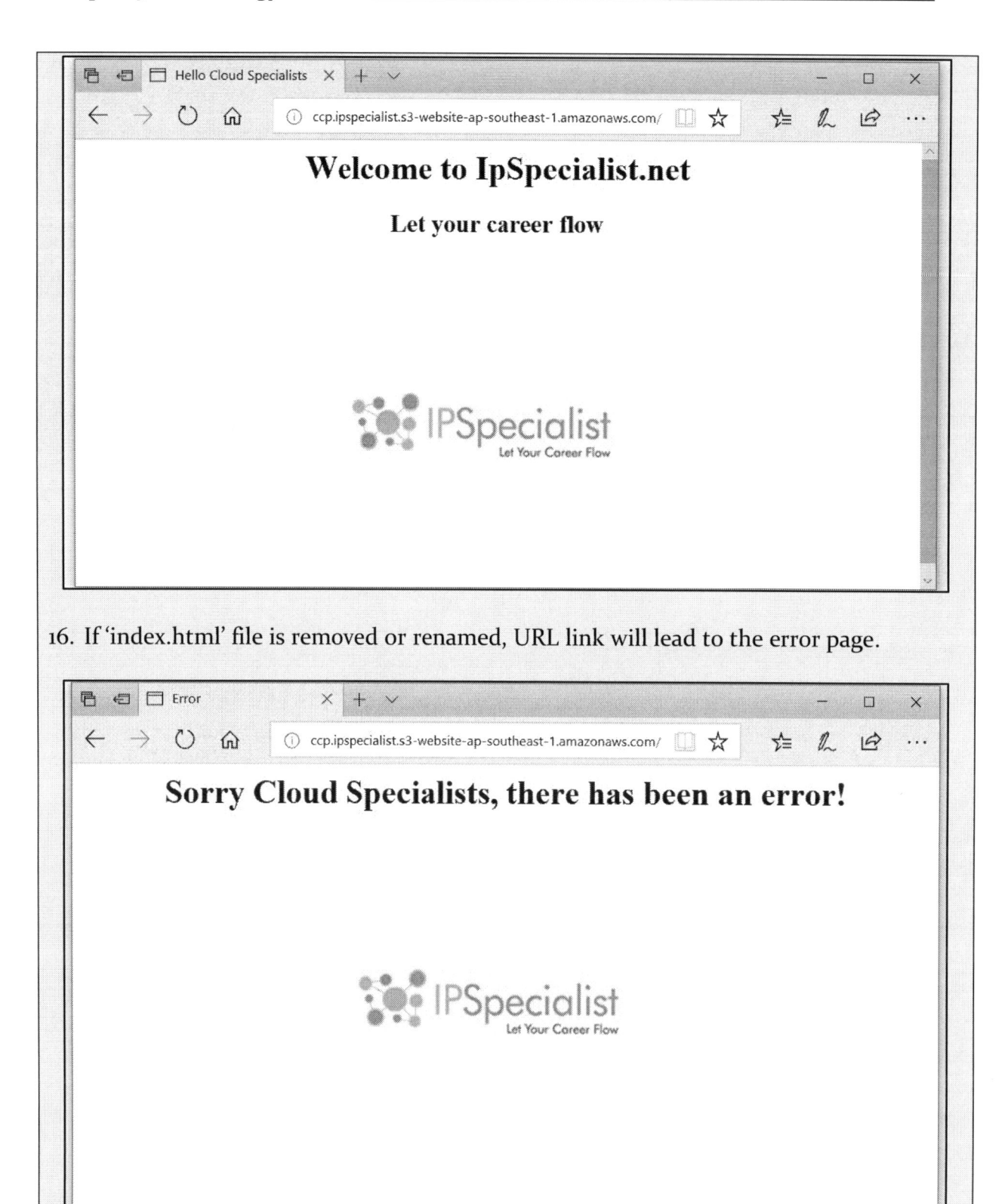

16. If 'index.html' file is removed or renamed, URL link will lead to the error page.

Chapter 3: Technology

> **EXAM TIPS:**
> - Use S3 to host static websites only (such as .html). Websites that require database connections such as WordPress cannot be hosted on S3.
> - S3 scales automatically to meet your demands. Many enterprises will put static websites on S3 when they think there is going to be a large number of requests.

Amazon Glacier

Amazon Glacier is an exceptionally low-cost storage service, which offers durable, secure and flexible storage for data archival and long-term backup. Users can store any amount of data reliably for as low as $0.004 per gigabyte per month, which results in significant savings as compared to on-premises solutions. Amazon Glacier is optimized for data that is infrequently accessed and does not require immediate availability, for which retrieval times of 3 to 5 hours are suitable. It easily and cost effectively retain data for months, years, or decades for future analysis or reference. It provides three options for access to archives to cater varying retrieval needs, from a few minutes to several hours.

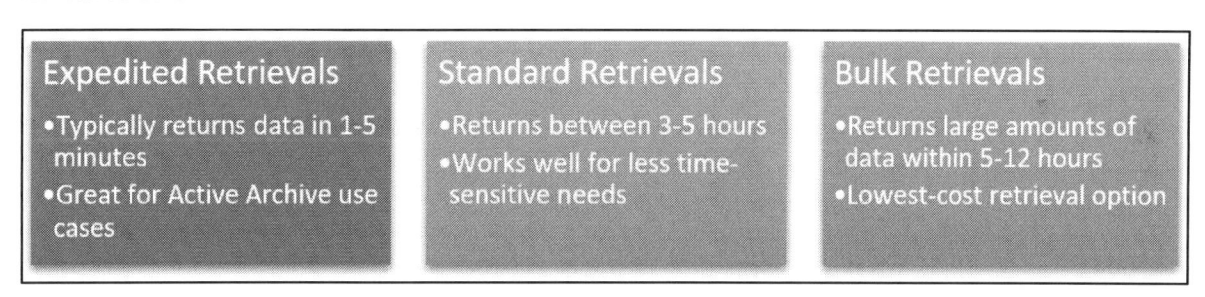

Expedited Retrievals	Standard Retrievals	Bulk Retrievals
•Typically returns data in 1-5 minutes •Great for Active Archive use cases	•Returns between 3-5 hours •Works well for less time-sensitive needs	•Returns large amounts of data within 5-12 hours •Lowest-cost retrieval option

Figure 3-10. Amazon Glacier

Key Features:

- The extremelylow-cost design is ideal for long-term archive
- Designed for 99.999999999% durability of objects across multiple Availability Zones
- Redundantly stores data in multiple facilities and on multiple devices within each facility
- Data is resilient in the event of one entire Availability Zone destruction
- Supports SSL encryption of data in transit and at rest
- Vault Lock feature enforces compliance via a lockable WORM policy

- Lifecycle management for automatic migration of objects between storage classes
- Performs regular, systematic data integrity checks and is built to be automatically self-healing

> **EXAM TIP**: Understand the key differences between S3 and Glacier. S3 is for current data and Glacier is for archived data where a 3 to 5 hour retrieval time is acceptable. Use Amazon S3 if you need low latency or frequent access to your data. Use Amazon Glacier if low storage cost is vital, and you do not require instant access to your data.

Comparison of Amazon S3 and Amazon Glacier

	S3 Standard - IA	S3 One Zone - IA	Glacier
Durability	99.999999999%	99.999999999%	99.999999999%
Availability	99.9%	99.5%	N/A
Availability SLA	99%	99%	N/A
Availability Zones	≥ 3	1	≥ 3
Min. Object Size	128 KB	128 KB	N/A
Min. Storage Duration	30 days	30 days	90 days
Retrieval Fee	per GB retrieved	per GB retrieved	per GB retrieved
First Byte Latency	milliseconds	milliseconds	minutes or hours
Storage Type	Object level	Object level	Object level
Lifecycle Transitions	Yes	Yes	Yes

Table 3-3 S3 Vs. Glacier

Amazon Elastic Block Store (Amazon EBS)

Amazon Elastic Block Store (Amazon EBS) provides persistent block storage volumes to use with Amazon EC2 instances in the AWS Cloud. EBS allows you to create storage volumes and attach them to Amazon EC2 instances in the same Availability Zone. Once attached, it appears as a mounted device similar to any hard drive or other block device and the instance can interact with the volume just as it would with a local drive. You can format it with a file system, run a database, install applications on it directly or use them in any other way you would use a block device.

Each Amazon EBS volume is replicated automatically within its Availability Zone to protect you from the failure of a single component. A volume can only be attached to one instance at a time, but many volumes can be attached to a single instance. This increases I/O, and throughput performance as your data is striped across multiple volumes. This is useful for database applications that come across many random reads and writes frequently. If an instance fails or is detached from an EBS volume, the volume can be attached to any other instance in that Availability Zone.

Amazon EBS volumes provide reliable, low-latency performance needed to run your workloads while allowing you to scale your usage up or down within minutes by paying a low price for only what you provision. Amazon EBS is intended for application workloads that benefit from fine-tuning for performance, cost, and capacity. Typical use cases include Big Data analytics engines (like the Hadoop/HDFS ecosystem and Amazon EMR clusters), relational and NoSQL databases (like Microsoft SQL Server and MySQL or Cassandra and MongoDB), stream and log processing applications (like Kafka and Splunk), and data warehousing applications (like Vertica and Teradata).

Amazon EBS volumes can also be used as boot partitions for Amazon EC2 instances, which lets you preserve your boot partition data irrespective of the life of your instance, and bundle your AMI in one-click. You can also stop and restart instances that boot from Amazon EBS volumes while preserving state, with very fast start-up times.

Amazon EBS Volume Types

- General Purpose SSD(gp2)
    - General purpose SSD balances price and performance for a variety of transactional workloads.
    - Use Cases: Boot-volumes, low-latency interactive apps, dev & test
    - Volume Size: 1 GB - 16 TB
    - Max IOPS: 10,000
    - Max throughput/volume: 160 MB/s
- Provisioned IOPS SSD (io1)
    - Highest performance SSD, designed for latency-sensitive transactional workloads

- Use Cases: I/O-intensive applications, NoSQL, and relational databases
- Volume Size: 4 GB - 16 TB
- Max IOPS: 32,000
- Max throughput/volume: 500 MB/s

- **Throughput Optimized HDD (st1)**
  - Low-cost HDD, designed for frequently accessed, throughput-intensive workloads
  - Use Cases: Big data, data warehouses, log processing
  - Volume Size: 500 GB - 16 TB
  - Max Volume: 500
  - Max throughput/volume: 500 MB/s

- **Cold HDD (sc1)**
  - Lowest cost HDD, designed for less frequently accessed workloads
  - Use Cases: Colder data requiring fewer scans per day such as File Servers
  - Volume Size: 500 GB - 16 TB
  - Max Volume: 250
  - Max throughput/volume: 250 MB/s

Amazon EBS Magnetic Volumes

Amazon EBS Magnetic volumes are previous generation volumes backed by hard disk drives (HDDs). Ideal for workloads with smaller data sets where data is infrequently accessed and where primary importance is of lowest storage cost and not performance consistency. EBS Magnetic volumes offer approximately 100 IOPS on average, with an ability to burst to hundreds of IOPS, and support volumes from 1GB to 1TB in size. These are the lowest cost per gigabyte of all EBS volume types that are bootable.

> **EXAM TIP**: EBS is simply a virtual disk where you install your operating system and all relevant files. SSD-backed storage is for transactional workloads and HDD-backed storage is for throughput workloads.

Lab 3-7: Using AWS Command Line

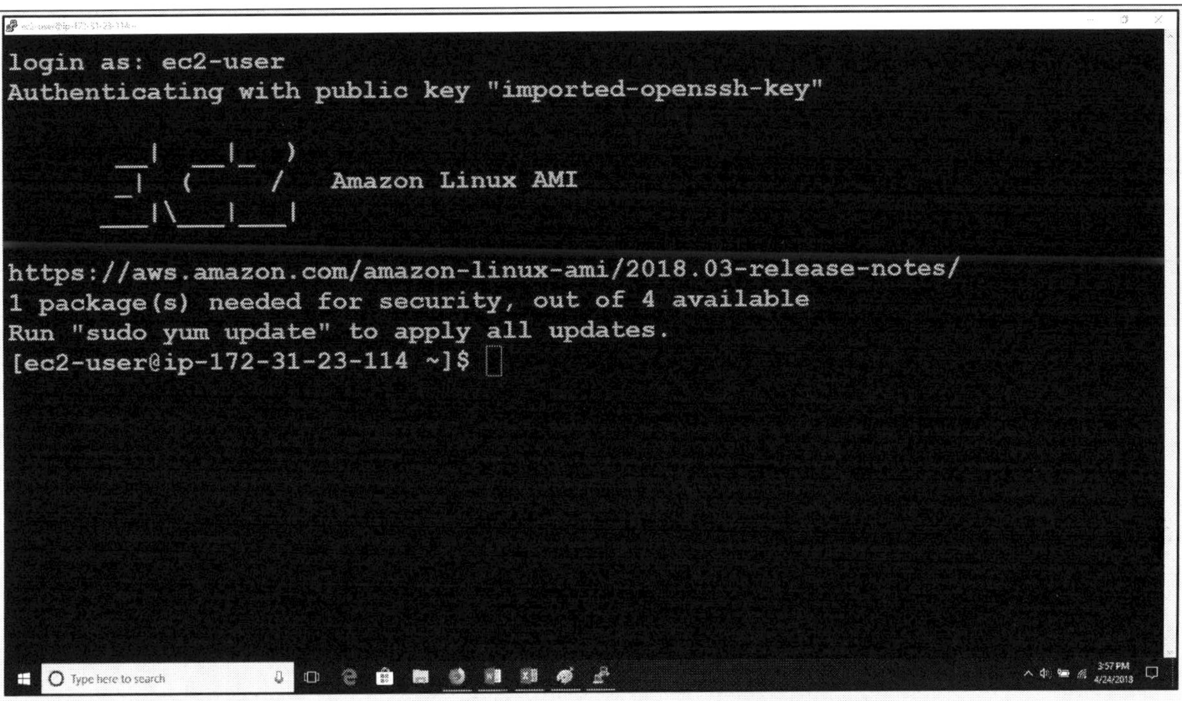

1. Once logged in to the EC2 instance, raise your privileges to root.

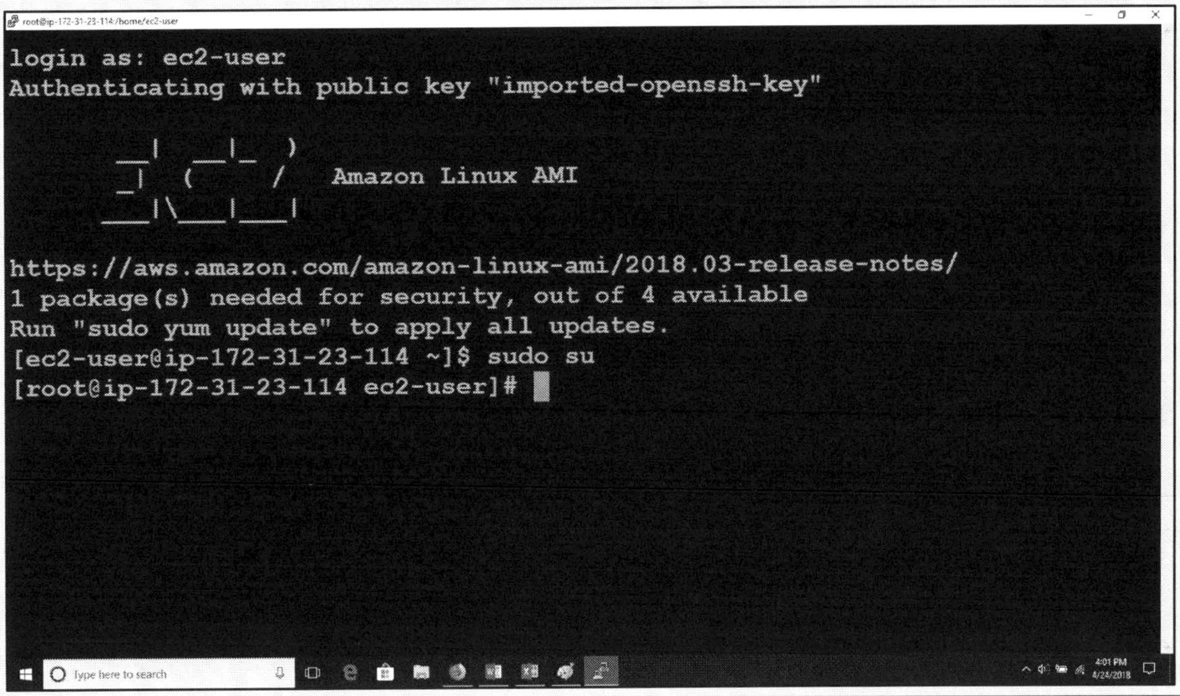

Chapter 3: Technology

2. By typing '**sudosu**', you can raise your privileges. Now, use the command line to work with your EC2 instance.

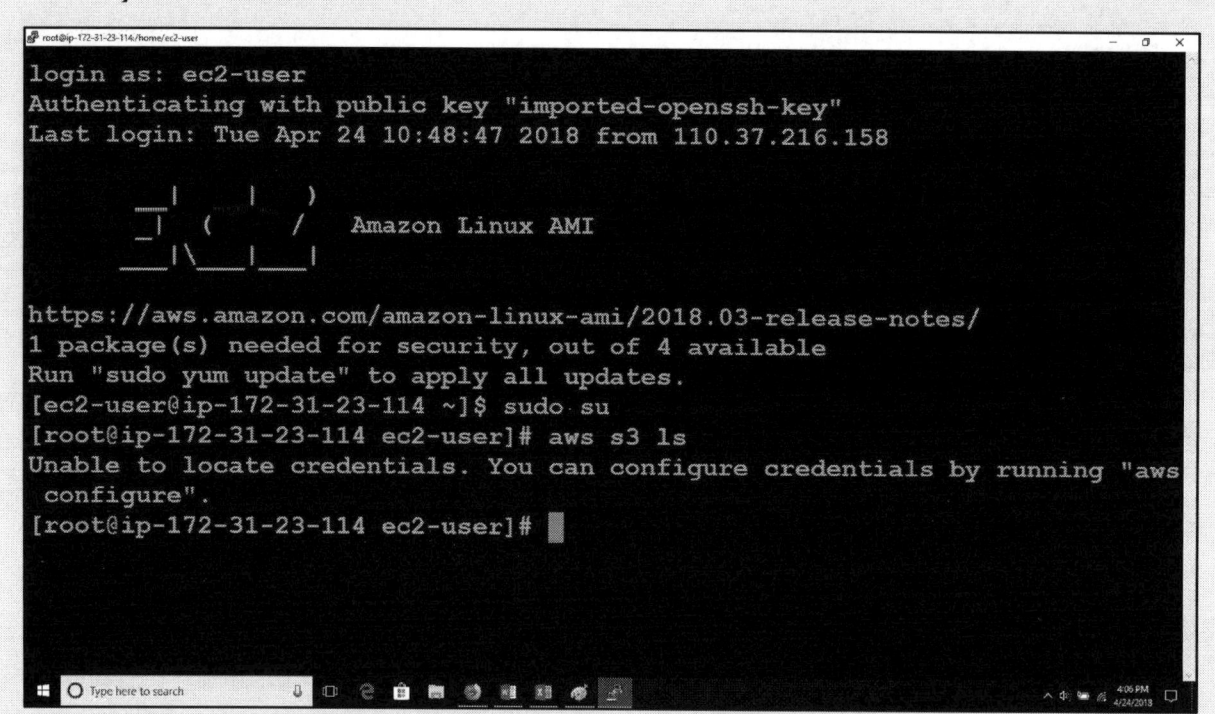

```
login as: ec2-user
Authenticating with public key "imported-openssh-key"
Last login: Tue Apr 24 10:48:47 2018 from 110.37.216.158

       _|  _|  )
       _|  (   /    Amazon Linux AMI
       ___|\___|___|

https://aws.amazon.com/amazon-linux-ami/2018.03-release-notes/
1 package(s) needed for security, out of 4 available
Run "sudo yum update" to apply all updates.
[ec2-user@ip-172-31-23-114 ~]$ sudo su
[root@ip-172-31-23-114 ec2-user]# aws s3 ls
Unable to locate credentials. You can configure credentials by running "aws configure".
[root@ip-172-31-23-114 ec2-user]#
```

3. By typing 'aws s3 ls', you can list all the items in your Amazon S3 storage. However, here, it is unable to locate credentials. You can configure credentials using the command 'awsconfigure'.

Chapter 3: Technology

```
login as: ec2-user
Authenticating with public key "imported-openssh-key"
Last login: Tue Apr 24 10:48:47 2018 from 110.37.216.158

       __|  __|_  )
       _|  (     /   Amazon Linux AMI
      ___|\___|___|

https://aws.amazon.com/amazon-linux-ami/2018.03-release-notes/
1 package(s) needed for security, out of 4 available
Run "sudo yum update" to apply all updates.
[ec2-user@ip-172-31-23-114 ~]$ sudo su
[root@ip-172-31-23-114 ec2-user]# aws s3 ls
Unable to locate credentials. You can configure credentials by running "aws
 configure".
[root@ip-172-31-23-114 ec2-user]# aws configure
AWS Access Key ID [None]:
```

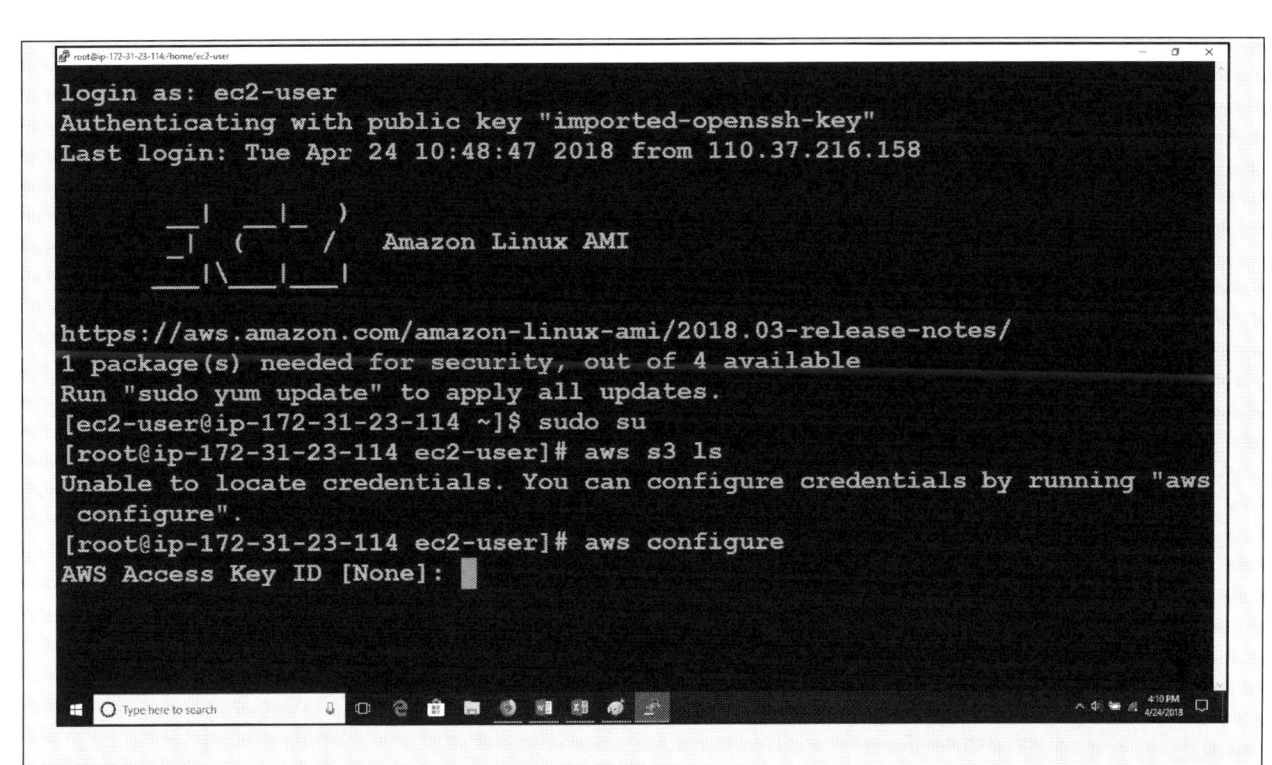

4. It will prompt you for the AWS Access Key ID. Open up the credentials file you downloaded when you created your IAM User (e.g. Saima_Talat) and copy paste the credentials here at the command line.

```
login as: ec2-user
Authenticating with public key "imported-openssh-key"
Last login: Tue Apr 24 11:21:43 2018 from 110.37.216.158

       __|  __|_  )
       _|  (     /   Amazon Linux AMI
      ___|\___|___|

https://aws.amazon.com/amazon-linux-ami/2018.03-release-notes/
1 package(s) needed for security, out of 4 available
Run "sudo yum update" to apply all updates.
[ec2-user@ip-172-31-23-114 ~]$ sudo su
[root@ip-172-31-23-114 ec2-user]# aws s3 ls
Unable to locate credentials. You can configure credentials by running "aws
 configure".
[root@ip-172-31-23-114 ec2-user]# aws configure
AWS Access Key ID [None]: AKIAJ3VFLC7IZDHEVHSQ
AWS Secret Access Key [None]: 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
Default region name [None]:
```

Chapter 3: Technology

5. After entering the Access Key ID and Secret Access Key, you will be prompted for default region name. Let us say your EC2 server is in the region 'us-west-2b'.

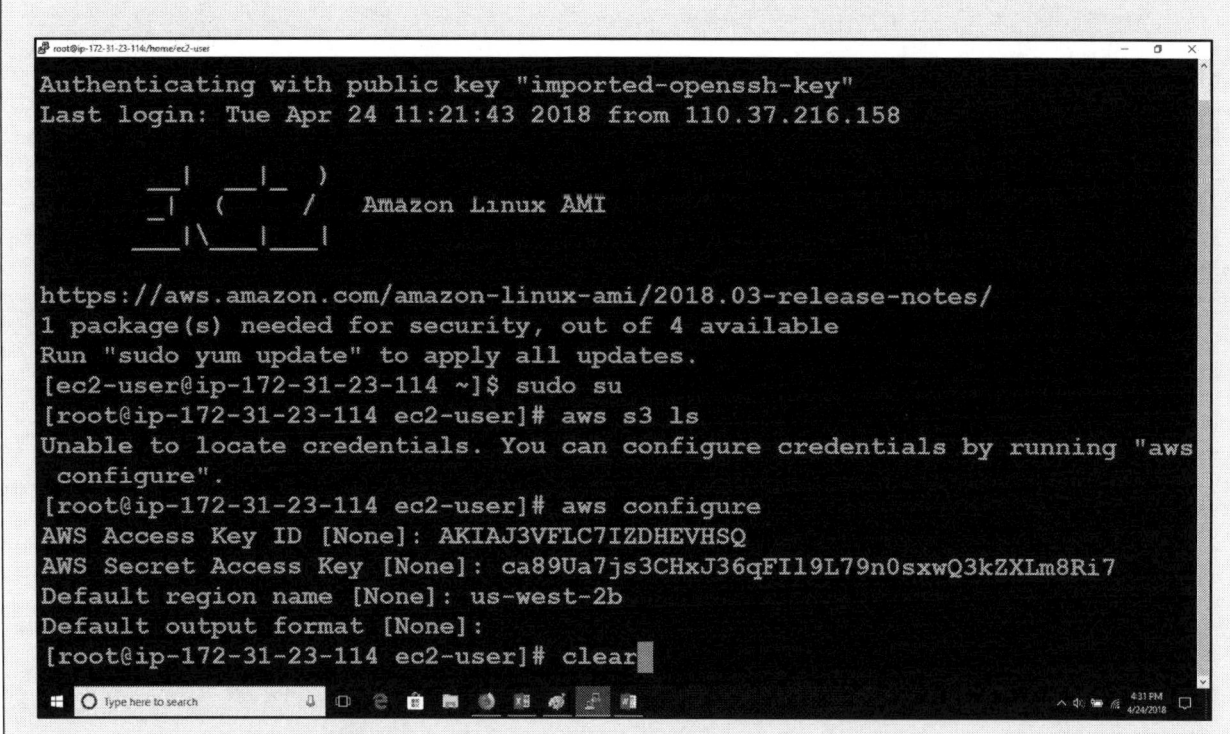

```
Authenticating with public key "imported-openssh-key"
Last login: Tue Apr 24 11:21:43 2018 from 110.37.216.158

       __|  __|_  )
       _|  (     /   Amazon Linux AMI
      ___|\___|___|

https://aws.amazon.com/amazon-linux-ami/2018.03-release-notes/
1 package(s) needed for security, out of 4 available
Run "sudo yum update" to apply all updates.
[ec2-user@ip-172-31-23-114 ~]$ sudo su
[root@ip-172-31-23-114 ec2-user]# aws s3 ls
Unable to locate credentials. You can configure credentials by running "aws configure".
[root@ip-172-31-23-114 ec2-user]# aws configure
AWS Access Key ID [None]: AKIAJ3VFLC7IZDHEVHSQ
AWS Secret Access Key [None]: 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
Default region name [None]: us-west-2b
Default output format [None]:
[root@ip-172-31-23-114 ec2-user]# clear
```

6. Leave the default output format as blank and clear the screen by typing 'clear'.

```
[root@ip-172-31-23-114 ec2-user]#
```

7. The IAM User 'Saima_Talat' you created in the IAM section had administrative access. So you are now able to perform all the administrative actions.

```
[root@ip-172-31-23-114 ec2-user]# aws s3 ls
2018-04-20 07:41:18 ccp.bucket
2018-04-23 17:00:45 ccp.ipspecialist
[root@ip-172-31-23-114 ec2-user]#
```

Chapter 3: Technology

8. Now if you type in again 'aws s3 ls' to list the content of Amazon S3 storage, you will be able to see the two buckets 'ccp.bucket' and 'ccp.ipspecialist'. Now, let us create a bucket from the command line.

```
[root@ip-172-31-23-114 ec2-user]# aws s3 ls
2018-04-20 07:41:18 ccp.bucket
2018-04-23 17:00:45 ccp.ipspecialist
[root@ip-172-31-23-114 ec2-user]# aws s3 mb s3://ccp.commandline.bucket
make_bucket: ccp.commandline.bucket
[root@ip-172-31-23-114 ec2-user]# aws s3 ls
2018-04-20 07:41:18 ccp.bucket
2018-04-24 11:50:07 ccp.commandline.bucket
2018-04-23 17:00:45 ccp.ipspecialist
[root@ip-172-31-23-114 ec2-user]#
```

9. Here we created a new bucket by the name 'ccp.commandline.bucket.' using the command 'aws s3 mb', where 'mb' stands for make bucket. Then we run the list command to see that the new bucket has been created.

```
[root@ip-172-31-23-114 ec2-user]# echo "Hello Cloud Practitioner" > hello.txt
[root@ip-172-31-23-114 ec2-user]# ls
hello.txt
[root@ip-172-31-23-114 ec2-user]# nano hello.txt
```

10. Here we created a text file named 'hello.txt' using the command 'echo' to display "Hello Cloud Practitioner". We then run the list command to see that the file has been created. To open up the file, we have used the text editor 'nano'.

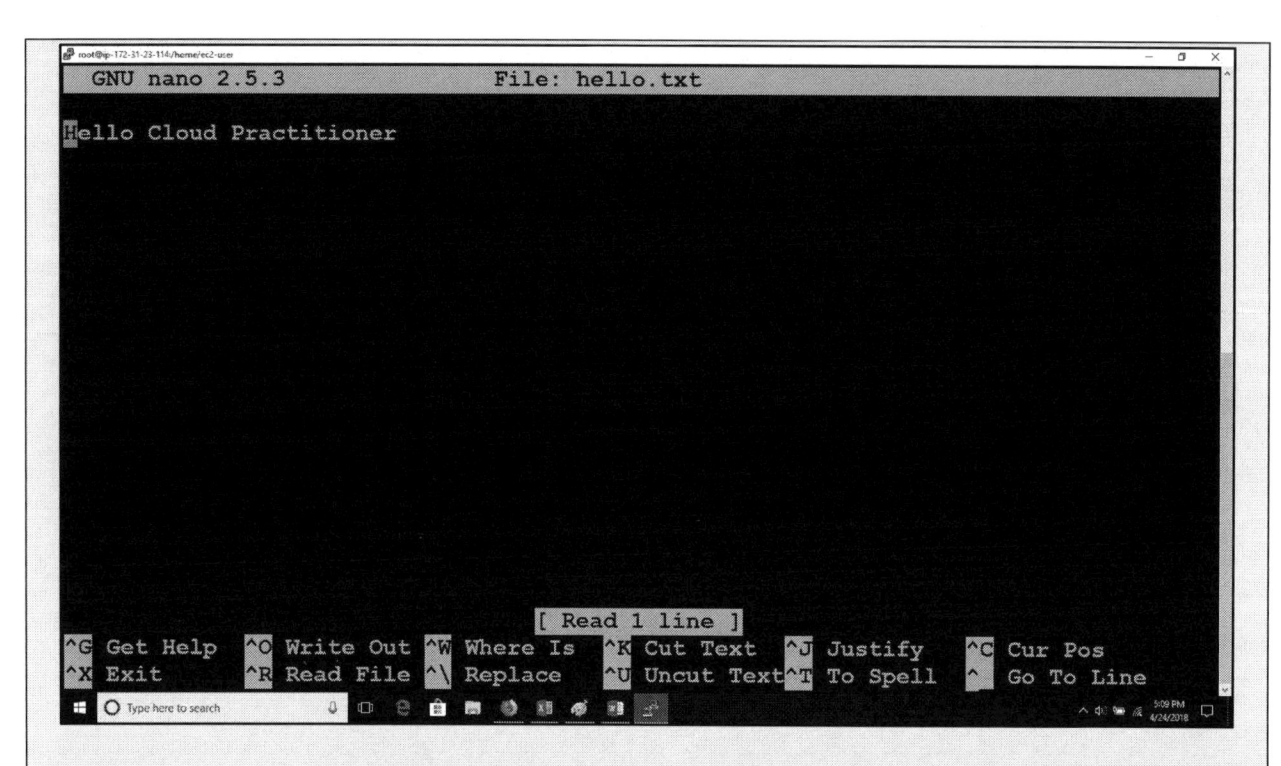

Chapter 3: Technology

[Screenshot of GNU nano 2.5.3 editor showing File: hello.txt with content "Hello Cloud Practitioner"]

11. This is the text editor displaying the content "Hello Cloud Practitioner". Press ctrl+x to exit the editor.

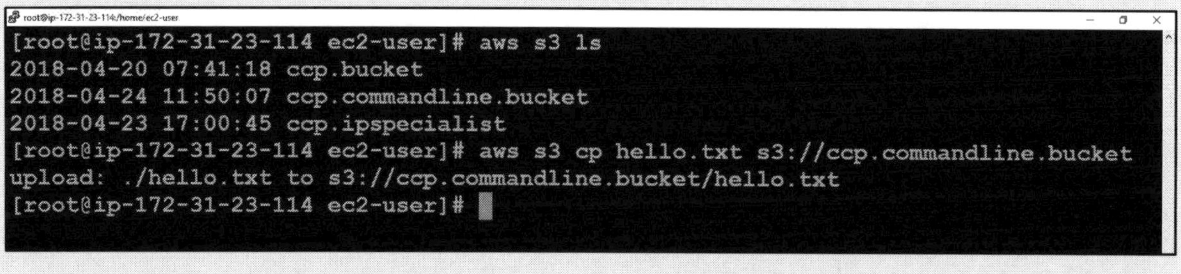

[Screenshot of terminal showing:]
```
[root@ip-172-31-23-114 ec2-user]# aws s3 ls
2018-04-20 07:41:18 ccp.bucket
2018-04-24 11:50:07 ccp.commandline.bucket
2018-04-23 17:00:45 ccp.ipspecialist
[root@ip-172-31-23-114 ec2-user]# aws s3 cp hello.txt s3://ccp.commandline.bucket
upload: ./hello.txt to s3://ccp.commandline.bucket/hello.txt
[root@ip-172-31-23-114 ec2-user]#
```

12. Here we are copying the text file 'hello.txt' from our EC2 instance to S3 bucket 'ccp.commandline.bucket' using the command 'cp', which means copy.

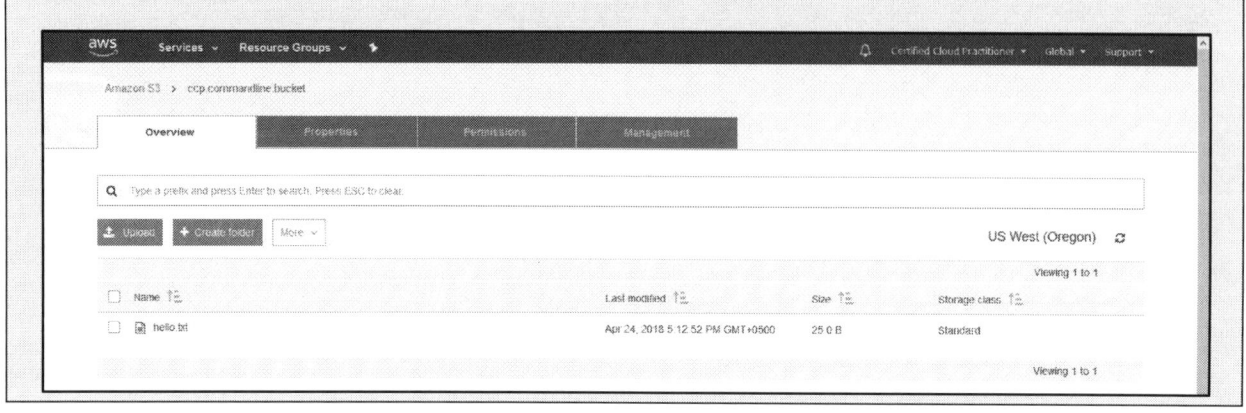

[Screenshot of AWS S3 console showing ccp.commandline.bucket with hello.txt file, Last modified Apr 24, 2018 5:12:52 PM GMT+0500, Size 25.0 B, Storage class Standard]

Chapter 3: Technology

> 13. If you log in through the AWS console, you will be able to see that 'hello.txt' file has now been copied into the S3 bucket 'ccp.commandline.bucket'.

Lab 3-8: Using Roles

> 1. Log in to the AWS command line as described before.

```
[root@ip-172-31-23-114 ec2-user]# cd ~/.aws
[root@ip-172-31-23-114 .aws]# ls
config  credentials
[root@ip-172-31-23-114 .aws]# nano credentials
```

> 2. The command 'cd ~/.aws' is used to change directory to AWS root. The list command displays the files stored on it which include the 'credentials' file as well. If we open it with the 'nano' text editor, we will be able to see the credentials.

```
GNU nano 2.5.3                File: credentials

[default]
aws_access_key_id = AKIAJ3VFLC7IZDHEVHSQ
aws_secret_access_key = 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




                              [ Read 3 lines ]
^G Get Help   ^O Write Out  ^W Where Is   ^K Cut Text   ^J Justify    ^C Cur Pos
^X Exit       ^R Read File  ^\ Replace    ^U Uncut Text ^T To Spell   ^_ Go To Line
```

165

Chapter 3: Technology

3. If someone hacks into the EC2 instance, he/she can easily get access to the Access Key ID and Secret Access Key and this can compromise security. To avoid this breach of security, we use Roles instead.

```
[root@ip-172-31-23-114 ec2-user]# cd ~/.aws
[root@ip-172-31-23-114 .aws]# ls
config  credentials
[root@ip-172-31-23-114 .aws]# nano credentials
[root@ip-172-31-23-114 .aws]# rm -rf credentials
[root@ip-172-31-23-114 .aws]# ls
config
[root@ip-172-31-23-114 .aws]# aws s3 ls
Unable to locate credentials. You can configure credentials by running "aws configure".
[root@ip-172-31-23-114 .aws]#
```

4. First, delete the credentials stored on your EC2 instance, as storing credentials on the EC2 instance is not safe. For this, use the 'rm' command to remove the credentials. If you type in 'ls', the credentials are now gone. To test this, if you run 'aws s3 ls', it will prompt unable to locate credentials. Now open up the AWS Console and select 'IAM' from services.

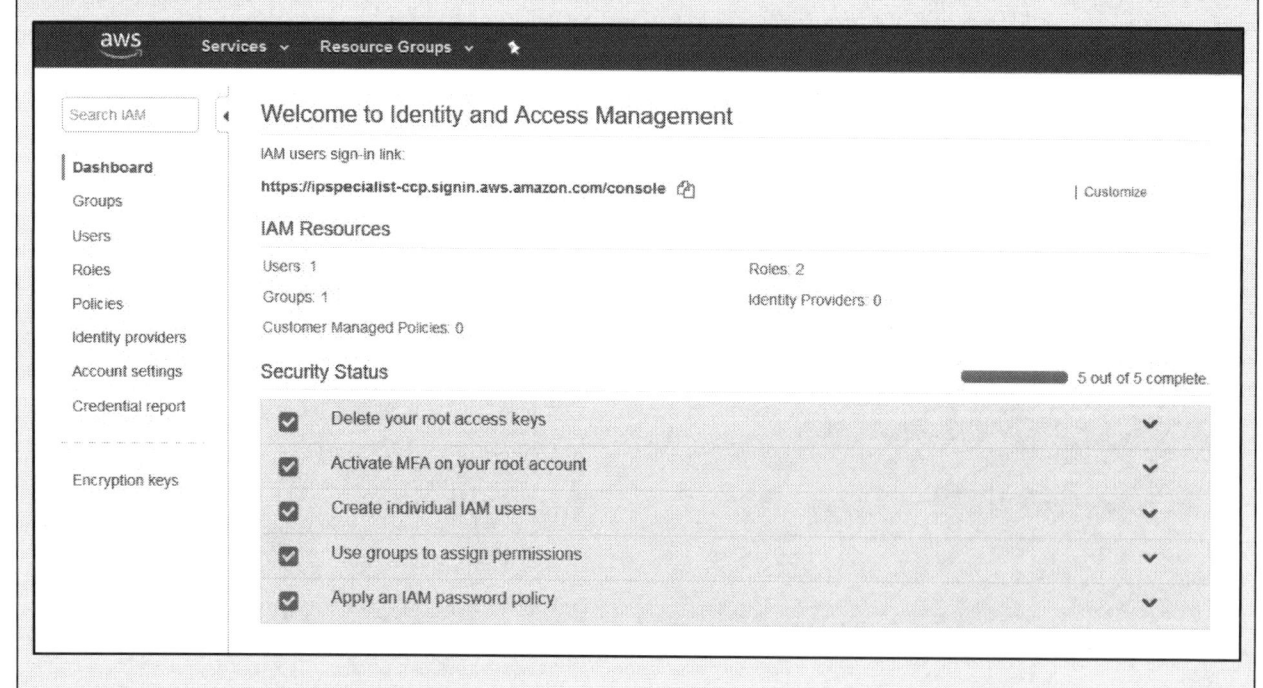

5. Select 'Roles' from the left side pane.

Chapter 3: Technology

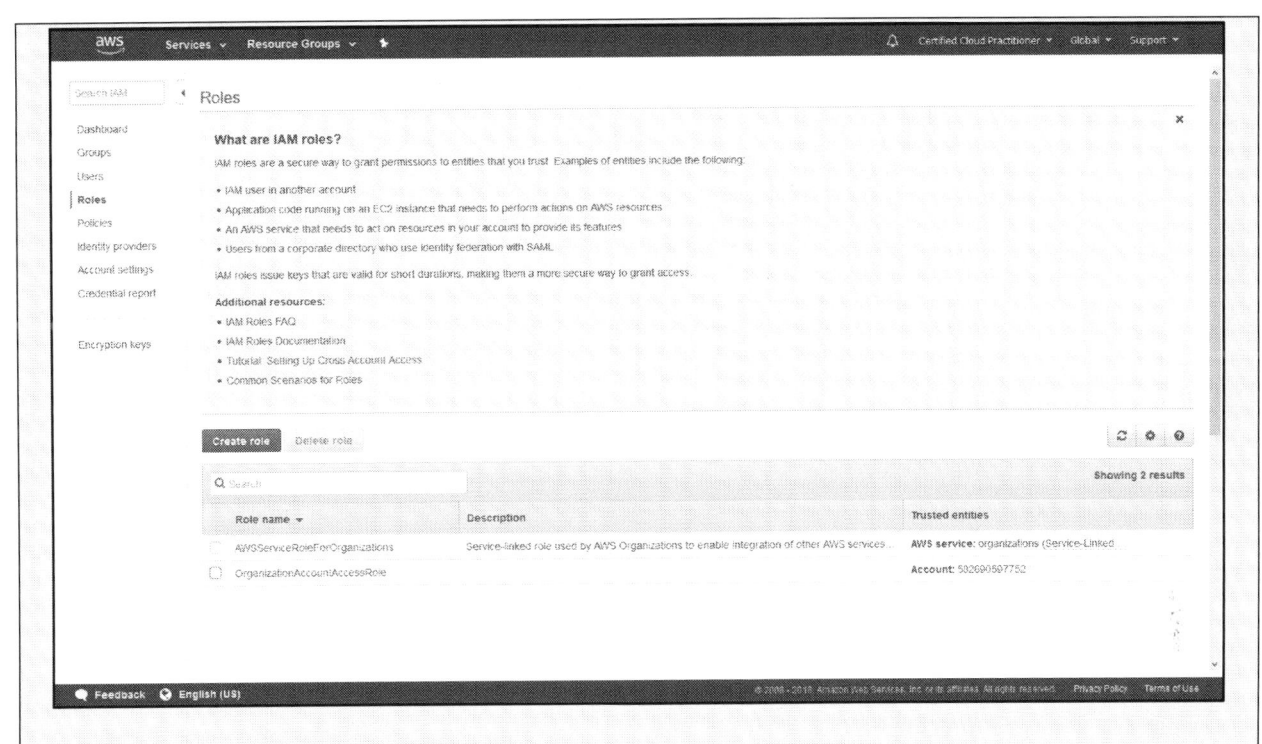

6. Here we are going to create a new Role. Roles are a secure way to grant permissions to entities. Click on 'Create role'.

Chapter 3: Technology

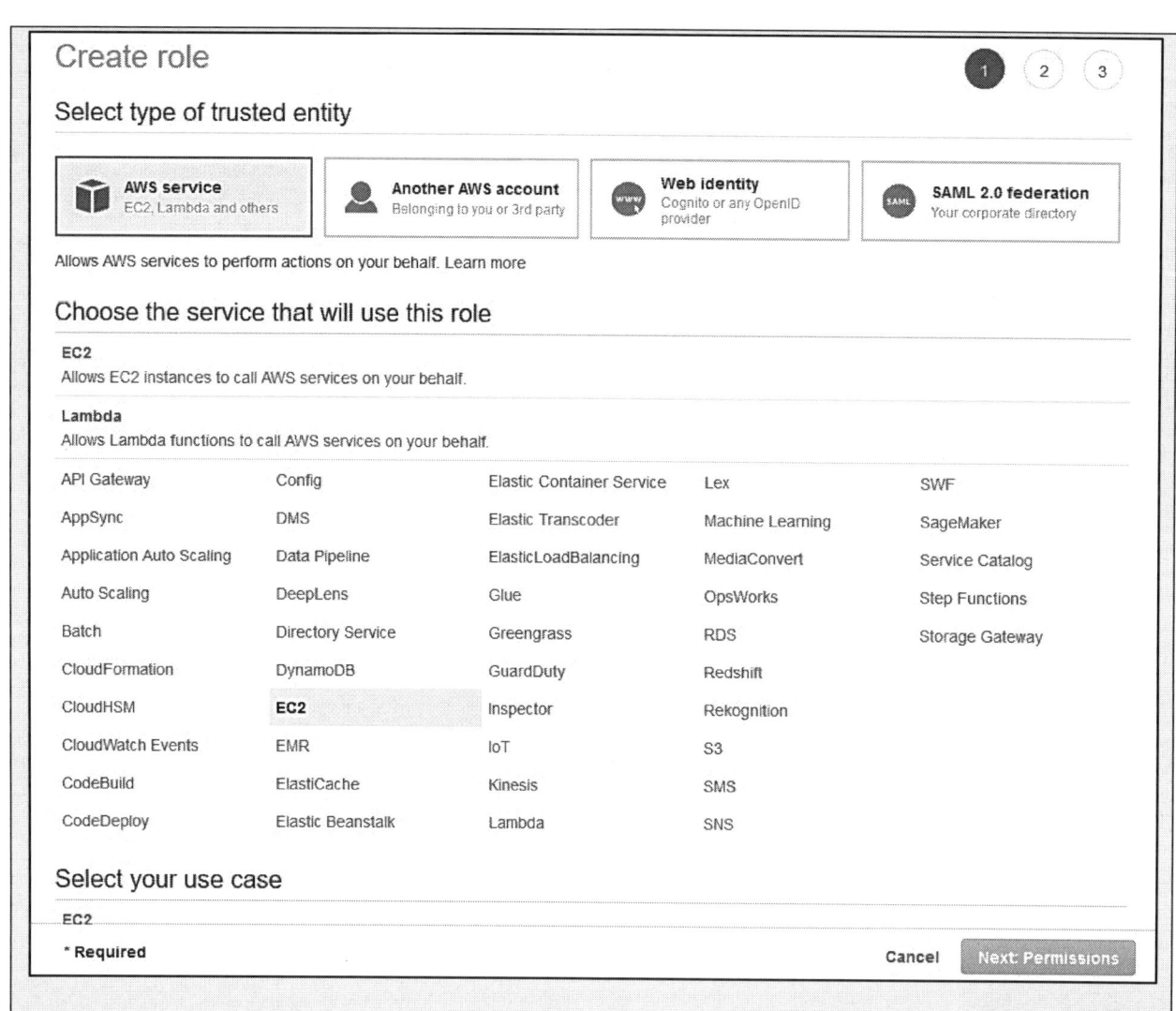

Create role

Select type of trusted entity

AWS service EC2, Lambda and others	Another AWS account Belonging to you or 3rd party	Web identity Cognito or any OpenID provider	SAML 2.0 federation Your corporate directory

Allows AWS services to perform actions on your behalf. Learn more

Choose the service that will use this role

EC2
Allows EC2 instances to call AWS services on your behalf.

Lambda
Allows Lambda functions to call AWS services on your behalf.

API Gateway	Config	Elastic Container Service	Lex	SWF
AppSync	DMS	Elastic Transcoder	Machine Learning	SageMaker
Application Auto Scaling	Data Pipeline	ElasticLoadBalancing	MediaConvert	Service Catalog
Auto Scaling	DeepLens	Glue	OpsWorks	Step Functions
Batch	Directory Service	Greengrass	RDS	Storage Gateway
CloudFormation	DynamoDB	GuardDuty	Redshift	
CloudHSM	**EC2**	Inspector	Rekognition	
CloudWatch Events	EMR	IoT	S3	
CodeBuild	ElastiCache	Kinesis	SMS	
CodeDeploy	Elastic Beanstalk	Lambda	SNS	

Select your use case

EC2

* Required   Cancel   Next: Permissions

7. We need to select the AWS service for which we are creating this role. So click on 'EC2' from the list of services.

Chapter 3: Technology

Auto Scaling	DeepLens	Glue	OpsWorks	Step Functions
Batch	Directory Service	Greengrass	RDS	Storage Gateway
CloudFormation	DynamoDB	GuardDuty	Redshift	
CloudHSM	**EC2**	Inspector	Rekognition	
CloudWatch Events	EMR	IoT	S3	
CodeBuild	ElastiCache	Kinesis	SMS	
CodeDeploy	Elastic Beanstalk	Lambda	SNS	

Select your use case

EC2
Allows EC2 instances to call AWS services on your behalf.

EC2 - Scheduled Instances
Allows EC2 Scheduled Instances to manage instances on your behalf.

EC2 - Spot Fleet
Allows EC2 Spot Fleet to launch and manage spot fleet instances on your behalf.

EC2 - Spot Fleet Auto Scaling
Allows Auto Scaling to access and update EC2 spot fleets on your behalf.

EC2 - Spot Fleet Tagging
Allows EC2 to launch spot instances and attach tags to the launched instances on your behalf.

EC2 - Spot Instances
Allows EC2 Spot Instances to launch and manage spot instances on your behalf.

EC2 Role for Simple Systems Manager
Allows EC2 instances to call AWS services like CloudWatch and SSM on your behalf.

EC2 Spot Fleet Role
Allows EC2 Spot Fleet to request and terminate Spot Instances on your behalf.

* Required   Cancel   **Next: Permissions**

8. Select your use case from the list. You need to allow EC2 instance to call AWS services on your behalf, so select the first option and click 'Next: Permissions'.

Chapter 3: Technology

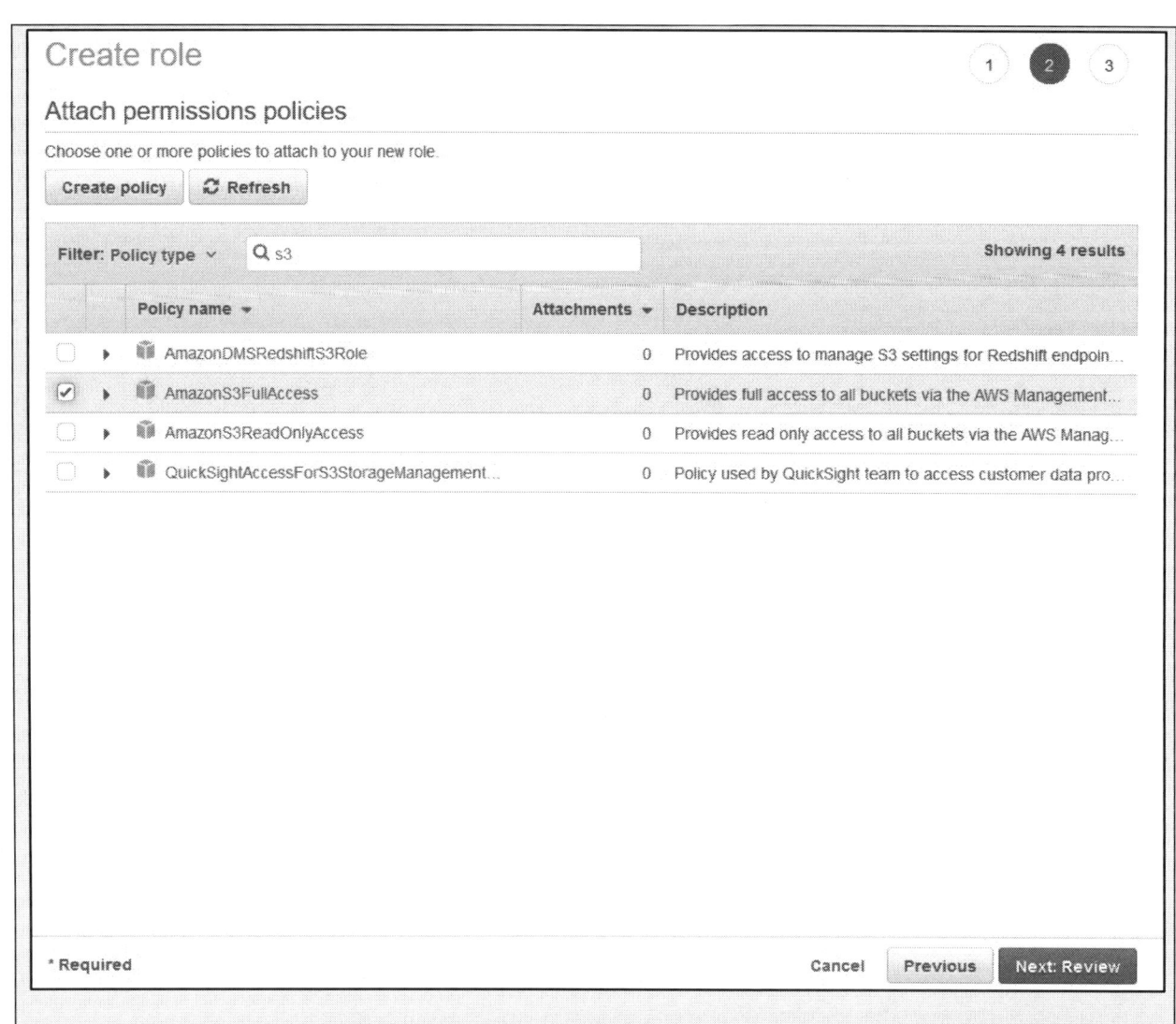

9. Type in S3 in the search bar to find S3 permission policies and select 'AmazonS3FullAccess' to grant S3 administrative access. Click 'Next: Review'.

Chapter 3: Technology

Create role

Review

Provide the required information below and review this role before you create it.

- **Role name*** : MyS3AdminAccess
  Use alphanumeric and '+=,.@-_' characters. Maximum 64 characters.

- **Role description** : Provides admin access to S3
  Maximum 1000 characters. Use alphanumeric and '+=,.@-_' characters.

- **Trusted entities** : AWS service: ec2.amazonaws.com

- **Policies** : AmazonS3FullAccess

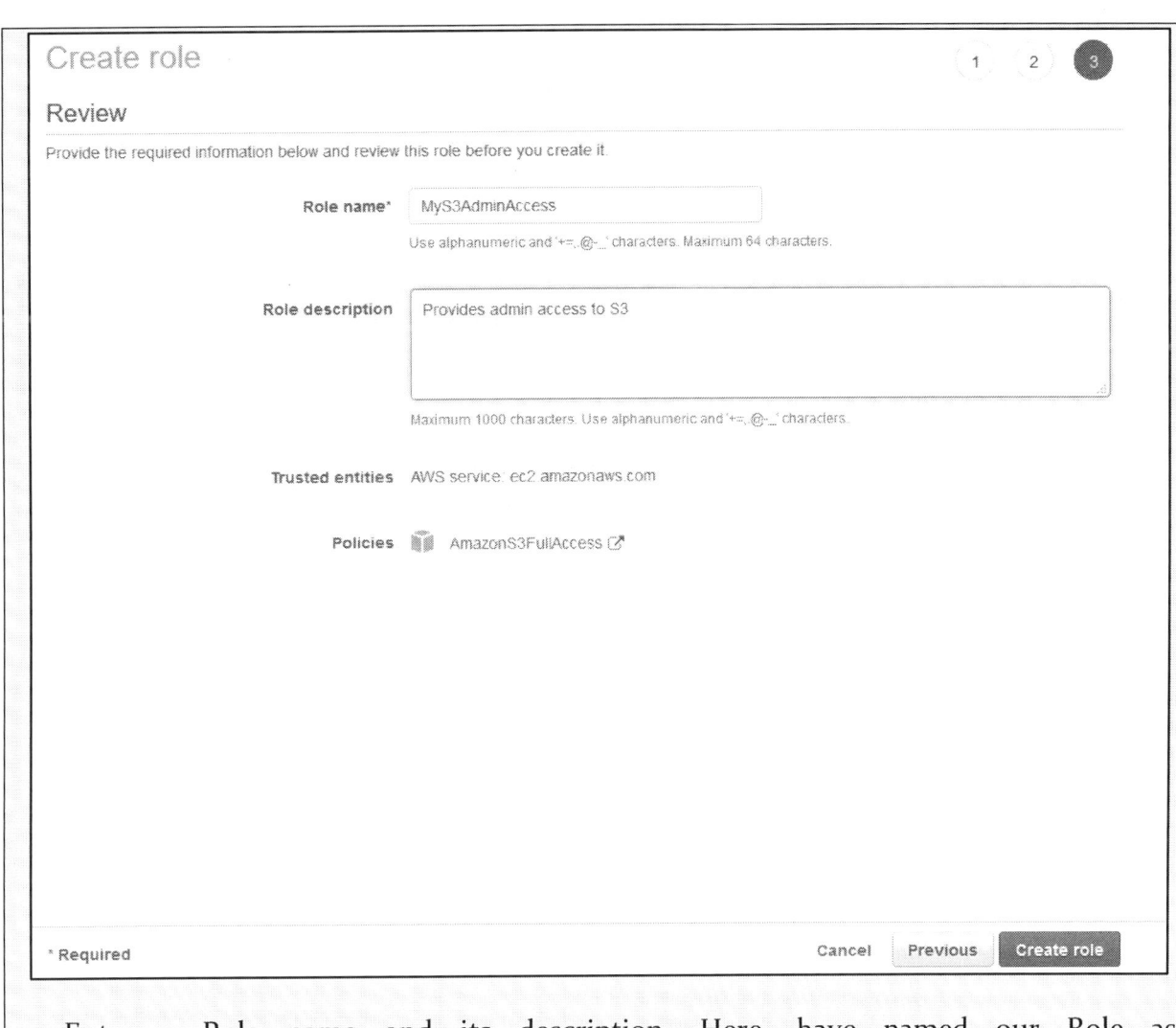

10. Enter a Role name and its description. Here, have named our Role as 'MyS3AdminAccess'. Click 'Create role'.

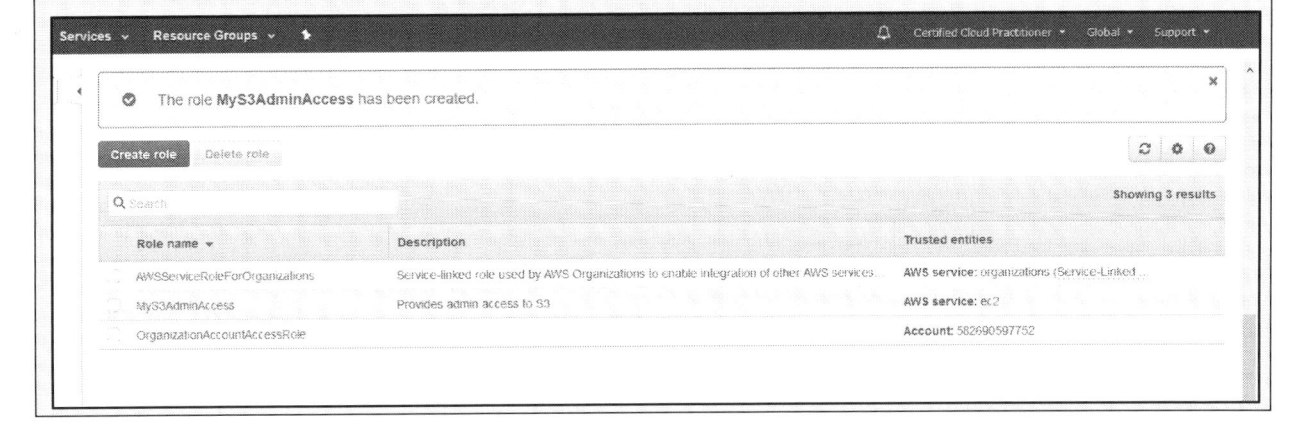

The role **MyS3AdminAccess** has been created.

Role name	Description	Trusted entities
AWSServiceRoleForOrganizations	Service-linked role used by AWS Organizations to enable integration of other AWS services...	AWS service: organizations (Service-Linked...
MyS3AdminAccess	Provides admin access to S3	AWS service: ec2
OrganizationAccountAccessRole		Account: 582690597752

Chapter 3: Technology

11. The Role 'MyS3AdminAccess' has been created. We now need to attach this role to our EC2 instance. So, click on 'Services' and select 'EC2'.

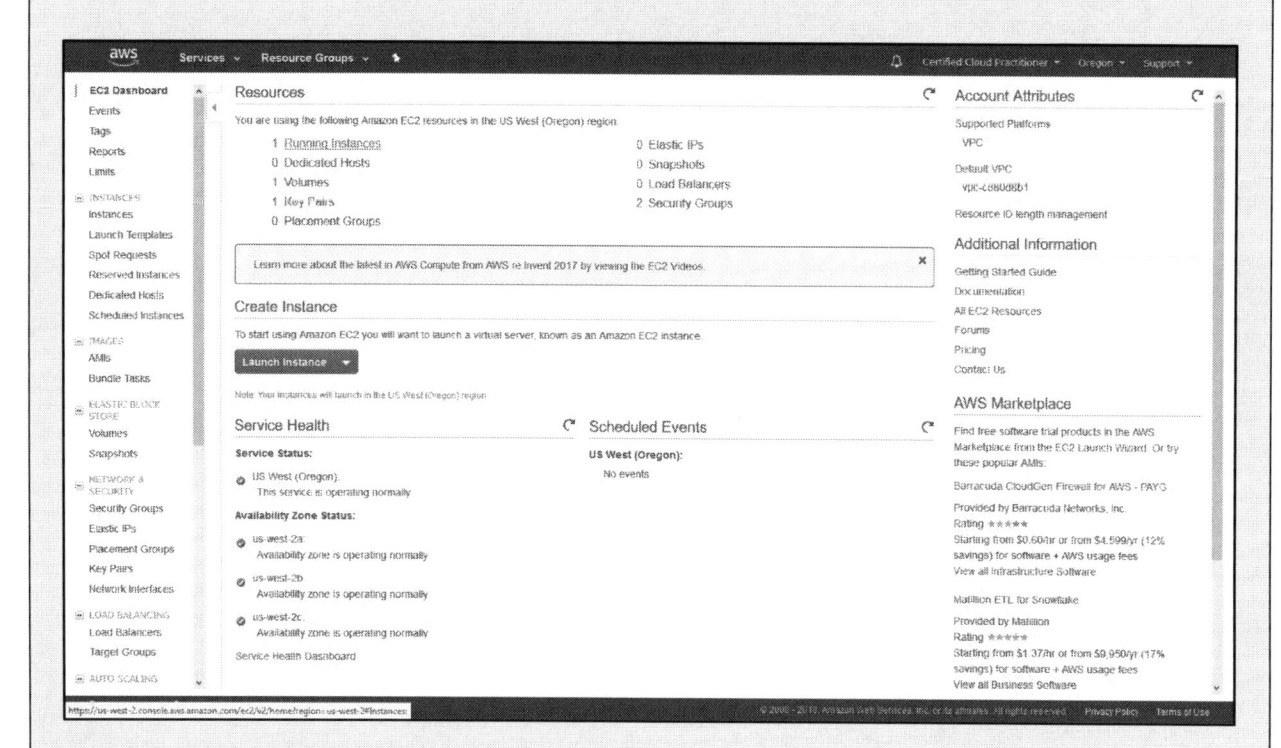

12. Click on 'Running Instances'.

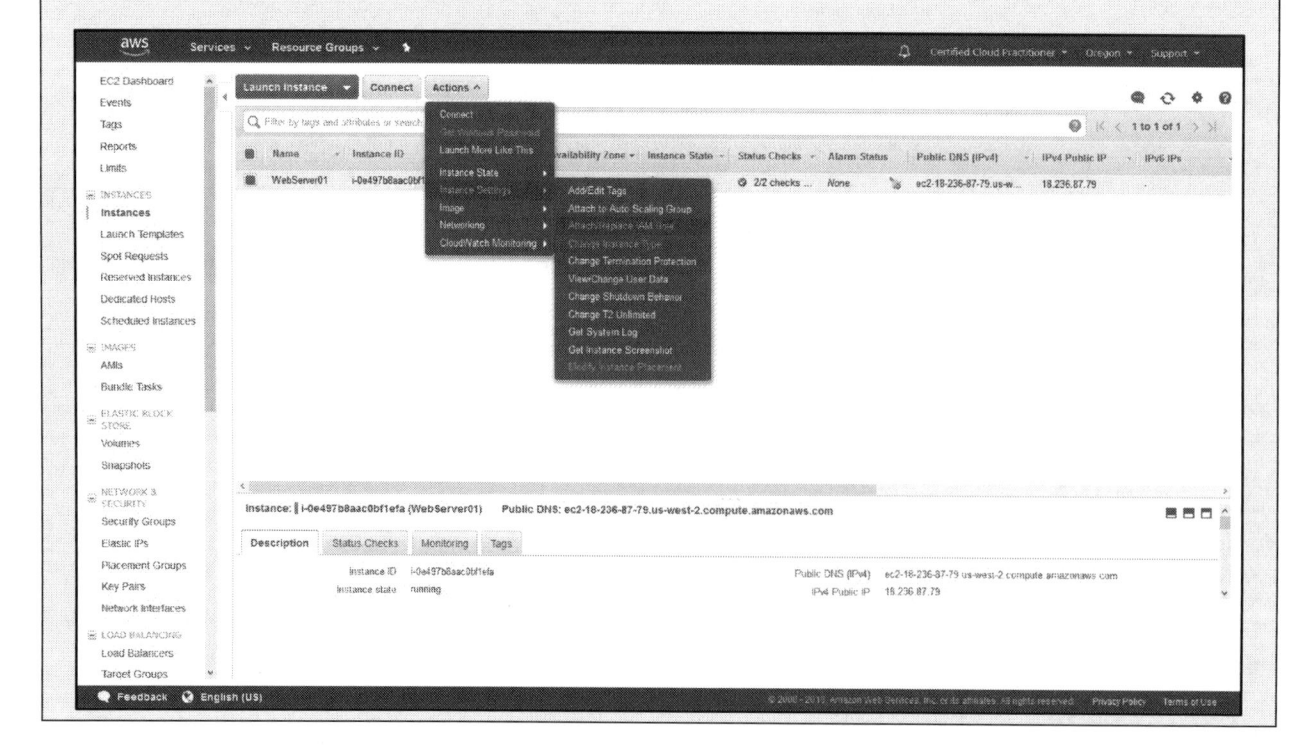

Chapter 3: Technology

13. Select your EC2 instance and click on 'Actions' to open up a drop-down menu. Navigate to 'Instance Settings' and select 'Attach/Replace IAM Role'.

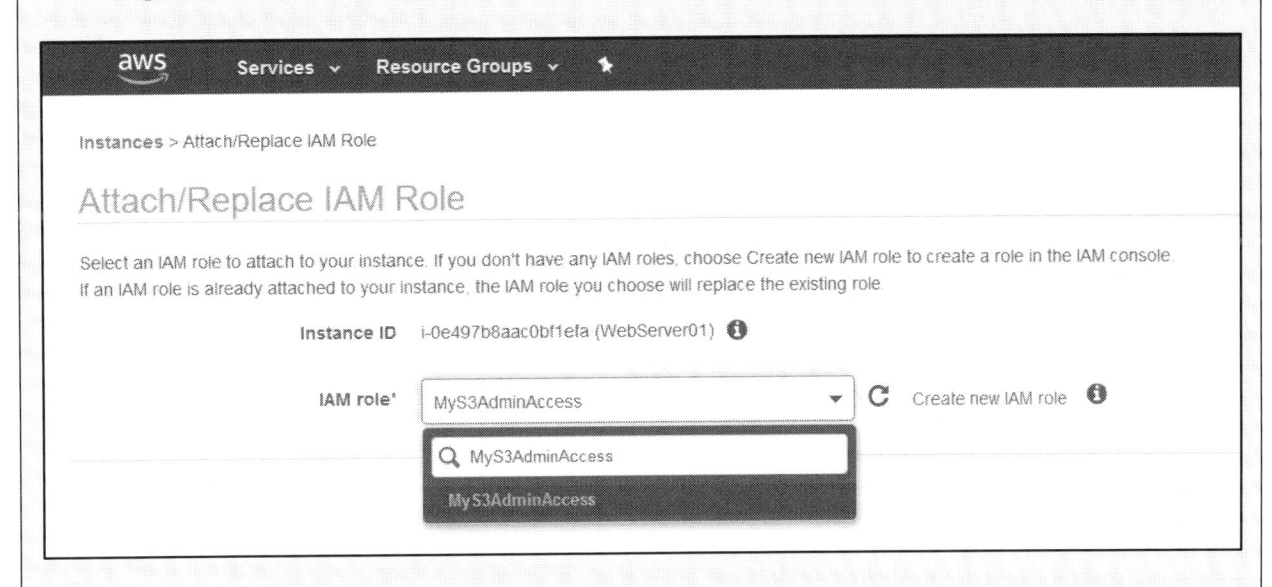

14. Select the IAM Role you just created from the drop-down list and click 'Apply'.

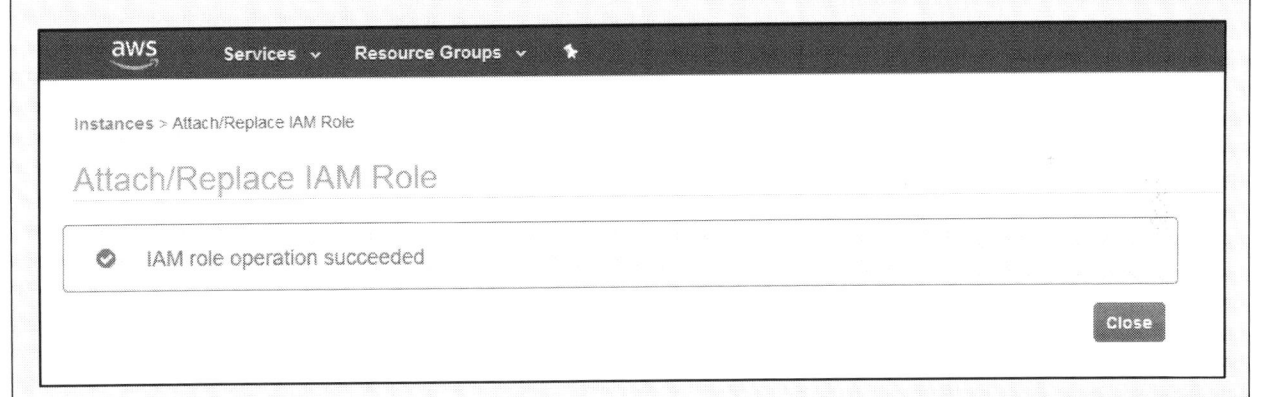

15. Click 'close' and open up your terminal for Mac and PuTTY for windows again where you left off.

Chapter 3: Technology

```
[root@ip-172-31-23-114 ec2-user]# cd ~/.aws
[root@ip-172-31-23-114 .aws]# ls
config  credentials
[root@ip-172-31-23-114 .aws]# nano credentials
[root@ip-172-31-23-114 .aws]# rm -rf credentials
[root@ip-172-31-23-114 .aws]# ls
config
[root@ip-172-31-23-114 .aws]# aws s3 ls
Unable to locate credentials. You can configure credentials by running "aws configure"
[root@ip-172-31-23-114 .aws]# aws s3 ls
2018-04-20 07:41:18 ccp.bucket
2018-04-24 11:50:07 ccp.commandline.bucket
2018-04-23 17:00:45 ccp.ipspecialist
[root@ip-172-31-23-114 .aws]# ls
config
[root@ip-172-31-23-114 .aws]#
```

16. Now if you run the same command 'aws s3 ls' to list objects of S3, you will be able to see the buckets. Also here, running the command 'ls' does not show the credential files. Hence, your EC2 instance can communicate with S3 in a much more secured way using Roles.

EXAM TIPS:

- Roles are much more secured than using Access Key IDs and Secret Access Keys and are easier to manage.
- You can apply roles to EC2 instances at any time; the change takes place immediately whenever applied.
- Roles are universal. You do not need to specify Region for it, similar to Users.

Lab 3-9: Building a Web Server

1. Log in to the 'AWS Console'.
2. Click on 'Services'.
3. Select 'EC2' from Compute.
4. Click on 'Running Instances'.

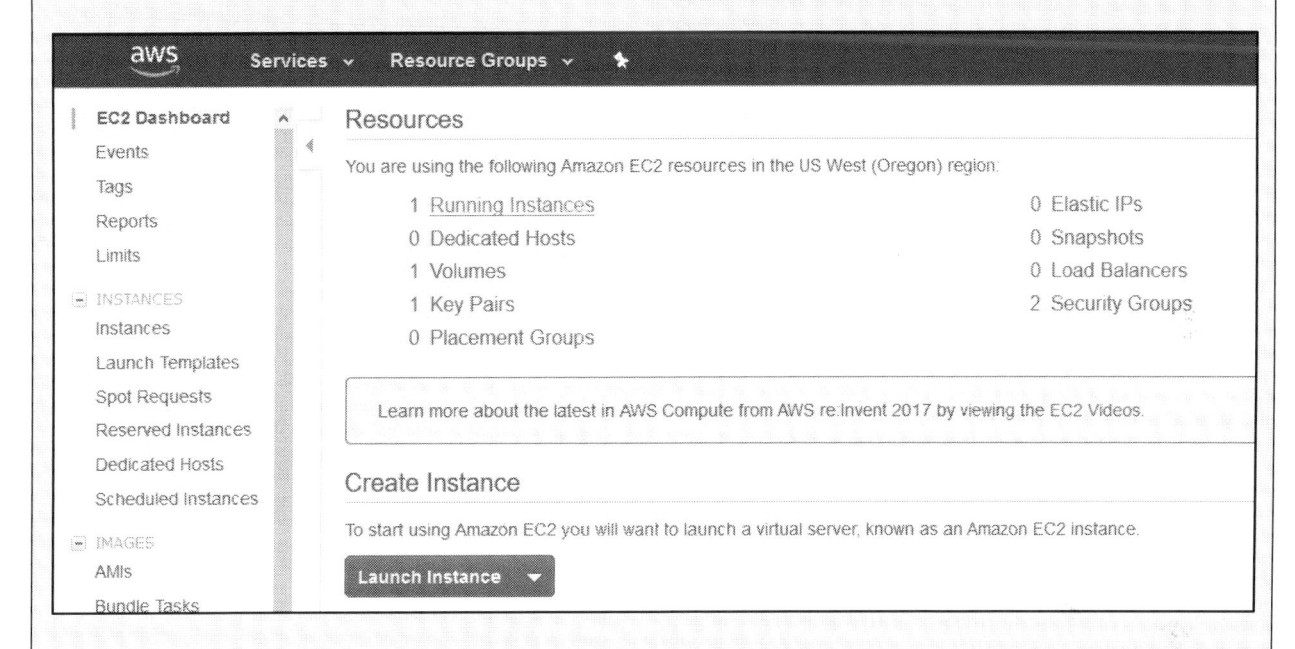

5. Copy the public IP address of the EC2 instance to log in through the AWS command line. Open up Terminal for Mac or PuTTY for Windows.

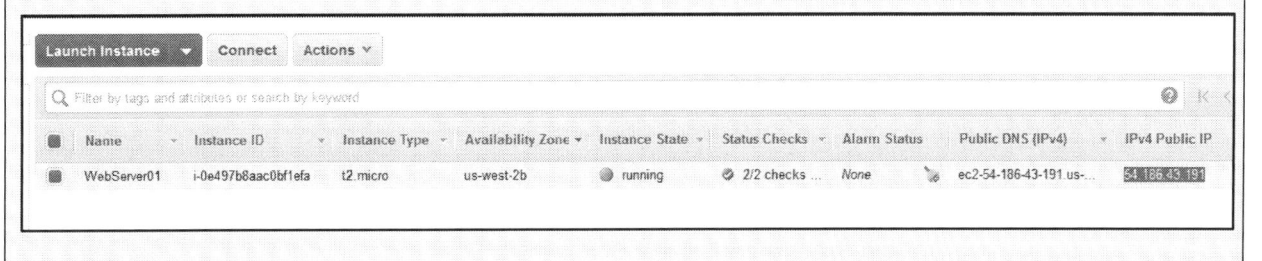

6. Type in 'sudosu' to get super-user access and clear the screen.

Chapter 3: Technology

```
login as: ec2-user
Authenticating with public key "imported-openssh-key"
Last login: Tue Apr 24 12:08:16 2018 from 110.37.216.158

       __|  __|_  )
       _|  (     /   Amazon Linux AMI
      ___|\___|___|

https://aws.amazon.com/amazon-linux-ami/2018.03-release-notes/
1 package(s) needed for security, out of 4 available
Run "sudo yum update" to apply all updates.
[ec2-user@ip-172-31-23-114 ~]$ sudo su
[root@ip-172-31-23-114 ec2-user]# clear
```

7. All webservers need Apache or IIS to make them a webserver. Apache is for Linux and IIS (Internet Information Service) is the Windows version of a webserver. 'httpd', here you can install Apache.

```
[root@ip-172-31-23-114 ec2-user]# yum install httpd -y
```

8. Once Apache is installed, you need to start the Apache server.

```
  Installing  : httpd-tools-2.2.34-1.16.amzn1.x86_64           3/5
  Installing  : apr-util-ldap-1.5.4-6.18.amzn1.x86_64          4/5
  Installing  : httpd-2.2.34-1.16.amzn1.x86_64                 5/5
  Verifying   : httpd-tools-2.2.34-1.16.amzn1.x86_64           1/5
  Verifying   : apr-util-1.5.4-6.18.amzn1.x86_64               2/5
  Verifying   : httpd-2.2.34-1.16.amzn1.x86_64                 3/5
  Verifying   : apr-1.5.2-5.13.amzn1.x86_64                    4/5
  Verifying   : apr-util-ldap-1.5.4-6.18.amzn1.x86_64          5/5

Installed:
  httpd.x86_64 0:2.2.34-1.16.amzn1

Dependency Installed:
  apr.x86_64 0:1.5.2-5.13.amzn1
  apr-util.x86_64 0:1.5.4-6.18.amzn1
  apr-util-ldap.x86_64 0:1.5.4-6.18.amzn1
  httpd-tools.x86_64 0:2.2.34-1.16.amzn1

Complete!
[root@ip-172-31-23-114 ec2-user]#
```

Chapter 3: Technology

9. Type in 'service httpd start', this will start the Apache server. Once again, clear the screen.

```
[root@ip-172-31-23-114 ec2-user]# service httpd start
Starting httpd:                                           [  OK  ]
[root@ip-172-31-23-114 ec2-user]#
```

10. Command 'cd' is used to change the directory. Type in the landing page path, which is '/var/www/html'. You can see that it is currently empty by running the 'ls' command. Now, put up a sample text file 'welcome.txt' in it using the 'echo' command. Once done, you can open it up in 'nano' editor to view the file.

```
[root@ip-172-31-23-114 ec2-user]# cd /var/www/html
[root@ip-172-31-23-114 html]# ls
[root@ip-172-31-23-114 html]# echo "Hello Cloud Practitioner" > welcome.txt
[root@ip-172-31-23-114 html]# ls
welcome.txt
[root@ip-172-31-23-114 html]# nano welcome.txt
```

11. Press Ctrl+X to exit the editor and open up your browser to browse your landing page using the EC2 instance public IP address followed by the file name 'welcome.txt'.

Chapter 3: Technology

12. You now know that your webserver is working. Deploy the same 'index.html' and 'error.html' codes here that you previously used during static website hosting using S3 buckets.

Chapter 3: Technology

13. This is the S3 bucket 'ccp.ipspecialist' that contains the previously used code that you used in static website hosting. It contains your code files 'index.html' and 'error.html.' Now copy these files to the landing page directory.

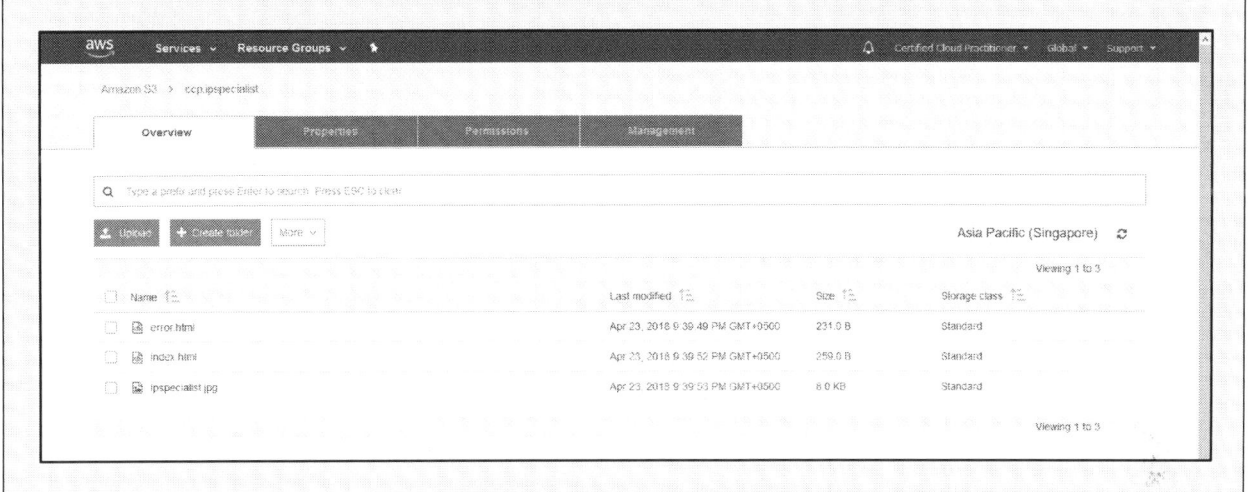

14. Use to 'cp' command to copy contents from 'ccp.ipspecialist' bucket to the landing page directory '**/var/www/html**'.

15. If your instance reboots, the Apache server will not start automatically. To do this, run the command '**chkconfighttpd on**'.

Chapter 3: Technology

```
[root@ip-172-31-23-114 html]# aws s3 ls
2018-04-20 07:41:18 ccp.bucket
2018-04-24 11:50:07 ccp.commandline.bucket
2018-04-23 17:00:45 ccp.ipspecialist
[root@ip-172-31-23-114 html]# aws s3 cp s3://ccp.ipspecialist /var/www/html --recursive
download: s3://ccp.ipspecialist/error.html to ./error.html
download: s3://ccp.ipspecialist/ipspecialist.jpg to ./ipspecialist.jpg
download: s3://ccp.ipspecialist/index.html to ./index.html
[root@ip-172-31-23-114 html]# ls
error.html  index.html  ipspecialist.jpg  welcome.txt
[root@ip-172-31-23-114 html]# chkconfig httpd on
[root@ip-172-31-23-114 html]#
```

16. Next, open up your browser and test your website.

Welcome to IpSpecialist.net

Let your career flow

17. Enter the public IP address in the browser, and you will be able to see your webpage 'index.html'.

AWS Database

AWS offers a wide range of databases that are designed purposely to cater the needs of specific application use cases. AWS fully managed database services include relational databases for transactional applications, non-relational databases for internet-scale applications and a data warehouse for analytical reporting and analysis.

> **EXAM TIP**: You will be quizzed on which services and database technologies you should use based on the scenario presented. Understand the different types of databases, their services, and typical use cases thoroughly.

Amazon Relational Database Service (Amazon RDS)

Amazon Relational Database Service (Amazon RDS) is a managed relational database service that makes it easy to set up, operate, and scale a relational database in the AWS cloud. It provides cost-efficient and resizable capacity while managing time-consuming database administration tasks.

Relational databases are more like a traditional worksheet. A typical database includes tables, rows, and fields (columns). A simple example of a table in a database is:

Employee ID	Employee Name	Department	Designation
001	John Smith	Finance	Manager
002	George Stanley	Human Resources	Senior Officer
003	Harry Walter	Human Resources	Clerk
004	David Anthony	IT	Network Engineer

Table 3-4 A Relational Database

Where Employee ID, Employee Name, Department, and Designation are fields and each row are an individual record. Relational databases are used for transactional applications like ERP, CRM, and eCommerce to log transactions and store structured data.

Amazon RDS Supported Databases

Amazon RDS offers six familiar database engines to choose from, including Amazon Aurora, MySQL, MariaDB, Oracle, Microsoft SQL Server, and PostgreSQL. Amazon RDS handles routine database tasks such as provisioning, patching, backup, recovery, failure detection, and repair. Amazon RDS can automatically back up your database and keep the database software up to date with the latest version.

Amazon RDS Key Features

Amazon RDS makes it easy to use replication to enhance database availability, improve data durability, and scale beyond the capacity constraints of a single database instance for read-heavy database workloads. Amazon RDS provides two distinct replication options to serve different purposes:

- Multi-Availability Zones
- Read Replicas

Multi-Availability Zones:

In Multi-AZ mode, Amazon RDS automatically provisions and manages a standby replica in a different Availability Zone (independent infrastructure in a physically separate location). In the event of planned database maintenance, DB instance failure, or an Availability Zone failure, Amazon RDS automatically failover to the standby replica so that database operations can resume quickly without administrative intervention.

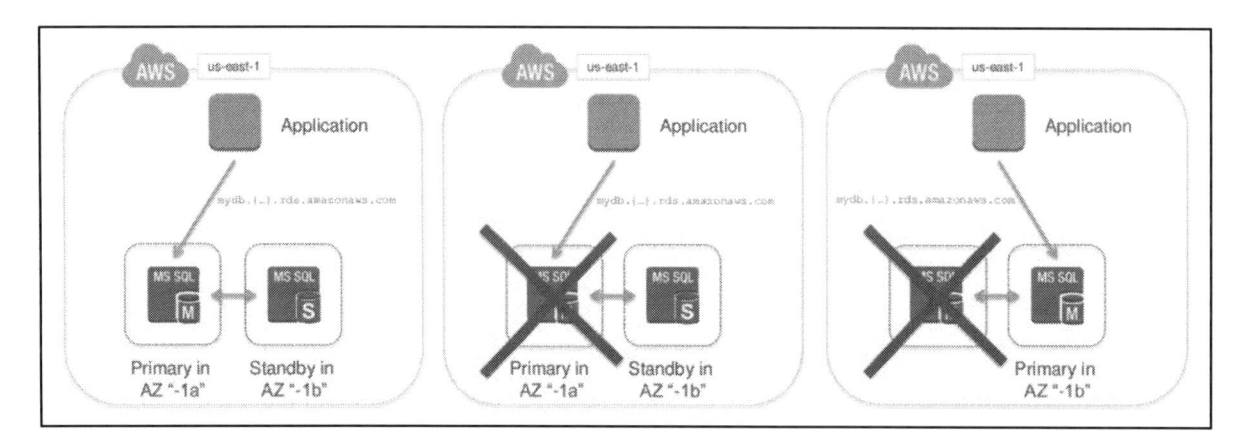

Figure 3-11. Multi-AZ Deployment

Multi-AZ deployments utilize synchronous replication, making database write concurrently on both the primary and standby so that the standby will be up-to-date in the event a failover occurs. With Multi-AZ deployments, replication is transparent, that is you do not interact directly with the standby and it cannot be used for reading operations.

Read Replicas:

Amazon RDS offers Read Replicas to scale beyond the capacity constraints of a single DB Instance for read-heavy database workloads. A Read Replica of a given source DB

Instance can be created using the AWS Management Console, the RDS API, or the AWS Command Line Interface.

Once the Read Replica is created, database updates on the source DB instance are asynchronously replicated to the Read Replica. Replication lag can vary significantly as the updates are applied to Read Replicas after they occur on the source DB Instance. This means database updates made to a standard (non-Multi-AZ) source DB instance may not be present on associated Read Replicas in the event of an unplanned outage on the source DB instance.

Multiple Read Replicas can be created for a given source DB Instance to distribute application's read traffic amongst them. Typical reasons for deploying Read Replicas are scaling beyond the capacity of a single DB instance, serving read traffic in case of unavailability of the source DB instance and running business-reporting queries.

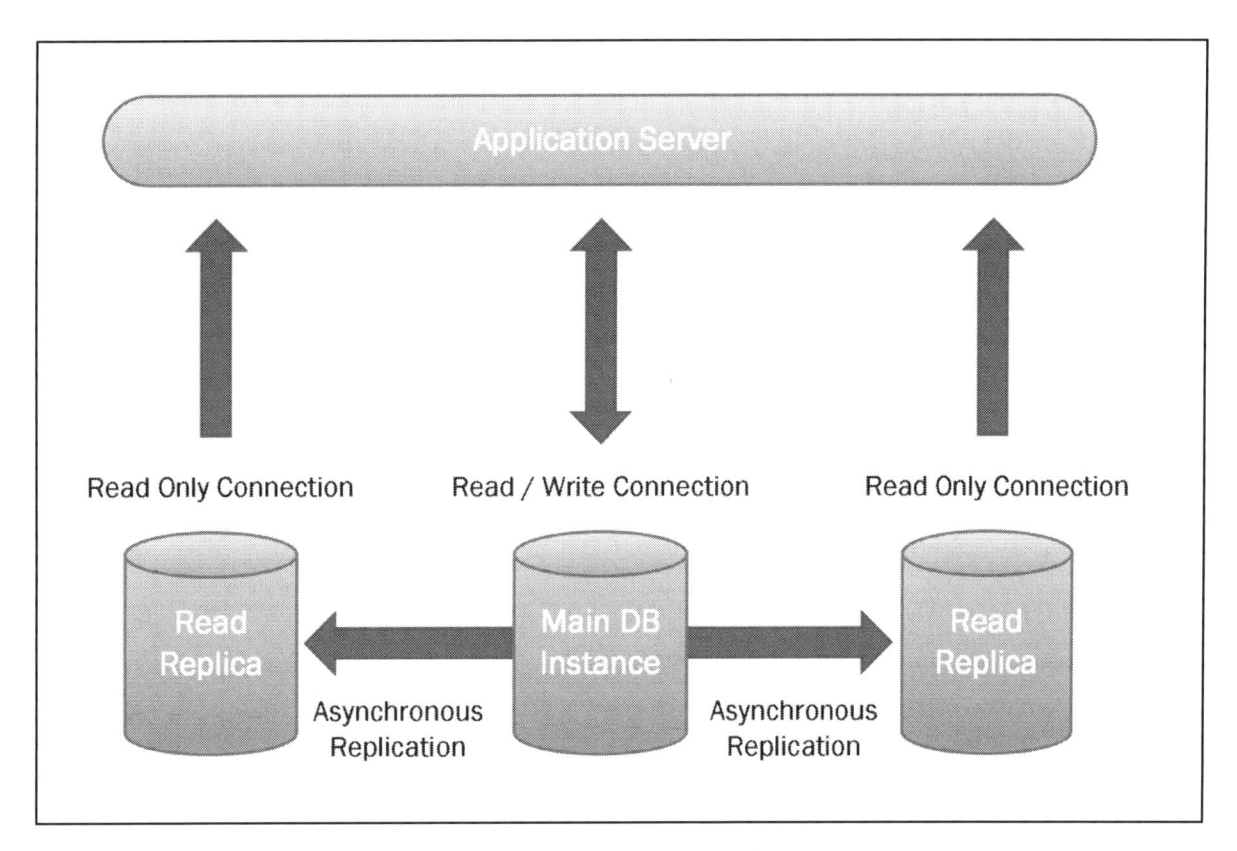

Figure 3-12. Read Replicas Deployment

Multi-AZ deployments and Read Replicas when used together in combination offer the benefits of both. By specifying a given Multi-AZ deployment as the source DB instance for the Read Replica, you get both the data durability and availability benefits of Multi-AZ deployments and the read scaling benefits of Read Replicas.

> **EXAM TIP:** RDS has two key features, Multi Availability Zones for disaster recovery and Read Replicas for performance improvement.

Amazon Aurora

Amazon Aurora is a MySQL and PostgreSQL-compatible relational database engine built for the cloud that combines the speed and availability of high-end commercial databases with the easiness and cost-effectiveness of open source databases. Amazon Aurora delivers up to five times better performance than MySQL and up to three times better performance than PostgreSQL. It provides the reliability, security, and availability of commercial-grade databases at 1/10th of the cost.

Amazon Aurora is entirely managed by Amazon Relational Database Service (RDS), which automates time-consuming administration tasks like hardware provisioning, database setup, patching, backup, recovery, failure detection, and repair. Amazon Aurora database instance can be quickly launched from the RDS Management Console. Amazon Aurora is designed to be compatible with MySQL and with PostgreSQL so that existing applications and tools can run without requiring modification.

Amazon Aurora delivers high performance and availability with auto-scaling up to 64TB per database instance. Its storage is fault-tolerant and self-healing where disk failures are repaired in the background without the loss of database availability. It is designed to detect database crashes automatically and start over without needing crash recovery or rebuilding the database cache. If the entire instance fails, Amazon Aurora automatically fails over to one of up to 15 read replicas, having a continuous backup to Amazon S3, and replication across three Availability Zones.

Amazon DynamoDB

Amazon DynamoDB is a fully managed, fast and flexible NoSQL database service for all applications that require consistent and predictable performance with seamless scalability. DynamoDB offloads the administrative burden of operating and scaling distributed databases so that the customers do not have to worry about hardware provisioning, setup, and configuration, throughput capacity planning, replication, software patching, or cluster scaling.

Chapter 3: Technology

Non-Relational databases such as NoSQL consist of collection, documents, and key-value pairs. You can change the design of the database by adding in extra fields. Example of a document within a collection can be:

```
JSON/NoSQL Code
{
  "_id" : "5834",
  "firstname" : "John",
  "surname" : "Smith",
  "age" : "23",
  "address" : [
              {"street" : "21 jump street",
               "suburb" : "Richmond",}
              ]
}
```

Figure 3-13. Example

Amazon DynamoDB supports both document and key-value store models. It's flexible data model, reliable performance, and automatic scaling of throughput capacity make it as the appropriate choice for web, mobile, gaming, IoT, ad tech, and many other applications. Internet-scale applications like socializing, hospitality, and ride sharing to serve content and store structured and unstructured data are good examples for Amazon DynamoDB.

DynamoDB Accelerator (DAX)

Amazon DynamoDB Accelerator (DAX) is a fully managed, highly available, in-memory cache that can reduce DynamoDB response times from milliseconds to microseconds, even at millions of requests per second.

DynamoDB scales automatically with your applications by turning on DynamoDB accelerator.

> EXAM TIP: Selecting the type of database: Choose Amazon RDS (specifically Amazon Aurora) if you have a relational database. Choose Amazon DynamoDB if you have a non-relational database or need automatic scaling.

Amazon Redshift

Amazon Redshift is a fast, fully managed, petabyte-scale data warehouse that is simple and cost-effective in analyzing large data sets using standard SQL and existing Business Intelligence (BI) tools. It runs complex analytic queries against petabytes of structured data by means of sophisticated query optimization, columnar storage on high-performance local disks, and massively parallel query execution. Queries are distributed and parallelized across multiple physical resources, and most results return in seconds.

Data Warehousing is used for business intelligence activities such as reporting and data analysis where huge data queries run on the database to pull in large and complex data sets. Using big data queries and business intelligence tools on your production database may take it down due to the amount and load of queries being made, hence a copy of the production database is maintained as a data warehouse where this reporting and querying operations can be performed.

Traditional data warehouses require time and resources to manage large data sets. Furthermore, dealing with the financial cost of building, maintaining, and growing self-managed, on-premise data warehouses is challenging. As the data increases, you need to compromise on what data to load into your data warehouse and what data to archive in storage to manage costs, retain low ETL complexity, and deliver good performance. Amazon Redshift greatly lowers cost and operational overhead of a data warehouse.

Amazon Redshift data warehouse can easily be scaled up or down, using the AWS Management Console or with a single API call. Amazon Redshift automatically patches and backs up your data warehouse. It uses replication and continuous backups to increase availability and enhance data durability and can automatically recover from component and node failures.

Like other Amazon Web Services, Amazon Redshift lets you pay as you go, with no up-front investments or commitments. You only pay for the resources use.

> EXAM TIP: You will use Amazon Redshift for the purposes of Business Intelligence and Data Warehousing.

AWS Networking & Content Delivery

AWS networking products offer you features and services that enable you to isolate your cloud infrastructure, scale your request handling capacity, and connect your physical network to your private virtual network. The services include content delivery network, virtual private cloud, direct connections, load balancing, and DNS.

These AWS networking products work together to fulfill your application requirements. For example, Elastic Load Balancing works with Amazon Virtual Private Cloud (VPC) to provide robust networking and security features.

Amazon Virtual Private Cloud (Amazon VPC)

Amazon VPC lets you provision a logically isolated section of the AWS cloud where you can launch AWS resources in a virtual network that you define. You have complete control over your virtual networking environment, including a selection of your own IP address ranges, the creation of subnets, and configuration of route tables and network gateways.

A Virtual Private Cloud is a cloud computing model which offers an on-demand configurable pool of shared computing resources allocated within a public cloud environment while providing a certain level of isolation from other users of the public cloud. Since the cloud (pool of resources) is only accessible to a single client in a VPC model, it, therefore, offers privacy with greater control and a secured environment where only the specified client can operate.

You can easily customize the network configuration for your Amazon VPC. For example, you can create a public-facing subnet for your web servers that have access to the Internet and place your backend systems such as databases or application servers in a private-facing subnet with no Internet access. You can leverage multiple layers of security, including security groups and network access control lists, to help control access to Amazon EC2 instances in each subnet. You can also create a hardware Virtual Private Network (VPN) connection between your corporate datacenter and your VPC and leverage the AWS cloud as an extension of your corporate datacenter.

Features & Benefits

Multiple Connectivity Options:

- Connect directly to the Internet (public subnets)
- Connect to the Internet using Network Address Translation (private subnets)
- Connect securely to your corporate datacenter
- Connect privately to other VPCs
- Privately connect to AWS Services without using an Internet gateway, NAT or firewall proxy through a VPC Endpoint
- Privately connect to SaaS solutions supported by AWS PrivateLink

- Privately connect your internal services across different accounts and VPCs within your own organizations

Secure:

- Advanced security features such as security groups and network access control lists, to enable inbound and outbound filtering at the instance level and subnet level
- Store data in Amazon S3 and restrict access so that it's only accessible from instances in your VPC
- For additional isolation launch dedicated instances which run on hardware dedicated to a single customer

Simple:

- Setup VPC quickly and easily using the AWS Management Console
- Easily select common network setups that best match your needs
- Subnets, IP ranges, route tables, and security groups are automatically created using VPC Wizard

Scalability & Reliability:

- Amazon VPC provides all of the benefits of the AWS platform

Amazon VPC Functionality

With Amazon Virtual Private Cloud (Amazon VPC), you can:

- Create an Amazon VPC on AWS's scalable infrastructure and specify its private IP address range from any range you choose.
- Expand your VPC by adding secondary IP ranges.
- Divide your VPC's private IP address range into one or more public or private subnets to facilitate running applications and services in your VPC.
- Assign multiple IP addresses and attach multiple elastic network interfaces to instances in your VPC.
- Attach one or more Amazon Elastic IP addresses to any instance in your VPC so it can be reached directly from the Internet.
- Bridge your VPC and your onsite IT infrastructure with an encrypted VPN connection, extending your existing security and management policies to your VPC instances as if they were running within your infrastructure.

- Enable EC2 instances in the EC2-Classic platform to communicate with instances in a VPC using private IP addresses.
- Associate VPC Security Groups with instances on EC2-Classic.
- Use VPC Flow Logs to log information about network traffic going in and out of network interfaces in your VPC.
- Enable both IPv4 and IPv6 in your VPC.

Components of Amazon VPC

- *A Virtual Private Cloud:* A logically isolated virtual network in the AWS cloud. You define a VPC's IP address space from ranges you select.
- *Subnet:* A segment of a VPC's IP address range where you can place groups of isolated resources.
- *Internet Gateway:* The Amazon VPC side of a connection to the public Internet.
- *NAT Gateway:* A highly available, managed Network Address Translation (NAT) service for your resources in a private subnet to access the Internet.
- *Hardware VPN Connection:* A hardware-based VPN connection between your Amazon VPC and your data center, home network, or co-location facility.
- *Virtual Private Gateway:* The Amazon VPC side of a VPN connection.
- *Customer Gateway:* Your side of a VPN connection.
- *Router:* Routers interconnect subnets and direct traffic between Internet gateways, virtual private gateways, NAT gateways, and subnets.
- *Peering Connection:* A peering connection enables you to route traffic via private IP addresses between two peered VPCs.
- *VPC Endpoints:* Enables private connectivity to services hosted in AWS, from within your VPC without using an Internet Gateway, VPN, Network Address Translation (NAT) devices, or firewall proxies.
- *Egress-only Internet Gateway:* A stateful gateway to provide egress only access for IPv6 traffic from the VPC to the Internet.

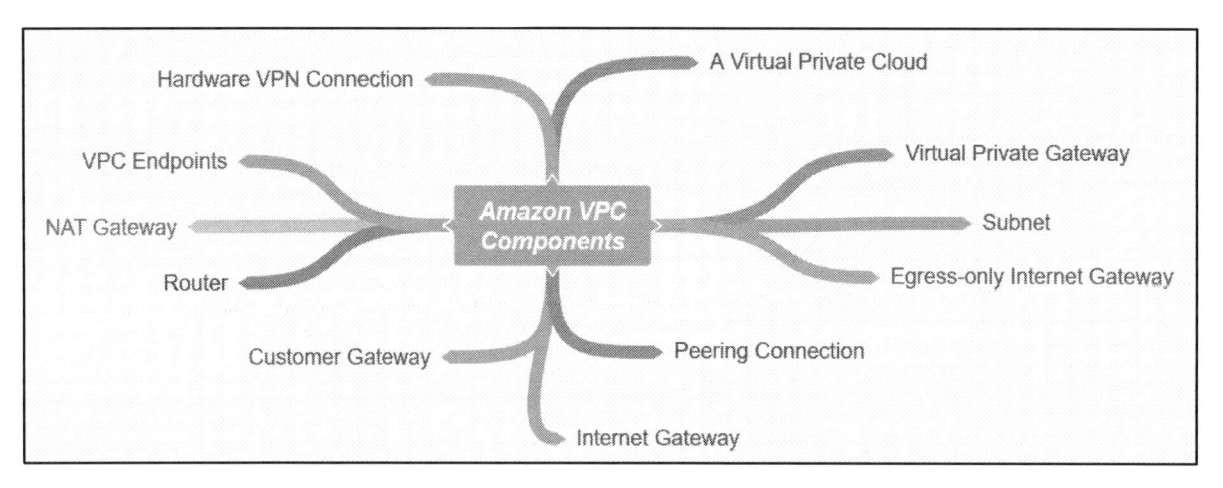

Figure 3-14. Mind Map of Amazon VPC Components

> **EXAM TIP**: Use Amazon VPC to isolate cloud resources in a private virtual network.

Amazon CloudFront

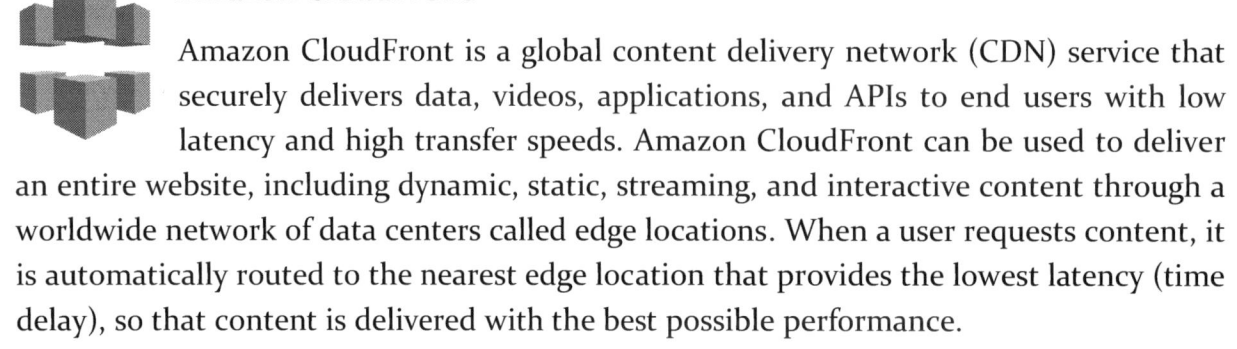

Amazon CloudFront is a global content delivery network (CDN) service that securely delivers data, videos, applications, and APIs to end users with low latency and high transfer speeds. Amazon CloudFront can be used to deliver an entire website, including dynamic, static, streaming, and interactive content through a worldwide network of data centers called edge locations. When a user requests content, it is automatically routed to the nearest edge location that provides the lowest latency (time delay), so that content is delivered with the best possible performance.

- If the content is already in the edge location with the lowest latency, CloudFront delivers it immediately.

- If the content is not currently in that edge location, CloudFront retrieves it from an Amazon S3 bucket or an HTTP server (for example, a web server) that you have identified as the source for the definitive version of your content.

A content delivery network (CDN) is a system of distributed servers (network) that deliver webpages and other web content to end users based on the geographic locations of the user, the origin of the webpage, and a content delivery server using edge locations.

Chapter 3: Technology

- Origin: Source of the files that the CDN will distribute. This can be an S3 bucket, an EC2 instance, an Elastic load balancer, or Route53.

- Distribution: Name given to the CDN, consisting of a collection of edge locations.

Amazon CloudFront has several regional edge cache locations globally, at close proximity to the end users. These regional edge caches are located between the origin web server and the global edge locations that serve content directly to the end users. As objects become less popular, individual edge locations remove those objects to make room for more popular content. Regional Edge Caches have a larger cache width than any individual edge location, so objects remain in the cache longer at the nearest regional edge caches. This helps keep more of your content closer to your viewers, reducing the needs for CloudFront to go back to your origin webserver and improving overall performance for viewers. For example, CloudFront edge locations in Europe now go to the regional edge cache in Frankfurt to fetch an object before going back to your origin webserver.

> **EXAM TIP**: Amazon CloudFront is a way of caching very big objects, image files, video files, etc. in the cloud.

How CloudFront Delivers Content?

1. A user accesses your website or application and requests one or more objects, such as an image file and an HTML file.

2. DNS routes the request to the CloudFront edge location that can best serve the request, typically the nearest CloudFront edge location in terms of latency.

3. In the edge location, CloudFront checks its cache for the requested files. If the files are in the cache, CloudFront returns them to the user. If the files are not in the cache, it does the following:

    a. CloudFront compares the request with the specifications in your distribution and forwards the request to the applicable origin server for the corresponding file type. For example, to your Amazon S3 bucket for image files and to your HTTP server for the HTML files.

    b. The origin servers send the files back to the CloudFront edge location.

    c. As soon as the first byte arrives from the origin, CloudFront begins to forward the files to the user. CloudFront also adds the files to the cache in the edge location for the next time someone requests those files.

Chapter 3: Technology

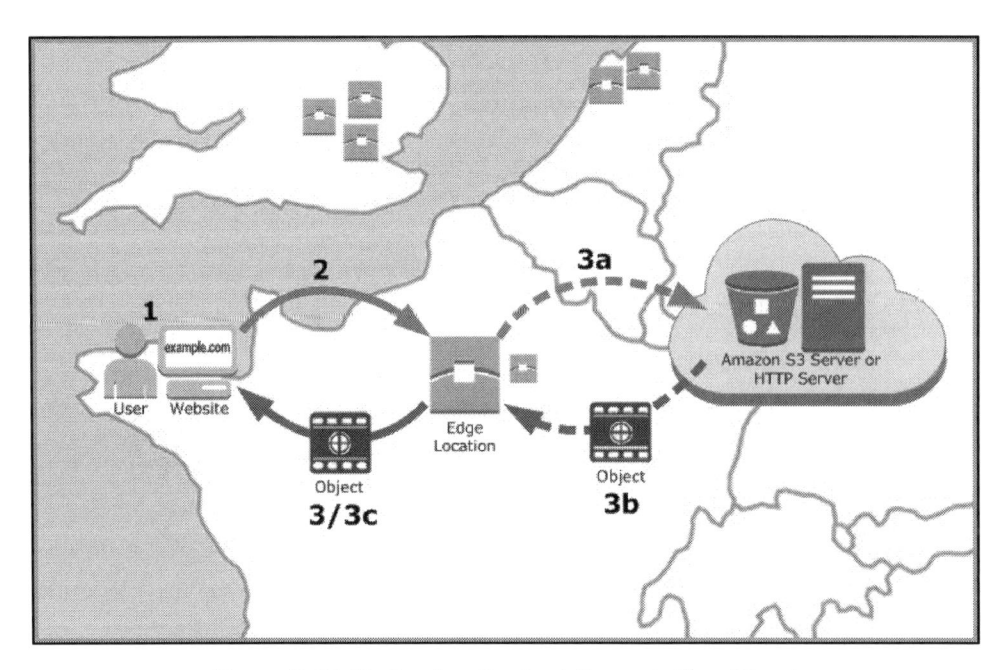

Figure 3-15. Delivering Content through CloudFront

Chapter 3: Technology

Amazon CloudFront Benefits:

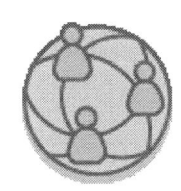

- Global, Growing Content Delivery Network

The Amazon CloudFront content delivery network is built on the expanding global AWS infrastructure that currently includes 54 Availability Zones within 18 geographic regions.

- Secure Content at the Edge

Amazon CloudFront provides both network and application level protection. It is seamlessly integrated with AWS WAF and AWS Shield Advanced to protect your applications from sophisticated threats and DDoS attacks with automatic protections of AWS Shield Standard, at no additional cost.

- Programmable CDN

All Amazon CloudFront features can be programmatically configured by using APIs or the AWS Management Console. With Lambda@Edge you can easily run your code across AWS locations worldwide, allowing you to respond to your end users with the lowest latency.

- High Performance

CloudFront is directly connected with hundreds of end-user ISPs and uses the AWS backbone network to accelerate the delivery of your content end-to-end. CloudFront also offers regional edge cache locations as part of the standard offering, to ensure consistently high cache hit ratios across the globe.

- Cost Effective

Like other AWS products, there are no long-term contracts or minimum monthly usage commitments for using Amazon CloudFront. You pay only for as much or as little content as you

Chapter 3: Technology

actually deliver through the content delivery service.

- Deep Integration with Key AWS Services

    Amazon CloudFront is optimized to work with other services in AWS, such as Amazon S3, Amazon EC2, Elastic Load Balancing, and Amazon Route 53. Amazon CloudFront also works seamlessly with any non-AWS origin server that stores the original, definitive versions of your files.

Lab 3-10: Create CloudFront Distribution for Large Files

1. Log in to the 'AWS Console'.
2. Click on 'Services'.
3. Select 'S3' from Storage.

4. We will now upload a large image file to our bucket. Select the bucket 'ccp.bucket' to upload your image file.

Chapter 3: Technology

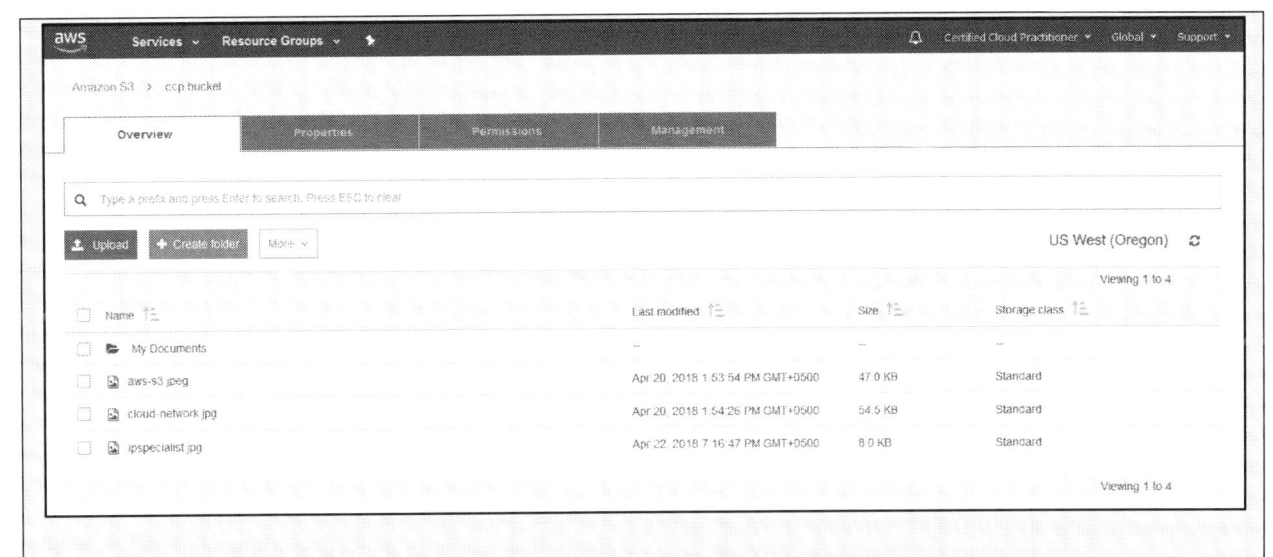

5. Click on 'Upload'.

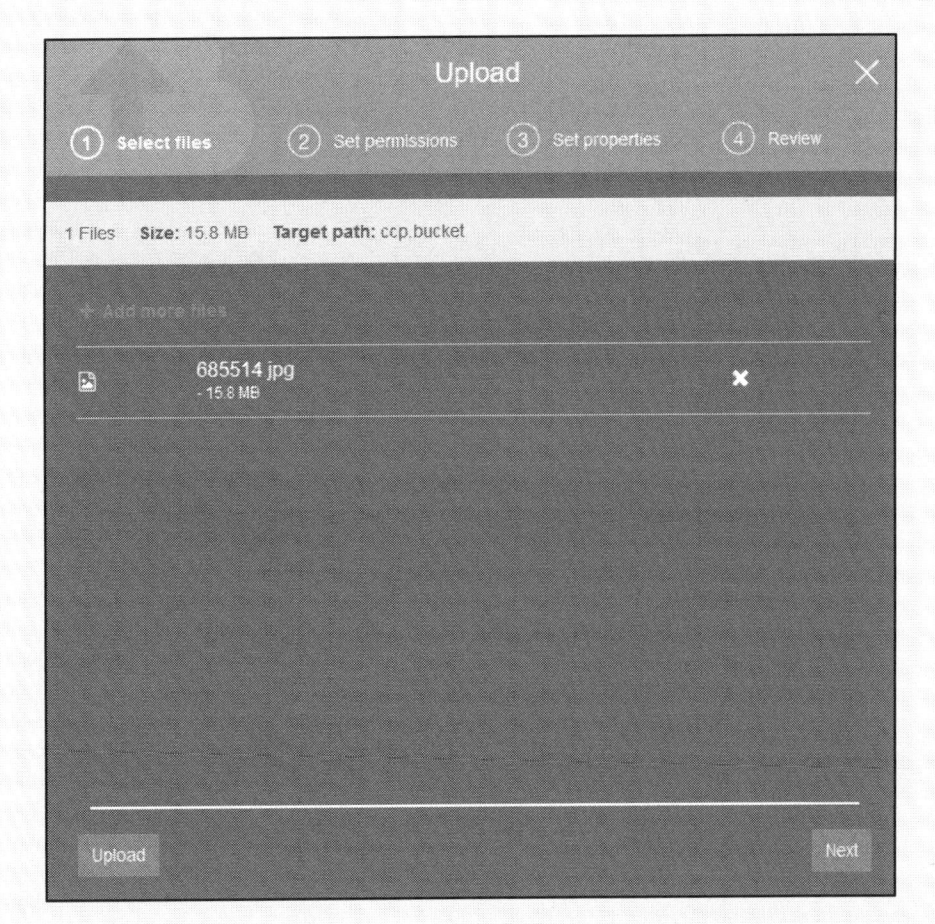

6. Add a large file and click 'Upload.' It will take some time to upload depending on the region and size of the file.

Chapter 3: Technology

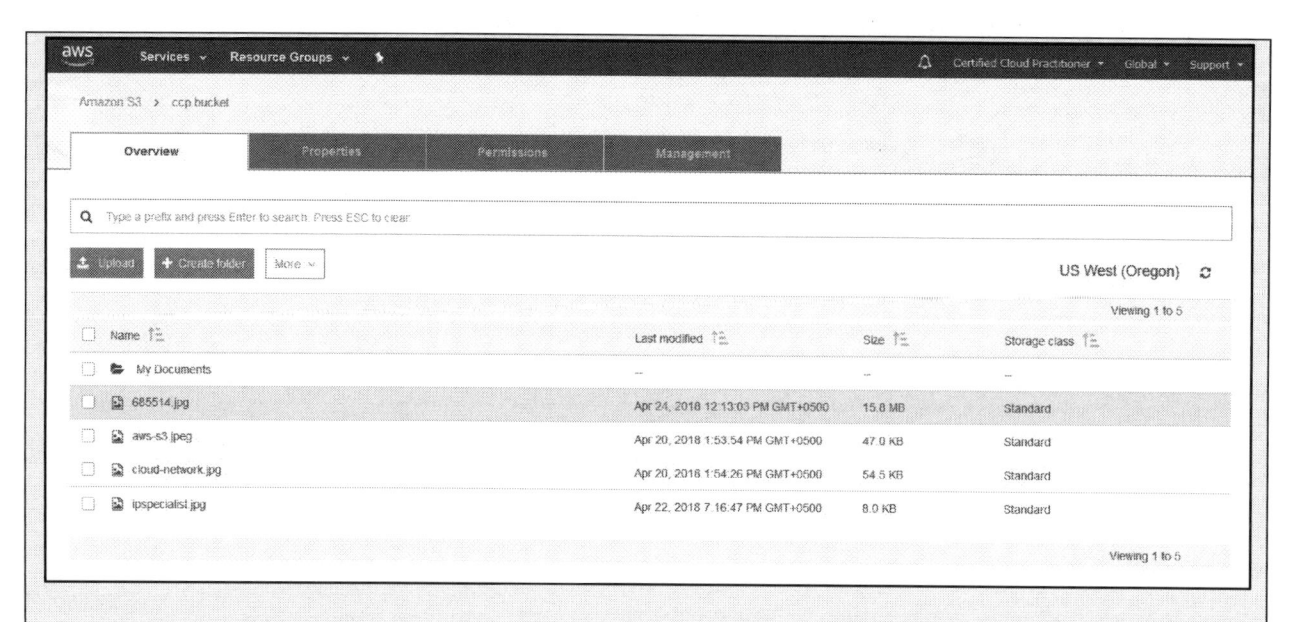

[Screenshot of AWS S3 console showing ccp.bucket with files: My Documents, 685514.jpg (15.8 MB, Standard), aws-s3.jpeg (47.0 KB, Standard), cloud-network.jpg (54.5 KB, Standard), ipspecialist.jpg (8.0 KB, Standard).]

7. Once the file '685514.jpg' is uploaded, you need to make it public so that it can be accessible.

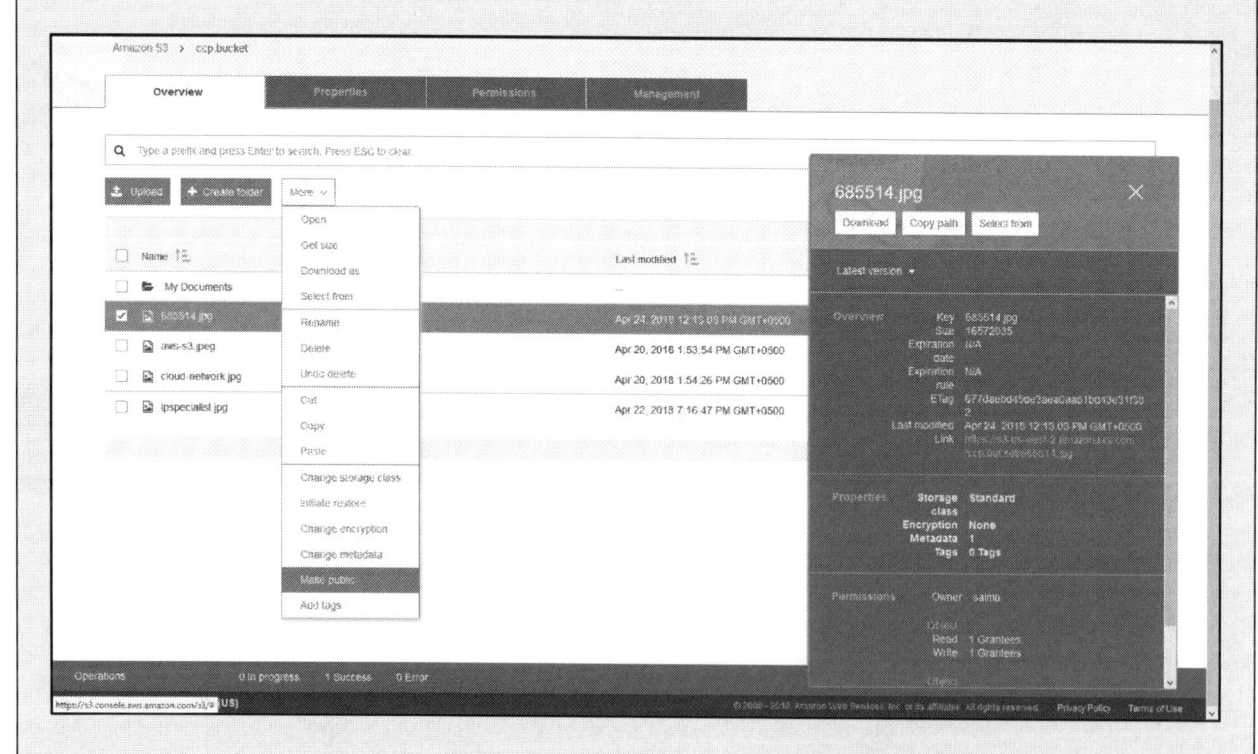

[Screenshot of AWS S3 console showing the 'More' dropdown menu with options including Open, Get size, Download as, Select from, Rename, Delete, Undo delete, Cut, Copy, Paste, Change storage class, Initiate restore, Change encryption, Change metadata, Make public, Add tags. A side panel shows details for 685514.jpg.]

8. Select the image file, click 'More' and then select 'Make public'.
9. Once done, go back to the main AWS console and select 'Services'.
10. Scroll down to Network & Content Delivery and select 'CloudFront'.

196

Chapter 3: Technology

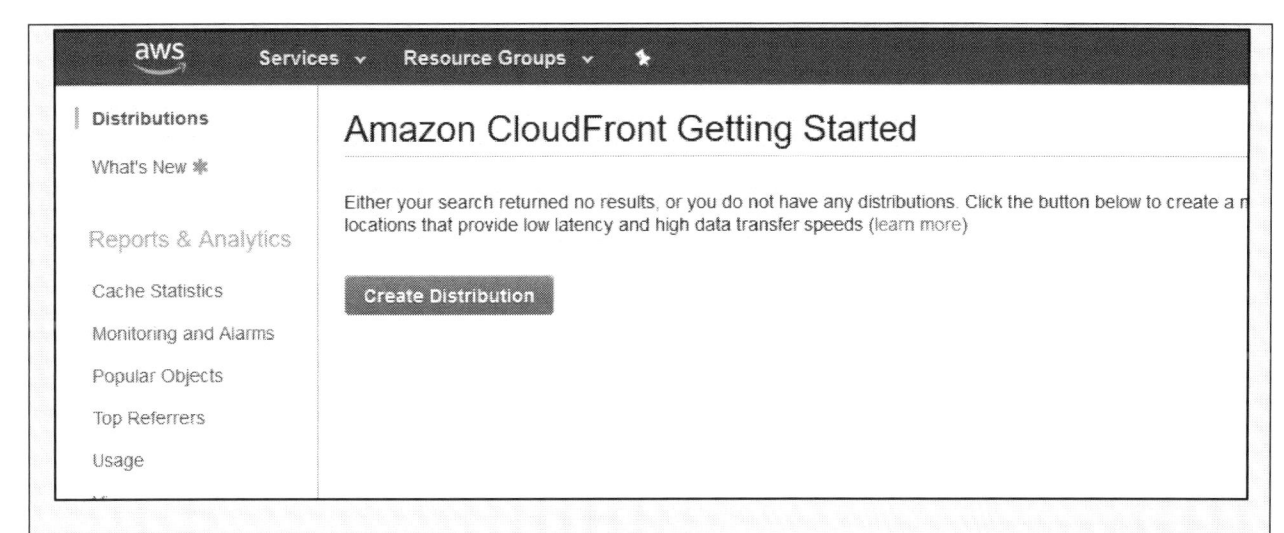

> **Amazon CloudFront Getting Started**
>
> Distributions / What's New / Reports & Analytics / Cache Statistics / Monitoring and Alarms / Popular Objects / Top Referrers / Usage
>
> Either your search returned no results, or you do not have any distributions. Click the button below to create a [new distribution]. Locations that provide low latency and high data transfer speeds (learn more)
>
> **Create Distribution**

11. Click 'Create Distribution'.

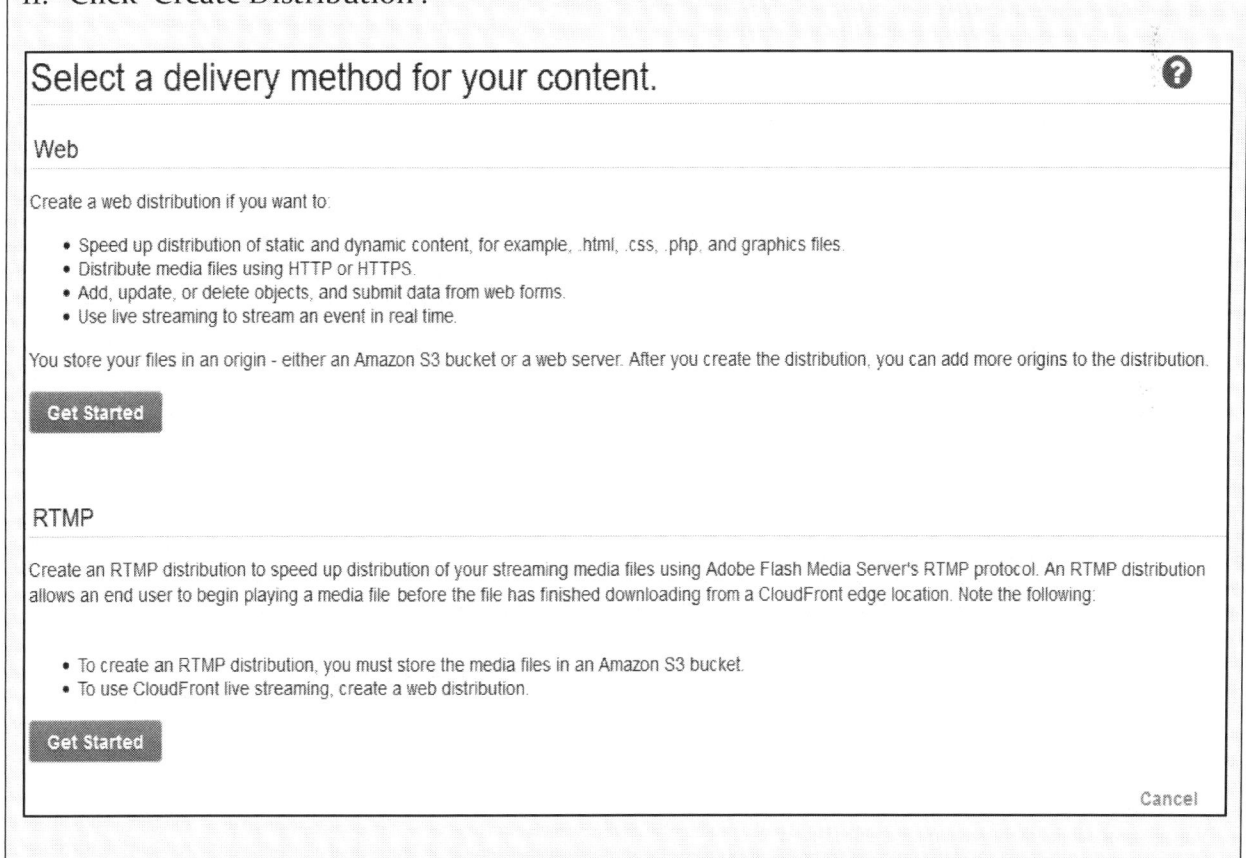

> **Select a delivery method for your content.**
>
> **Web**
>
> Create a web distribution if you want to:
> - Speed up distribution of static and dynamic content, for example, .html, .css, .php, and graphics files.
> - Distribute media files using HTTP or HTTPS.
> - Add, update, or delete objects, and submit data from web forms.
> - Use live streaming to stream an event in real time.
>
> You store your files in an origin - either an Amazon S3 bucket or a web server. After you create the distribution, you can add more origins to the distribution.
>
> **Get Started**
>
> **RTMP**
>
> Create an RTMP distribution to speed up distribution of your streaming media files using Adobe Flash Media Server's RTMP protocol. An RTMP distribution allows an end user to begin playing a media file before the file has finished downloading from a CloudFront edge location. Note the following:
>
> - To create an RTMP distribution, you must store the media files in an Amazon S3 bucket.
> - To use CloudFront live streaming, create a web distribution.
>
> **Get Started**
>
> Cancel

12. You will be given two options, Web distribution, and RTMP distribution. Here you want to distribute an image file, therefore you will use Web distribution. Select 'Get Started'.

Chapter 3: Technology

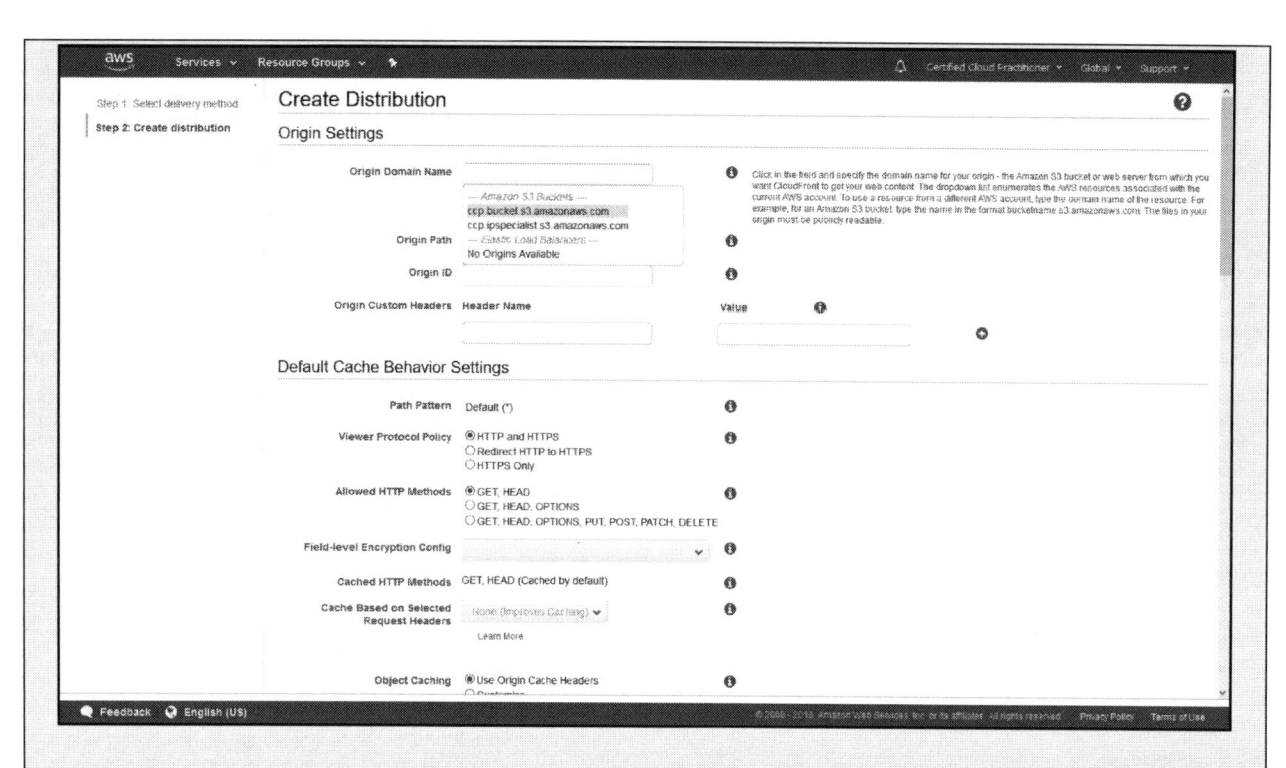

13. First, you need to select the Origin Domain Name. The origin of your image file is the S3 bucket 'ccp.bucket'.

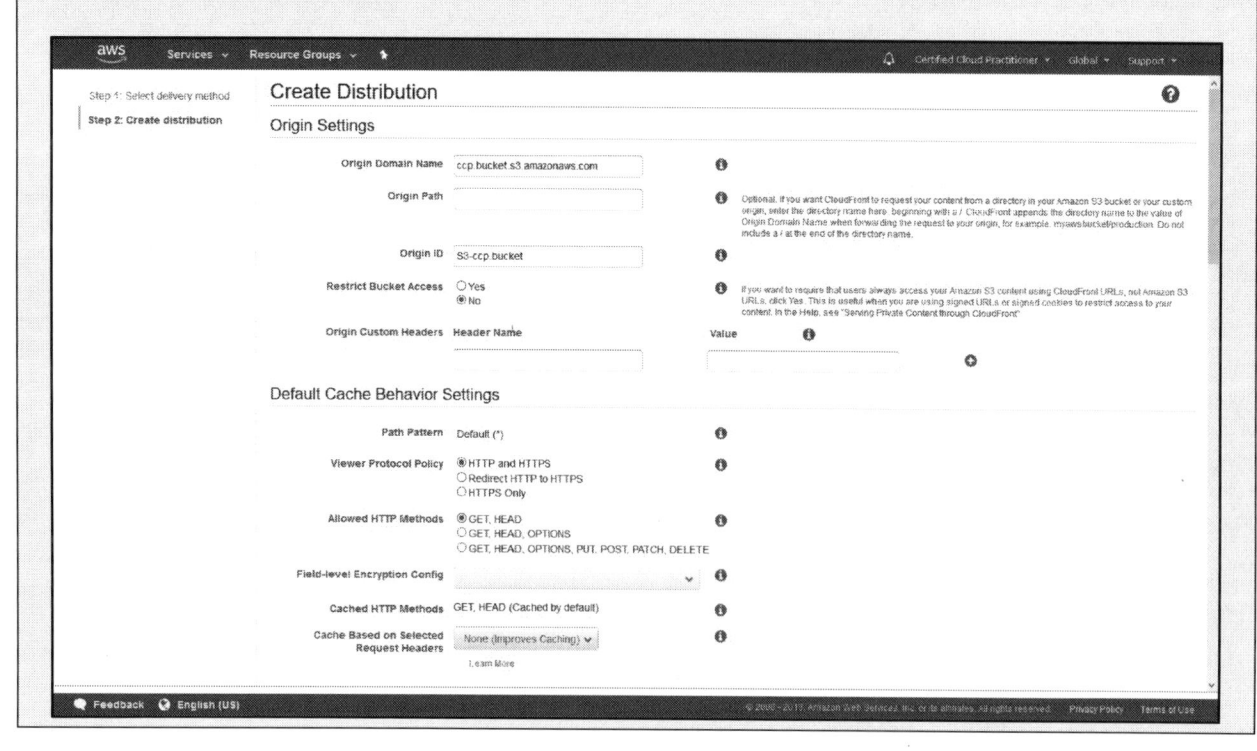

Chapter 3: Technology

14. If you have sub-directories or folders in your bucket, you can define the path of your file in the Origin Path field.
15. You can also restrict access to the content using Amazon S3 URL and only allow access to CloudFront URL.
16. Scroll down to the end of the distribution settings.

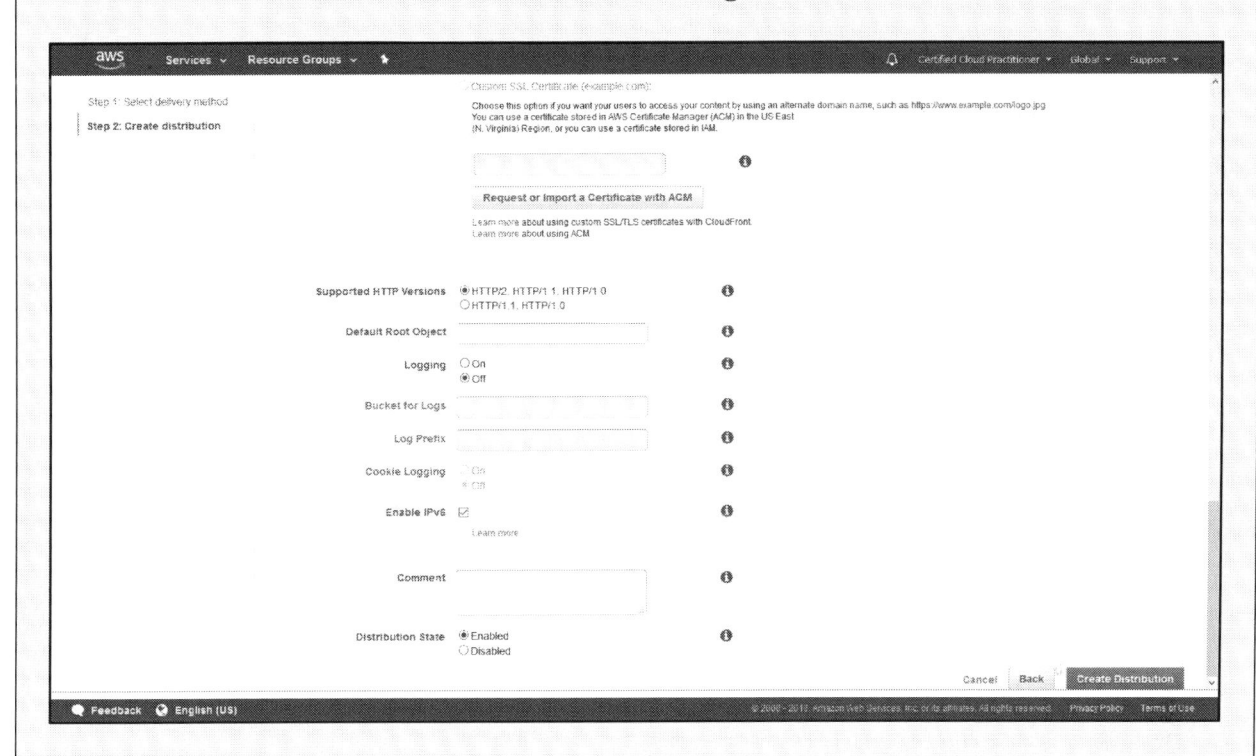

17. For now, leave everything as it is and click 'Create Distribution'. CloudFront Distribution does take some time to deploy.

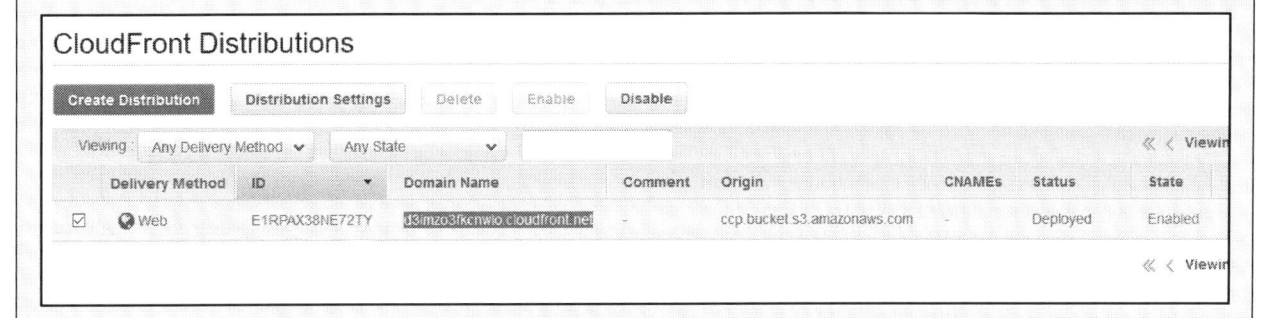

18. Once the distribution is deployed, copy the domain name and paste it into your browser followed by the image file name '685514.jpg'.

199

Chapter 3: Technology

19. As soon as you hit enter to browse your file, the CloudDistribution contacts your nearest edge location to check whether the file is present there. Since you are accessing the file for the first time, the file is not available at the edge location and is ultimately fetched from the origin bucket location. You will see that the image file took time to load on your browser this time.
20. Since the image file has now been requested once already, it is therefore present at the nearest edge location. If you refresh your page once again, you will noticeably see how fast your image file loads the second time.

EXAM TIPS:

- CDN Edge location is where the content is cached. This is separate to an AWS Region or Availability Zone.
- Web Distribution is typically used with websites.

Elastic Load Balancing

Elastic Load Balancing (ELB) automatically distributes incoming application traffic across multiple EC2 instances. It seamlessly provides necessary load balancing capacity required for application traffic distribution so that you can achieve greater levels of fault tolerance in your applications.

Elastic Load Balancing supports three types of load balancers, Application Load Balancers, Network Load Balancers, and Classic Load Balancers. You can select a load balancer based on your application needs. These load balancers feature high availability, automatic scaling, and robust security.

Application Load Balancer	Network Load Balancer	Classic Load Balancer
• Makes routing decisions at the application layer (layer 7) and is best suited for load balancing of HTTP and HTTPS traffic. • Application Load Balancer routes traffic to targets - EC2 instances, containers and IP addresses within Amazon Virtual Private Cloud (Amazon VPC) based on the content of the request. • Ideal for applications requiring advanced routing capabilities, microservices, and container-based architectures.	• Makes routing decisions at the transport layer (Layer 4) and is best suited for load balancing of TCP traffic where extreme performance is required. • Network Load Balancer routes connections to targets - Amazon EC2 instances, containers and IP addresses based on IP protocol data. • Optimized to handle sudden and volatile traffic patterns and is capable of handling millions of requests per second while maintaining ultra-low latencies.	• Makes routing decisions at the transport layer (TCP/SSL) or the application layer (HTTP/HTTPS) and supports either EC2 Classic or a VPC. However, it is recommended to use Application Load Balancer for Layer 7 and Network Load Balancer for Layer 4 when using Virtual Private Cloud (VPC). • Classic Load Balancer routes traffic based on either application or network level information. • Ideal for simple load balancing of traffic across multiple EC2 instances.

Figure 3-16. Elastic Load Balancing

Use Application Load Balancer for flexible application management and TLS termination. If extreme performance and static IP is needed for your application, then use Network

Load Balancer. Use Classic Load Balancer if your application is built within the EC2 Classic network.

Lab 3-11: Using a Load Balancer

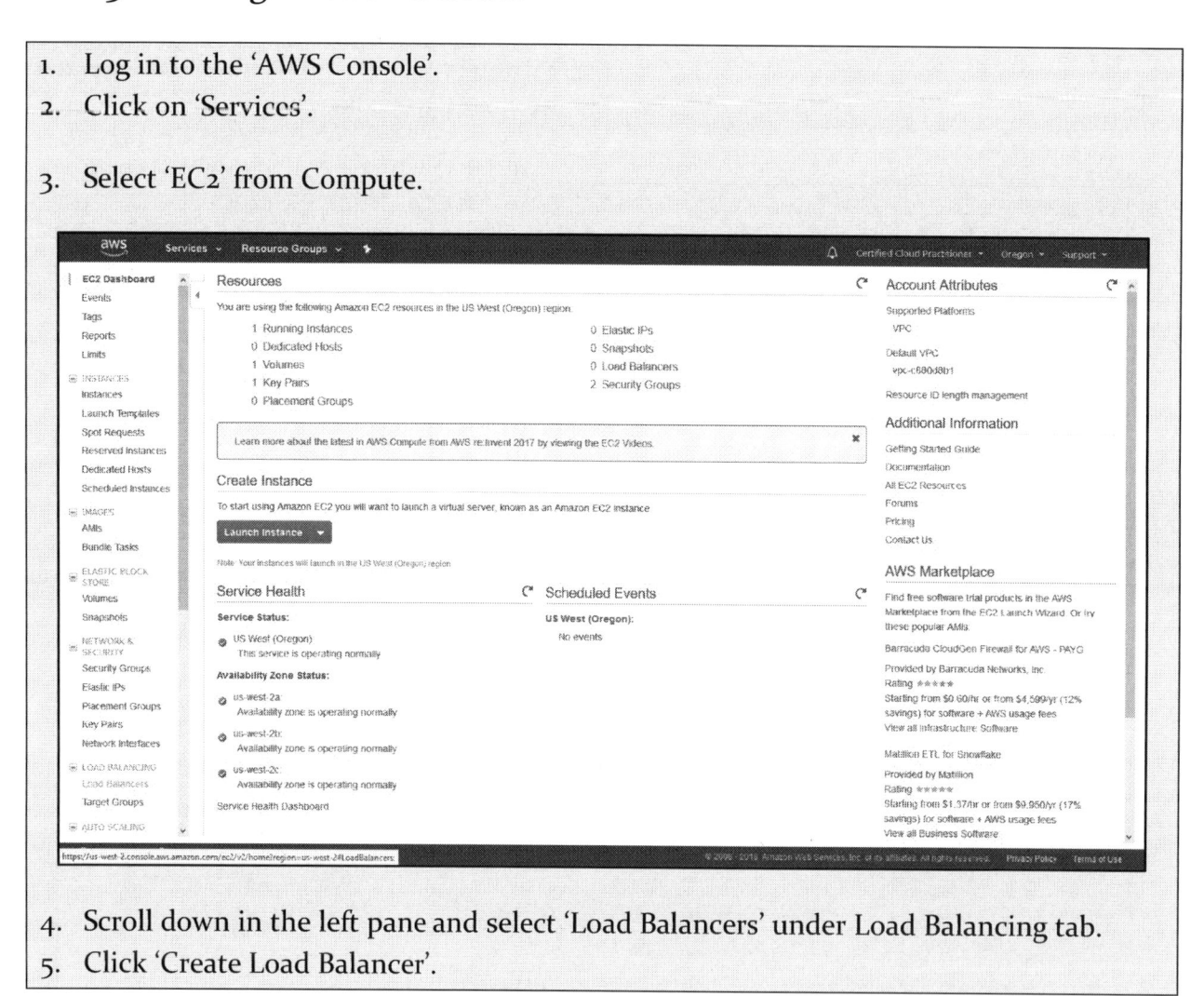

1. Log in to the 'AWS Console'.
2. Click on 'Services'.
3. Select 'EC2' from Compute.

4. Scroll down in the left pane and select 'Load Balancers' under Load Balancing tab.
5. Click 'Create Load Balancer'.

Chapter 3: Technology

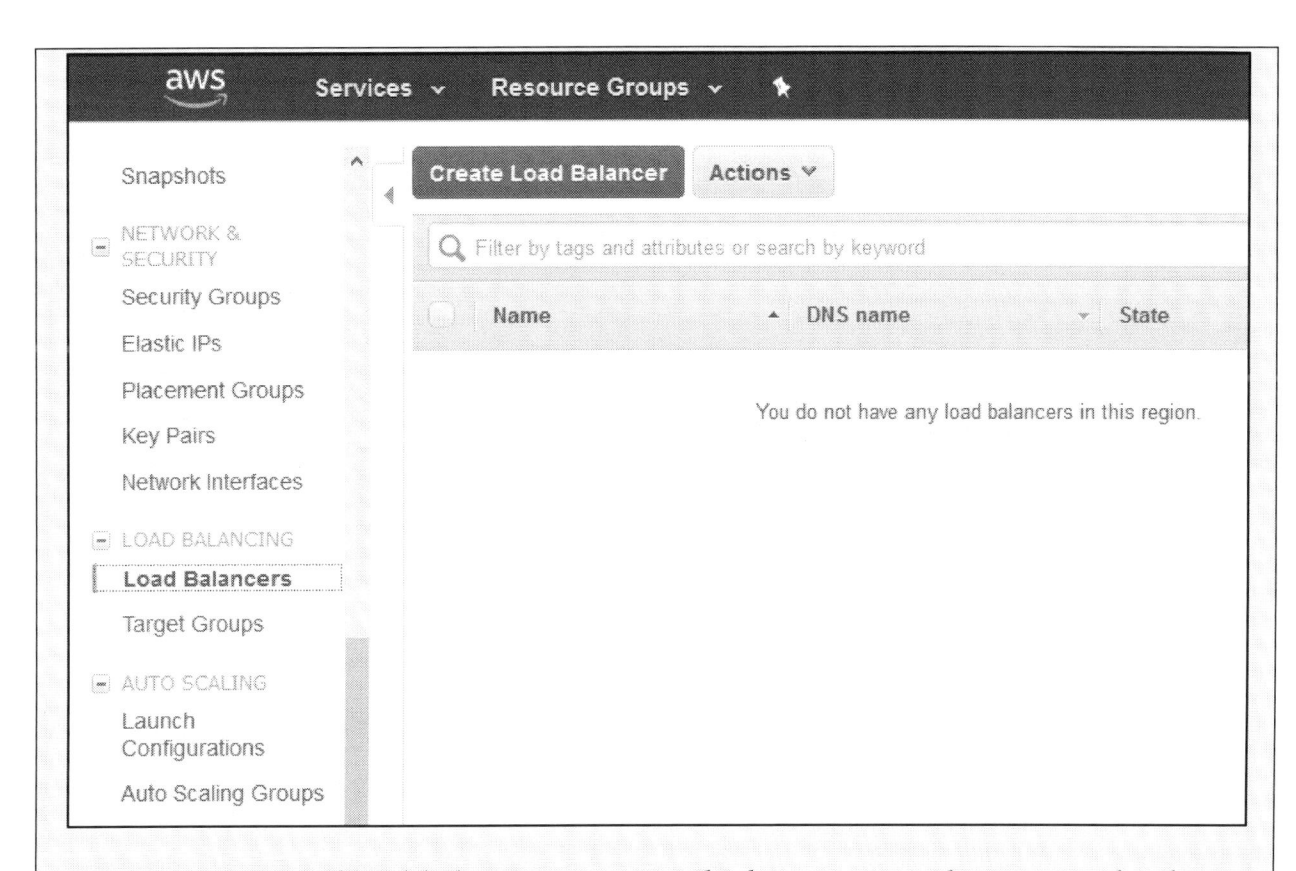

6. Select the type of load balancer. For example, let us use Application Load Balancer. Click 'Create' for Application Load Balancer.

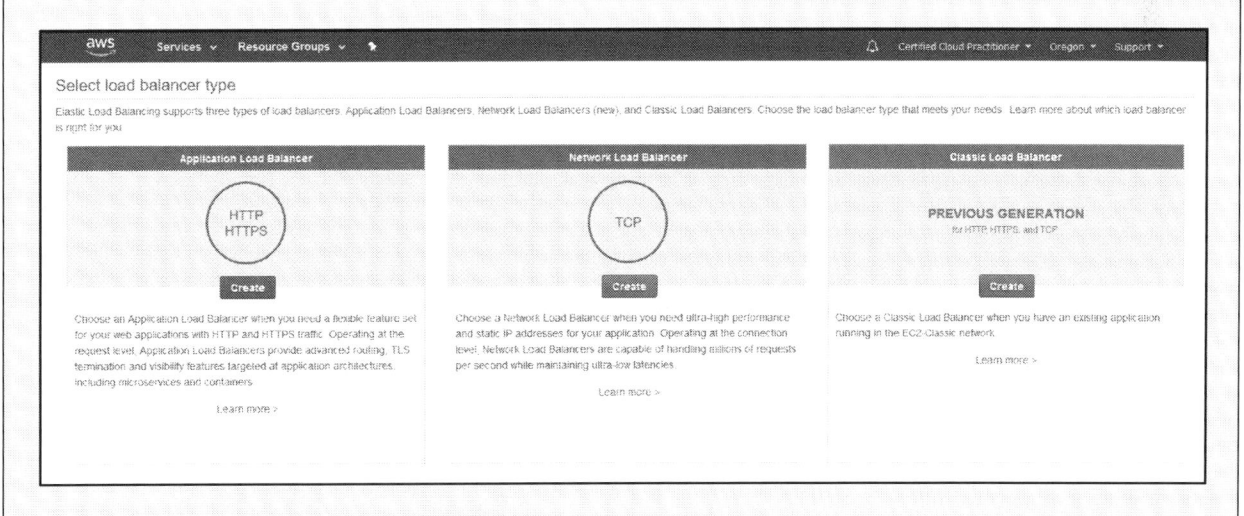

7. Enter a name for your load balancer. You will be using this load balancer as internet facing, and the address type is IPv4. Its open to http port 80. Select all the availability zones for the load balancer. Click 'Next: Configure Security Settings'.

Chapter 3: Technology

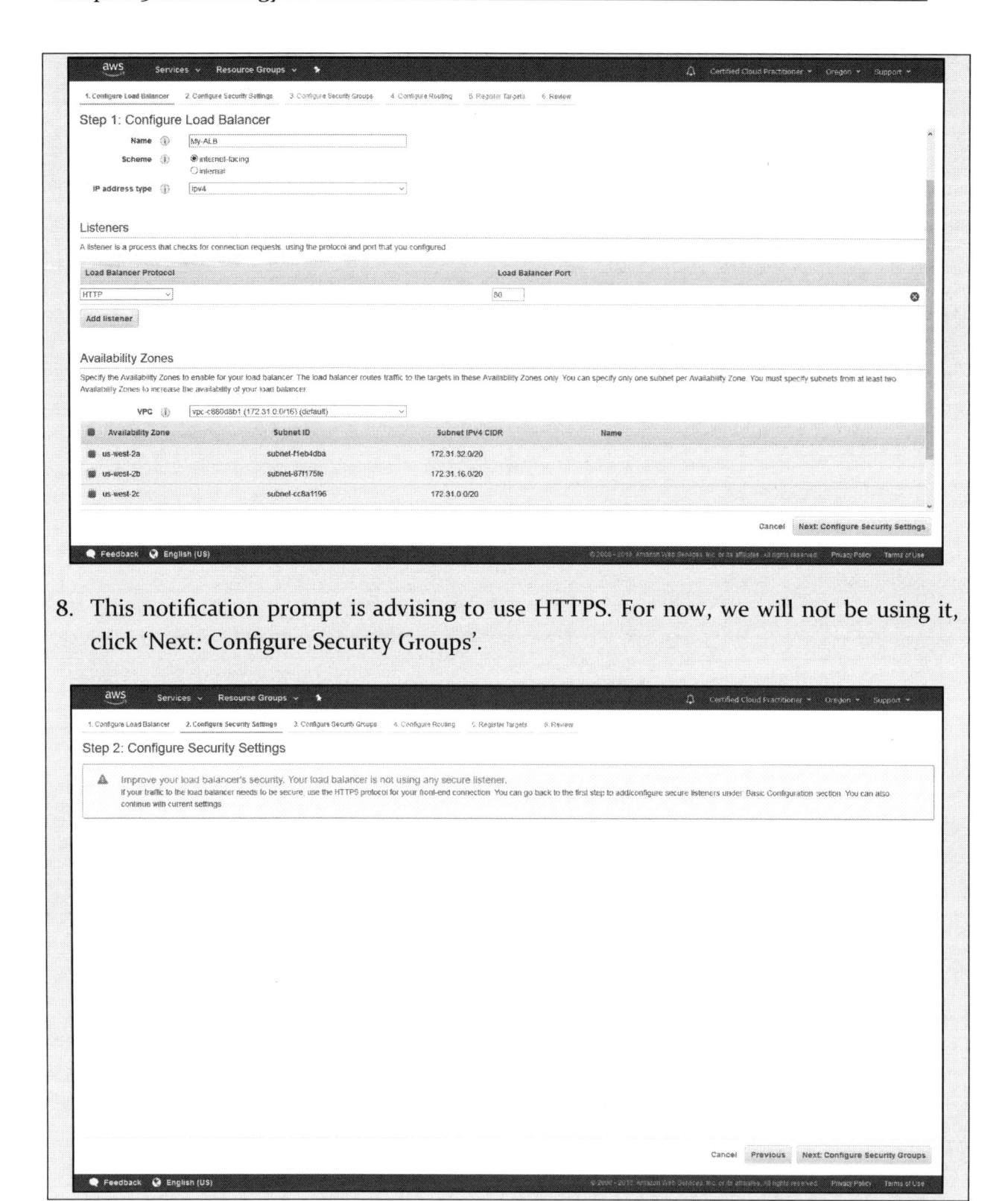

8. This notification prompt is advising to use HTTPS. For now, we will not be using it, click 'Next: Configure Security Groups'.

Chapter 3: Technology

9. Select the security group you already created for your web servers 'My Web Group' and click 'Next: Configure Routing'.

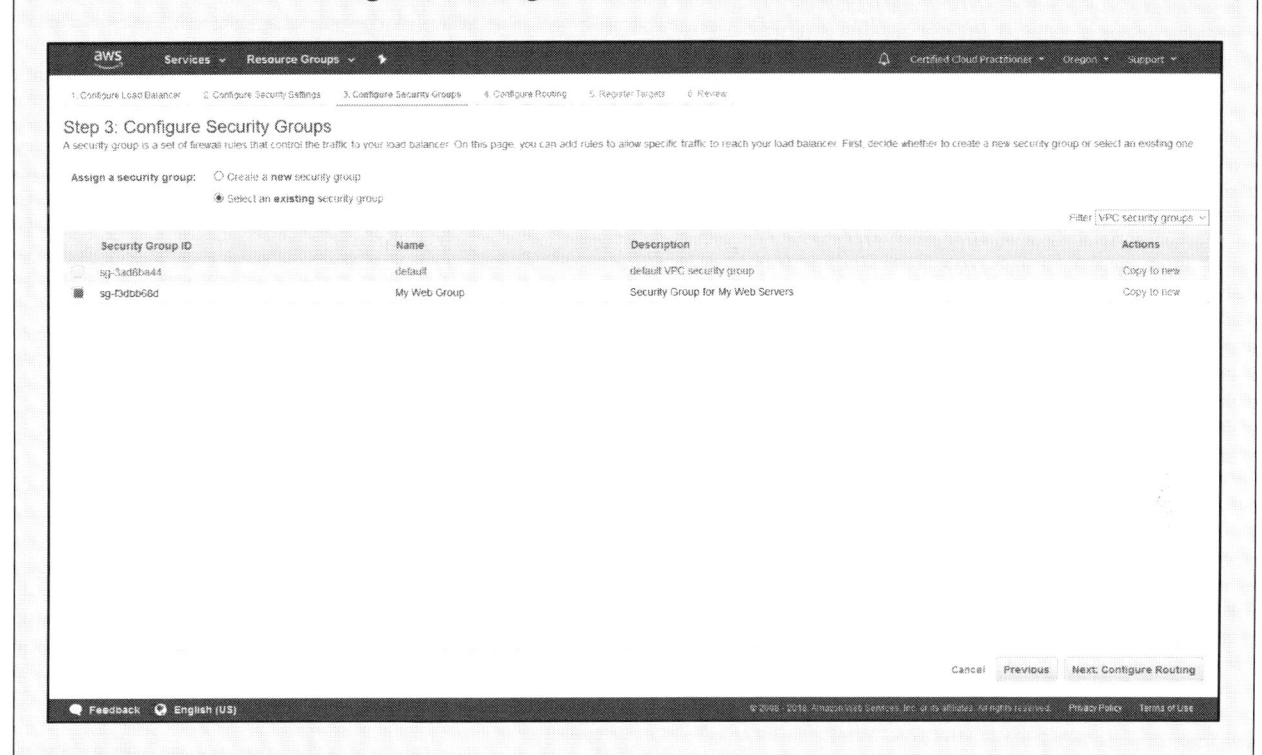

10. Here you will create a new target group for our load balancer. Enter a name for the target group. Select HTTP port 80, and your target type is an instance. For now, you do not need to define any specific path for health checks such as index.html or error.html. Let it be the default directory. Click 'Next: Register Targets'.

Chapter 3: Technology

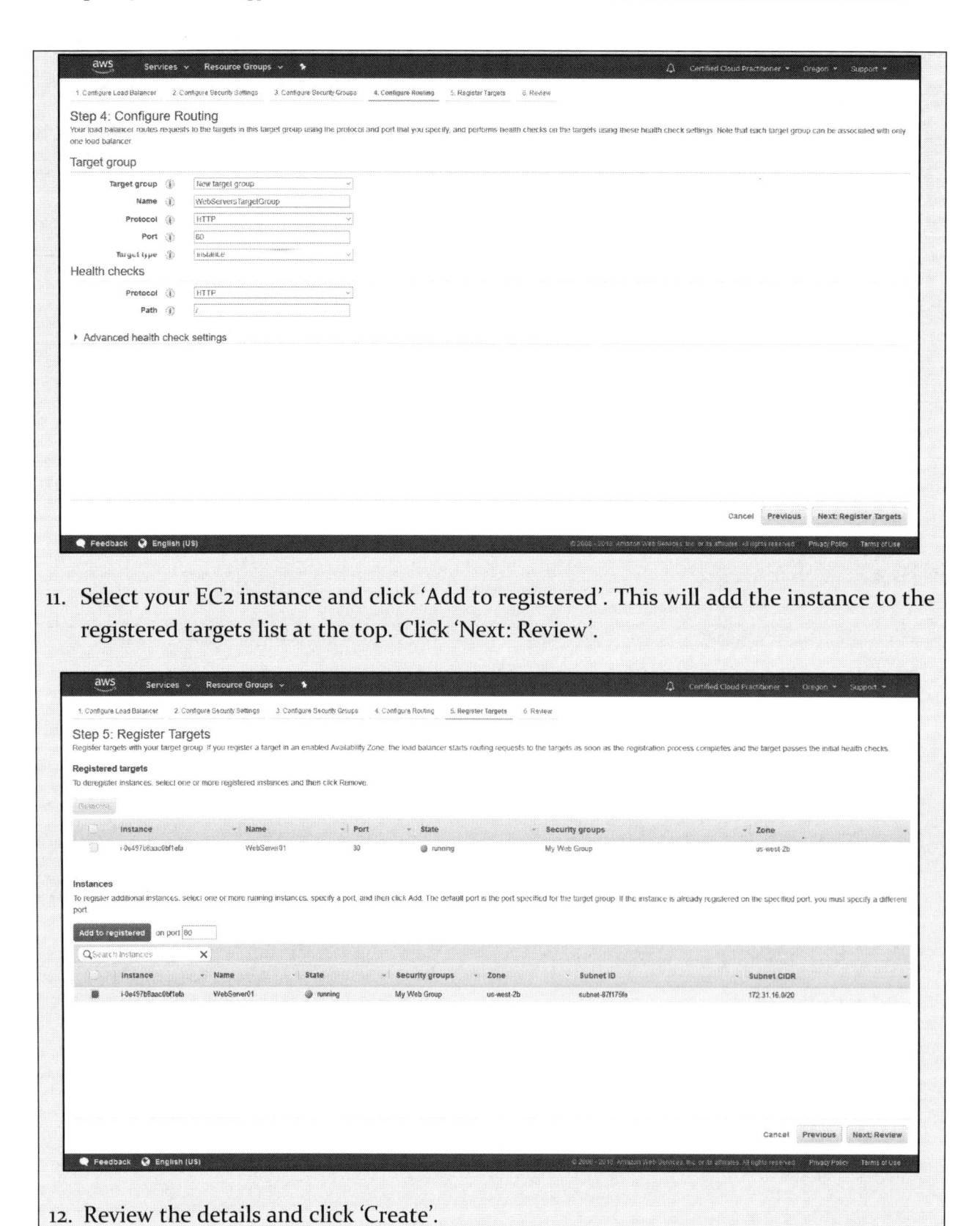

11. Select your EC2 instance and click 'Add to registered'. This will add the instance to the registered targets list at the top. Click 'Next: Review'.

12. Review the details and click 'Create'.

Chapter 3: Technology

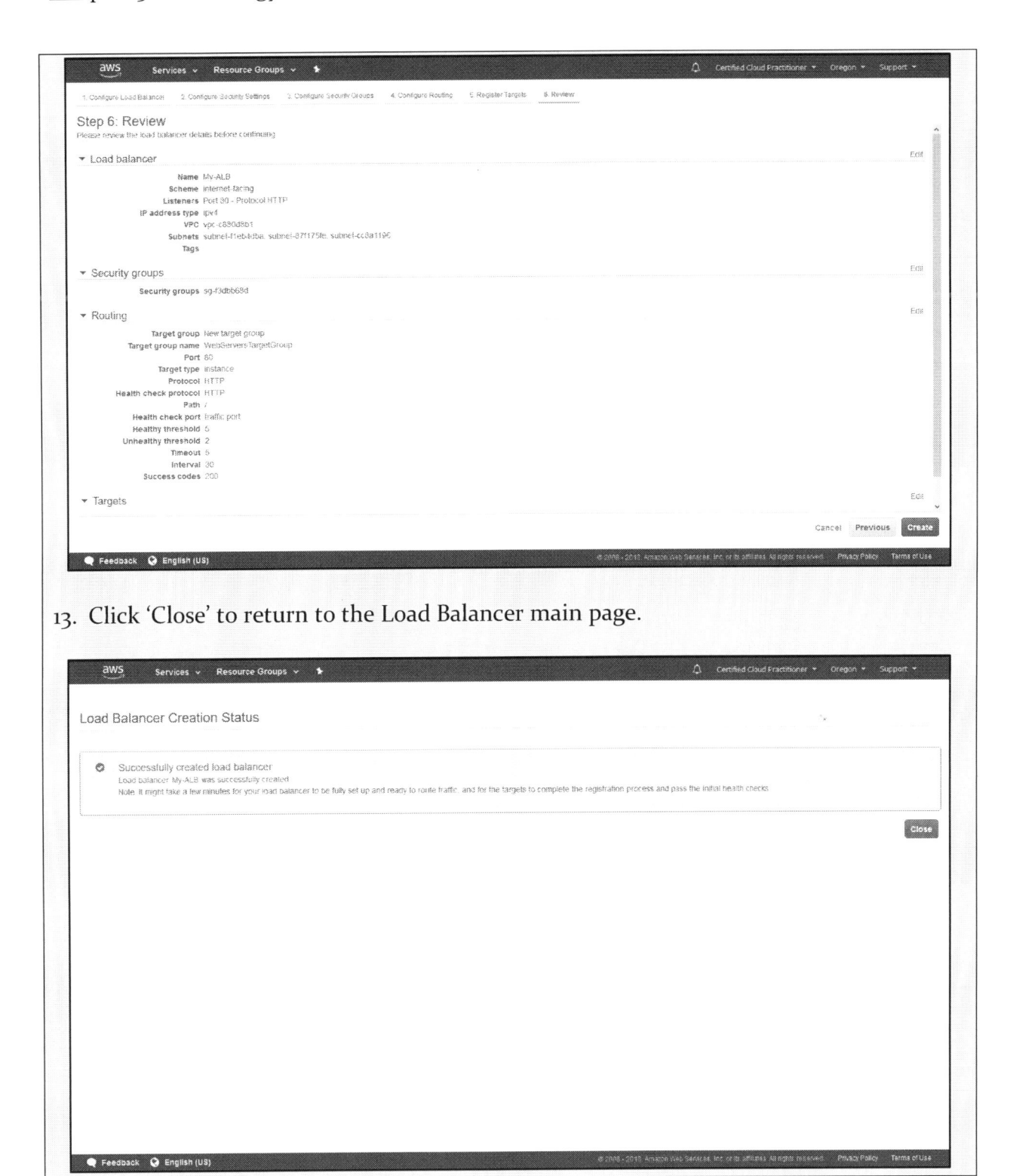

13. Click 'Close' to return to the Load Balancer main page.

Chapter 3: Technology

14. The load balancer is active now. Go ahead and create another webserver to add behind this load balancer. Go to EC2 to launch another instance by following the same steps as you did before.

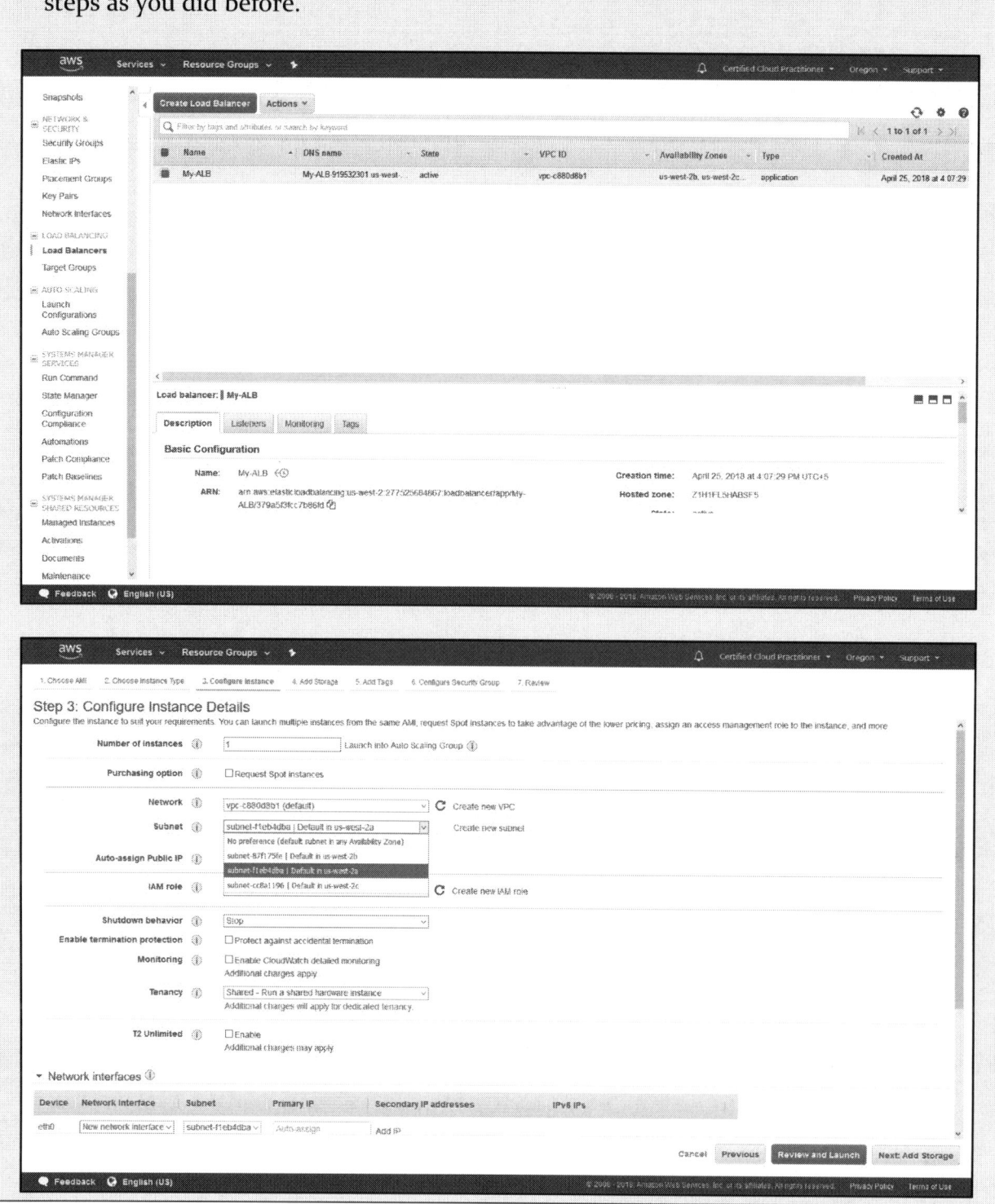

Chapter 3: Technology

15. When you reach to Configuring Instance Details, make sure you select a different availability zone for this instance. Your previous EC2 instance is in the availability zone 'us-west-2b'. Therefore, you have to selecte 'us-west-2a' for this instance. Scroll down to 'Advanced Details' section.
16. In this section, you can pass user data to the instances. You can configure commands that you want to run when this instance is booting up. Click 'Next: Add Storage' after adding the following code:

- #!/bin/bash
- yum update -y
- yum install httpd -y
- service httpd start
- chkconfighttpd on
- echo "Welcome to IPSpecialist" >> /var/www/html/index.html

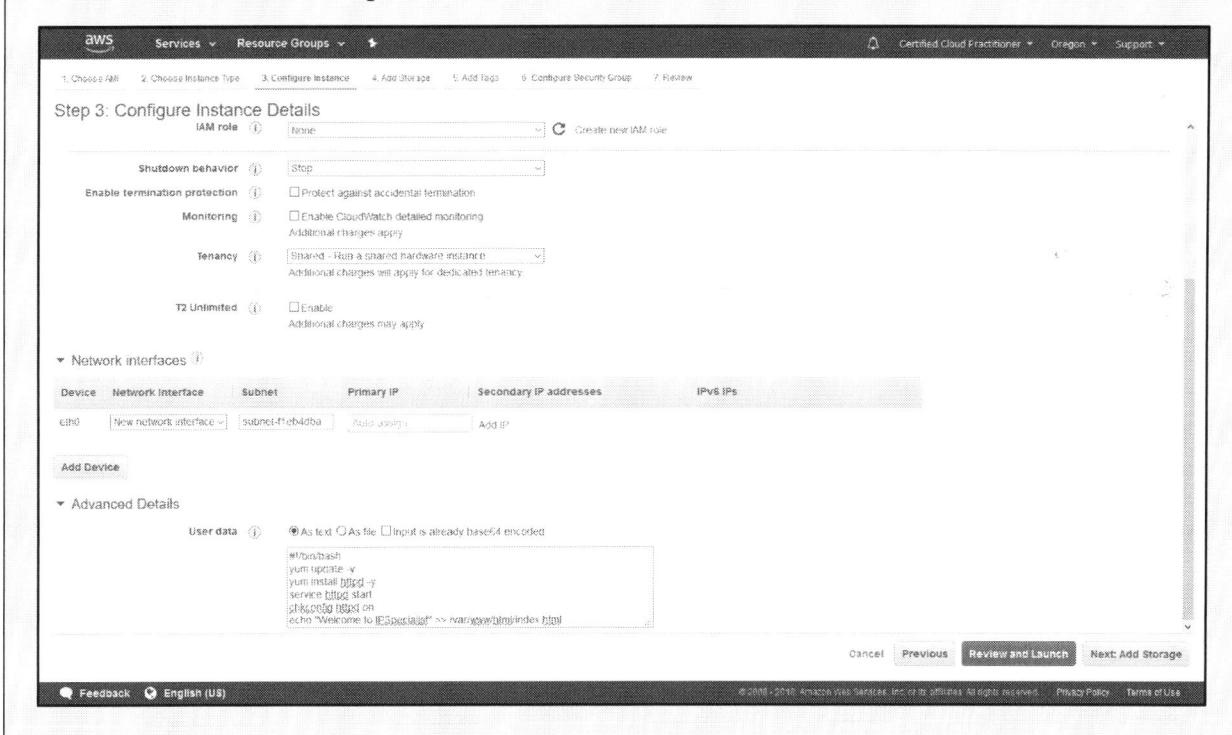

17. Leave this section as it is and click 'Next: Add Tags'.

Chapter 3: Technology

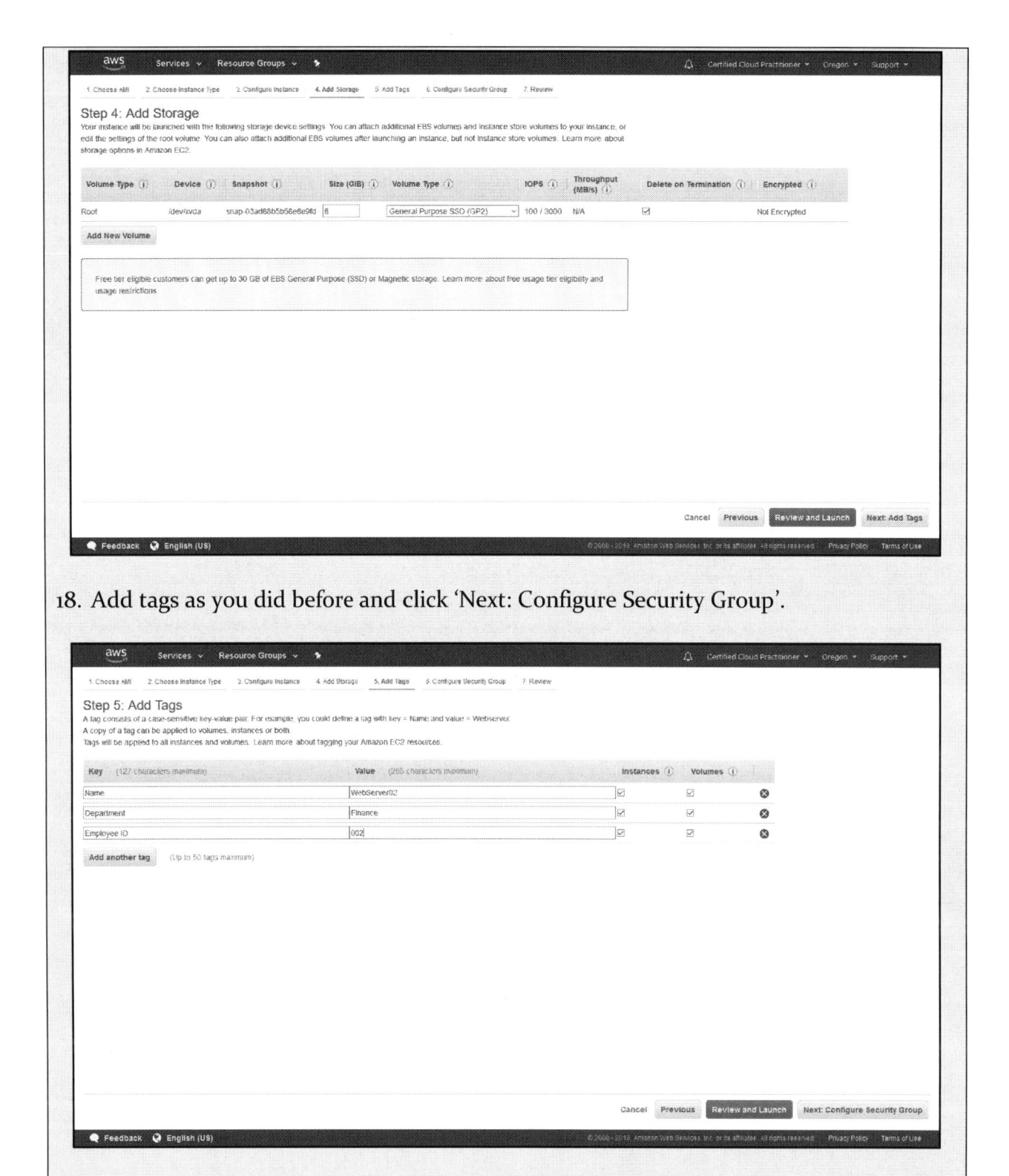

18. Add tags as you did before and click 'Next: Configure Security Group'.

19. Here you will select the existing security group that you made already 'My Web Group' and click 'Review and Launch'.

Chapter 3: Technology

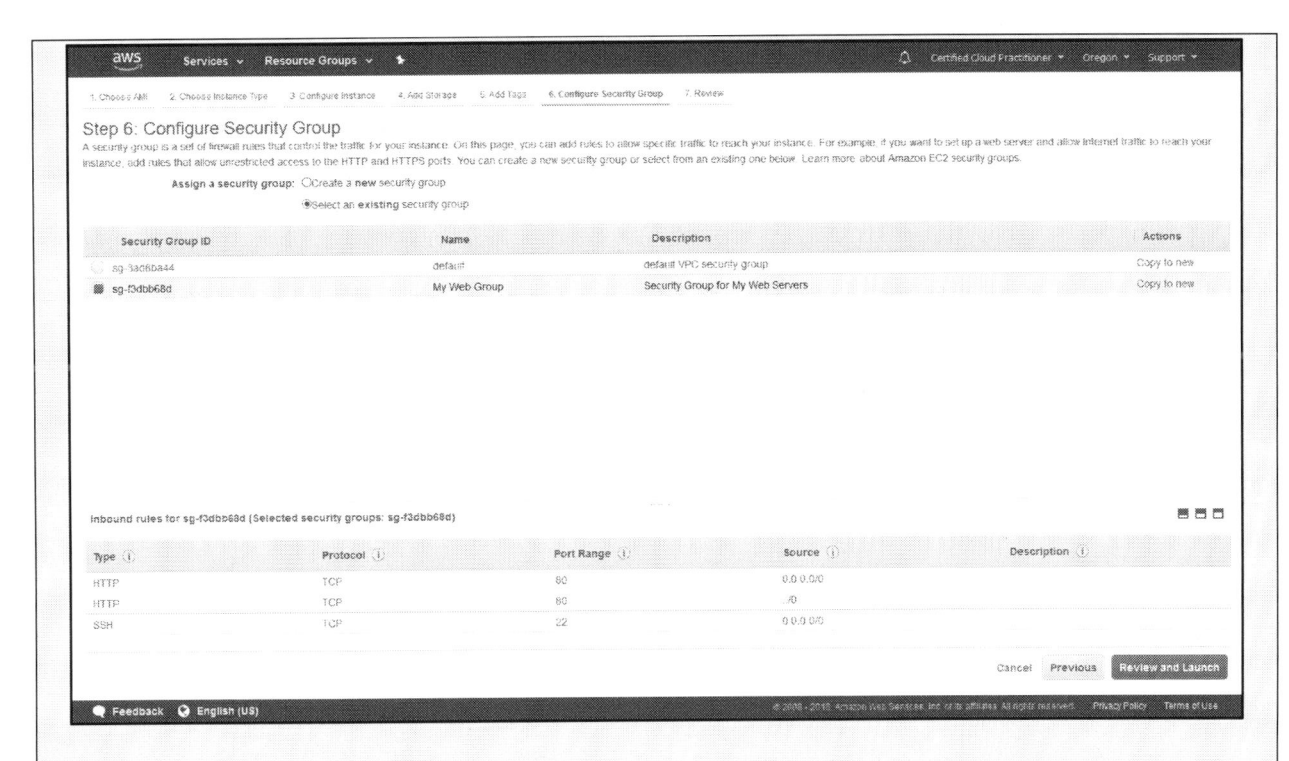

20. Select the existing key pair and click 'Launch Instance'.

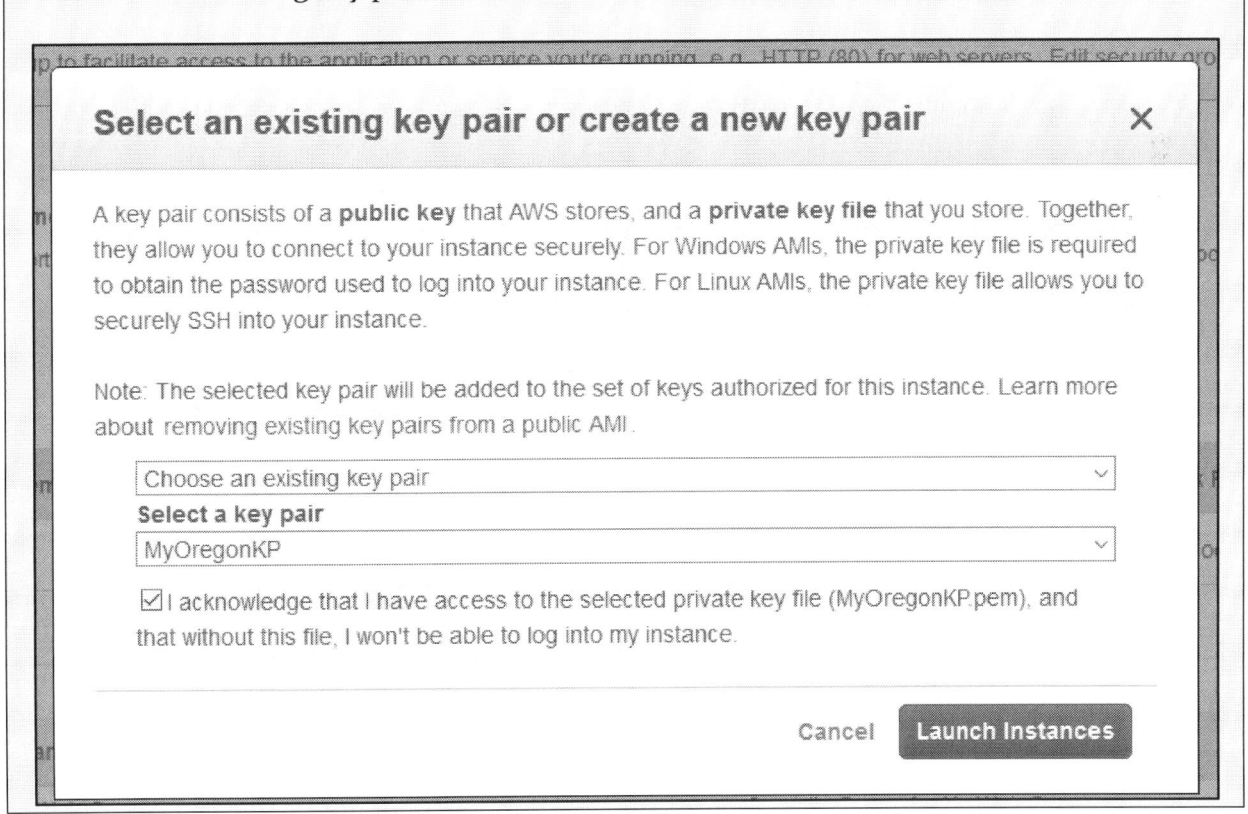

21. You can now see that both instances are up and running and both are in different availability zones. You have already added one instance to our load balancer; you now need to add the new instance to the load balancer's target group as well. Select 'Target Groups' from under the Load Balancing tab.

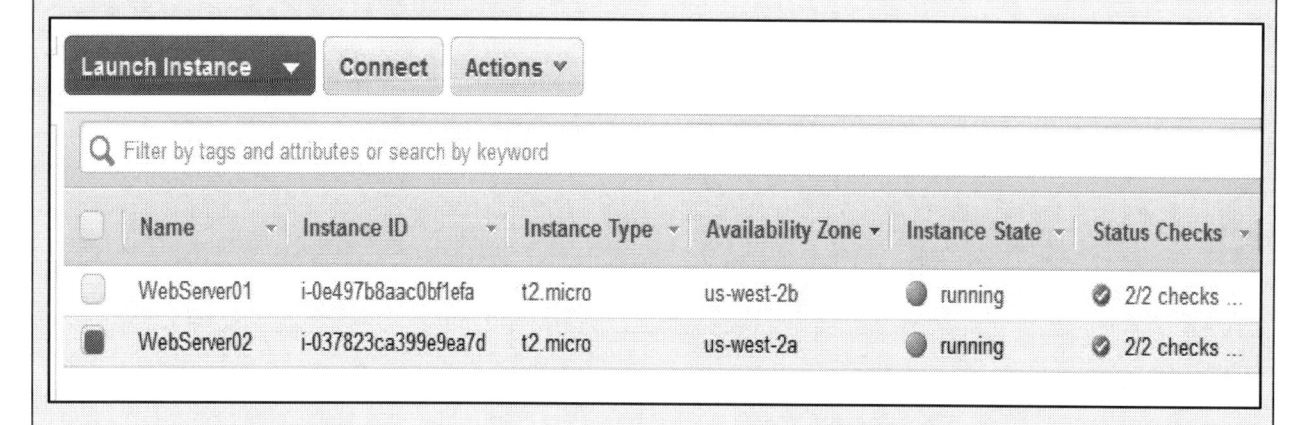

22. Select the 'Targets' tab from the list of tabs and click 'Edit' to edit the target group.

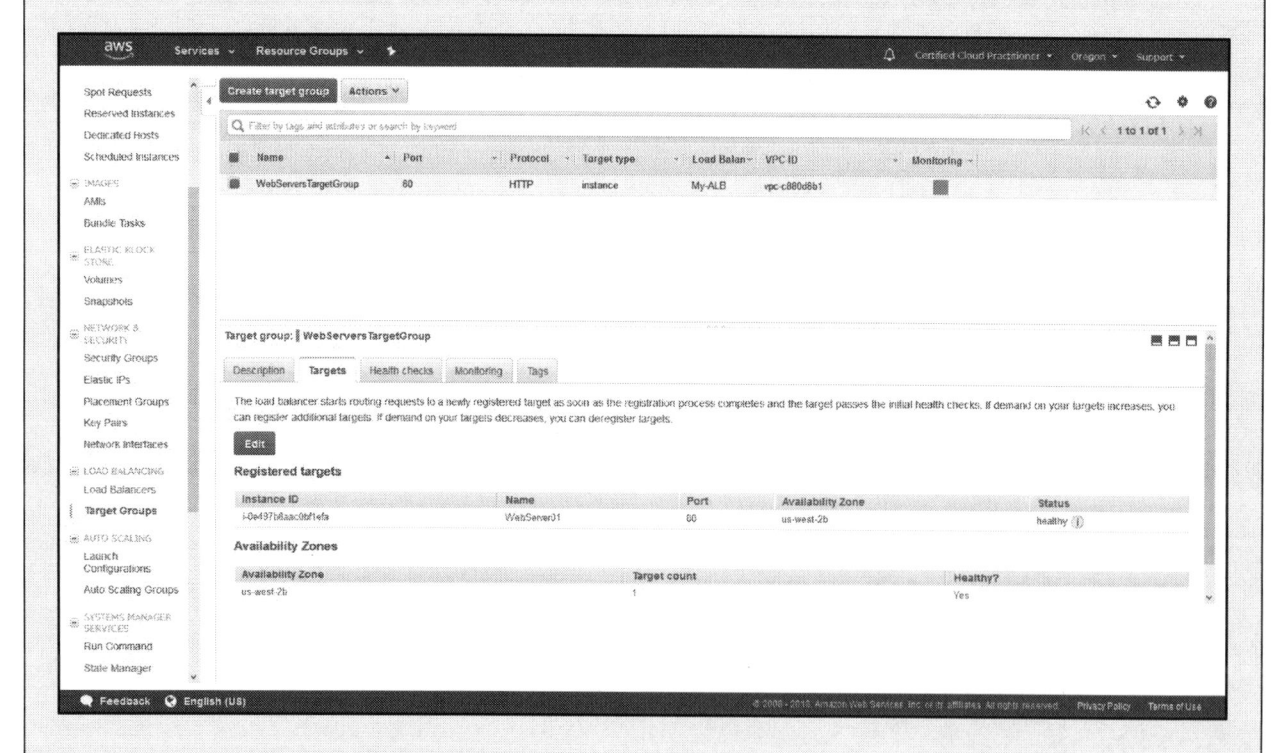

23. Select the instance that needs to be added and click 'Add to registered' to register the instance in the Registered targets list above. Click 'Save'.

Chapter 3: Technology

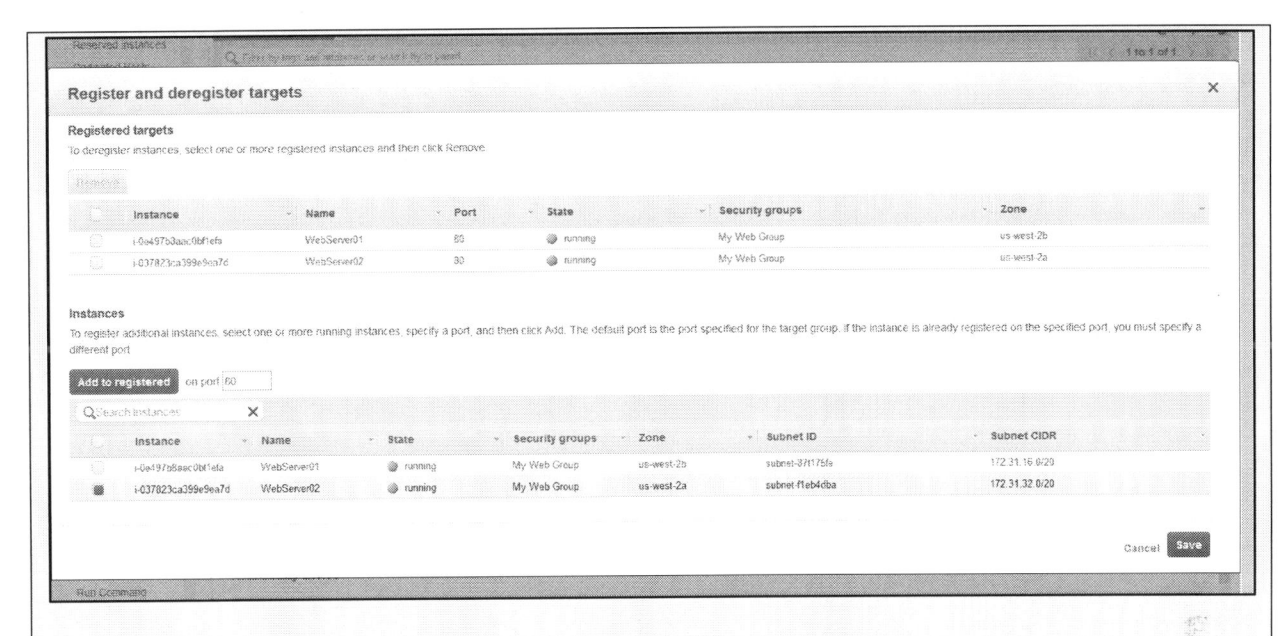

24. Now, both the webservers are behind your load balancer. Now, click 'Load Balancers' from under the Load Balancing tab.

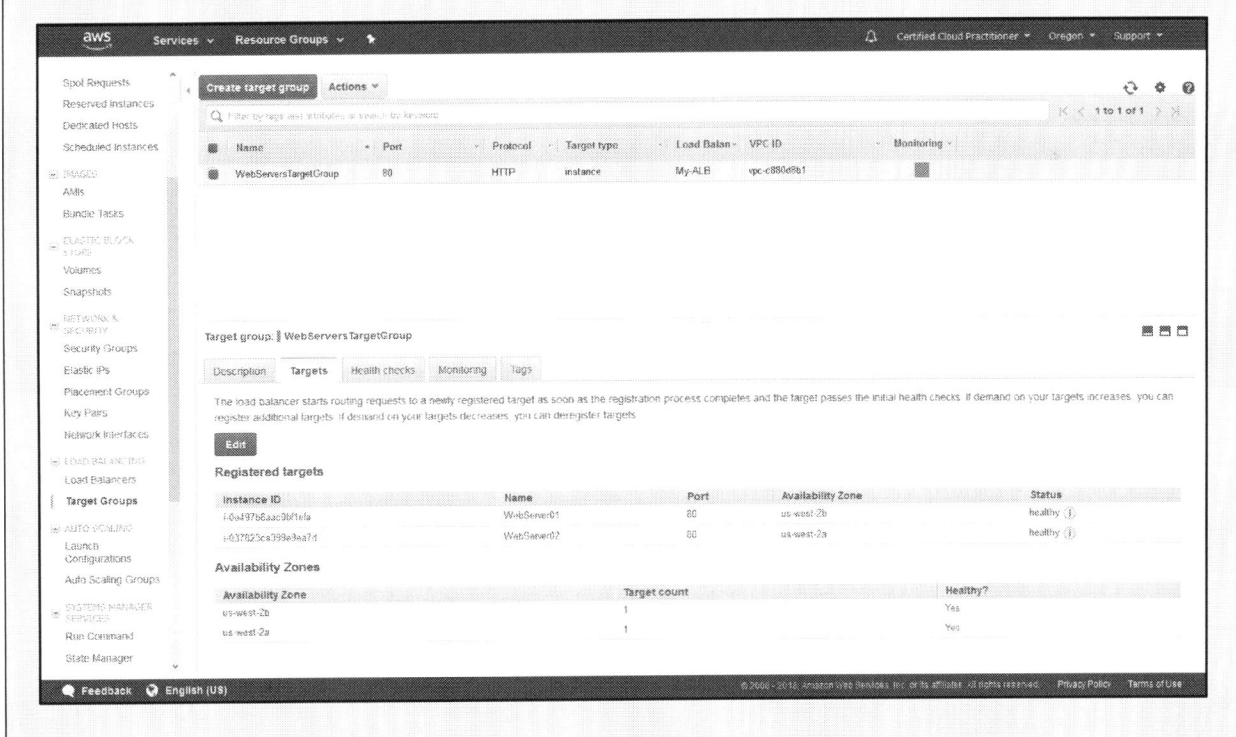

25. Copy the DNS name and open it up in your browser.

Chapter 3: Technology

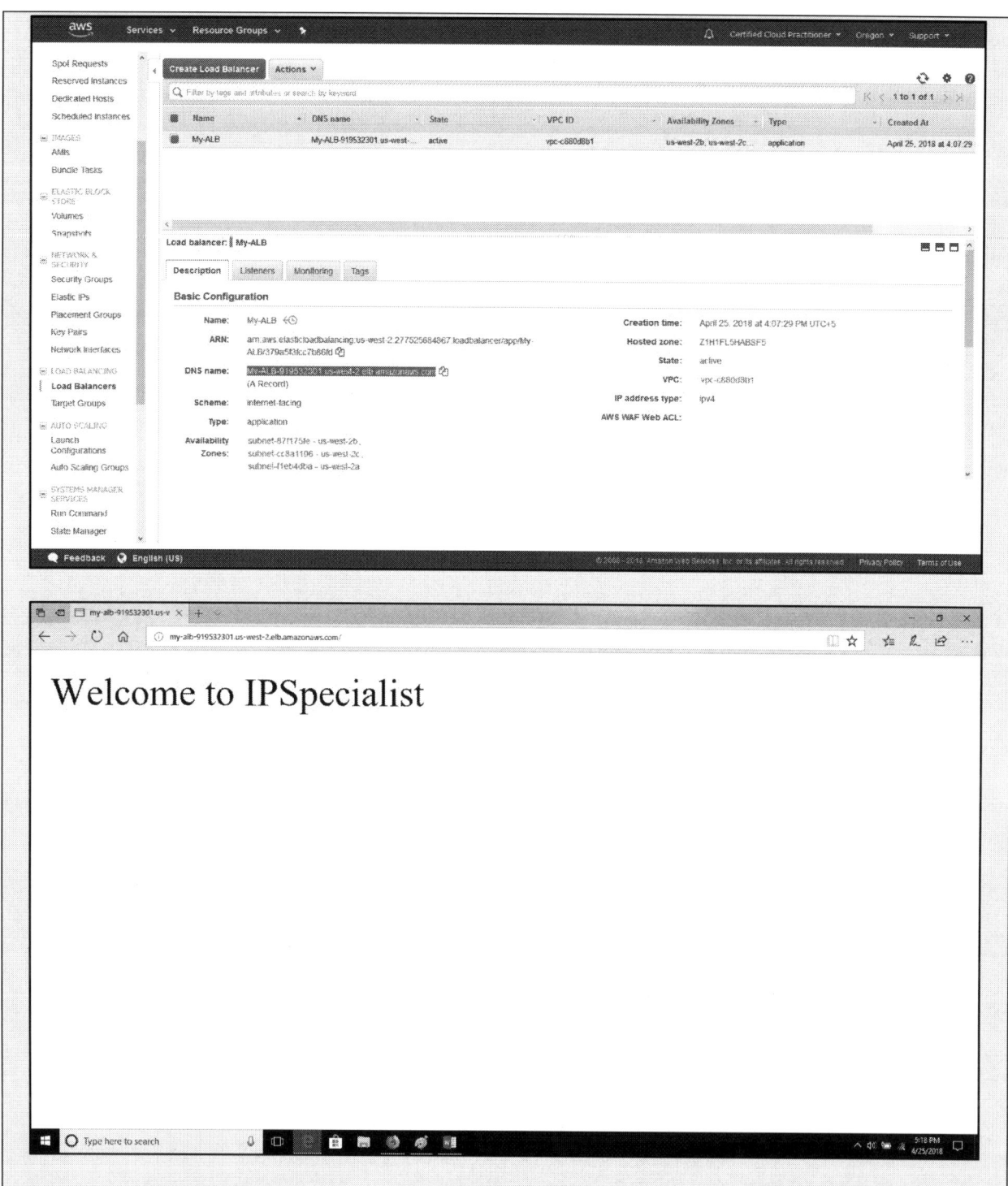

26. For now, this DNS name is leading to the new webserver we just created. If you terminate this instance and then use the same DNS name, the load balancer will detect that one of the webservers is down and will redirect to the other webserver. Go back to the EC2 instances and stop one instance.

Chapter 3: Technology

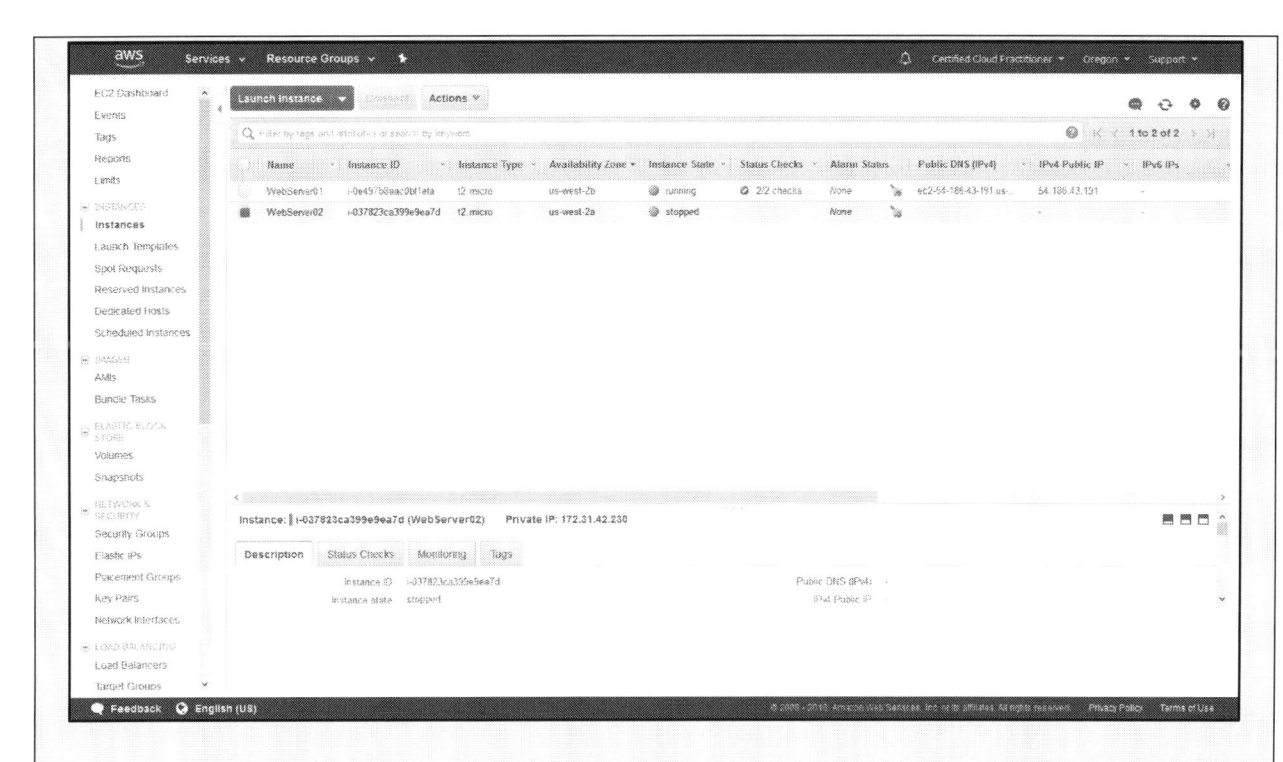

27. Here we have stopped the new instance we created. Go back to the browser and again use the same DNS name.

215

> 28. This time it leads to the other webserver as the load balancer detects one of them is down and redirects to the active webserver.

Amazon Route 53

Amazon Route 53 provides highly available and scalable cloud DNS web service that effectively connects user requests to infrastructure running in AWS such as EC2 instances, Elastic Load Balancers, or Amazon S3 buckets. It can also be used to route users to infrastructure outside of AWS. DNS (Domain Name System) is a globally distributed service that translates human-readable domain names like www.example.com to the numeric machine-readable IP addresses like 192.0.2.1 that computers use to connect to each other.

Amazon Route 53 traffic flow makes it easy for you to manage traffic globally through a variety of routing types, including latency-based routing, Geo DNS, and weighted round robin, all of which can be combined with DNS Failover in order to enable a variety of low-latency, fault-tolerant architectures.

You can use Amazon Route 53 to register new domains, transfer existing domains, route traffic for your domains to your AWS and external resources, and monitor the health of your resources.

- **DNS Management:**

    If you already have a domain name, such as example.com, Route 53 can tell the Domain Name System (DNS) where on the internet to find web servers, mail servers, and other resources for your domain.

- **Traffic Management:**

    Route 53 traffic flow provides a visual tool that you can use to create and update sophisticated routing policies to route end users to multiple endpoints for your application, whether in a single AWS Region or distributed around the globe.

- **Availability Monitoring:**

    Route 53 can monitor the health and performance of your application as well as your web servers and other resources. Route 53 can also redirect traffic to healthy resources and independently monitor the health of your application and its endpoints.

Chapter 3: Technology

- **Domain Registration:**

    If you need a domain name, you can find an available name and register it by using Route 53. Amazon Route 53 will automatically configure DNS settings for your domains. You can also make Route 53 the registrar for existing domains that you registered with other registrars.

> **EXAM TIP:** Route 53 is Amazon's DNS service. If you own a domain name and want to host a website on it using Amazon S3, you need to have the exact same bucket name as the domain name for it to work.

Resource Groups and Tagging

Resource Groups

Resource Groups allow you to easily create, maintain, and view a collection of resources that share one or more common tags or portions of tags. You can use resource groups to organize your AWS resources by marking resources from multiple services and regions with a common tag, and then view those resources together in a customizable pane of the AWS Management Console.

To create a resource group, you simply identify the tags that contain the items that members of the group should have in common. Resource Groups can display metrics, alarms, and configuration details and make it easier to manage and automate tasks on large numbers of resources at one time. Examples of these bulk actions include:

- Applying updates or security patches
- Upgrading applications
- Opening or closing ports to network traffic
- Collecting specific log and monitoring data from your fleet of instances

Lab 3-12: Creating Resource Groups

1. Log in to the 'AWS Console'.
2. Click on 'Resource Groups'.

Chapter 3: Technology

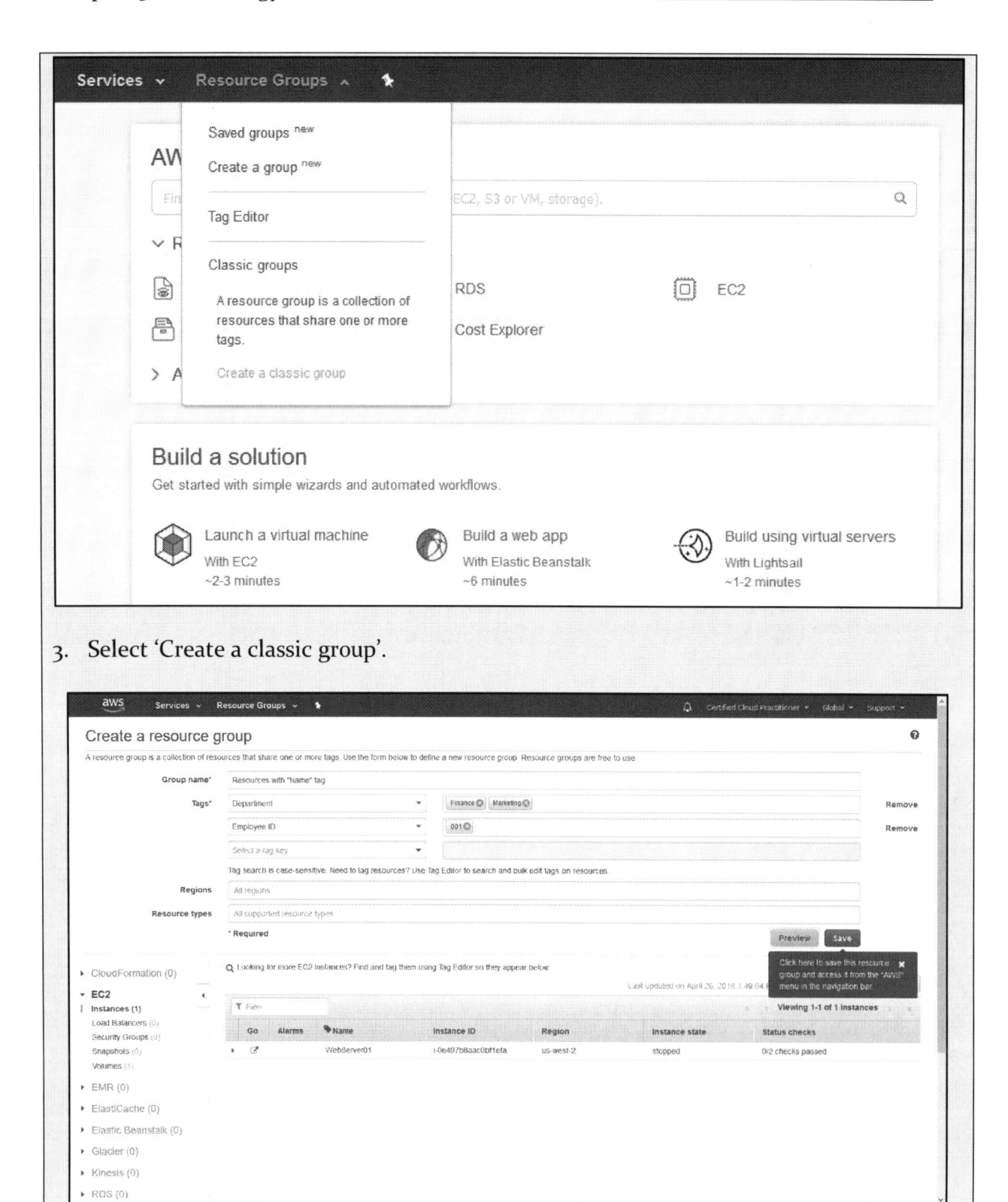

3. Select 'Create a classic group'.

Chapter 3: Technology

4. Here, we will make a resource group using the tags we created while provisioning resources. Enter a resource group name and the tags you want to include in this group. For Example, we have selected 'Department' tag with values 'Finance' and 'Marketing' and also another tag of 'Employee ID' with only the values '001'. Click 'Preview' to view the resources falling in the above criteria and then click 'Save'.

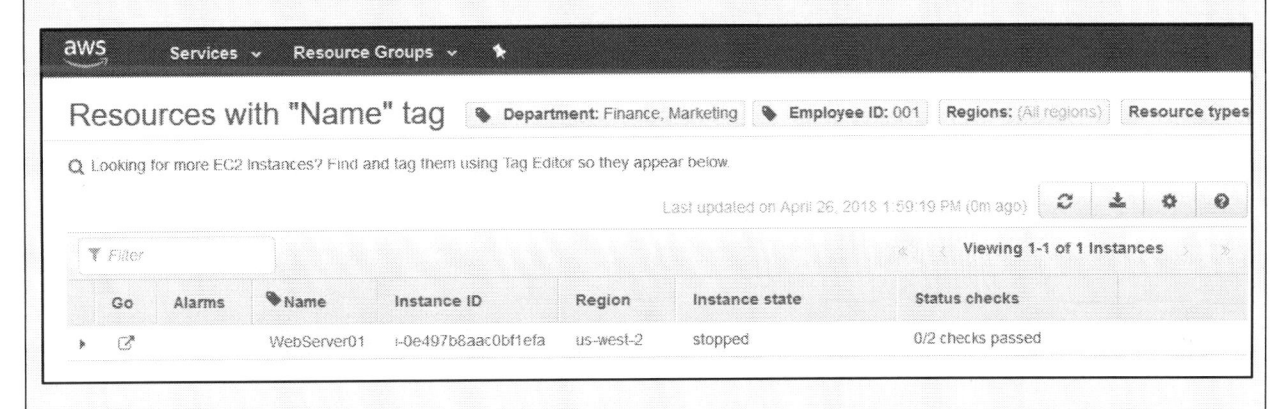

Go	Alarms	Name	Instance ID	Region	Instance state	Status checks
▸ ☐		WebServer01	i-0e497b8aac0bf1efa	us-west-2	stopped	0/2 checks passed

5. Your Resource Group has been created displaying all the resources with the tags and values you mentioned.

Chapter 3: Technology

Tags

Tags are words or phrases that act as metadata for identifying and organizing your AWS resources. It is a label that you assign to an AWS resource. Each tag consists of a key and a value, both of which you define. The tag limit varies with the resource, but most can have up to 50 tags.

With most AWS resources, you have the option of adding tags when you create the resource, whether it's an Amazon EC2 instance, an Amazon S3 bucket, or another resource. You can also add, change, or remove those tags one resource at a time within each resource's console. Whereas, adding tags to multiple resources at once can be done by using Tag Editor.

Tags can sometimes be inherited. When we use services such as Autoscaling, CloudFormation, and Elastic Beanstalk, they can provide other resources with the inherited tags. If you delete a resource, any tags for the resource are also deleted. You can edit tag keys and values, and you can remove tags from a resource at any time. With Tag Editor, you search for the resources that you want to tag, and then add, remove, or edit tags for the resources in your search results. Tag Editor provides a central, unified way to easily create and manage your user-defined tags across services and Regions.

The tags function like properties of a resource, so they are shared across the entire account. It enables you to categorize your AWS resources in different ways, for example, by purpose, owner, or environment. This is useful when you have many resources of the same type; you can quickly identify a specific resource based on the tags you have assigned to it. Tagging can help you organize your resources and enables you to simplify resource management, access management, and cost allocation.

Assigning tags to resources allows higher levels of automation and ease of management. You can execute management tasks at scale by listing resources with specific tags, then executing the appropriate actions. For example, you can list all resources with a particular tag and value, then for each of the resources either delete or terminate them. This is useful to automate shutdown or removal of a set of resources at the end of the working day. Creating and implementing an AWS tagging standard across your organization's accounts will enable you to manage and govern your AWS environments in a consistent and uniform manner.

Lab 3-13: Using Tag Editor

1. Log in to the 'AWS Console' and Click on 'Resource Groups'.

Chapter 3: Technology

2. Select 'Tag Editor'.

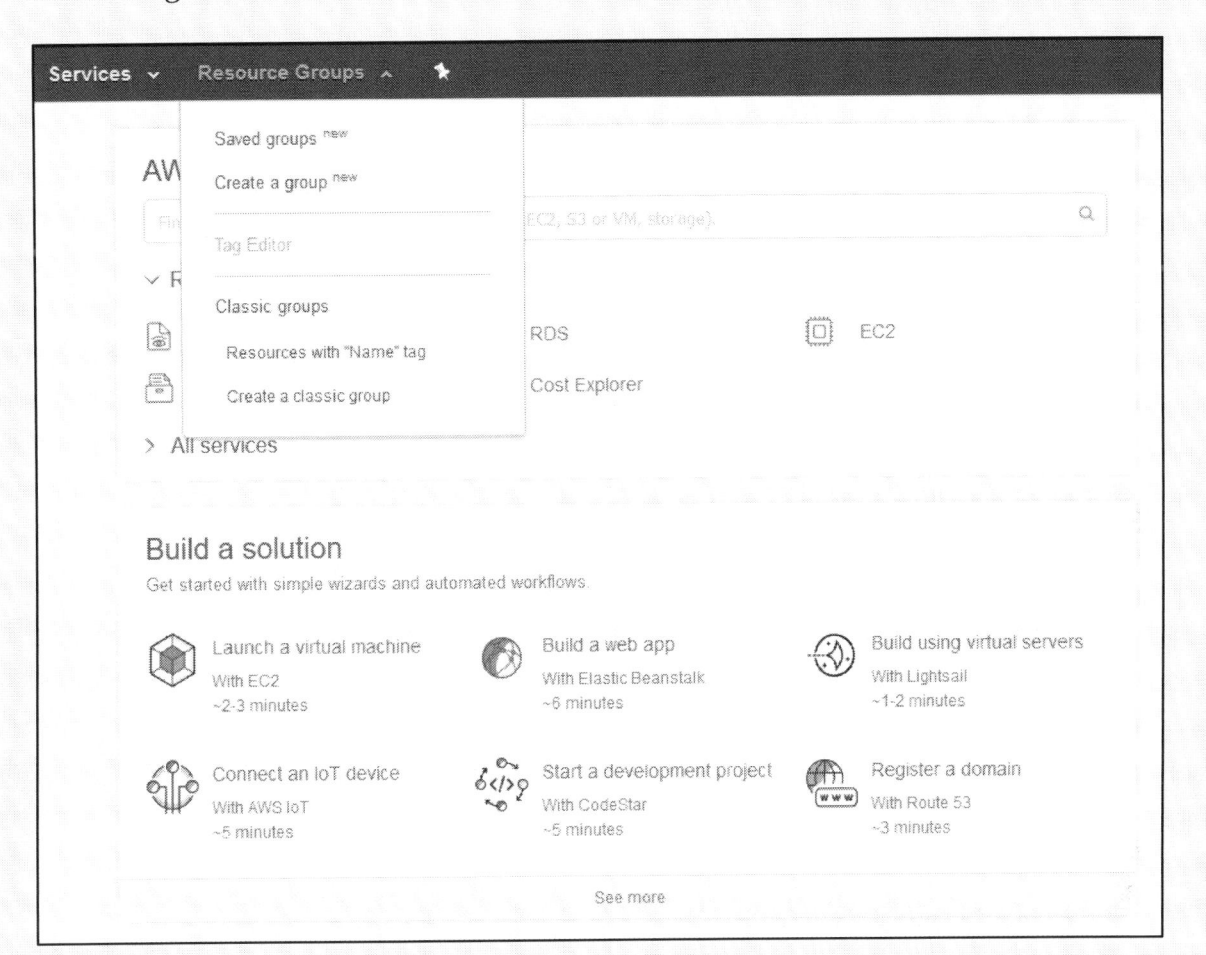

3. Using the tag editor, you can find resources easily by the tags created at the time of provisioning resources. The editor allows you to add, edit and delete tags. Click 'Create a new tag key' to add a new tag field.

Chapter 3: Technology

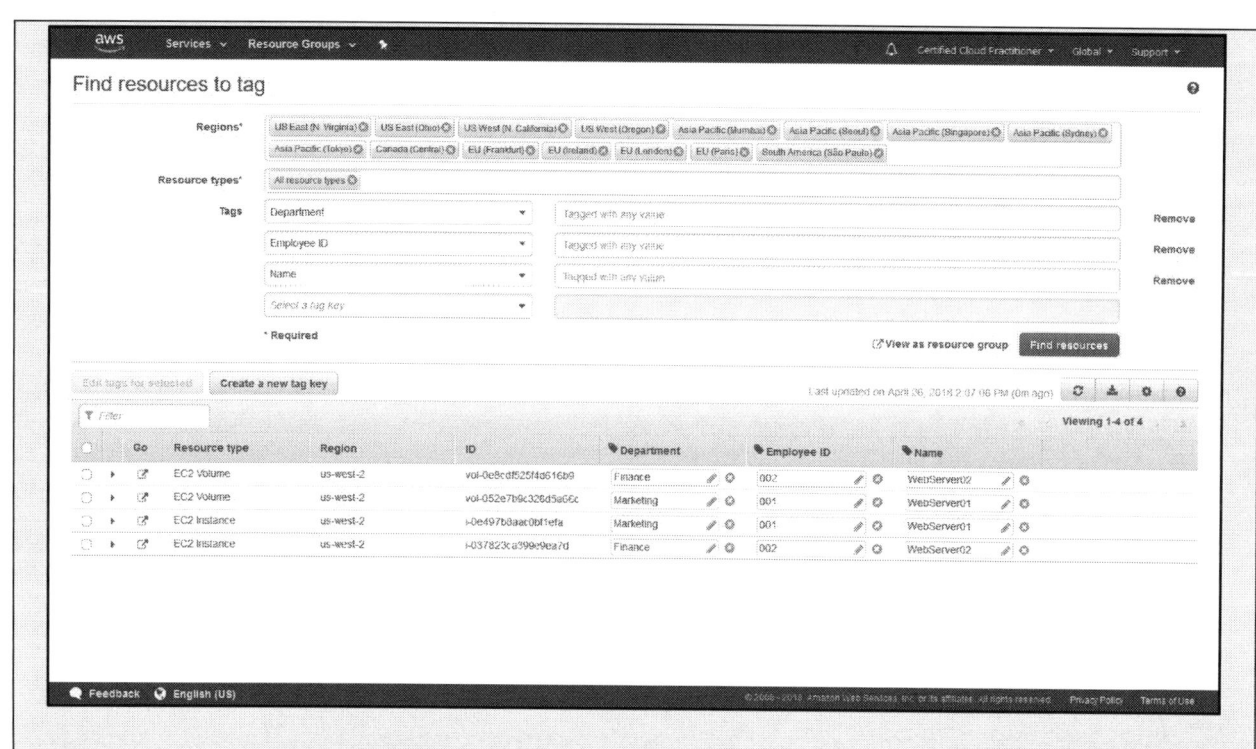

4. Enter a new Key name and click 'Add key'.

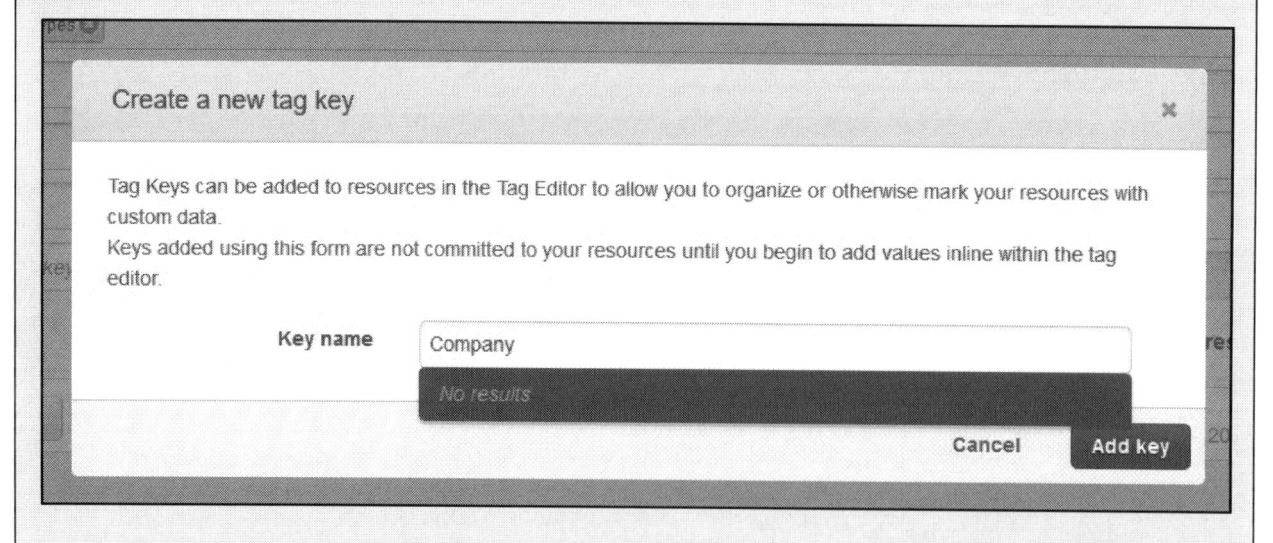

5. Now our new tag 'Company' has been added. You can click on the '+' button to add values to the tag.

Chapter 3: Technology

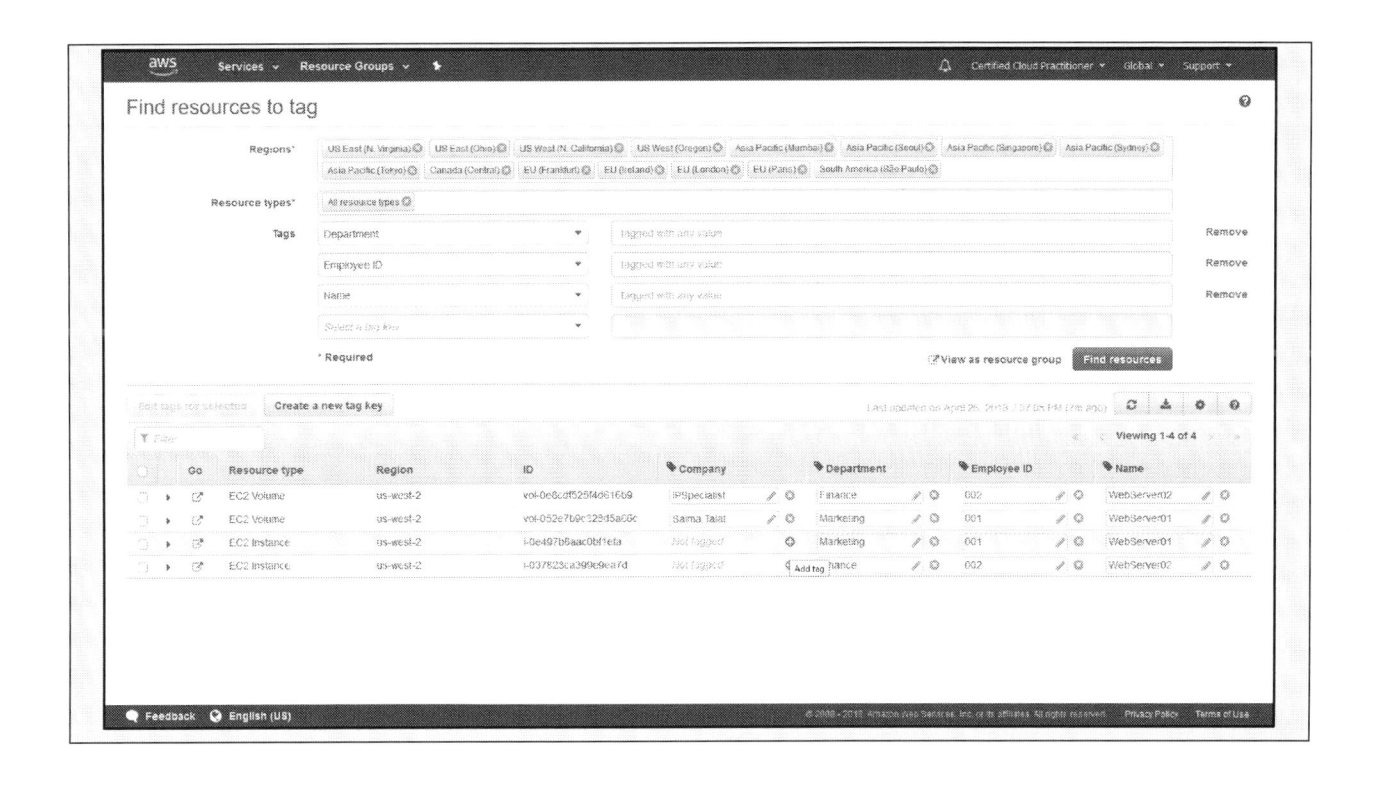

# Chapter 4: Billing and Pricing

Introduction

AWS runs with a pay-as-you-go pricing approach for over 70 cloud services. While the number and types of services offered by AWS have increased dramatically, the philosophy of pricing has not changed. At the end of each month, you pay only for what you use, and you can start or stop using a product at any time. No long-term contracts are required.

AWS is based on the strategy of pricing each service independently to provide customers with remarkable flexibility by allowing them to choose the services they need for their project and to pay only for what they use. AWS pricing is comparable to how you pay for utilities like water or electricity. You only pay for the services consumed with no additional costs or termination fees once you stop using them.

AWS Pricing Policy

Amazon Web Services (AWS) provides a variety of cloud computing services with a utility-style based pricing model. For every service, you pay for exactly the amount of resources needed. The following pricing policies apply all across AWS for all the different services it offers:

- **Pay as you go**
  With AWS, replace upfront capital expense with low variable cost and pay only for what you use, as long as you need it. The charges are based on the underlying infrastructure and services consumed. This allows you to easily adapt to changing business needs without paying upfront for excess capacity and improving your responsiveness to changes. No minimum commitments or long-term contracts required with no complex licensing dependencies. For compute resources, you pay on an hourly basis from the time you launch a resource until the time you terminate it. For data storage and transfer, you pay on a per gigabyte basis.

Chapter 4: Billing and Pricing

- **Pay less when you reserve**

  You can get volume-based discounts for certain products by investing in reserved capacity and gaining a significant discounted hourly rate. This results in overall savings up to 60% (depending on the type of instance you reserve and whether you do upfront or partial payments) over equivalent On-Demand capacity. To optimize savings, choosing the right combinations of storage solutions to help reduce costs while preserving performance, security, and durability. As a result, you benefit from the economies of scale by keeping costs under control.

- **Pay even less per unit by using more**

  Save more, as you grow bigger. For storage and data transfer OUT, pricing is tiered, meaning the more you use, the less you pay per gigabyte. While data transfer IN is always free of charge. For compute, you get up to 10% volume discounts when you reserve more. Whereas if you buy Reserved Instances, the larger the upfront payment, the greater the discount. Paying all up-front can maximize your savings with greater discounts. Partial up-front RI's offer lower discounts, but you get to spend less up front. By choosing to spend nothing up front gives you a smaller discount, it allows you to free up capital to spend on other projects.

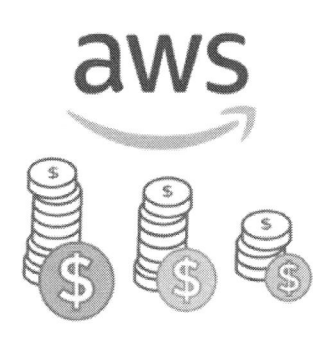

- **Pay even less as AWS grows**

  AWS concentrate on decreasing data center hardware expenses, improving operational efficiencies, reducing power consumption, and overall lowering the cost of doing business. These optimizations and AWS's extensive and increasing economies of scale results in the transfer of savings back to you in the form of lower pricing. AWS has reduced pricing 44 times since 2006.

Chapter 4: Billing and Pricing

- **Custom pricing**

    If none of the pricing models suits your needs, AWS also offers custom pricing for high volume projects with distinctive requirements. If you are using AWS in an enterprise environment, you can acquire custom pricings as well.

> EXAM TIP: Follow the pricing policy of AWS while attempting any scenario-based question; i.e., you only pay for what you use at the end of each month with no long-term contracts and can start or stop using a product anytime. However, if you do enter into a long-term contract and pay for everything upfront, you are going to get the maximum amount of savings.

AWS Free Tier

AWS offers a free usage tier to assist new AWS customers in getting familiarized with the cloud. A Free Tier account offers the benefit of getting free, hands-on experience with the AWS platform, products, and services. Some of the AWS services are free for 12 months while some are always free. A new AWS customer can run a free Amazon EC2 Micro Instance for a year while also having the opportunity of acquiring a free usage tier for Amazon S3, Amazon Elastic Block Store, Amazon Elastic Load Balancing, AWS data transfer and other AWS services.

Free Services

AWS also provides a variety of services that are free with no additional charge:

- *Amazon VPC*

    Amazon Virtual Private Cloud (Amazon VPC) enables you to provision a private logically isolated section of the AWSCloud for launching AWS resources in a virtual network that you define.

Chapter 4: Billing and Pricing

- **AWS Elastic Beanstalk**

   AWS Elastic Beanstalk facilitates you to quickly deploy and manage applications in the AWS cloud easily and effortlessly. The actual service itself is free; the resources it provisions are not, like EC2 instances or RDS instances.

- **AWS CloudFormation**

   AWS CloudFormation service can be used by developers and system administrators. It allows you to easily create a group of related AWS resources and provision them in an arranged and predictable manner. AWS CloudFormation service is free; the resources it provisions are not.

- **AWS Identity and Access Management (IAM)**

   AWS IAM securely control users' access to AWS services and resources by allowing access to who is authenticated (signed in) and authorized (has permissions) to use resources.

- **Auto Scaling**

   Auto Scaling adds (scale up) or removes (scale down) Amazon Elastic Compute Cloud (EC2) instances automatically according to your defined conditions. By using AutoScaling, you can increase the number of Amazon EC2 instances seamlessly during demand spikes to maintain performance and decrease automatically when demand subsidies to minimize costs.

- **AWS OpsWorks**

   AWS OpsWorks is an application management service that simplifies the deployment and operation of applications of all forms and sizes.

- **Consolidated Billing**

   Consolidated Billing can be used to combine all your accounts billing into one bill and get tiering benefits.

> EXAM TIP: It is essential to remember all the free services offered by Amazon while preparing for the exam. The services themselves are free, but the resources they provision, are not.

Fundamental Pricing Characteristics

While Using the AWS Cloud platform, there are three fundamental characteristics you are charged for:

- Compute
- Storage
- Data Transfer Out

These characteristics vary to some extent depending on the AWS product being used. However, essentially these core characteristics have the greatest influence on cost. The outbound data transfer is combined across Amazon EC2, Amazon S3, Amazon RDS, Amazon SimpleDB, Amazon SQS, Amazon SNS, and Amazon VPC to be charged at the outbound data transfer rate. This charge appears on the monthly statement as AWS Data Transfer Out.

Free Inbound Data Transfer

While Data Transfer outcomes with a price, there is no charge for inbound data transfer across all Amazon Web Services in all regions. In addition, there are no outbound data transfer charges between Amazon Web Services within the same region.

> **EXAM TIP:** If you get a scenario-based question, think through the fundamental charges; whether it involves compute service, requires storage or if data is being transferred out to the internet. If yes, then you are going to be charged. Whereas data transfer in is free.

Amazon Elastic Compute Cloud (Amazon EC2)

Amazon EC2 is a web service that enables you to obtain and configure resizable compute capacity in the cloud. Amazon only charges for the computing capacity you actually use. The following factors need to be considered while estimating the cost of using Amazon EC2:

Chapter 4: Billing and Pricing

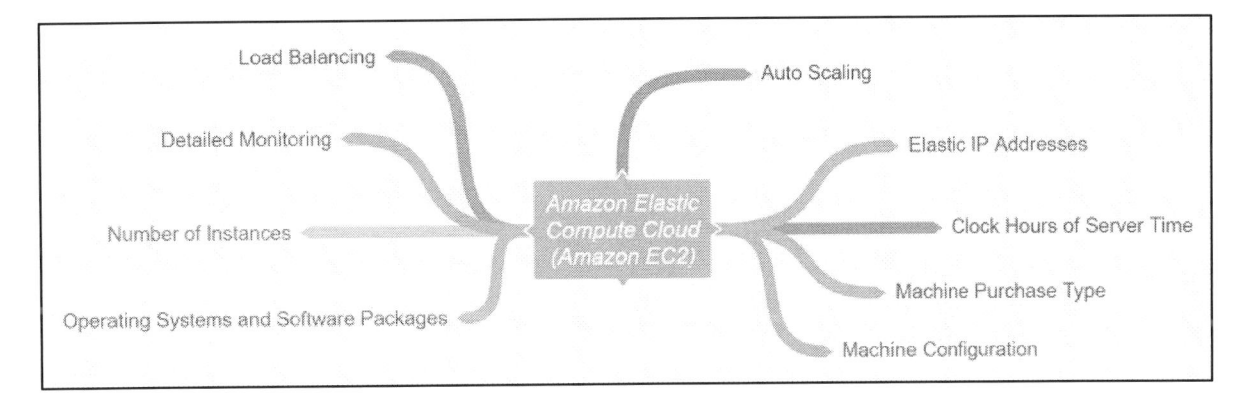

Figure 3-01. Mind Map of EC2 Cost Factors

- **Clock Hours of Server Time** – Running resources incur charges. For example, the time from which Amazon EC2 instances are launched up until they are terminated, or from the time Elastic IPs are allocated until the time they are de-allocated.

- **Machine Configuration** – Instance pricing varies depending upon the physical configuration of the Amazon EC2 instances such as the operating system, number of cores, memory and the AWS region as well.

- **Machine Purchase Type** – These purchase types can be On-Demand Instances, Reserved Instances or Spot Instances. With On-Demand Instances, you pay by the hour with no commitments. With Reserved Instances, you receive a significant discount on the hourly usage by either paying a low one-time payment or no payment at all for each instance of the compute capacity you reserve. With Spot Instances, you can bid for unused Amazon EC2 capacity.

- **Number of Instances** – Multiple resources of Amazon EC2 and Amazon EBS can be provisioned for managing and handling peak loads.

- **Load Balancing** – Using an Elastic Load Balancer for distributing traffic among the Amazon EC2 instances can contribute to the monthly cost determined by the number of hours the Elastic Load Balancer runs and the volume of data it processes.

- **Detailed Monitoring** – Amazon CloudWatch can be used to monitor your EC2 instances. Basic monitoring is supported by default without any additional cost. However, you can subscribe for detailed monitoring at a fixed monthly rate, which contains seven preselected metrics logged once a minute. Partial months are charged on an hourly pro rata basis, at a per instance-hour rate.

- ***Auto Scaling*** – Auto Scaling scales the number of Amazon EC2 instances up or down automatically to adjust accordingly to the deployment needs you define. The service is accessible at no additional cost except for the Amazon CloudWatch fees.

- ***Elastic IP Addresses*** – One Elastic IP (EIP) address linked with a running instance is free of charge.

- ***Operating Systems and Software Packages*** – Operating Systems prices are included in the instance prices.

Amazon Simple Storage Service (Amazon S3)

Amazon S3 is a web service that provides storage in the cloud. The simple web services interface can be used to store and retrieve any volume of data, at any time, from anywhere on the web. The following factors should be considered while estimating the cost of Amazon S3:

Figure 4-02. Mind Map of S3 Cost Factors

- ***Storage Class*** – Different storage classes have different rates;
  - *Standard Storage* is best for frequently accessed data, designed to provide 99.999999999% durability and 99.99% availability.
  - *Standard – Infrequent Access* is used for storing less frequently access data with lower levels of redundancy than standard storage. It offers cheaper storage over time, but higher charges to retrieve or transfer data.

- ***Storage*** - The number and size of objects stored in your Amazon S3 buckets plus the type of storage used.

- ***Requests*** - The number and type of requests. For Example, GET requests charges cost at different rates than other requests, such as PUT and COPY requests.

- ***Data Transfer*** - The amount of data transferred out of the Amazon S3 buckets. Whereas Data Transfer In is free of charge.

Amazon Relational Database Service (Amazon RDS)

Amazon RDS is a relational database web service in the cloud that allows you to easily set up, operate, and scale as per your needs. It lets you concentrate on your applications and business by offering cost-efficient and resizable capacity while handling the database administration tasks itself. When estimating the cost of Amazon RDS, the following factors need to be considered:

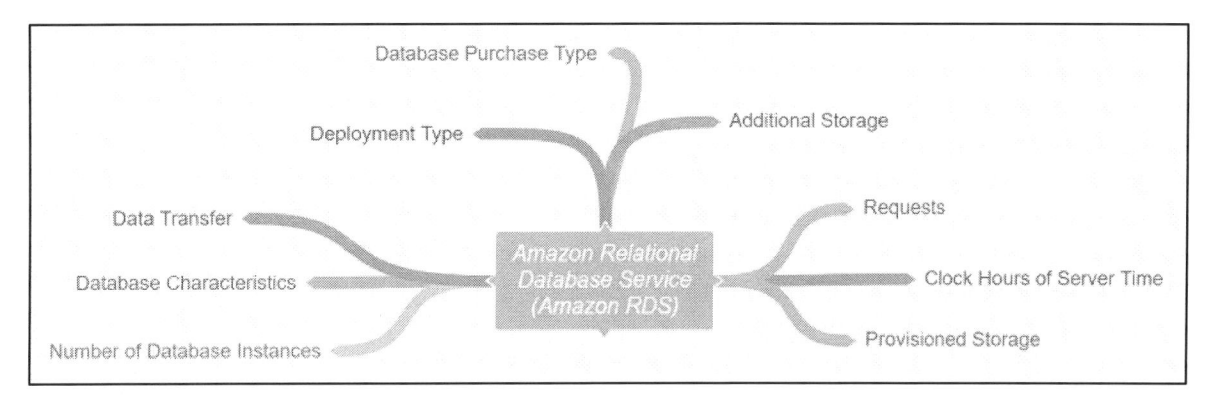

Figure 4-03. Mind Map of RDS Cost Factors

- ***Clock Hours of Server Time*** – Resources incur charges when they are running. For example, from the time you launch a DB instance until you terminate the DB instance.

- ***Database Characteristics***–The physical characteristics of the database such as database engine, size, and memory class affect how much you are charged.

- ***Database Purchase Type*** – With On-Demand DB Instances, you pay for compute capacity for each hour your DB Instance runs, with no minimum commitments. With Reserved DB Instances, you receive a significant discount on the hourly usage charge by paying a low one-time, up-front payment for each DB Instance you reserve for a 1-year or 3-years term.

- ***A number of Database Instances*** – Multiple DB instances can be provisioned with Amazon RDS to handle peak loads.

- ***Provisioned Storage*** – For an active DB instance, there is no extra charge for backup storage of up to 100% of your provisioned database storage. Backup storage incurs charges for per gigabyte per month after the DB Instance is terminated.

- **_Additional Storage_** – Along with the provisioned storage amount, the amount of backup storage also incurs charges for per gigabyte per month.

- **_Requests_** – The number of input and output requests to the database.

- **_Deployment Type_** – DB instance can be deployed in a single Availability Zone that is similar to a stand-alone data center or in multiple Availability Zones, which works like a secondary data center for increased availability and durability. The charges for storage and I/O differ depending upon the number of Availability Zones used for deployment.

- **_Data Transfer_** – Inbound data transfer is free, whereas outbound data transfer costs are tiered.

Amazon CloudFront

Amazon CloudFront is a web service for content delivery. It incorporates with other Amazon Web Services to distribute content to end users with low latency, high data transfer speeds, with no minimum commitments. For Amazon CloudFront cost estimation, the following factors need to consider:

Figure 4-04. Mind Map of CloudFront Cost Factors

- **_Traffic Distribution_** – The data transfer and request pricing differ across geographic regions and depends upon the edge location through which the content is served.

- **_Requests_** – The number and type of requests (HTTP or HTTPS) made, and the geographic region in which the requests are made.

- **_Data Transfer Out_** – The amount of data transferred out of your Amazon CloudFront edge locations.

Amazon Elastic Block Store (Amazon EBS)

Amazon EBS offers block level storage volumes to be used with Amazon EC2 instances. These EBS volumes carry on independently irrespective of the EC2 instance lifespan. They are off-instance storage, similar to virtual disks in the cloud. Amazon EBS offers three types of volume, General Purpose (SSD), Provisioned IOPS (SSD), and Magnetic, all with different costs and performance characteristics.

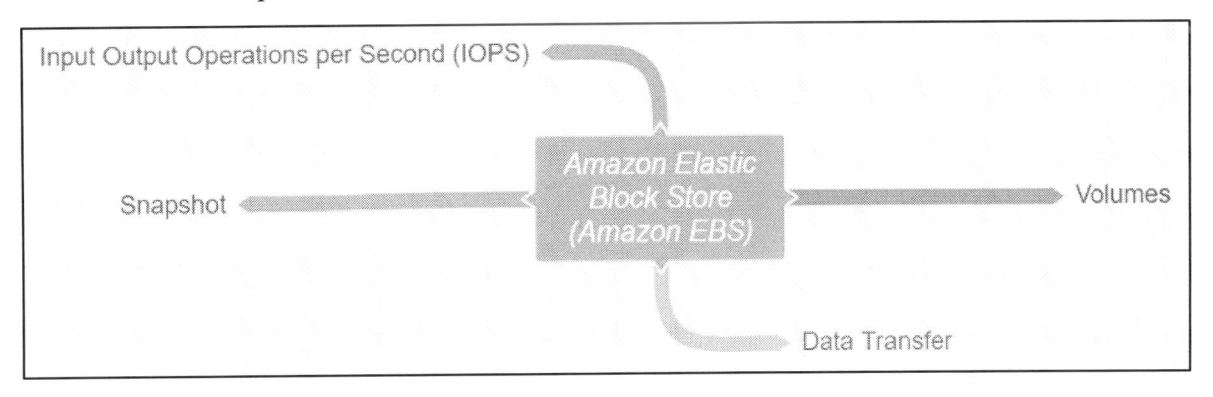

Figure 4-05. Mind Map of EBS Cost Factors

- **_Volumes_** – The amount of storage volume you provisioned is charged in GB per month for all EBS volume types until you release the storage.

- **_Input Output Operations per Second (IOPS)_** – When using EBS Magnetic volumes, I/O is charged by the number of requests made to your volume. For Provisioned IOPS (SSD) volumes, you are charged by the amount you provision in IOPS (multiplied by the percentage of days you provision for the month). While for General Purpose (SSD) volumes, I/O is included in its price.

- **_Snapshot_**– Amazon EBS offers the facility of backing up snapshots of your data to Amazon S3 for a durable recovery, with an added cost of per GB-month of data stored.

- **_Data Transfer_** –Inbound data transfer is free, while the outbound data transfer charges are tiered.

Saving Further Costs

Many large enterprise organizations customize their contracts with AWS to further optimize their costs and meet their needs. Different pricing models are available for some of the AWS products, offering you the flexibility to access services according to your requirements.

On-Demand Instance

With on-demand instances, you pay for computing capacity by the hour, with no minimum commitments required.

Reserved Instance

Reserved Instances allow you to reserve compute capacity in advance for long-term savings. It provides significant discounts (up to 60 percent) compared to On-Demand Instance pricing.

The following table compares one-year and three-year savings from the use of reserved instances versus on-demand instances. The figures are based on pricing as of January 2015 on an m3.large Linux instance type in the US East (N. Virginia) region.

	No Upfront	Partial Upfront	All Upfront	On-Demand
1 Year	$876.00	$767.12	$751.00	$1226.40
3 Years		$1461.40	$1373.00	$3679.20
Savings 1 Year	29%	37%	39%	
Savings 3 Years		60%	63%	

Table 4-1 Reduced Instances Vs. On-Demand Instances

Spot Instance

You can bid for unused Amazon Elastic Compute Cloud (Amazon EC2) capacity. Instances are charged at Spot Price, which is set by Amazon EC2 and fluctuates, depending on supply and demand. If your bid exceeds the current Spot Price, your requested instances will run until either you terminate them or the Spot Price increases above your bid.

Pricing is tiered for storage and data transfer. The more you use, the less you pay per gigabyte (GB). Volume discounts are also available.

AWS Support Plans

AWS provides access to tools and expertise under a range of support plans that support the operational health and success of your AWS solutions. You can opt for a support plan according to your organizational requirements; whether you need technical support or additional resources to assist you in planning, deploying and optimizing your AWS environment. AWS offers four support plans to its customers, which are Basic, Developer, Business, and Enterprise.

Basic — Get familiar with AWS

- The Basic plan is the account you get on Free Tier. It offers its customers support for account and billing queries and service limit increases as well as:
  - Receiving basic support with access to support forums
  - Accessing to 24x7 to customer service
  - Accessing to AWS documentation and whitepapers

Developer — Experimenting with AWS

- The Developer Support plan offers resources for customers testing or doing early development on AWS, as well as any customer who:
  - Wants access to guidance and technical support
  - Is exploring how to quickly put AWS to work
  - Uses AWS for non-production workloads or applications

Business — Production use of AWS

- The Business Support plan offers resources for customers running production workloads on AWS as well as any customer who:
  - Runs one or more applications in production environments
  - Has multiple services activated, or uses key services extensively
  - Depends on business solutions to be available, scalable, and secured

Enterprise — Mission-critical use of AWS

- The Enterprise Support plan offers resources for customers running business & mission critical workloads on AWS, as well as any customer who wants to:
  - Focus on proactive management to increase efficiency and availability
  - Build and operate workloads following AWS best practices
  - Leverage AWS expertise to support launches and migrations

Features of AWS Support Plans

Different AWS Support plans have different features, which they offer to their customers. The Basic plan is free of charge whereas the other plans offer pay-by-the-month pricing with no long-term contracts and an unlimited number of technical support cases to provide you the level of support that you require.

All AWS customers inherently have 24x7 access to these Basic support plan features:

- Customer Service: one-on-one responses to account and billing queries
- AWS Community Support forums
- Service health checks
- Documentation, whitepapers, and best-practice guides

Additionally, Developer support plan customers have access to these features:

- Best-practice guidance
- Client-side diagnostic tools
- Building-block architecture support: Guidance on using AWS products, features, and services collectively

Furthermore, Business and Enterprise support plan customers get these features as well:

- Use-case guidance: What AWS products, features, and services to use to best support your particular needs
- Identity and Access Management (IAM) to control users' access to AWS Support
- AWS Trusted Advisor, for inspecting users' environments, identifying cost-saving prospects, closing security gaps and optimizing your infrastructure.
- AWS Support API for automating support cases and Trusted Advisor operations
- Third-party software support: help with Amazon EC2 instance operating systems, configurations, and performance of third-party software components

In addition to all the above features, Enterprise support plan customers enjoy the benefits of the following features as well:

- Application architecture guidance: Consultative partnership supporting specific use cases and applications
- Infrastructure event management: Support for product launches, architectural and scaling guidance for seasonal promotions/events and migrations depending on your use case
- AWS Concierge, for billing and account analysis/assistance
- Technical Account Manager, dedicated customer service personnel
- White-glove case routing
- Management business reviews

Chapter 4: Billing and Pricing

Comparison of Support Plans

The following table lists the key comparison factors among the four support plans that AWS offers:

	Basic	**Developer**	**Business**	**Enterprise**
Pricing	Free	From $29 per month	From $100 per month	From $15k per month
Technical Support		Business hours access to Cloud Support Associates via email	24x7 access to Cloud Support Engineers via email, chat & phone	24x7 access to Sr.Cloud Support Engineers via email, chat & phone
Technical Account Manager	No	No	No	Yes
Who can open cases?	None	One prime contact/ Unlimited cases	Unlimited contacts/ Unlimited cases	Unlimited contacts/ Unlimited cases
Trusted Adviser	Access to 6 core Trusted Advisor checks	Access to 6 core Trusted Advisor checks	Access to full set of Trusted Advisor checks	Access to full set of Trusted Advisor checks
Programmatic Case Management			AWS Support API	AWS Support API

Table 4-2 AWS Support Plans

Chapter 4: Billing and Pricing

The table below describes the case severities and their respective response times under different support plans:

Case Severity	Response Time	Support Plan	Description
General guidance	< 24 business hours	Developer, Business, and Enterprise	General development question, or request a feature
System impaired	< 12 business hours	The developer, Business, and Enterprise	Non-critical functions of the application behaving abnormally, or having a time-sensitive development question
Production system impaired	< 4 hours	Business and Enterprise	Important functions of the application are impaired or degraded
Production system down	< 1 hour	Business and Enterprise	Business is significantly impacted. Important functions of the application are unavailable
Business-critical system down	< 15 minutes	Enterprise Only	Business is at risk. Critical functions of the application are unavailable

Table 4-3 Case Severity and Response Times

> **EXAM TIP**: Remember the different response times for the corresponding case severity in any particular plan. Also, keep in mind that Technical Account Manager (TAM) is only available for the Enterprise Support Plan.

AWS Organizations

AWS Organizations is an account management service that allows you to consolidate multiple AWS accounts into an organization, enabling you to create a hierarchical structure that can be managed centrally.

With AWS Organizations, you can create multiple groups of AWS accounts known as the Organizational Units and then apply policies to those Organizational Units, commonly referred to as Service Control Policies (SCPs). These policies centrally control the use of AWS services across multiple AWS accounts, without the need for custom scripts and manual processes. Entities in the AWS accounts can only use the AWS services allowed by both the SCP and the AWS IAM policy for the account.

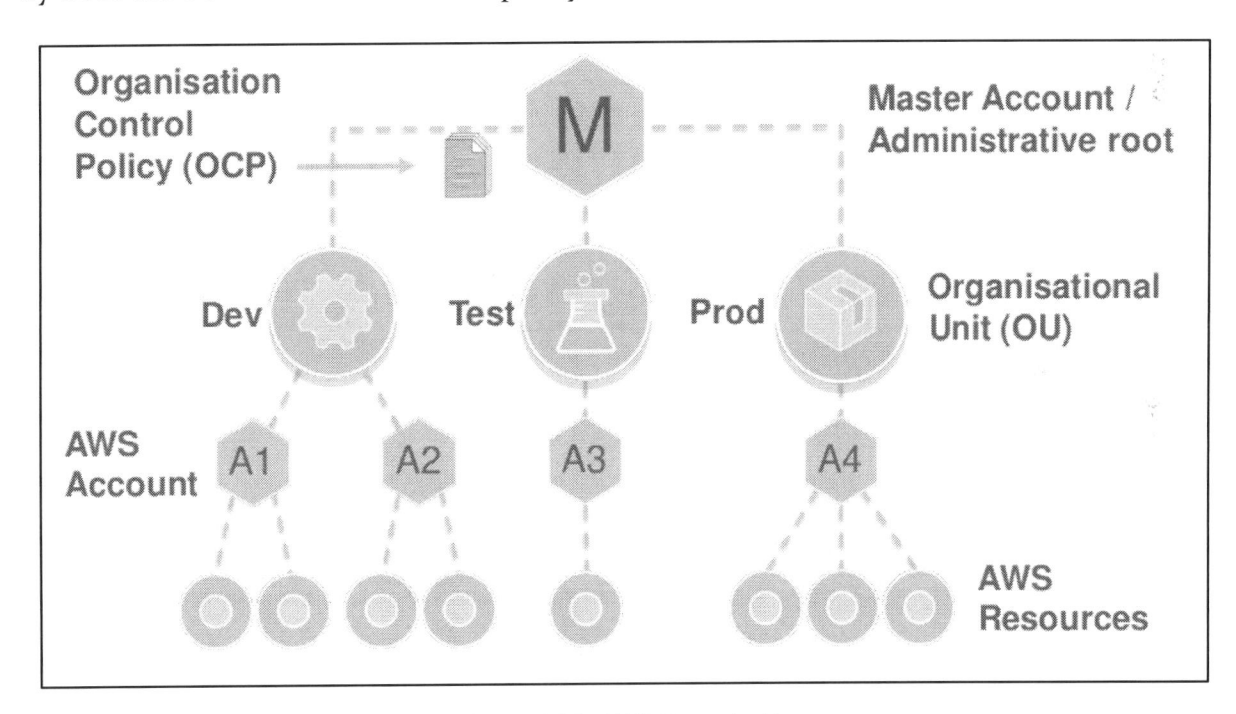

Figure 4-06. AWS Organization

AWS Organizations is available to all AWS customers at no additional charge in two feature sets:

- Only Consolidated billing features: This mode only provides the consolidated billing features and does not include the other advanced features of AWS Organizations, such as the use of policies to restrict what users and roles in different accounts can access.

- **All features:** This mode is the complete feature set that includes all the functionality of consolidated billing in addition to the advanced features that provides more control over the accounts in your organization.

Key Features of AWS Organizations

- ***Group-based account management:***
  Create separate groups of AWS accounts to use with development and production resources, and then apply different policies to each group.

  - ***Policy framework for multiple AWS accounts:***
    AWS Organizations provides a policy framework for multiple AWS accounts. Apply policies to a group of accounts or all the accounts in your organization.

- ***API level control of AWS services:***
  Use service control policies (SCPs) to manage and centrally control access to AWS services at an API level across multiple AWS accounts.

  - ***Account creation and management APIs***
    Automate the creation and management of new AWS accounts through APIs. APIs create new accounts programmatically.

- ***Consolidated billing***
  Set up a single payment method for all the AWS accounts in your organization through consolidated billing. It provides combined view of charges incurred by all your accounts.

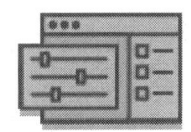

  - ***Enable only consolidated billing features***
    Create new organizations with only the consolidated billing features enabled. Advanced policy controls such as Service Control Policies (SCPs) are not enabled.

Consolidated Billing

One of the key features of AWS Organizations is the consolidation of the billing of all the AWS accounts in your organization, where you have a single AWS account as the paying master account linked with a set of all other AWS accounts to form a simple one-level hierarchy. At the end of the month, you obtain a combined view of charges incurred by all of your AWS accounts. It also provides a cost report for each member account that is associated with the master paying account. Consolidated billing is available at no additional cost.

Consolidated billing has the following key benefits:

- One Bill – Get one bill for multiple accounts.
- Easy Tracking – Easily track each account's charges.
- Combined Usage – Combine usage from all accounts in the organization results in volume discounts.

> **EXAM TIP**: Paying Account should be used for billing purposes only. Do not deploy resources to the Paying Account. When monitoring is enabled on the Paying Account, billing data for all linked accounts are included. You can also create billing alerts for individual accounts separately.

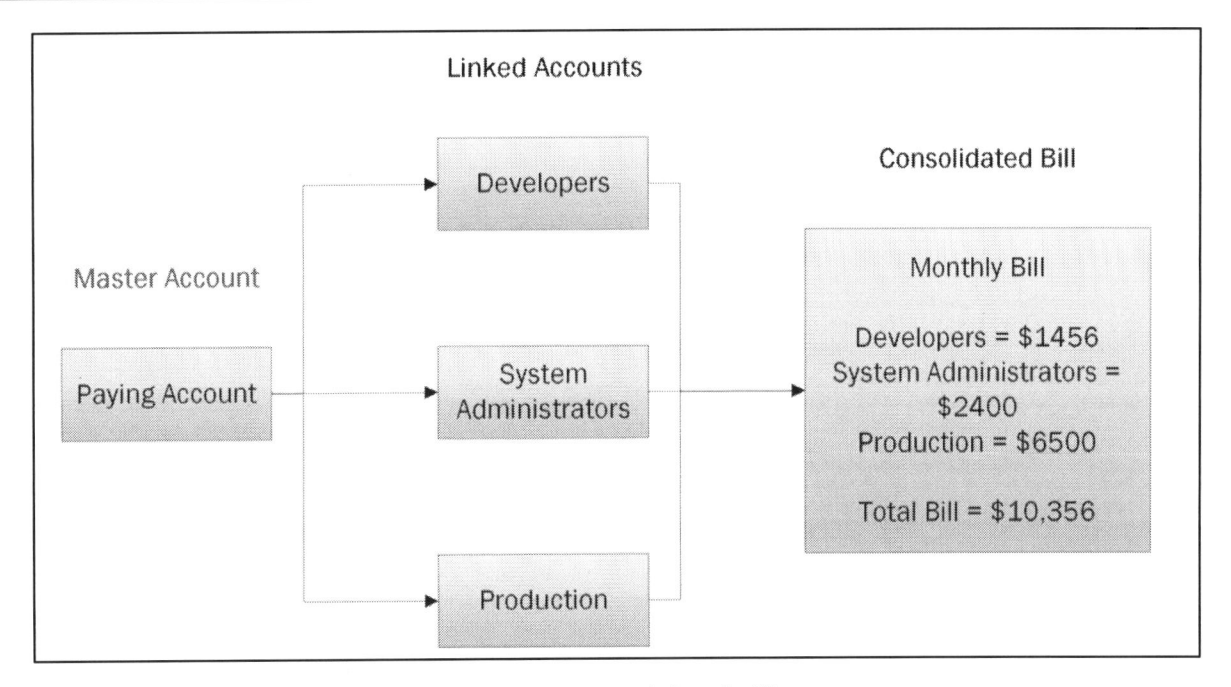

Figure 4-07. Consolidated Billing

With only the consolidated billing feature enabled, each member account is independent of the other member accounts. Unless the master account explicitly restricts linked accounts using policies, the owner of each member account can independently access resources, sign up for AWS services and use AWS Premium Support. Account owners use their own IAM username and password with independently assigned account permissions in the organization.

Currently, there is a soft limit of 20 accounts per organization and a hard limit of one level of billing hierarchy; i.e., a master (paying) account cannot be in the same organization as another master (paying) account.

> **EXAM TIP**: AWS CloudTrail is a service used to monitor account activity and deliver generated event logs to the associated account S3 Bucket. You can aggregate Log Files from multiple regions to a single S3 bucket of the Paying Account.

Consolidated Billing Examples

1. **Volume Discounts**

Services such as Amazon EC2 and Amazon S3 have tiered volume pricing that offers lower prices, the more you use the service, the less you will be charged. With consolidated billing, AWS determines which volume pricing tiers to apply by combining the usage from all accounts. Consider the following scenario:

Account Name	Data Transfer OUT
Developers	8 TB
System Administrators	5 TB
Production	3 TB

The Data Transfer OUT rates from Amazon S3 to the internet for US East (N. Virginia) Region are as follows:

Data Transfer Volume	Pricing
Up to 1 GB / Month	$0.00 per GB
Next 10 TB / Month	$0.09 per GB
Next 40 TB / Month	$0.085 per GB

Chapter 4: Billing and Pricing

Without Consolidated billing, the cost will be calculated as:

- 8 TB will be charged as (8 * 1024) * $0.09 = $ 737.28
- 5 TB will be charged as (5 * 1024) * $0.09 = $ 460.80
- 3 TB will be charged as (3 * 1024) * $0.09 = $ 276.48
- Total Bill = $ 1474.56 for 16 TB of data transfer

With Consolidated billing, data transfer charges for a total of 16 TB will be:

- Tier 1: First 10 TB will be charged as (10 * 1024) * $0.09 = $ 921.60
- Tier 2: Next 6 TB will be charged as (6 * 1024) * $0.085 = $ 522.24
- Total Consolidated Bill = $ 1443.84 for 16 TB of data transfer

2. **Reserved Instances:**

As AWS Organizations deals with all the linked accounts in the organization as a single account, every member account can get the hourly cost-benefit of Reserved Instances purchased by any other member account within the organization. Consider the following scenario of two linked accounts:

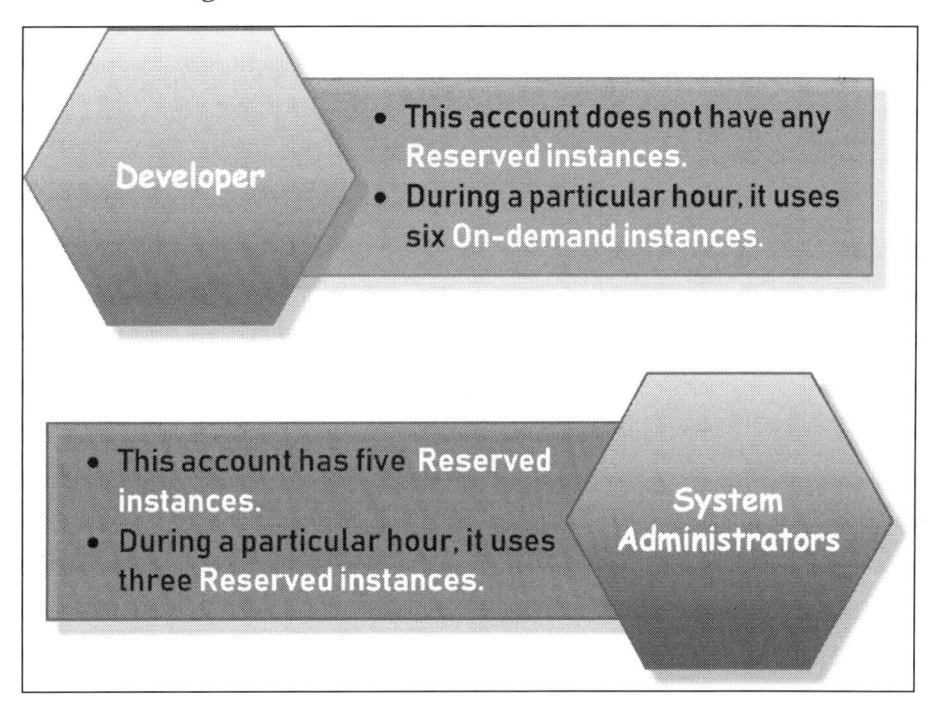

Figure 4-08. Linked Accounts with Reserved Instances

On the organization's consolidated bill, only nine instances will be charged, from which five of them will be charged as Reserved Instances and the remaining four as regular On-Demand Instances. If the accounts were not linked to a single consolidated bill, six On-Demand Instances and five Reserved Instances would have been charged.

The linked accounts receive the cost-benefit from each other's Reserved Instances only if the launched instances are in the same Availability Zone having the same instance size and belonging to the same family of instance types.

> **EXAM TIP:** Consolidated Billing allows you to get volume discounts on all your accounts. When consolidated billing is enabled, unused reserved instances for EC2 are applied across the group.

> **EXAM TIP:** During the exam, you are going to get scenario-based questions asking about how you can save cost, the answer to it is 'Consolidated Billing'.

AWS Cost Calculators

AWS helps you calculate your costs using a couple of calculators. There are two calculators available for this:

- AWS Simple Monthly Calculator
- AWS TCO (Total Cost of Ownership) Calculator

AWS Simple Monthly Calculator

The AWS Simple Monthly Calculator provides an estimation of monthly bill depending on the resources configuration. Whether you are running a single instance or dozens of individual services, you organize your planned resources by service, and the Simple Monthly Calculator provides an estimated cost per month for that configuration.

The calculator provides per service cost breakdown, as well as an aggregate monthly estimate. You can also use the calculator to see an estimation and breakdown of costs for common solutions.

Chapter 4: Billing and Pricing

Lab 4-1: AWS Simple Monthly Calculator

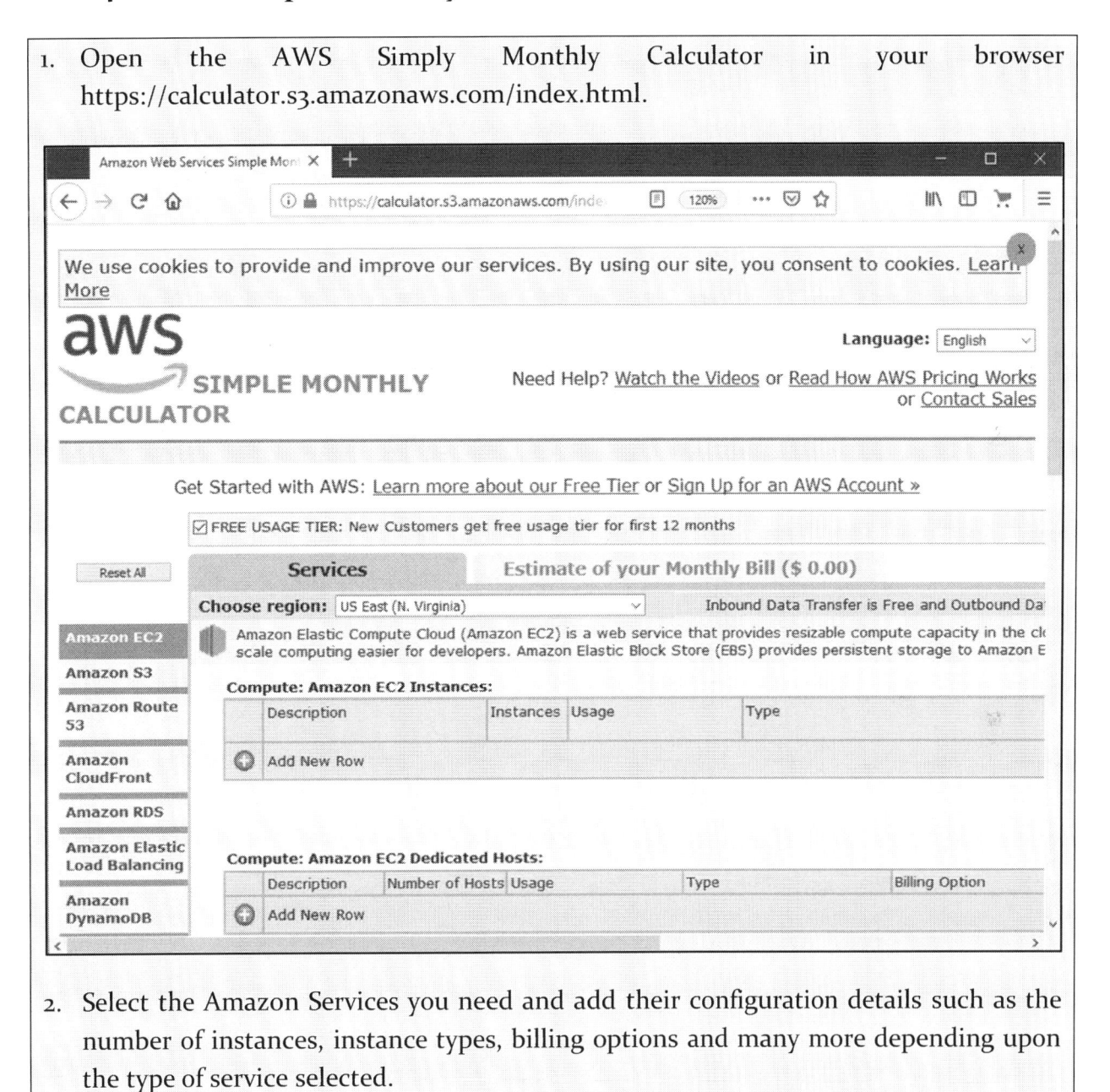

1. Open the AWS Simply Monthly Calculator in your browser https://calculator.s3.amazonaws.com/index.html.

2. Select the Amazon Services you need and add their configuration details such as the number of instances, instance types, billing options and many more depending upon the type of service selected.

Chapter 4: Billing and Pricing

Select Instance Type

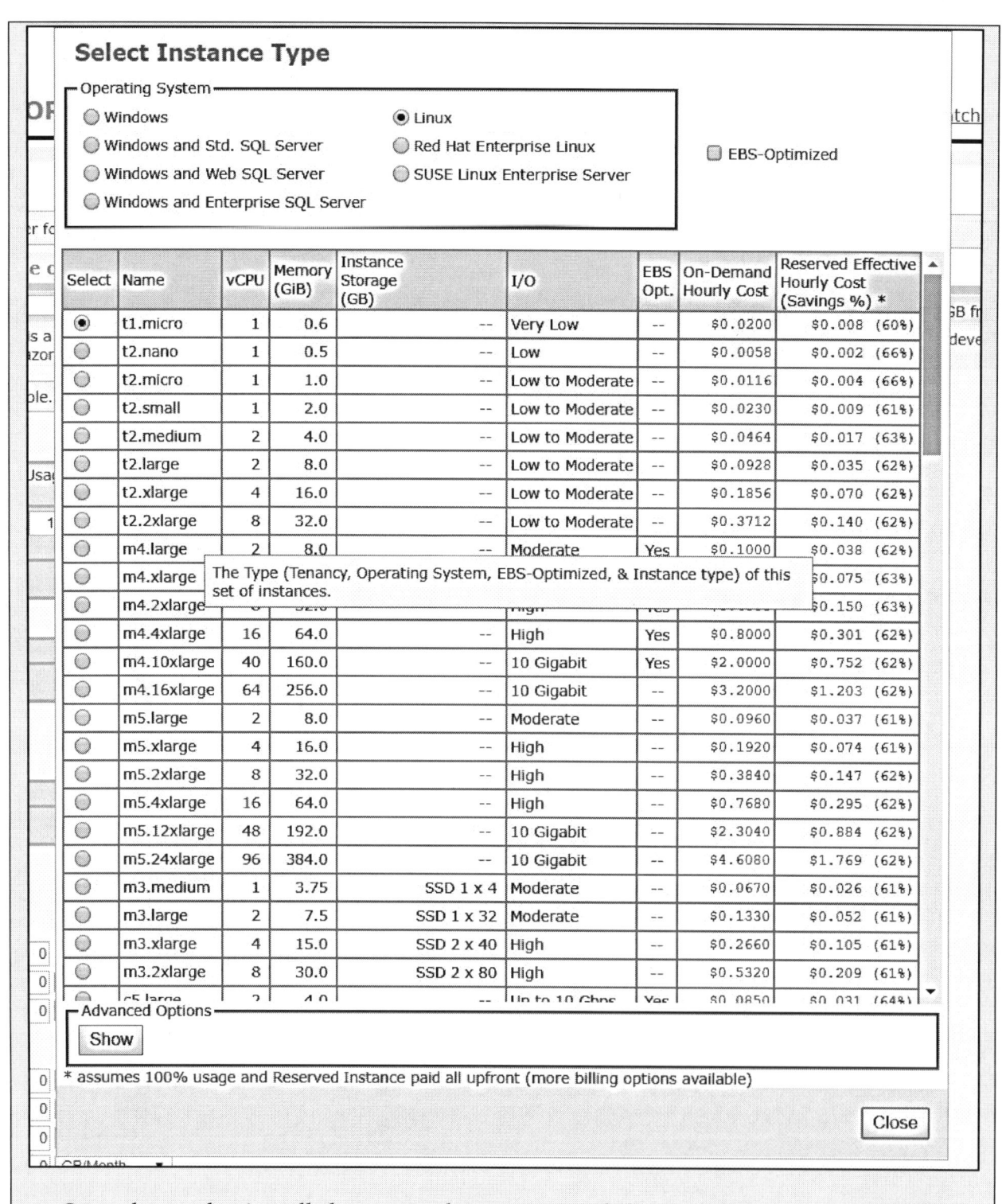

Operating System
- ○ Windows
- ● Linux
- ○ Windows and Std. SQL Server
- ○ Red Hat Enterprise Linux
- ○ Windows and Web SQL Server
- ○ SUSE Linux Enterprise Server
- ○ Windows and Enterprise SQL Server

☐ EBS-Optimized

Select	Name	vCPU	Memory (GiB)	Instance Storage (GB)	I/O	EBS Opt.	On-Demand Hourly Cost	Reserved Effective Hourly Cost (Savings %) *
●	t1.micro	1	0.6	--	Very Low	--	$0.0200	$0.008 (60%)
○	t2.nano	1	0.5	--	Low	--	$0.0058	$0.002 (66%)
○	t2.micro	1	1.0	--	Low to Moderate	--	$0.0116	$0.004 (66%)
○	t2.small	1	2.0	--	Low to Moderate	--	$0.0230	$0.009 (61%)
○	t2.medium	2	4.0	--	Low to Moderate	--	$0.0464	$0.017 (63%)
○	t2.large	2	8.0	--	Low to Moderate	--	$0.0928	$0.035 (62%)
○	t2.xlarge	4	16.0	--	Low to Moderate	--	$0.1856	$0.070 (62%)
○	t2.2xlarge	8	32.0	--	Low to Moderate	--	$0.3712	$0.140 (62%)
○	m4.large	2	8.0	--	Moderate	Yes	$0.1000	$0.038 (62%)
○	m4.xlarge			The Type (Tenancy, Operating System, EBS-Optimized, & Instance type) of this set of instances.			$0.075 (63%)
○	m4.2xlarge							$0.150 (63%)
○	m4.4xlarge	16	64.0	--	High	Yes	$0.8000	$0.301 (62%)
○	m4.10xlarge	40	160.0	--	10 Gigabit	Yes	$2.0000	$0.752 (62%)
○	m4.16xlarge	64	256.0	--	10 Gigabit	--	$3.2000	$1.203 (62%)
○	m5.large	2	8.0	--	Moderate	--	$0.0960	$0.037 (61%)
○	m5.xlarge	4	16.0	--	High	--	$0.1920	$0.074 (61%)
○	m5.2xlarge	8	32.0	--	High	--	$0.3840	$0.147 (62%)
○	m5.4xlarge	16	64.0	--	High	--	$0.7680	$0.295 (62%)
○	m5.12xlarge	48	192.0	--	10 Gigabit	--	$2.3040	$0.884 (62%)
○	m5.24xlarge	96	384.0	--	10 Gigabit	--	$4.6080	$1.769 (62%)
○	m3.medium	1	3.75	SSD 1 x 4	Moderate	--	$0.0670	$0.026 (61%)
○	m3.large	2	7.5	SSD 1 x 32	Moderate	--	$0.1330	$0.052 (61%)
○	m3.xlarge	4	15.0	SSD 2 x 40	High	--	$0.2660	$0.105 (61%)
○	m3.2xlarge	8	30.0	SSD 2 x 80	High	--	$0.5320	$0.209 (61%)
○	c5.large	2	4.0	--	Up to 10 Gbps	Yes	$0.0850	$0.031 (64%)

Advanced Options
[Show]

* assumes 100% usage and Reserved Instance paid all upfront (more billing options available)

[Close]

3. Once done selecting all the required resources and their configuration specifications, select 'Estimate of your monthly bill' tab at the top to see you estimated monthly cost calculation.

Chapter 4: Billing and Pricing

Get Started with AWS: Learn more about our Free Tier or Sign Up for an AWS Account »	
FREE USAGE TIER: New Customers get free usage tier for first 12 months	

Services | **Estimate of your Monthly Bill ($ 9678.39)**

Estimate of Your Monthly Bill
☑ Show First Month's Bill (include all one-time fees, if any)

Below you will see an estimate of your monthly bill. Expand each line item to see cost breakout of each service. To save this bill and input values, click on 'Save and Share' button. To remove the service from the estimate, jump back to the service and clear the specific service's form.

[Export to CSV] [Save and Share]

Amazon EC2 Service (US East (N. Virginia))		$ 43.92
Compute:	$ 43.92	
Amazon S3 Service (US East (N. Virginia))		$ 1.15
Standard Storage:	$ 1.15	
Amazon S3 Service (EU (London))		$ 2.82
Standard Storage:	$ 2.16	
Standard - IA Storage:	$ 0.66	
Amazon RDS Service (Asia Pacific (Sydney))		$ 8765.76
DB instances:	$ 8754.72	
Storage:	$ 11.04	
AWS Support (Business)		$ 879.86
Support for all AWS services:	$ 879.86	
Free Tier Discount:		$ -15.12
Total Monthly Payment:		$ 9678.39

AWS TCO (Total Cost of Ownership) Calculator

AWS Total Cost of Ownership (TCO) Calculator provides a comparative analysis of the cost estimation by comparing on premises and co-location environments to the AWS.

It estimates the costs of migrating on-premises infrastructure to AWS and gives you the option to evaluate the savings with the infrastructure running on AWS.

The TCO calculator matches your existing or planned infrastructure to the most cost-effective AWS offering. This tool considers all the costs to run a solution, including physical facilities, power, and cooling, providing a realistic end-to-end comparison of

Chapter 4: Billing and Pricing

your costs in the form of a detailed set of reports. The calculator also gives you the option to modify assumptions that best meet your business needs.

Lab 4-2: AWS Total Cost of Ownership Calculator

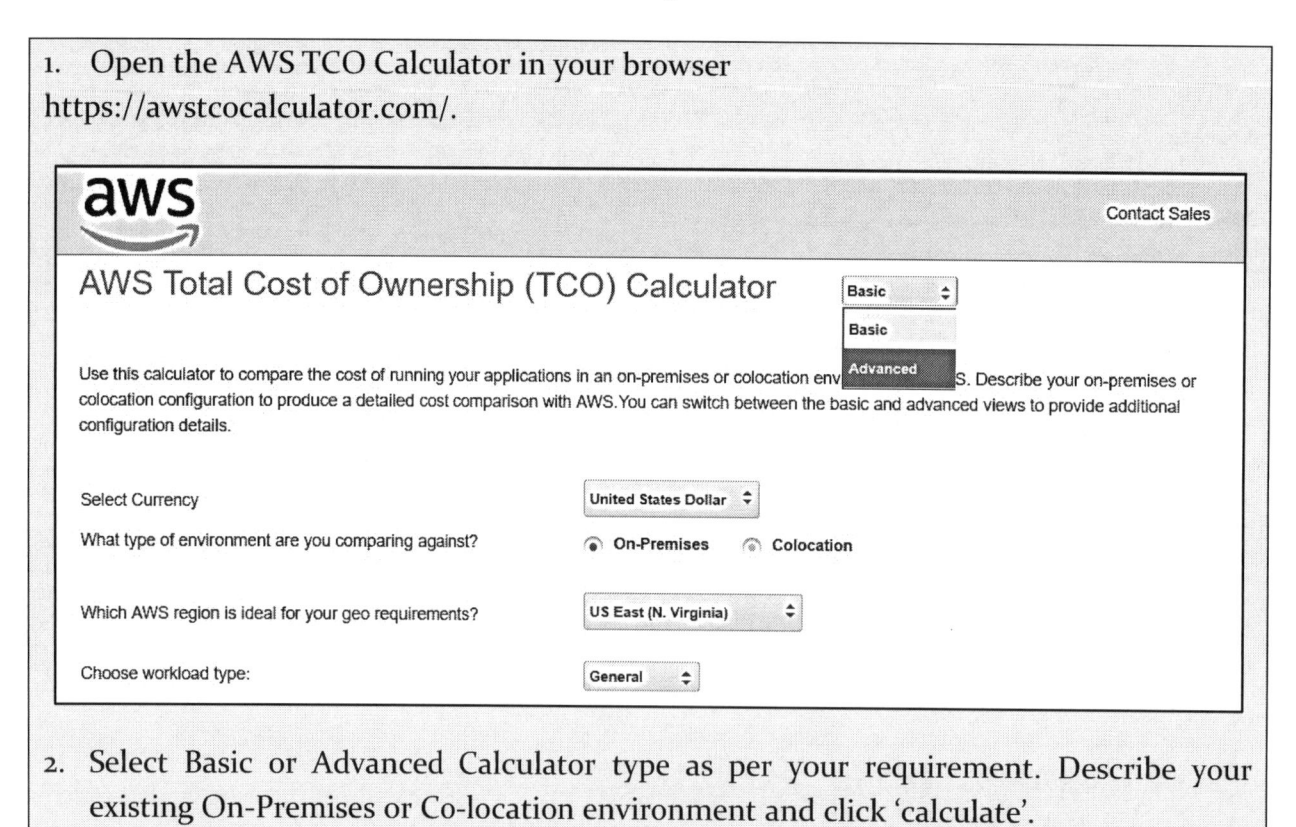

1. Open the AWS TCO Calculator in your browser https://awstcocalculator.com/.

AWS Total Cost of Ownership (TCO) Calculator

Use this calculator to compare the cost of running your applications in an on-premises or colocation environment vs. AWS. Describe your on-premises or colocation configuration to produce a detailed cost comparison with AWS. You can switch between the basic and advanced views to provide additional configuration details.

Select Currency: United States Dollar
What type of environment are you comparing against? ● On-Premises ○ Colocation
Which AWS region is ideal for your geo requirements? US East (N. Virginia)
Choose workload type: General

2. Select Basic or Advanced Calculator type as per your requirement. Describe your existing On-Premises or Co-location environment and click 'calculate'.

Chapter 4: Billing and Pricing

AWS Total Cost of Ownership (TCO) Calculator

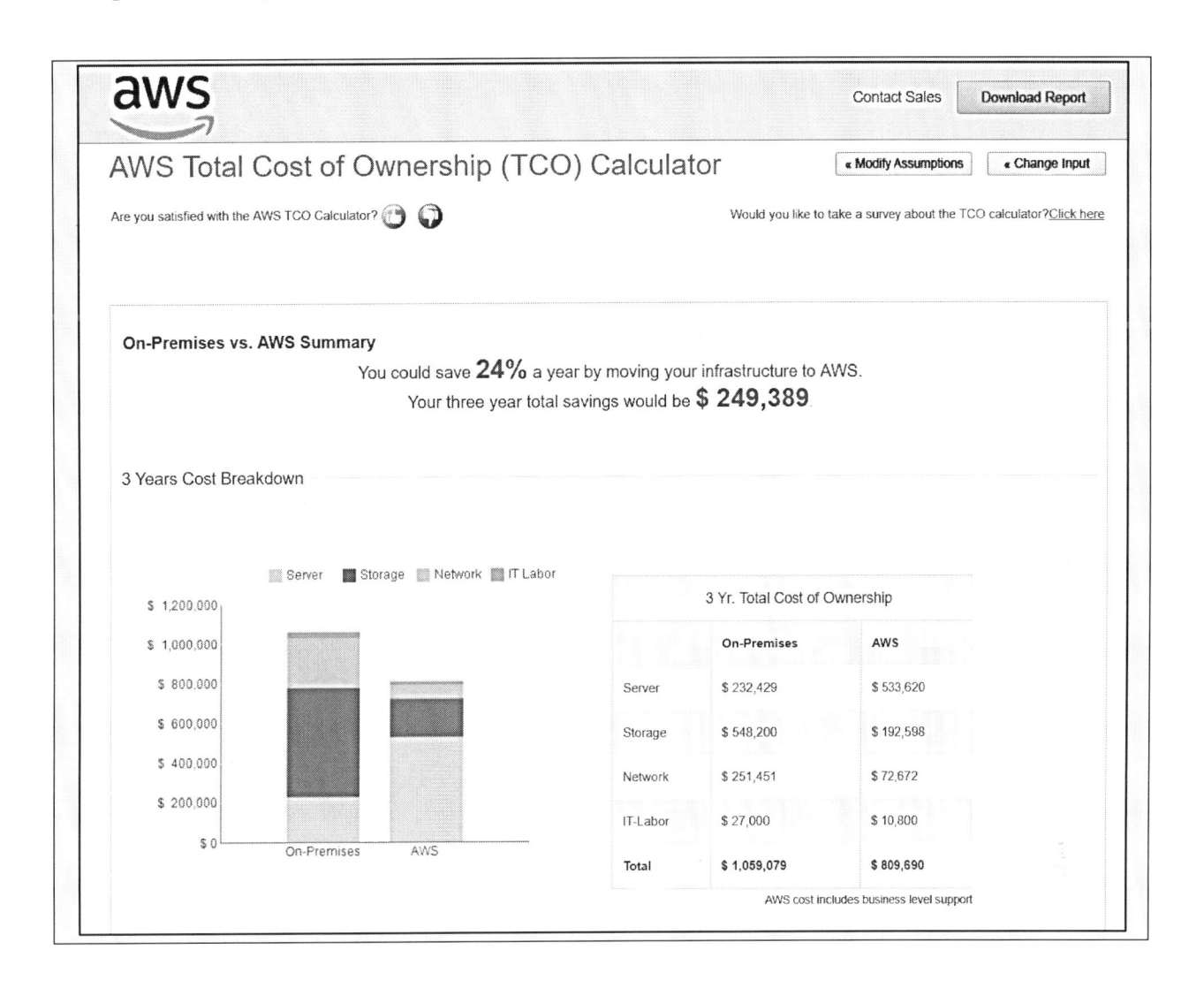

Are you satisfied with the AWS TCO Calculator?

Would you like to take a survey about the TCO calculator? Click here

On-Premises vs. AWS Summary

You could save **24%** a year by moving your infrastructure to AWS.
Your three year total savings would be **$ 249,389**

3 Years Cost Breakdown

3 Yr. Total Cost of Ownership	On-Premises	AWS
Server	$ 232,429	$ 533,620
Storage	$ 548,200	$ 192,598
Network	$ 251,451	$ 72,672
IT-Labor	$ 27,000	$ 10,800
Total	$ 1,059,079	$ 809,690

AWS cost includes business level support

Chapter 4: Billing and Pricing

AWS TCO Calculator

AWS cost includes business level support

Environment Details

Your On-Premises environment

Environment : Physical

# Servers	# Cores	RAM (GB)	OS	Avg.Util.	Optimize by
3	8	100	Linux	100%	RAM

Storage (TB)			Bandwidth (Mbps)	
SAN	NAS	Object	Pipe Size	Peak/Avg. Ratio
100	0	0	2,000	3

Your AWS environment : US East (N. Virginia)

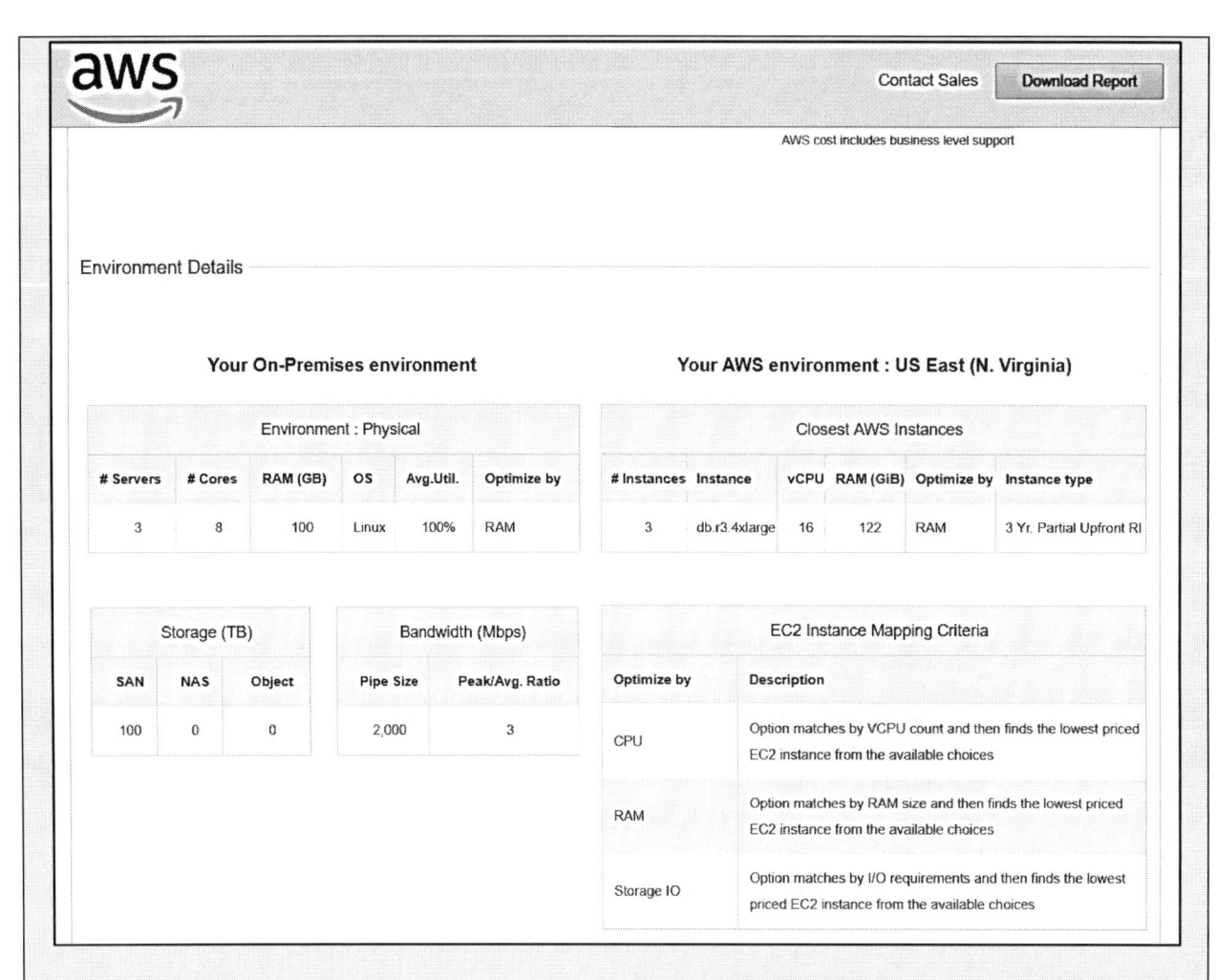

Closest AWS Instances

# Instances	Instance	vCPU	RAM (GiB)	Optimize by	Instance type
3	db.r3.4xlarge	16	122	RAM	3 Yr. Partial Upfront RI

EC2 Instance Mapping Criteria

Optimize by	Description
CPU	Option matches by VCPU count and then finds the lowest priced EC2 instance from the available choices
RAM	Option matches by RAM size and then finds the lowest priced EC2 instance from the available choices
Storage IO	Option matches by I/O requirements and then finds the lowest priced EC2 instance from the available choices

3. You will get an instant summary report of the three-year TCO comparison by cost categories that you can download. The report also includes detailed cost breakdowns, Methodology, Assumptions, and FAQs.

Chapter 4: Billing and Pricing

Cost Breakdown

Your On-Premises Cost Breakdown

Server
- Hardware: $ 39,485 [17%]
- Software: $ 133,812 [58%]
- Overhead: $ 59,132 [25%]

Storage
- Raw Capacity: $ 409,600 [75%]
- Backup: $ 48,600 [9%]
- Overhead: $ 54,000 [10%]
- Admin: $ 36,000 [7%]

Network

Your AWS Cost Breakdown

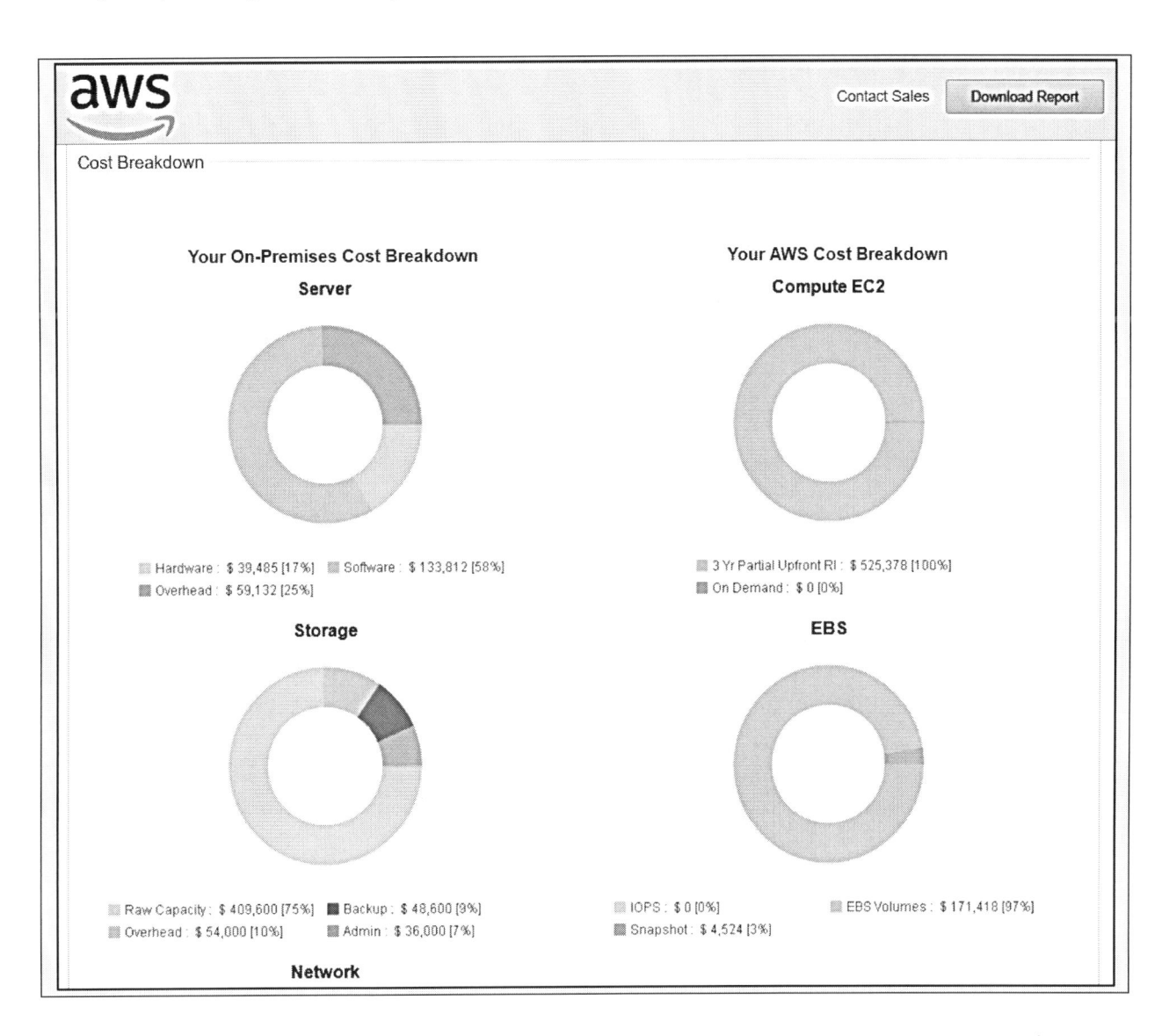

Compute EC2
- 3 Yr Partial Upfront RI: $ 525,378 [100%]
- On Demand: $ 0 [0%]

EBS
- IOPS: $ 0 [0%]
- EBS Volumes: $ 171,418 [97%]
- Snapshot: $ 4,524 [3%]

> 💡 **EXAM TIP**: Do not get confused between the two calculators. TCO is a cost comparison tool to compare the on-premises cost with the cloud cost and how much you would save by moving to the cloud. The simple monthly calculator allows you to calculate your monthly AWS bill based on the resources consumed.

Chapter 4: Billing and Pricing

Cost Management Using Tags

Tags allow you to add business and organizational statistics to your billing and usage data. This helps in categorizing and tracking costs by significant, relevant business information. Tags can be applied that represent business categories (such as cost centers, application names, projects, or owners) to organize costs across various services and teams.

AWS provides two types of cost allocation tags; an AWS generated tag and user-defined tags. AWS defines, creates, and applies the AWS generated a tag for you, whereas the User-defined tags are tags that you define, create, and apply to resources yourself. After creating and applying the tags to the resources, you can activate them on the Billing and Cost Management console for cost allocation tracking. You must activate both types of tags separately before they can appear in Cost Explorer or on a Cost Allocation Report.

The Cost Allocation Report contains all of your AWS costs for each billing period. The report includes both tagged and untagged resources so that you can clearly organize the charges for your resources. For example, if you tag resources with an application name, you can track the total cost of a single application that runs on those resources.

References

AWS Cloud Certifications

- o https://aws.amazon.com/certification/
- o https://cloudacademy.com/blog/choosing-the-right-aws-certification/

AWS Certified Cloud Practitioner

- o https://aws.amazon.com/certification/certified-cloud-practitioner/

Cloud Concepts

- o https://aws.amazon.com/what-is-cloud-computing/
- o https://aws.amazon.com/types-of-cloud-computing/

Cloud Compliance

- o https://aws.amazon.com/compliance/

Identity and Access Management

- o https://aws.amazon.com/iam/

Security Support

- o https://aws.amazon.com/products/security/

Cloud Deployment and Management

- o https://do.awsstatic.com/whitepapers/overview-of-deployment-options-on-aws.pdf

AWS Global Infrastructure

- o https://cloudacademy.com/blog/aws-global-infrastructure/

AWS Compute

- o https://aws.amazon.com/products/compute/

AWS Storage

- o https://aws.amazon.com/products/storage/

AWS Database

- o https://aws.amazon.com/products/databases/

Amazon Virtual Private Cloud

Chapter 4: Billing and Pricing

- o https://en.wikipedia.org/wiki/Virtual_private_cloud
- o https://aws.amazon.com/vpc/

Network & Content Delivery

- o https://aws.amazon.com/cloudfront/details/
- o https://aws.amazon.com/elasticloadbalancing/
- o https://aws.amazon.com/route53/

AWS Free Tier

- o https://aws.amazon.com/free/

AWS Support Plans

- o https://aws.amazon.com/premiumsupport/compare-plans/

AWS Organizations

- o https://aws.amazon.com/organizations/

AWS Cost Calculators

- o https://calculator.s3.amazonaws.com/index.html
- o https://awstcocalculator.com/

Acronyms

- AAD — Additional Authenticated Data
- ACL — Access Control List
- ACM PCA — AWS Certificate Manager Private Certificate Authority
- ACM Private CA — AWS Certificate Manager Private Certificate Authority
- ACM — AWS Certificate Manager
- AMI — Amazon Machine Image
- ARN — Amazon Resource Name
- ASN — Autonomous System Number
- AUC — Area Under a Curve
- AWS — Amazon Web Services
- BGP — Border Gateway Protocol
- CDN — Content Delivery Network
- CIDR — Classless Inter-Domain Routing
- CLI — Command Line Interface
- CMK — Customer Master Key
- DB — Database
- DKIM — DomainKeys Identified Mail
- DNS — Domain Name System
- EBS — Elastic Block Store
- EC2 — Elastic Cloud Compute
- ECR — Elastic Container Registry
- ECS — Elastic Container Service
- EFS — Elastic File System
- EMR — Elastic Map Reduce
- ES — Elasticsearch Service
- ETL — Extract, Transform, and Load
- FBL — Feedback Loop
- FIM — Federated Identity Management
- HMAC — Hash-based Message Authentication Code
- HPC — High Performance Compute
- HSM — Hardware Security Module
- IAM — Identity and Access Management

Chapter 4: Billing and Pricing

- IdP — Identity Provider
- ISP — Internet Service Provider
- JSON — JavaScript Object Notation
- KMS — Key Management Service
- MFA — Multi-factor Authentication
- MIME — Multipurpose Internet Mail Extensions
- MTA — Mail Transfer Agent
- OU — Organizational Unit
- RDS — Relational Database Service
- S3 — Simple Storage Service
- SCP — Service Control Policy
- SDK — Software Development Kit
- SES — Simple Email Service
- SMTP — Simple Mail Transfer Protocol
- SNS — Simple Notification Service
- SOAP — Simple Object Access Protocol
- SQS — Simple Queue Service
- SSE — Server-Side Encryption
- SSL — Secure Sockets Layer
- SSO — Single Sign-On
- STS — Security Token Service
- SWF — Simple Workflow Service
- TLS — Transport Layer Security
- VERP — Variable Envelope Return Path
- VPC — Virtual Private Cloud
- VPG — Virtual Private Gateway
- WAF — Web Application Firewall
- WAM — WorkSpaces Application Manager
- WSDL — Web Services Description Language

Chapter 4: Billing and Pricing

About Our Products

Other products from IPSpecialist LTD regarding AWS technology are:

AWS Certified Cloud Practitioner Technology Workbook

AWS Certified SysOps Admin - Associate Workbook

AWS Certified Solution Architect - Associate Technology Workbook

AWS Certified Developer Associate Technology Workbook

Upcoming products from IPSpecialist LTD regarding AWS technology are:

AWS Certified DevOps Engineer - Professional Technology Workbook

AWS Certified Solution Architect - Professional Technology Workbook

AWS Certified Advance Networking – Specialty Technology Workbook

AWS Certified Big Data – Specialty Technology Workbook

Chapter 4: Billing and Pricing

Note from the Author:

Reviews are gold for authors! If you have enjoyed this book and it has helped you along your certification, would you consider rating it and reviewing it?

Made in the USA
Columbia, SC
25 June 2023